A History
of
Sunderland

THIRD EDITION

Glen Lyndon Dodds

Albion
Press

For my parents
and in memory of
Sheila Ann Woodroffe (1947–2004)

Albion Press
40 Park Parade Roker Sunderland Tyne & Wear
ISBN 978 0 9932527 3 0

First published November 1995
Second edition published January 2001
Third edition December 2011
Reprinted 2013 with minor revisions
Reprinted 2018

For more information on Albion Press titles
email albionpress@gmail.com

Typeset and designed by UpStyle Book Design
www.upstyledesign.co.uk

CONTENTS

PREFACE

Sunderland has a long and fascinating history and in this book I have endeavoured to trace the story of human activity on Wearside from earliest times to the present in as comprehensive, authoritative, and lucid a manner as space would permit.

I first set eyes on Sunderland on a lovely day in early June 1974 upon arriving here with my parents and brothers after emigrating from Rhodesia. Though keenly interested in history, for some years little of Sunderland's past appealed to me. The bulk of the information concerning the town's past was too recent for my taste. However, I have since developed a great fondness for the history of Sunderland in general and I hope that this is reflected in the text.

On the whole writing this book has been a pleasurable experience and I wish to thank all those, past and present, whose work on Sunderland, or aspects of its history, rendered the task less arduous than it would otherwise have been. I also wish to thank my family for their support. In particular, I wish to thank my brother, Gavin Dodds, for taking and developing many of the photographs and for rendering technical assistance. I also wish to thank Geoffrey Milburn, Norman Dennis, George Patterson and John Pearson, for reading and commenting on sections of the text. Thanks must also go to Stephen Speak, Keeper of Field Archaeology for Tyne and Wear Museums, for corroborating certain information. I also wish to thank the staff of Sunderland Museum and the Local Studies Section of The City Library for their services, and Eric Balmer, the Librarian of the Sunderland Antiquarian Society, for setting aside time to enable me to obtain copies of photographs and engravings belonging to its collection.

Glen Lyndon Dodds
Sunderland, 7 July 1995

Preface to the Second Edition

I have taken the opportunity afforded by the decision to reprint the book not only to revise and update the text, but to deal in more detail with certain topics than had been the case. Moreover, I have also discussed themes that were omitted in the first edition owing to limited space. In all, the text is thus nearly 25,000 words longer than was originally the case.

Glen Lyndon Dodds
Sunderland, 4 December 2000

Preface to the Third Edition

Once again, in addition to updating and refining the text, I have provided additional information on various aspects of Sunderland's history and have included previously omitted themes. Inevitably, I have benefited from the research of other students of the city's past. However, as with the previous editions I have also used medieval records and other primary sources.

I wish to thank John Wood and the other staff of Local Studies in Sunderland City Library. I also want to thank Peter Watson for the photograph of Bishopwearmouth Choral Society, and Philip Curtis, Norman Kirtlan and Bill Hawkins of Sunderland Antiquarian Society for other pictures. I also want to thank Brian Dodds, Derek Haynes and Neil Mearns for providing information. Above all, I wish to thank my brother Gavin for providing the maps, technical expertise and proofreading.

It is over 20 years since I began work on the first edition. The idea of writing the book was suggested to me in August 1990 by the editorial director of a publishing firm based in Sussex. Initially, I was not enthusiastic about accepting the proposal. For one thing, it was only a couple of years since the appearance of an excellent publication, *Sunderland, River, Town & People*, by several accomplished historians including Geoffrey Milburn and Stuart Miller. Furthermore, in 1989 Miller had published a short but enjoyable work, *The Book of Sunderland*. Nonetheless, despite my reservations, during the closing months of 1990 I began planning the text of my own account of Sunderland's long and eventful history and set to work writing the first chapter at the beginning of 1991. In the event, although I later parted company with the publishing firm in Sussex (the number of illustrations required was a bone of contention) the first edition was published in late 1995 and sold better than I had anticipated.

Finally, I wish to mention the person to whose memory this book is dedicated. Sheila Woodroffe was vivacious, intelligent, courageous and immensely engaging. Above all, she was an extremely loving person who invariably put the needs of other people ahead of her own and was thus very popular. Sheila's death was a terrible blow to everyone who loved her, and she is remembered with the greatest of affection and respect. Words uttered by Edward I after he lost his beloved Eleanor of Castile in 1290, are also appropriate in Sheila's case: 'We always loved her for as long as she lived. We will not cease to love her now that she is dead.'

Glen Lyndon Dodds
Sunderland, 29 September 2011

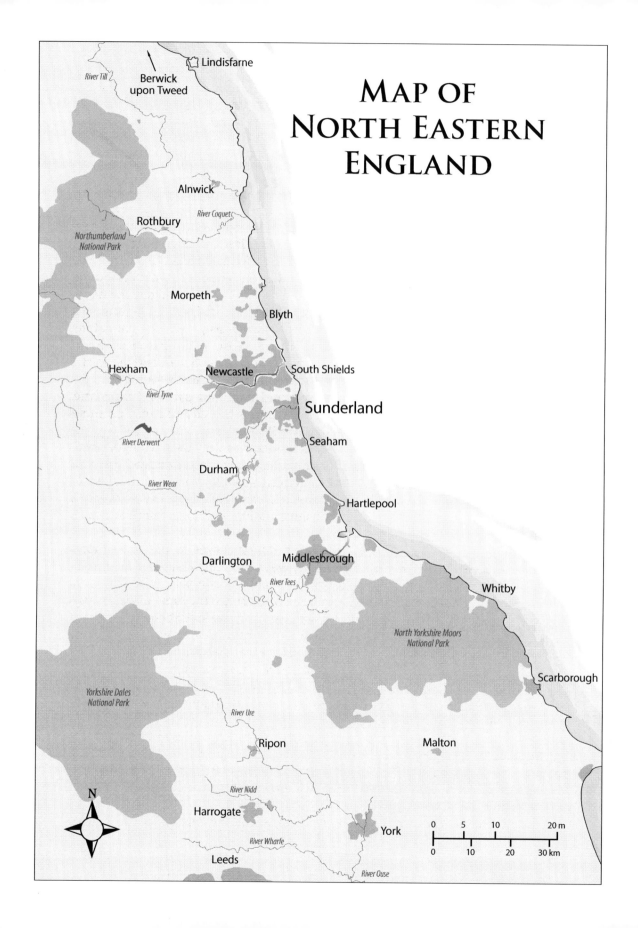

Map of North Eastern England

River Till

Lindisfarne

Berwick upon Tweed

Alnwick

Rothbury

River Coquet

Northumberland National Park

Morpeth

Blyth

Hexham

Newcastle

South Shields

River Tyne

Sunderland

River Derwent

Seaham

Durham

River Wear

Hartlepool

Darlington

Middlesbrough

River Tees

Whitby

North Yorkshire Moors National Park

Yorkshire Dales National Park

Scarborough

River Ure

Ripon

Malton

River Nidd

Harrogate

York

Leeds

River Wharfe

River Ouse

N

| 0 | 5 | 10 | 20 m |
| 0 | 10 | 20 | 30 km |

PREHISTORY TO SAXON TIMES

S underland lies at the mouth of the River Wear, one of the principal waterways in the North East of England, and is the region's second largest city. It straddles both sides of the river. A sizeable percentage of the population live to the north of the Wear and here one finds, in close proximity to the river mouth, St Peter's Church, which dates from the late 7th century and is famed for its connections with Bede and Benedict Biscop. Here too, less than a mile west of the church, which is located in a part of the city known as Monkwearmouth, is the Stadium of Light, the home of Sunderland's football team. Between St Peter's and the stadium lies Wearmouth Bridge, the most easterly of the bridges that link the city together. For generations, there were shipbuilding yards on both sides of the river near Wearmouth Bridge and beyond, and these played a major part in Sunderland's development and led to the town being justly described as 'the greatest shipbuilding port in the world.'[1]

South of the river is the most extensive and populous part of Sunderland. Indeed, upon crossing Wearmouth Bridge one enters the city centre. The showpiece here is the enclosed shopping mall, 'The Bridges', and it is as good a place as any to see large numbers of Sunderland's residents as they come and go, preoccupied no doubt for the most part by the thoughts and concerns of daily life, and thus unmindful that other people have lived in this locality before—other people who lived long before the cheering of fans first emanated from the Stadium of Light, long before the commencement of shipbuilding, and long before St Peter's Church came into being.

So let us now travel back in an imaginary time machine to the earliest days of human activity on Wearside. As we do so, we see the city disappear from view and ultimately find ourselves in a densely wooded environment inhabited by a wide variety of animal and bird life, a veritable wilderness: the same place but two different worlds. We have arrived in the Stone Age and as we look about us, bemused and no doubt apprehensive, we hear the sound of voices and soon see a small group of people coming into view, clad in animal skins and heading towards the river, chatting to one another in a language of which we know nothing.[2]

Artefacts from Mesolithic times—the Middle Stone Age—an era ascribed by some British archaeologists to the period from around 8000 BC to approximately 4000 BC have been found in significant quantity in and around Sunderland.[3] Birch, hazel, and pine trees dominated the region's landscape for much of this time span but as the climate warmed towards the close of the epoch these were largely replaced by elm and oak. Fauna included red deer, wolf, boar, pine marten, and wild cattle. Elk also roamed the area, especially in the early Mesolithic before the tree cover became extensive and thus a less inviting habitat.

Lithic material from the Mesolithic period, including microliths (tiny sharp-edged flints fashioned by man and primarily used to tip and barb spears and arrows) has been discovered in the vicinity of St Peter's Church, Monkwearmouth, evidently a popular location for local Mesolithic groups towards the close of the era.[4] Flints have also been uncovered elsewhere, including the former site of Vaux Brewery near the Magistrates Court in Bishopwearmouth, and the environs of Copt Hill on the outskirts of Houghton-le-Spring.

The small groups responsible for this, and other material, were hunter-gatherers whose food supply inevitably varied as the seasons came and went. Robert Young has for example stated that winter 'would have seen an influx of seabirds from further north, over wintering in the district and the sandy beaches and the area around the Wear mouth would probably have provided a large wader population.'[5] Some prehistorians are of the opinion that a substantial part of the Mesolithic diet came from plants. Meat may have only predominated during the winter months when plant foods were less plentiful than at other times of the year and when animals gathered in lowland areas rather than endure harsher conditions at higher altitudes.

Perhaps the Mesolithic bands that spent time on Wearside lived permanently along the coast. On the other hand, the discovery of Mesolithic flints inland, most notably in the Finchale area and in Weardale, has led to the plausible suggestion that the groups moved inland during the spring or summer and partly supported themselves by catching salmon and trout that had swum upstream to spawn. They could also hunt deer (which had migrated to their summer upland grazing territories) and aurochs that may likewise have had a migratory existence.

Evidently, the coastline witnessed encroachment by the sea during this period—the present shoreline, in general, is believed to date from around 4000 BC—and at low tide the remnants of submerged peat or 'forest' deposits have been located at several places along the North East coast. A case in point is Whitburn Bay, or Seaburn Bay as it is more widely known. Reportedly about 6ft thick in places, this deposit has for instance yielded the antlers of red deer, birch bark, charcoal and clusters of hazelnuts, and was most likely the provenance of a deer-horn harpoon-head picked up on the shore at Whitburn in 1852.

The pollen record of the Tyne-Tees region indicates that during the Neolithic or New Stone Age (c.4000–2000 BC)[6], woodland clearance was undertaken so that animals could be herded and crops cultivated—pastoral farming may have begun late in the Mesolithic. The commencement of, or at least increase in, farming evidently resulted in an expanding population which has left visible traces of its presence on the landscape.

It is interesting to note that aerial photographs of Hasting Hill (or Hastings Hill as it is more commonly known) on the western outskirts of Sunderland show crop-marks indicating the former presence of a causewayed camp and cursus. The camp was small and basic—approximately 1.5 acres in extent, and with a single ditch crossed by causeways on the northwest and southeast sides. It may very well have served as a meeting place for tribal rites and/or, trading. The cursus was just to the south of the enclosure. It had a pair of parallel banks and ditches about 154 ft apart

Aerial view of Hasting Hill showing cropmarks of
a causewayed camp, cursus and round barrows

and ran southwest for at least 1,312 ft. Formerly it was thought that cursuses served as prehistoric racing tracks. It is now believed that they had a ritual significance and at least some may have had astronomical functions. Of Hasting Hill it has been aptly said: 'This camp and cursus complex is one of the farthest north known, and indicates significant Neolithic activity in the area.'[7]

During the Neolithic some of the dead were buried in, or under, burial mounds known as cairns or barrows and this practice continued during the Bronze Age (c.2000–700 BC). A number of barrows were erected in the Sunderland area, at for example Copt Hill, Hasting Hill, Humbledon Hill and Warden Law, all sites on the East Durham Plateau, one of the four main landscape regions between the Tyne and the Tees.[8]

In 1877 the barrow at Copt Hill was excavated by Dr Greenwell and T.W.U. Robinson, and was found to contain a Neolithic deposit of several disarticulated and partially cremated skeletons, as well as a number of Bronze Age burials. The disarticulated state of the Neolithic burials suggests that the bodies had been left to rot in the open air—a practice known as excarnation—before the remains were brought to their final resting place and set alight.

The barrow is located on the edge of the plateau in a position commanding excellent views westward over the Wear Lowlands towards the Pennines. It is in

The Copt Hill barrow, Houghton-le-Spring

a false crest position and so when viewed from lower ground seems to be on the summit of the escarpment. This siting may have been intended to make the mound a prominent feature of the skyline for people in the valley. The barrow is chiefly constructed of limestone and sandstone. As no quarry ditch was located, it has been suggested that the barrow's makers were agriculturalists engaged in clearing the land of stones that would have hindered cultivating the ground in the vicinity, and disposed of the material in a useful manner when erecting the mound.

Another barrow, situated on the summit of Hasting Hill, was excavated by C.T. Trechmann and three companions in 1911. Although the overall quality of the grave goods was not impressive, the excavation nonetheless proved worthwhile, for as Trechmann later wrote: 'No fewer than ten definite interments were met with, comprising six burnt and four unburnt burials. In addition to these the remains of several skeletons were found, probably in part representing further disturbed unburnt burials.'[9]

The primary burial, at least as far as the definite interments are concerned, was of a contracted inhumation in a cist. The individual was male and aged about 50. Though rather short, at 5 ft 4 in., an analysis of the bones led T. Coke Squance to declare that he had 'been extremely muscular.' He had, moreover, 'suffered from a fractured rib and rheumatism.'[10] Associated with the burial was a degenerate Beaker pot which, according to an authority on early ceramics, 'has a form not unlike a bipartite Food Vessel.'[11] It thus seems likely that the burial dates from the early 2nd millennium, a period that witnessed the final phase of Beakers—a style of pot first used in the 3rd millennium—and the commencement of the use of Food Vessels.

Of the artefacts, Trechmann observed:

> In contrast with the richness of the number of burials, is the poverty in workmanship and decoration of the objects found with the remains. Much of the pottery is of a somewhat inferior description, and the few flints which have been intentionally deposited with the unburnt bones were of an unusually meagre description in remarkable contrast to those I have found in some other barrows in the neighbourhood.[12]

Presumably, the deceased had either not possessed many objects of good quality or their relatives were not prepared to use such items as grave goods.

Cist burials from Hasting Hill of a man aged about fifty, and an infant who had suffered from rickets

Another interesting site is Carley Hill on the northern outskirts of Sunderland, where several burials believed to date from prehistoric times had been discovered. In view of the reports of early burials, Carley Hill was deemed a site where trial excavations might prove fruitful. Hence in 1990 trenches were dug on waste ground just to the north of Earlston Street. This led to the discovery of a number of ditches (whose layout was rather irregular) which it was hoped were part of a settlement. This proved not to be the case, though one must have been near at hand. At least some of the ditches were cobbled. Thus it was plausibly concluded by Stephen Speak, the archaeologist in charge of the excavations, which continued intermittently until early 1992, that they had served as drove ways for a large land allotment scheme—now undoubtedly partly built over—dating from the mid 2nd millennium. A pollen sample taken from the bottom of one of the ditches revealed that alder trees had grown in the vicinity and were gradually replaced by cereal cultivation.[13]

More recently, other material from the Bronze Age was uncovered in 2003–4 when eight trenches were dug as part of an archaeological evaluation of the former site of Vaux Brewery. In addition to lithic material—flakes, blades etc—characteristic of the Mesolithic and early Neolithic on the one hand, and of the Bronze and Iron Ages on the other, the finds included sherds of pottery. With the exception of two sherds that date from the late Bronze Age or early Iron Age, the pottery is from the middle Bronze Age. A large ditch with an associated bank was also discovered and may have formed part of an enclosure in the late Neolithic or early Bronze Age. Overall, the evidence suggests that the site was most utilised in the middle Bronze Age and may have been used continuously for an extended period.

For much of the Bronze Age the climate is believed to have been warmer and drier than that of today. As the 2nd millennium drew to a close it began to worsen, and by about 800 BC the weather was apparently colder and wetter than at present. This led to the abandonment of upland sites in places such as the Pennines and seems to have resulted in life becoming more violent, with communities competing for resources.

During the late Bronze Age, votive offerings were deposited in waterways and in the North East this practise evidently occurred most frequently on the Tyne, where many bronze swords have been recovered from the river, especially around an island near Elswick. However, the River Wear has likewise yielded weapons dating from the same period, namely a bronze rapier from Claxheugh and two bronze swords from Hylton, probably the location of a river crossing. Furthermore, a bronze socketed axe of perhaps comparable date was found in the same stretch of the river and these objects may well have been ritually deposited in the water.

In 1888 an oak logboat was recovered from the river bottom at Offerton Haugh, some years after a comparable vessel—which has not survived—was found a short distance downstream at Hylton. According to N.R. Whitcomb, the logboats were probably made in the late Bronze Age, but they may in fact date from the subsequent Iron Age (c.700 BC–AD 71), as is the case with some dugout canoes found elsewhere. Of the vessels, Whitcomb has stated:

> The two canoes are so alike that it would seem reasonable to consider them contemporary or even a pair. They may even have been intended to be fastened together to make a catamaran. Cords through the matching holes in the gunwhales with additional lashing at the bows would have transformed the two canoes into a single more stable craft for taking across the river bulky material or livestock such as sheep.[14]

Sooner or later, and most probably during the Iron Age, Celts settled in Britain from the continent and by the 1st century AD at the very latest Celtic speech was the dominant tongue nationwide. The name of the River Wear is of Celtic origin and is often said to derive from a word meaning 'water' or 'river.' Andrew Breeze, though, has provided another etymology—that the name comes from a word meaning 'bend, curve' and is due to the meandering nature of the river.[15]

During the Iron Age, human exploitation of the area undoubtedly continued.

Some of the farmsteads that existed on Wearside were likely enclosed by banks and ditches, as was the case elsewhere in the region where the enclosures were generally rectangular in plan, a state of affairs also found at some late Bronze Age sites. Presumably, unenclosed settlements could also be found, as was true at South Shields where an Iron Age homestead and its cultivation plots have been discovered by archaeologists while excavating a Roman fort.[16]

Wearside and the Romans

In the 1st century AD if not before, the most powerful tribe in the north of England were the Brigantes, a people centred on Yorkshire, and it is believed that their north-eastern frontier rested on the River Tyne or even the Coquet, in either case thereby embracing Wearside. According to the Roman historian Tacitus, the Brigantes were 'numerically the largest tribe in Britain.' However, this did not prevent their territory from being overrun by the Romans—whose conquest of Britain commenced in AD 43—for in AD 71 Roman soldiers began subjugating Brigantia and this process was brought to a conclusion by Tacitus' father-in-law, Agricola, a decade or so later. Indeed, Agricola pressed on far into Scotland. But by the early years of the 2nd century the Romans had fallen back to the Tyne-Solway isthmus, across which Hadrian's Wall was subsequently built during the reign of Emperor Hadrian (117–38) and this remained the northern frontier for most of the Roman period.

The Roman occupation of Britain lasted for nearly four hundred years. During this era many towns and cities and hundreds of villas were founded and members of native society, high and low, could enjoy the fruits of civilization to the extent that their circumstances allowed—imported pottery, for instance, has been found on many humble native sites. Wearsiders, though, lived in one of the least Romanized parts of *Britannia*, a militarized zone that contrasted greatly with conditions further south. The closest town, Corbridge (most likely known to the Romans as *Coriosopitum* rather than the more widely known alternative *Corstopitum*), was many miles away, whilst the nearest known definite villa was just to the south of present day Durham City. Both were inferior to some of the towns and villas found elsewhere.

In contrast, military installations were closer to home. Substantial forts existed at Chester-le-Street (*Congcangium*) and at South Shields (*Arbeia*). The latter was likely the location of a Roman fort from the late 1st century onward—a stone fort was certainly in existence from c.160—and, in common with most Roman forts, was associated with a civil settlement that developed beside it. Any Wearsiders who visited South Shields would have found themselves in a thriving cosmopolitan environment. Arabs, for instance, were sometimes present.

Various objects from the Roman period have been discovered on Wearside. One such was found near the quarry at Carley Hill, Fulwell, in 1820. It is a bronze figurine, possibly of the smith god Jupiter Dolichenus, and dates from the 2nd or 3rd century. Jupiter Dolichenus was a deity of eastern origin (from Syria) whose worship was apparently introduced into Britain in the 2nd century and became popular in the 3rd. Religion was central to people's lives during the Roman period, as was no doubt true of preceding epochs, and Jupiter Dolichenus was one of a large number of gods and goddesses worshipped in Roman Britain. These included deities of the classical world such as the Romans' principal god Jupiter (the father of gods and men); native cults; and deities worshipped by non-Roman peoples serving in the army. Christianity also had devotees in late Roman times—a possible 4th century church has been located at South Shields—although to what extent, if any, its beliefs were accepted on Wearside is unknown.

A bronze figurine found at Fulwell

In addition to the bronze figurine, other material from the Roman period found in Sunderland includes Roman coins—some of these have been located in the heart of the city and at Carley Hill and Hylton. Pottery has also been uncovered by archaeologists during excavations, or found by chance. Some writers have stated that a probable Roman pottery came to light in Sunderland in 1849, close to the south side of the mouth of the River Wear, but in this case the material in question was not Roman.

It has been plausibly suggested that a number of Roman signal stations were constructed along the coast between the Tees and the Tyne—at Seaham and on Wearside for example—and that these were a continuation of the chain of stations certainly built along the coast of Yorkshire in the second half of the 4th century to give warning of seaborne raids by barbarians like the Picts of Scotland.

Monkwearmouth has sometimes been proposed as the location of such an installation on Wearside, where Roman material has been found at St Peter's. For one thing, Rosemary Cramp notes that in 'the Anglo-Saxon fabric of the church there are several stones with Roman cross-tooling or with lewis-holes … [and] it is possible that the sandstone blocks which formed the quoins and door openings could all have been recovered from a Roman site.'[17] Admittedly, Roman material was sometimes transported for subsequent building purposes—for instance Wilfrid's crypt at Hexham was erected in the late 7th century using stone brought from a Roman bridge a few miles away at Corbridge. Nevertheless, limited Roman occupation may thus have occurred at, or in close proximity to, the location of St Peter's where, moreover, two Roman coins as well as 'a scattering of pottery in the form of eight sherds of Samian and colour-coated wares' were uncovered during a programme of excavation.[18]

The reconstructed west gate of the Roman fort at South Shields. The fort, and substantial associated settlement, must have been familiar to some Wearsiders

Another location on Wearside suggested for the presumed signal station, is that of the former Vaux Brewery on the south side of the river. Of the site, which over-looks the Wear and had commanding views of the sea, William Cranmer Mitchell wrote early in the 20th century: 'An ancient building once stood at the place ... and in 1873 the late Mr John Moore examined the foundations, which were four feet thick, and found the worked stones and cement were in keeping with Roman work-manship.'[19] Furthermore an inscribed stone, reading 'V.S.L.M.' within a scroll, was discovered in the vicinity in 1903; a discovery that led one cautious authority to conclude that 'on the whole this would add to the possibility of a Roman station' in the neighbourhood.[20]

Indeed, some have contended that instead of a signal station there was a stronger military presence—a fort—located at the Vaux site. This view seemed unlikely. If a fort had existed there a much larger quantity of Roman material would no doubt have been found over the years than has been the case, and during excavations conducted in 2003–4 no evidence of a Roman presence was detected.[21]

According to John Robinson, at the turn of the 19th century 'a section of ancient roadway' was uncovered at nearby Low Row.[22] Robinson conjectured that the discovery was part of a Roman coastal road that connected Hartlepool with South Shields and crossed the Wear a few miles upstream from Bishopwearmouth at

Hylton. There, massive stones regularly shaped and bound together by iron bands, were removed from the Wear in the mid 19th century, and were accepted as Roman work by several experts, including Dr Bruce and C.S. Collingwood.

Additional evidence for a presumed Roman road was furnished by the discovery of a Roman milestone in the vicinity of the suggested crossing. If a Roman coastal road did exist (the idea does not enjoy strong support among modern scholars) it would have been of minor importance in comparison with some other roads in the region, one of which ran northward via Chester-le-Street to Newcastle upon Tyne. An even more important highway, Dere Street, lay further inland and headed north from Piercebridge towards Corbridge and beyond.

Whether the stones removed from the Wear at Hylton had formed a bridge or a causeway has been strongly disputed—the evidence supports the latter—and if the structure were Roman it was erected near a stretch of the Wear apparently used as a crossing since prehistoric times, part of the route of a presumed ancient trackway that perhaps headed northward to the Wear via Copt Hill and Hastings Hill.

For his part, David Heslop (the County Archaeologist for Tyne and Wear) leans towards the view 'that the Roman presence around Sunderland was not significant, and that while there may well have been some form of crossing of the Wear at Hylton, that road, however ancient in origin, wasn't significant in terms of the Roman military network, and so a substantial investment on a large stone structure is, on balance, unlikely.'[23]

An alternative view was proposed by Ray Selkirk. He maintained that the Romans dammed the Wear and that the Hylton stones were a 'solid causeway' which formed 'a Roman navigation weir, to make the Vedra [as the river was known to the Romans] navigable at all stages of the tide' so that heavy cargoes, brought by sea, could be carried upstream by barge to Chester-le-Street.[24] However, this theory has not gained wide support among Roman archaeologists.

It is reasonable to suppose that the Roman occupation stimulated the local economy to some degree. Food and other commodities such as hides, would have been required by the troops stationed in the region and by inhabitants of the settlements that developed outside the forts, and although at least some of their needs were transported from elsewhere, the native rural populace no doubt supplemented these provisions. In this context it is interesting to note that an analysis of grain found during excavations at South Shields Roman Fort indicated that some of the grain stored there, namely spelt wheat, was grown by local farmers. It is also conceivable that young local males were enrolled in the Roman Army, much of whose manpower was derived from subject peoples: some units garrisoning Hadrian's Wall for instance were of Germanic origin.

The Arrival of the English

In 409 Roman rule in Britain ceased. However, within a few generations Wearsiders came under the sway of other conquerors—the Anglo-Saxons or English. In general terms, the arrival of the Anglo-Saxons is one of the most fascinating and controversial subjects in English history. Some historians, echoing the views of the 8th century historian, Bede, have argued that immigration from the north German coastlands and adjacent areas was large-scale. In contrast, revisionists maintain that the great changes that occurred in most of what is now England in the post-Roman era, can be attributed to the natives adopting the speech and culture of numerically insignificant, but politically dominant, Germanic newcomers.[25]

In the North East, Anglo-Saxon settlement occurred later than in much of the country and the majority of the immigrants were Angles whose immediate forebears had settled in Britain after migrating from Schleswig-Holstein and Denmark. Settlement evidently commenced in the Tyne-Tees region in, or about, the first quarter of the 6th century, a hundred years or more later than in the South and eastern Midlands. Apparently, moreover, it was less intense in scale, a view partly derived from the greater survival of native institutions, and the scarcity of Anglo-Saxon archaeological remains, in comparison with what has been found elsewhere.

A 6th century Anglian brooch was discovered at Cleadon, a short distance to the north of Sunderland, in 1983 shortly after a comparable brooch had been found at Hylton. But the most important of the early Anglo-Saxon material located in the vicinity of Sunderland has been uncovered near Easington, a few miles to the south of the city, where a cemetery located on the brow of a hill was excavated in 1991–2. The burials found were inhumations. Associated artefacts (the majority datable to the 6th century) include cruciform brooches and wrist-clasps: the latter would have been sewn on to long-sleeved garments to serve as a form of cuff-link and were a characteristic feature of Anglian female costume introduced from southern Scandinavia. The Anglo-Saxons were pagans and worshipped a number of deities, such as Twi, Woden, Thor and Frig—after whom Tuesday, Wednesday, Thursday and Friday are named—and the grave goods were perhaps intended to be of use in the afterlife.

The first notable Germanic leader to emerge in the North East was Aethelfrith, who came to power in the late 6th century and proceeded to create the kingdom of Northumbria. Thus Wearsiders (if indeed they had not already done so) came under Teutonic rule and sooner or later the native tongue was supplanted by English, albeit a form of English that is unintelligible today unless studied like a foreign language.[26]

Other changes were to occur in the region: changes effected in the 7th century by men fighting a very different type of warfare to that of rulers like Aethelfrith. The combatants were warriors of Christ, and their endeavours paved the way for Wearside to become a place of renown.

AN ISLAND OF MEDITERRANEAN CULTURE
IN A BARBARIAN SEA

In 597 a band of monks from Rome came ashore in the kingdom of Kent, the most advanced Anglo-Saxon state. Their mission?—to convert the Anglo-Saxons to Christianity. Though they were to have some notable successes (such as the conversion of the Kentish king) it was to be many years before the bulk of the English people renounced paganism. Indeed, in neighbouring Sussex, the South Saxons were still heathen in the latter half of the 7th century. By the time they were finally won over, a monastery had come into existence at the mouth of the River Wear that would become one of the most celebrated of the Anglo-Saxon era.

It was founded by a remarkable Northumbrian nobleman called Benedict Biscop. As a young man, Biscop—who was born in about 628—served as a military retainer of King Oswy of Northumbria and would have accompanied the monarch as he travelled around his kingdom to places such as Yeavering (in the Cheviot foothills) and Bamburgh, the latter located near the tidal island of Lindisfarne, where a monastery had been founded in 635 by a saintly Celtic monk named Aidan.

Benedict Biscop grew to manhood at a time when missionaries such as Aidan were converting the Northumbrians to Christianity. Evidently, he was profoundly affected by the new faith for in about 653 he renounced the world and journeyed to Rome by land and sea, no doubt accompanied by a number of attendants. It was the first of several prolonged absences from Britain during which he became familiar with Mediterranean culture and continental monasticism. In fact, following a second visit to Rome, Biscop made his way to the famous monastery of Lérins—on an island near Cannes—where he took monastic vows and stayed for two years. He then returned to Rome, apparently with the intention of residing there for the rest of his life. However, in 668 he was entrusted by the pope with the task of escorting a newly appointed Archbishop of Canterbury to Britain and upon therefore returning to England the following year, served for perhaps two years as abbot of the monastery of St Peter and St Paul, Canterbury. He later returned to Rome yet again, primarily it seems to acquire books.

Thus by the 670s Biscop was a widely travelled and experienced man, a man who commanded respect. Oswy's son and successor King Ecgfrith certainly respected him, for according to the monastic historian Bede (whose account dates from the early 8th century), after hearing first-hand about Biscop's many adventures and love of the religious life, the king granted him 70 hides of land upon which to found a monastery of his own. Another early source, the anonymous *Life of Ceolfrith*, states that the endowment comprised 50 hides and was later augmented by the king and other benefactors. Either way, given that the smallest known hides in England were approximately 40 acres in extent while others comprised 120 acres, the grant constituted a substantial estate.

Some Anglo-Saxon monasteries were nondescript places where a few people lived communal lives of devotion. Ecgfrith's generous endowment, likely made in 673, gave Biscop the opportunity to found something grander. An ambitious man, he seized the chance, determined to establish a notable monastery at *Wiuraemuda*— Wearmouth.

Bede, who was probably born on Wearside and whose parents entrusted him to Biscop's care a few years after the monastery's foundation, relates that about a year after Ecgfrith's endowment, Biscop crossed to Gaul. He did so to hire craftsmen who could build him a church 'in the Roman style that he had always loved,' i.e., a sophisticated stone church, and construction commenced in 674 (or perhaps 675) and proceeded rapidly.[1] Then, as work on the place of worship neared completion, Benedict Biscop sent men to Gaul to hire glassmakers, 'craftsmen as yet unknown in Britain, to glaze the windows of the church, its side-chapels and upper storey.'[2] Thus by the standards of the age, an impressive church dedicated to St Peter came into being, together with fine monastic quarters adjoining it to the south. The construction work must have amazed the local populace for stone buildings were extremely rare in England. Indeed, to see something comparable in the region they would have had to travel to Hexham where an aristocratic churchman named Wilfrid, a former associate of Biscop, had recently founded an impressive monastery with the assistance of foreign craftsmen.

To regulate life at Wearmouth, Biscop devised a Rule by which the monks would live. This was based on his experience of life in 17 monasteries, and in particular on the Rule of the celebrated 6th century Italian abbot, St Benedict, which enjoined on those who vowed to obey it a self-sacrificing lifestyle devoted to the service of God. Consequently, at regular intervals both day and night, the monks would have gathered to observe the canonical Hours, while the periods in between would have been devoted to various activities such as providing for the physical needs of the community. The latter necessitated manual labour—ploughing the monastic lands for instance.

Closely linked to Biscop's desire that Wearmouth should be an admirable centre of the religious life, was his wish for it to be a place of learning where the monks could acquire knowledge by reading a variety of works, including scriptural commentaries by the Church Fathers. Therefore, he set himself to establish a splendid library. In fact, in the years that preceded the monastery's foundation, this Greek and Latin scholar had acquired a notable collection of books during his continental travels and he was eager to add to it.

So, in the late 670s, he left Wearmouth in the care of a cousin named Eosterwine and, accompanied by a monk called Ceolfrith, set off for Rome again to acquire 'a plentiful supply of sacred books … relics, pictures … and other gifts from overseas.'[3] They duly returned 'with a greater variety of spiritual treasures than ever before', including 'a great mass of books of every sort.'[4] Other items included paintings with sacred themes (such as scenes from the Gospels) that were used to adorn St Peter's Church for the edification of those who beheld them.

St Peter's Church from the west. The west wall of the nave and lower stages
of the tower date from the days of the Anglo-Saxon monastery

But this was not all. With the approval of Pope Agatho, Biscop returned to
Wearmouth accompanied by John, the chief-cantor of St Peter's, Rome, who came
to teach the community the chant for the liturgical year as performed at Rome.
Bede relates that 'John taught the monks at first hand how things were done in the

churches in Rome and also committed a good part of his instruction to writing. This is still preserved in memory of him in the monastery library.'[5] Furthermore, Bede adds that monks from elsewhere visited Wearmouth to receive instruction and so John's visit greatly influenced the development of English church music in general.

Moreover, the pope had conferred upon Benedict Biscop a letter of privilege, ensuring the monastery of Wearmouth from interference from both secular and episcopal powers in perpetuity. The letter was subsequently publicly ratified by King Ecgfrith. It is clear that the monarch was impressed by events at Wearmouth, for he granted Biscop an additional estate of 40 hides upon which to found a religious house beside the Tyne at Jarrow. The new monastery, established in 682 by a party sent from Wearmouth under Ceolfrith, likewise had stone buildings and was dedicated to St Paul.

In or about 684, Biscop travelled to Rome again in order to obtain more books and other items. He left Wearmouth and Jarrow respectively in the care of trusted subordinates, Eosterwine and Ceolfrith. In 682 Biscop had made Eosterwine an abbot as a result of his own frequent attendance at the court of King Ecgfrith, to whom he acted as an adviser, thereby necessitating the assistance of someone else to handle the affairs of the monastery.

During Biscop's absence on the continent, Ecgfrith was slain in battle campaigning against the Picts beyond the Firth of Forth, and this event was followed by a major plague that ravaged the region and took a heavy toll. It was especially deadly in monasteries like Wearmouth where so many lived in close proximity and one of the victims was Eosterwine, who died on 7 March 686 aged 36. Eosterwine, one of the original members of the monastic community, had been a cheerful man of great humility. Bede states that despite his high birth, Eosterwine 'took his share of the winnowing and threshing, the milking of the ewes and the cows' and 'laboured in bakehouse, garden and kitchen, taking part cheerfully and obediently in every monastery chore. He was no different when he attained to the rank and authority of abbot.'[6] He also engaged in other tasks such as helping to plough the monastic lands.

Benedict Biscop returned to Wearmouth in March 687, bringing with him many fine treasures acquired during his pilgrimage. Among these were two excellent silk cloaks that ultimately caught the eye of Ecgfrith's half-brother and successor, King Aldfrith. In exchange for them, the king gave Biscop three hides of land on the south side of the River Wear in proximity to the North Sea.

Other items Biscop brought home included more paintings. One group of these, portraying the story of Christ, was used by him to adorn 'the chapel of the Holy Mother of God which he had built within the main monastery, setting them, as its crowning glory, all the way round the walls.'[7] The building in question was a church dedicated to the Virgin Mary at Wearmouth and so distinct from the principal monastic church dedicated to St Peter.

Following his return, Biscop fell ill. According to Bede, his lower limbs were paralysed to such a degree that they were 'as good as dead.'[8] He lingered on, enduring creeping paralysis, until death overtook him on 12 January 689. He was buried to the east of the altar in St Peter's Church.

One of his last instructions to the monks was that Wearmouth and Jarrow should be ruled by the same abbot, and that abbots should be chosen for their ability, not because of their relationship to him. In this, Biscop differed from some other senior figures in Anglo-Saxon monasticism such as Wilfrid, who favoured the principle of family succession at religious houses they had founded.

Benedict Biscop was one of the most remarkable men of his generation. When he renounced the world as a young man, Wearmouth was a place of no consequence, perhaps solely inhabited by rustic folk. However, by the time of his death, and primarily due to his drive and vision, it had been transformed into a place of note in Northumbria and in lands beyond. As a great Anglo-Saxonist, Sir Frank Stenton observed, Biscop 'had brought into being two neighbouring monasteries, governed as a single community, which possessed an endowment in relics, religious ornaments, and books unparalleled in England.'[9]

Ceolfrith and the *Codex Amiatinus*

At the time of Biscop's death, Wearmouth and Jarrow, which Bede describes as 'the one monastery…founded on two separate sites', were administered by Ceolfrith, whom Biscop had appointed to run both houses in 688.

Ceolfrith is undoubtedly one of the central figures in the history of the monastery. He was born into the Northumbrian aristocracy and, when aged 18, entered monastic life at Gilling in present day North Yorkshire. He subsequently moved to a monastery at Ripon—where he was ordained a priest—and spent time elsewhere in England before returning to Ripon, where he was invited by Biscop to become one of the founding members of the monastic community at Wearmouth. But here, shortly after the monastery's foundation and during Biscop's journey abroad to secure the services of master-builders and stonemasons to construct St Peter's, Ceolfrith quarrelled with some monks of aristocratic birth who resented the discipline of the Rule: 'He suffered acutely from the bitter attacks of certain noblemen who could not endure regular discipline.'[10] Ceolfrith therefore returned to Ripon, but was entreated to come back by Biscop when the latter heard of his departure. Ceolfrith did so and, as noted, was duly placed in charge at Jarrow before eventually becoming abbot of both houses, whereupon he presumably moved to Wearmouth, evidently the senior house.

Bede wrote that Ceolfrith was 'industrious in everything he did…and intensely dedicated to the religious life…. All the splendid works of piety begun by his predecessor he set himself to complete with equal energy.'[11] Among other things, Ceolfrith doubled the number of books in each of the monastic libraries and had three Bibles, largely based on Jerome's Vulgate translation, transcribed by monks under his charge. The size of the monastic community likewise expanded, as did its landed endowment. For instance, the community received an estate of 10 hides at *Daltun* (believed to be Dalton-le-Dale) from Witmaer, an elderly man who entered the monastery and was described by Bede as 'well-versed in every branch of secular learning as well as in the scriptures.'[12]

In 716, by which time the joint monastic community reportedly numbered over 600 monks, the elderly Ceolfrith decided to resign the abbacy, intent on spending his last days in Rome.[13] Ceolfrith kept his intention secret until the last possible moment. Then, despite the entreaties of the monks who wished him to stay—Bede says that he was so distraught by Ceolfrith's departure that he was unable to proceed for some time with a literary project on which he was engaged—Ceolfrith set off on his pilgrimage.

He commenced his journey by crossing the River Wear on the first Thursday in June and as 'the ship sailed across the river, he looked towards the brothers mourning his departure and heard the sublime

A monk at work in a scriptorium (Lindisfarne Priory Museum)

sound of their song mixed with grief.'[14] Upon reaching the south bank, he continued his pilgrimage on horseback and duly sailed from the Humber, no doubt with fond memories and eager expectations. Sadly, the journey proved too much for him. On 25 September, he died in meadowland on the outskirts of Langres, France, far from home and his intended destination. While some of the monks travelling with him began the long homeward journey with news of his demise, others pressed on to Rome taking gifts that Ceolfrith had intended to give to the pope.

Among the gifts was one of the three Bibles mentioned above that had been transcribed by Ceolfrith's monks—the volume may always have been intended as a present for the pope and, if so, was perhaps the most magnificent of the three pandects. It contained a dedicatory inscription describing Ceolfrith as an 'abbot from the furthest ends of the earth.' The Bible, the work of several scribes, is now known as the *Codex Amiatinus* (it is sometimes referred to by local historians as the 'Wearmouth Bible') and is in the Laurenziana Library, Florence. Strongly influenced by Italian exemplars both in terms of script and decoration, it is a work of great importance for it is one of the finest uncial volumes in existence and testifies to the high calibre of the monks working in the scriptoria of Wearmouth/Jarrow.[15] The codex, which contains 2,060 pages and weighs over 75 pounds, also highlights the wealth of Ceolfrith's monastery. It has been estimated that the skins of 1,550 calves were required to provide the vellum needed for the codex and its two companion volumes that Ceolfrith had made for Wearmouth and Jarrow.

Of the codex, Michelle Brown comments:

> The varied textual affiliations of the *Codex Amiatinus*…indicate that…the scriptoria of Wearmouth/Jarrow conceived of a major editorial project…. Amiatinus was not an antiquarian facsimile of an Italian pandect… but an active, dynamic work of scholarly compilation and emendation. The Ceolfrith Bibles were in themselves a 'new edition' [albeit representing] … a version of the Vulgate.[16]

Presumably, Bede played a role in this major editorial task. Alan Thacker has observed that the great scholar's 'involvement in this project is indicated by his production of an important commentary on the biblical book of Ezra, whose image is such a striking element in the adornment' of the *Codex Amiatinus*.[17]

Bede tells us that at Wearmouth on Whit Sunday following Ceolfrith's departure, the remaining brethren, including some monks from Jarrow, chose a new abbot for the monastery, having gathered for the occasion.

Their choice was Hwaetberht, a learned priest who had been resident in the monastery since boyhood, save for a lengthy stay in Rome. He was also a musician and a skilled writer with a taste for composing complex Latin riddles. Hwaetberht is known to have been still alive in 746, for in that year an English missionary in Germany, St Boniface, wrote to him asking for copies of Bede's works.

Bede and Beyond

By this date Bede had died. He did so in 735, and the place of his death is almost universally believed to have been Jarrow. Of the personal life of this humble and attractive man little is known. At the end of his most famous work, his *Ecclesiastical History of the English People*, he describes himself as 'a servant of Christ and priest of the monastery of the blessed apostles Peter and Paul at Wearmouth and Jarrow' and states that he was born on the territory of this monastery—'*natus in territorio eiusdem monasterii*'.[18]

The date of his birth was either 672 or 673, and the place where it occurred is disputed. Monkton, in the parish of St Paul, Jarrow, is often accorded the honour. In contrast, some historians are of the opinion that Bede was born on Wearside. Interestingly, when Bede's *Ecclesiastical History* was translated into Old English in the second half of the 9th century during the reign of Alfred the Great, the Latin phrase quoted above was rendered '*acenned on sundurlonde paes ylcan mynstres*'. Did the translator thus believe that Bede was born in Sunderland? This is the conclusion to which some have come. On the other hand, an eminent Bedan, the late Peter Hunter Blair, stated that 'it is wiser to regard [the use of *sundurlonde*, a word used to indicate land set aside for a special purpose]...in this passage as translating *territorium* [*territorio* is the ablative case] rather than as referring to the place now called Sunderland.'[19]

The entrance porch of St Peter's, added to the church by the year 716

What is certain is that when Bede was entrusted to the care of Benedict Biscop at the age of seven, he resided at Wearmouth for the sister house at Jarrow had not yet been founded. It is generally maintained that following a brief residence at Wearmouth as a child, Bede spent most of his life at Jarrow. Although he never states that he made such a move, several factors have been used to deduce that Bede went to Jarrow and likely did so when Ceolfrith was entrusted with overseeing the establishment of a monastic presence there.

For instance, it is widely assumed that Bede is referred to in the anonymous *Life of Ceolfrith*. When referring to events at Jarrow, this mentions a member of the community 'who has been brought up and taught by him [Ceolfrith] and who until the present day holds the rank of a priest in the same monastery and commends the abbot's laudable actions in words and writings to all who wish to know them.'[20] In short, Peter Hunter Blair, concluded that the tradition of Bede's association with Jarrow, 'resting presumably on his own statement that he was educated first at the hands of Benedict Biscop and later of Ceolfrith whom we know to have been at Jarrow, is old enough to deserve respect.'[21]

If Bede did indeed move to Jarrow, it is reasonable to conclude that this strengthens the view that he was born on Wearside. After all, if he were born in the vicinity of Jarrow then surely even a scholar as reticent about himself as Bede would have been moved to mention the fact that in transferring from Wearmouth to Jarrow he was returning to the area of his birth and, presumably, early childhood.

Alternatively, Henry Robson (a former president of the Sunderland Antiquarian Society) maintained that Bede's statement that he had been educated by Biscop and Ceolfrith, should be taken to mean that Bede remained under the former's supervision until Biscop's death, whereupon Ceolfrith moved to Wearmouth—the more important of the monastic communities—and that Bede came under his tutelage. Among other things, Robson maintained that if Bede had gone to Jarrow as a boy he would have had far more to say about the foundation and early years of that monastery in his *Historia Abbatum* (written in the mid 720s and popularly known as the 'Lives of the Abbots of Wearmouth and Jarrow') than is in fact the case: it is Wearmouth, not Jarrow, that is the chief focus of Bede's attention. At one time, Robson believed that Bede resided at Wearmouth into his late forties and only moved to Jarrow during the abbacy of Hwaetberht. Subsequently, Robson went further and concluded that Bede never moved to Jarrow at all.[22]

Even if Bede did reside at Jarrow, it is possible that sooner or later he returned to Wearmouth (the senior component of the 'one monastery in two places'), which presumably possessed a larger library that would have facilitated his scholarship.

What is beyond doubt is that Bede was a great intellectual with a thorough knowledge of Latin who devoted much time to writing. His first works were school-books, doubtless intended for his pupils, for teaching was one of Bede's duties. His remarkable literary output includes biblical commentaries, history—through which he popularised the *Anno Domini* dating system—verse, and chronological and scientific studies. For instance, he made a significant study of tides, partly based on information supplied to him by correspondents at places such as Lindisfarne, Whithorn and the Isle of Wight. Of Bede, Thomas MacKay comments, 'In all his writings he demonstrates a care and methodical precision which speak highly of his reliability and integrity, his thoroughness and control.'[23]

Bede's works made him a celebrated figure at home and, following his death, abroad as well. Among those who valued his scholarship were the monks of Lindisfarne (links between Wearmouth-Jarrow and Lindisfarne were evidently close at the time) who commissioned him to write an account of their revered former leader St Cuthbert, who had died in 687.

Bede is our chief source for the history of Wearmouth. Hence our knowledge of events following his demise is fragmentary. We do know that in the 760s one of his former pupils, a monk named Cuthbert, was abbot of the monastery. Among those with whom Cuthbert corresponded was an Englishman called Lull, the Archbishop of Mainz in Germany, to whom Cuthbert, in a letter of 764, requested that a harpist and someone skilled in making glass vessels should be sent to Wearmouth.

During Cuthbert's abbacy, members of the monastic community made copies of Bede's work. Copying this, and other material, could be onerous as Cuthbert's letter to Lull makes clear. The abbot apologises for a delay that had occurred in sending copies of Bede's writings for which the prelate had asked: those involved on the task had had to suspend their work for long periods because of inclement weather. Cuthbert wrote:

> Now since you asked me for some of the works of the blessed father Bede, for your love I have prepared what I could with my young pupils, to the best of their ability…. And if I had been able I would gladly have done more. But during the past winter the island of our race has been very savagely oppressed with cold and ice and with long and widespread storms of wind and rain, so that the hand of the scribe became sluggish and could not produce a very large number of books. [24]

A better known figure than either Cuthbert or Lull, is Alcuin. Born in about 735, the son of a Northumbrian nobleman, Alcuin was educated at York and in 782 went to Gaul where he served at the court of the greatest ruler in the western world, Charlemagne, although he was again in Northumbria from 790 to 793 before returning to the continent.

Alcuin was a prominent intellectual and a prolific writer. For example, over 300 of his letters survive. Among recipients were the monks of Wearmouth and Jarrow who received the following exhortation to good living:

> Consider the splendour of your churches, the beauty of your buildings, your way of life according to the Rule…. Let the boys be present with praises of the heavenly king, and not be digging foxes out of holes or following the fleeting courses of hares…. Reflect upon that most noble teacher…Bede, how eager he was to learn when he was young, what praise he has now among men, and what much greater glory of reward with God. Therefore, stir up sluggish minds by his example. Be attentive to those who teach, open your books, look closely at what is written, understand what it means, so that you may succeed both in nourishing yourselves and in offering the food of spiritual life to others. Avoid secret feasts and furtive drinkings like the snare of the Devil.[25]

In Alcuin's day, storm clouds were beginning to appear on the horizon for English monasticism. Indeed, a foretaste of what was to come occurred in 793 when 'the harrying of the heathen' resulted in the devastation of the monastery of Lindisfarne. In 794, moreover, another Northumbrian monastery (generally believed to be Jarrow) suffered the same fate when it was likewise attacked by Vikings—Germanic raiders from Scandinavia. Although religious life at both sites resumed, during the course of the latter half of the 9th century large-scale Viking invasions of England resulted in a general cessation of monastic life and Wearmouth, which was possibly in a state of decline, was one of the houses that evidently ceased to exist. It did so either as a result of destruction or the departure of the monks, and a lack of pottery, metalwork and coinage from the site are noteworthy.[26]

The Viking onslaught also brought an end to the Anglo-Saxon kingdom of Northumbria. In fact, of the four English kingdoms in existence in 865 when the main Viking attack commenced, only the southern kingdom of Wessex survived the turbulent years that ensued. From 871 Wessex was ruled by Alfred the Great—one of the most remarkable figures in British history—who repelled the Vikings and began an expansionist policy that was pursued vigorously in the 10th century by his successors, such as his grandson Athelstan. This resulted in the creation of the kingdom of England.

Meanwhile, in 875 the religious community on Lindisfarne had abandoned that island. They took with them the relics of St Cuthbert and duly settled at Chester-le-Street in the early 880s, having been granted most of the land between the Rivers Tyne and Tees (including the land upon which Sunderland now stands) by a Danish king of York named Guthred. At Chester-le-Street the community erected, or at least took over, a timber church which they dedicated to St Cuthbert.[27]

In 934, Athelstan visited Chester-le-Street during one of his rare appearances in the region and, according to a mid 10th century work, the *History of St Cuthbert*, granted various gifts to the Church of St Cuthbert. One such comprised South Wearmouth—*Wiremuthe australem*, the future Bishopwearmouth—and its dependencies, namely the settlements

A statue of Alfred the Great, King of Wessex (871–99), in Winchester

of Westoe, Offerton, Silksworth, the Ryhopes, Burdon, Seaham, Seaton, Dalton-le-Dale, Dawdon and Cold Hesledon. However, some scholars maintain that the list of gifts attributed to Athelstan should not be taken at face value. It may contain material dating from when the *History* was revised in the mid 11th century: 'it is entirely possible', states David Rollason, 'that whoever revised the *Historia*...expanded the list of Athelstan's gifts with items which might have been received much later but which he considered would have been worthy of that king's largesse.'[28] Either way, Bishopwearmouth—which is now a part of Sunderland—was evidently in existence before the Norman Conquest.

At some point in the late Anglo-Saxon period, St Peter's was likely restored to serve as a parish church. It is sometimes held that this occurred in the days of Aldhun, the first Bishop of Durham (in 995 the seat of the bishopric was moved from Chester-le-Street to Durham), who is presumed to have sent secular clergy, who did not live by a monastic Rule, to Wearmouth. The tower of St Peter's, which surmounts the earlier west porch of the church, is often said to have been constructed at this time but Eric Cambridge has plausibly argued that it dates from the late 11th century or slightly thereafter.[29]

Archaeological Findings

Mention must be made of archaeological excavations conducted at Monkwearmouth, as the site is now known, under the direction of Rosemary Cramp of the University of Durham, a process that commenced in 1959.[30] These revealed, among other things, that there were evidently two cemeteries situated south and southwest of St Peter's Church. One served the monastic community; the other, in close proximity to the west, contained the skeletons of men, women and children, and was a Saxon lay cemetery, some of whose burials evidently predated the founding of the monastery.

In all, 190 groups of bone have been analysed, mostly by the palaeopathologist Calvin Wells. Of the findings, we read that the proportion of children to adults 'was comparatively high … but it is not possible to conclude whether this was due to a bias in the sample, or whether it was a true reflection of the original number of children interred.'[31] Almost two-thirds of the juveniles had died aged six or under and likely causes of death were dysentery and enteritis.

On the other hand, most of the men and women apparently 'survived into middle or old age.'[32] Moreover, compared with skeletons that Wells had examined elsewhere, the Monkwearmouth remains, and especially those of females, had significantly less evidence of osteoarthritis. He thus concluded that the deceased had enjoyed a good food supply and generally led less physically demanding lives than the East Angles with whom they were compared.[33]

Interestingly, one of the skeletons was of a man who had fractured his pelvis and femur but had recovered from his injuries. Likely, he incurred the fractures by falling from an elevated position, perhaps while engaged on construction work, for of course erecting buildings such as St Peter's Church was not without risk. It is said, for example, that while involved in constructing Wilfrid's monastic church at Hexham, a young man fell from a great height and received horrific wounds from which he would have died had it not been for prompt medical attention and the prayers of Wilfrid himself.

The excavations at Monkwearmouth also demonstrated that Biscop's church was not the only impressive building of those comprising the monastic complex. The core of this complex was formed by the church and an enclosure against its south side, delimited by walls on the east and west sides, and by a range of buildings to the south. The latter was aligned parallel to the church and attached to it by a covered passageway. In addition to serving as a link with the church, the passage may well have been used as a place where monks occupied time by, for example, reading and writing. If so, the passage was analogous to the cloister walks of medieval monasteries.

In short, as Rosemary Cramp has written:

> The importance of this site is that it has produced buildings regularly aligned on the church, in which the quality of construction is reminiscent of Roman work. The painted plaster, decorative stone-carving, and coloured window-glass associated with them, all indicate the reintroduction of an advanced stone technology into the area.[34]

In view of this, and other factors such as the splendid library containing many volumes acquired on the continent, it is easy to agree with the statement of another leading Anglo-Saxonist, the late Patrick Wormald, that the monastery founded by Benedict Biscop was akin to 'an island of Mediterranean culture in a barbarian sea.'[35]

MEDIEVAL AND TUDOR TIMES

To the inhabitants of the communities on Wearside, Saturday, 14 October 1066 was just another day. They were unaware that a battle was raging in Sussex that would determine the destiny of the nation. Even if they had known that William of Normandy would emerge triumphant it is probable that some of them would not have cared: so what if the southerner King Harold was replaced by the Norman duke, it would make little difference to them and their lifestyle.

We know, however, that many of the English were far from indifferent to William's success for in the years that followed his coronation on Christmas Day, 1066, rebellions occurred and in one or two of these Wearsiders may have participated.

One revolt began in early 1069, shortly after William appointed Robert de Comines Earl of Northumbria. Robert arrived in Durham City in late January and was hospitably received by the Bishop of Durham, an Englishman named Aethelwine, who had evidently submitted to William the Conqueror. Comines was probably intending to press on beyond the Tyne. In the event, he never left the city. As the *Anglo-Saxon Chronicle* tersely relates, 'the local men surprised him in the stronghold at Durham, and killed him and 900 men with him.'[1]

In response to this revolt and others that soon followed, William ravaged the North in the winter of 1069–70 with great ferocity, for he was 'stern beyond all measure to those men who opposed his will.'[2] We do not know what, if anything, occurred on Wearside by way of retribution but what we do know is that in December 1069 Bishop Aethelwine, who feared that Norman vengeance would be indiscriminate, fled to Lindisfarne where he remained for a few months before returning to Durham.

To add to the region's problems, in 1070 Malcolm III of Scotland invaded England and entered County Durham from the west. Wearside may have escaped visitation by William's wrathful Normans, but according to the *Historia Regum* ('History of the Kings') the Scottish monarch came here while heading up the coast after ravaging Teesdale and Cleveland, and supervised the destruction of St Peter's Church founded by Benedict Biscop.

On Wearside, Malcolm reportedly met Edgar Aetheling, a young English prince and the senior representative of the line of Alfred the Great, as well as other members of the fugitive English royal family, whom he offered sanctuary north of the border. Another source, a tract written in the first decade of the 12th century by a Durham monk named Symeon (who was once thought to have also written the *Historia Regum*) says that in 1070 Bishop Aethelwine likewise made his way to Wearmouth. Given the turbulent nature of the times, he had decided to abandon his bishopric and had thus had a ship provisioned for his departure. According to Symeon, the bishop set sail for Cologne but contrary winds duly set in and the ship was blown to Scotland instead. Aethelwine was not the only high ranking person from England who landed on the shores of Malcolm's kingdom that year. Edgar Aetheling also did so. Hence William Aird has suggested that it is possible 'that Aethelwine was travelling as part of Edgar's company.'[3]

Within a few years other people likewise came to Wearside. Unlike Malcolm, they were intent on restoration, not destruction. They arrived in 1075 and were led by Aldwin, a monk from Winchcombe. He had travelled north a year or so earlier

The tower of St Peter's, Monkwearmouth. The upper stages of the tower were perhaps added by Aldwin

to live a life of simple devotion in the land of saints, of whose deeds he had read in the works of Bede. Aldwin and his like-minded companions were sent to the mouth of the Wear by Aethelwine's French successor Bishop Walcher (whom the Conqueror had appointed to the see of Durham), a man who wished to encourage the revival of monasticism in the North.

Symeon relates that the monks, who lived under the Benedictine Rule—Aldwin served as abbot—constructed 'little habitations of wattle work' and 'took pains to clear out the church of St Peter, nothing more than the half-ruined walls of which were at this time standing.' Moreover, they 'cut down the trees, and rooted up the thorns and brambles which had taken possession of the whole site' and roofed the church with thatch.[4]

The work of Aldwin and his small number of associates (some of whom were French) must have been a source of interest, and perhaps pleasure, to members of the lay communities in the vicinity to whom they are said to have preached. For example, a settlement—subsequently named Monkwearmouth—lay a short distance to the northwest of St Peter's Church. However, like many other people in the region, local folk may well have resented Bishop Walcher whose knights acted in a tyrannical manner in the bishopric. Walcher (who often visited Aldwin and his monks) was naturally held accountable for their misdeeds and in 1080 was murdered at Gateshead by rebellious natives. King William responded by sending his own half-brother, Bishop Odo of Bayeux, to ravage and subdue the area. We can be sure that he was not averse to doing so. The Anglo-Norman historian

Orderic Vitalis relates that Odo was 'not a bishop, but a tyrant'[5] and it is possible that the inhabitants of the settlements on Wearside experienced his wrath.

In the early 1080s Walcher's successor, William de St Calais, enhanced the lands of the monastery at St Peter's by granting the monks the township of Southwick, over a mile to the west. Initially, the monks' estate had comprised Monkwearmouth and, perhaps, Fulwell. The latter has been described as 'Presumably an original possession as an appendage of Monkwearmouth.'[6] Fulwell was certainly in existence by the 1150s, when it was referred to as belonging to Durham Cathedral Priory in a papal confirmation of the monastery's possessions in 1157.

In May 1083, Bishop William de St Calais summoned Aldwin and his monks to Durham where he was founding a Benedictine monastery, whose landed endowment would include Monkwearmouth and Southwick and, possibly from the outset as well, Fulwell. At Durham, the bishop duly commenced building a splendid Norman cathedral. Henceforth, St Peter's is often thought to have served as a cell of Durham Cathedral Priory, occupied by one or two monks under a 'master.' That such a cell existed during the Middles Ages is certain. But a gap in occupation of the site evidently first occurred and apparently lasted into the early 13th century.

Puiset and his Charter

In 1153 a colourful young man who was to become a figure of some importance in the history of Sunderland was elected to the bishopric of Durham. His name was Hugh du Puiset, and as an eminent medievalist, Austin Lane Poole observed, he was 'an aristocrat of the old school, connected by family ties with kings and counts, a man who lived and did everything in the grand manner,' a prelate who 'loved his purse better than his Bible.'[7] He was undoubtedly one of the most significant of Durham's long line of so-called 'Prince Bishops', prelates who, with royal sanction, enjoyed prerogatives exercised elsewhere in England by the king: the palatine status of the bishops is sometimes said to have been created by William the Conqueror but was a gradual development that was still not complete in the days of Bishop Hugh.

During the 12th century England as a whole experienced a period of economic advancement, and one manifestation of this development was the creation of numerous boroughs, founded by the king or individual lords. Successive Bishops of Durham likewise created, or at least took an interest in, boroughs. Indeed, by 1183 there were five episcopal boroughs within the diocese: Durham, Gateshead, Norham on Tweed, Darlington, and the port of Wearmouth, i.e., Sunderland.

The latter, located on the south side of the River Wear opposite St Peter's Church, received a charter from Puiset which granted its citizens a number of customs also enjoyed by the burgesses of the royal borough of Newcastle upon Tyne, founded by Henry I (1100–35). It is sometimes said that the charter dates from about 1154, but this is erroneous, for it is evident that the charter was granted in, or shortly after, 1180. For one thing, Philip, the Sheriff of Durham, one of the men who witnessed the charter, only assumed that office in 1180.

Although it is often stated that Puiset's charter made the port of Wearmouth a borough, Gaillard Lapsley has stated that the document should be viewed as granting 'the constitution or customs of Newcastle' to the burgesses of an already existing one.[8] Furthermore, another distinguished historian, Geoffrey Scammell, has suggested that the port was perhaps made a borough by Bishop Flambard (1099–1128).[9] Hugh himself, though, seems a more likely candidate for the borough's creation. Either way, Puiset's charter should be seen as one that granted the burgesses some privileges enjoyed by their counterparts in Newcastle and a confirmation of ones they already had.

The charter begins as follows:

> Hugh, by the grace of God, Bishop of Durham to the prior, archdeacons, barons and all men of his whole bishopric, both French and English, greeting. Know you that we, by this present charter, have given and confirmed to our burgesses of Wearmouth free customs in their borough according to the customs of the burgesses of Newcastle.[10]

Among the customs in question, was the right of the burgesses to determine all pleas arising within the borough with the exception of Crown pleas—in County Durham, the latter, which involved more serious crimes, were dealt with by the bishop's judicial apparatus. The charter also granted burgesses the right to judge peasants and other rural inhabitants who were indebted to them (except any sent to the borough on the bishop's behalf), without having to secure the permission of the reeve, an episcopal appointee chosen from the ranks of the burgesses who would hold the borough court.

Moreover, they could purchase whatever merchandise they wished from ships visiting the port—with the exception of salt and herrings, the merchandise had to be landed before sale. They were also free to dispose of land bought with their own money without having to obtain the consent of their heirs. Among other things, the charter says that a burgess could export his corn whenever he desired except at a time when the bishop imposed an embargo; and was free to use the 'common pasture' (evidently a reference to what was later known as the Town Moor) which had already been granted to the community. He was also allowed to sell his land and move elsewhere unless a claim existed against his ownership of the property.

Additionally, the charter decreed that a villein (an unfree member of the peasantry) who came to live in the borough, and held land and a house in it for a year and a day, was henceforth free to enjoy the status of a burgess if he had not been reclaimed by his lord. Furthermore, in the borough, Hugh du Puiset waived his right to blodwite, merchet, heriot, and stengesduit. These were, respectively, a fine paid for the shedding of blood; a payment by a villein to his lord for permission to marry off a daughter; a fine payable to a lord by the successor of a deceased tenant; and a fine for an assault committed with a stick or comparable instrument. The charter also stipulates that the bishop retained the same custom arising from fish purchased at Wearmouth as a baron, Robert de Bruce, held from his own people at Hartlepool.

Hugh du Puiset no doubt hoped that the borough would prosper and be a good source of revenue from tolls etc. But success was not guaranteed. For one reason or another, while some boroughs flourished many others failed to do so. A case in point is Warenmouth, founded further up the coast near Bamburgh by Henry III in 1247, whose foundation charter—which includes the grant of a merchants' guild—is sometimes erroneously thought to refer to the borough of Wearmouth. The Northumbrian borough never prospered and was in fact moribund by the close of the 13th century.

And what of Wearmouth? Despite the privileges granted to its citizens, the port did not take off during the remainder of Puiset's pontificate (which ended in 1195) and of the episcopal boroughs was far surpassed in importance by Gateshead and Durham. It was also outclassed by Hartlepool, County Durham's premier port during the Middle Ages. Indeed, the borough was to remain a nondescript place for several centuries. For instance, none of the five orders of friars that became established in England during the 13th century—orders whose ministry was primarily based in urban areas—founded a friary at Sunderland, whereas by the close of the century they were all represented in Newcastle upon Tyne and Berwick upon Tweed.

Seal of Hugh du Puiset, Bishop of Durham (1153–95)

Nevertheless, Christine Newman has highlighted evidence that indicates that for part of the medieval period the borough was busier than previously supposed. For one thing, pottery finds from recent archaeological excavations on Low Street (along the riverfront) indicate that the port's level of trade was more significant than was imagined. What is more, in 1296 instead of a being called a reeve, the term normally used for the figure in charge of Sunderland's administration, Stephen Gare was described as the town's mayor: 'This unique designation...suggests that Sunderland was then prospering and becoming more urbanised. By 1319, however, the leading borough official is once again referred to as reeve, perhaps reflecting lower aspirations in the declining economic conditions of the time.'[11]

Pottery evidence shows that subsequently, in the late 14th century, some of the ships that visited Sunderland came from the Low Countries. By this date, however, the borough's fortunes were at a low ebb and this remained the case into the 15th and 16th centuries, by which time the borough court was defunct.[12]

Presumably, several factors were responsible for Wearmouth's general lacklustre performance. One may simply have been a scarcity of individuals with drive and ambition. Moreover in the late Middle Ages when Scottish raids blighted the North East, many merchants must have found Newcastle, with its strong town walls, mostly erected in the 13th and 14th centuries, a more attractive venue. Newcastle, in contrast to Sunderland, witnessed significant expansion. Primarily, its development was due to seaborne trade involving such cargoes as wool and coal and by 1334 the town's overall economic growth was such that it ranked fourth in wealth in the country, surpassed only by London, Bristol and York. Furthermore, in 1400 Newcastle (with the exception of the castle, a royal stronghold), was severed from Northumberland and made a county in its own right, a rare distinction at the time.[13]

Boldon Book and Beyond

As Geoffrey Scammell comments 'the last quarter of the twelfth century was a period of agricultural prosperity' in which some 'estates were surveyed and consolidated for their better administration and the profit of their owners.'[14] For example, in 1181 and 1182 the monks of St Paul's (London) and Bury St Edmunds, carried out such surveys of their lands. In view of Hugh du Puiset's great interest in financial matters, it is not surprising that a survey of settlements comprising his estate in the diocese of Durham was conducted—his extensive possessions elsewhere, such as in Yorkshire, were excluded as indeed were some settlements within the bishopric.

The survey, which is dated 1183, is known as *Boldon Book*. It is often said that it is so named because the village of Boldon, a short distance northwest of Sunderland, is the first entry, but that honour belongs to the City of Durham. The survey owes its name to the fact that the Latin phrase *'sicut ille de Boldon'* (as those of Boldon) is used when dealing with the renders and services due from peasants in 19 of the vills mentioned, thereby avoiding the need to repeatedly describe at length the obligations of the tenants to their lord.

One of the non Boldon-type entries is as follows: 'Sunderland is leased out and renders 100s. Roger of Audry pays one mark for the millpond built on the land of Sunderland.'[15]

Whether or not this entry refers to the Sunderland with whose history we are dealing has been disputed. One argument used to support the view that it does not, is the fact that the entry is not located in the section of the survey in which most of the bishop's properties on Wearside appear—in general vills are listed in association with others in the same locality. Instead, the Sunderland entry appears amid a number of sites on Tyneside and along the River Tees. Furthermore, Roger of Audry (or Audre) who belonged to an important family with lands in central Durham, and whose name appears as a witness on some episcopal charters, did not witness Puiset's charter to the port of Wearmouth or Sunderland. The fact that there is a reference to the borough of Wearmouth elsewhere in the survey likewise indicates that the entry quoted above relates to another site. The reference simply states that the *'Burgus de Wermuth'* yielded a mere 20s.[16] It is fitting to leave the last word on the matter to one of the foremost authorities on medieval Durham, the late H.S. Offler, who declared: 'Sunderland…is not to be identified as the port at the mouth of the Wear. It is the Sunderland from which Sunderland Bridge by Croxdale takes its name, as is indicated by the entry's reference to Roger of Audre, lord of Croxdale, Butterby and Coxhoe.'[17]

Although Puiset's survey mentions the borough of Wearmouth in a cursory manner, it contains a fuller entry for another Wearmouth—the future Bishopwearmouth—located on a low hill about a mile to the west and likewise south of the River Wear. The entry begins thus: 'In Wearmouth and Tunstall [a township approximately two miles to the southwest], there are 22 villeins and each holds, pays rent and works as those of Boldon.'[18]

The villeins owed certain renders and services to their lord in return for the land they held, and to gain information about their obligations, we must of course turn to the entry for Boldon.[19] This states that the 22 villeins of that community (the fact that the number of peasants was the same is coincidental) each held two bovates of land amounting to 30 acres. In return, each villein rendered annually, among other things, 2s. 6d. of scot-penny and as Frederick Bradshaw has suggested, this was 'an acknowledgement perhaps of 1d. for every acre of land he held.'[20] The villein also had to pay 16d. of carriage-penny in order to avoid carriage-service (a duty incumbent on peasants mentioned in other entries), and had to provide 'half a scot-chalder of oats', five wagon-loads of wood, two hens and 10 eggs.

Furthermore, in addition to working his land, each villein had to work three days a week on his lord's local farm (demesne) except for the weeks of Easter and Whitsun, and 13 days at Christmas. During autumn, the villein and his household, with the exception of the housewife (*excepta husewiva*)[21] had to do four days of special work when the lord's reaping had to be done. Added to these and other services, the villeins were collectively required to construct annually, if necessary, a house 40ft long and 15ft wide, in which case they were each exempted from paying 4d. of carriage-penny.

Returning to the entry for Bishopwearmouth and Tunstall, we read: 'Six cottagers hold and work as those of Boldon'.[22] There 12 cottagers each held 12 acres, and owed in return two days' work a week, except at Easter etc., and 12 hens and 60 eggs. Like villeins, cottagers were unfree peasants, but they held less land and so the services they had to provide were less onerous. Poole has said of cottagers in general: 'Their principal function was to provide a reserve of labour which could be called upon in times of stress.'[23] For instance, in addition to working their small tenements and performing labour for their lord, cottagers could, if required, help prosperous villeins cultivate their land in return for a wage.

The entry for Bishopwearmouth and Tunstall also mentions three specialist members of the associated communities: the carpenter, smith and pinder. The former, who is said to have been elderly, held 12 acres in return for making and repairing ploughs and harrows. The smith likewise possessed 12 acres. In his case he did so for providing the iron work for the ploughs, and for the '*carbone quem invenit*', a phrase that has been translated, 'the coal which he finds', or 'the coal which he provides.' Given that the 'coal' was likely charcoal, the latter reading seems preferable. The pinder, who impounded stray cattle in the pinfold until they were redeemed by their owners for a fee, also held 12 acres. He did so in return for 40 hens (one version of *Boldon Book* says 24 hens) and 500 eggs.[24]

We also read that Bishopwearmouth and Tunstall yielded 20s. of cornage, a payment made by the peasants for the right to pasture cattle. In addition, one version of the survey also mentions that they rendered '*ii vaccas de metride*', a problematic phrase sometimes translated 'two cows in milk' or 'two milk cows'.

The survey also says that the lordship farm was leased out 'with a stock of 20 oxen [some versions say 20 bovates], two harrows and 200 sheep,' and with the mill, rendered £20. The fishery (or fisheries) yielded £6. In some of the bishop's townships the demesne was in his hands and the unfree peasants worked it under the supervision of persons appointed by him, but here as noted, the lordship farm was leased out. It was the unnamed lessee's responsibility to see that it was worked by the tenants of the townships in accord with the requirements stipulated in *Boldon Book* and that the bishop received a share of the profits.

Boldon-type vills such as Bishopwearmouth and Tunstall (which form only a proportion of the 150 or so settlements mentioned) were all located in the east of County Durham, and of them Paul Harvey comments: 'Other twelfth-century estate surveys offer no parallel to a long series of manors sharing exactly the same set of customs and services...such total uniformity can only have been imposed from above, though not necessarily on a single occasion.'[25] Evidently, such uniformity was not of distant creation. One possible explanation for the nature of the Boldon-type vills has been provided by W.E. Kapelle, who has argued that they were places that had been re-established by Walcher, the Bishop of Durham, after being devastated by William the Conqueror's soldiers. Kapelle states that at the time of their reconstruction, and the reinstatement of the peasantry, heavy labour services were imposed on members of the revived communities by 'Walcher and his men [who]...manorialized the Boldon villages and imposed week work on the peasants.'[26] However, this view has not gained universal acceptance.

Puiset's survey also records the existence of other settlements that have since become part of Sunderland or lie in very close proximity. Some of these—Cleadon, Whitburn, Ryhope and Burdon—were Boldon-type vills, while among other local settlements were Washington and the 'two parts of Herrington' where other tenurial arrangements obtained.

A gentleman named William de Hartburn held the manor of Washington (*Wessyngton*) with the exception of the church and its property, in exchange for the township of Hartburn, a place located in the southeast of the county. In addition to paying £4 rent, William's obligations to the bishop included attending the annual great hunt, an event held in Weardale, with two greyhounds. On the other hand, the entry for Herrington mentions a dreng (a more exalted figure than unfree peasants) and notes that in accord with his tenure, he kept a dog and a horse (*pascit canem et equum*) and, among other things, did court duty.[27]

In 1195, during the reign of Richard the Lionheart, Hugh du Puiset went 'the way of all flesh', whereupon the bishopric of Durham was vacant until a successor was appointed in 1197. During the interim, the bishopric was administered by royal officials and a tallage (tax) was imposed, of which details were recorded on a Great

Roll of the Exchequer. Sunderland (the port of Wearmouth) was required to pay 58s., of which sum 27s. had so far been paid, whereas the 'township of Weremuth' (Bishopwearmouth) had nearly met its tallage requirement, 37s. 4d., for the treasury had so far received 31s. 1d.[28]

The use of the name 'Sunderland' for the port of Wearmouth at this time is the first known use of the name for the borough. It can simply mean 'separate land', or indicate land set apart for a special purpose, or separated from the main estate. It is usually stated that it was given to the place with whose history we are dealing because the community in question grew up on land separated by the River Wear from Monkwearmouth to the north. However, the name may very well have come into use to distinguish the borough from [Bishop]wearmouth.

The borough was linked to Bishopwearmouth by its principal thoroughfare, which was thus aligned east-west and would later become known as High Street. At Sunderland a number of burgages, narrow strips of land, ran southward from this street towards the town moor. Nevertheless, despite

Durham Cathedral, whose monks were major landholders on Wearside

its borough status, Sunderland, would have looked very rural. We have noted that Puiset's charter refers to the burgesses having their own lands and the right to common pasturage, which indicates that they had agricultural interests. For its part, Bishopwearmouth was of course inhabited by peasants primarily engaged in farming; peasants whose humble residences were doubtless overlooked by St Michael's and All Angels' Church (now Sunderland Minster) which apparently was of late Saxon origin.

As noted above, not all the settlements on Wearside belonged to the Bishop of Durham. Another landlord was an institution, Durham Cathedral Priory, which possessed settlements on the north side of the River Wear, namely Monkwearmouth, Southwick and Fulwell.

At Monkwearmouth (often simply referred to as Wearmouth in medieval sources), the settlement overlooked a central green and was aligned east-to-west. It extended eastward from where the *Wheatsheaf* now stands and probably terminated on the site of today's Church Street. Southwick was centred on the present green, and at Fulwell (located at the site of Station Road) the dwellings were likewise built in two rows on either side of a green.

In addition, in around 1195 part of the township of Silksworth came into the hands of the monks as a result of a grant by a man named Philip, son of Hamo. The township, in the parish of Bishopwearmouth, lay well to the south of the river. Like the three townships mentioned in the preceding paragraph, it has since become part of Sunderland.

According to a valuation of the priory's property of around 1230, its most valuable local possession was Southwick. The combined income from its tenants was £6 9s. 2d. a year, significantly more than was acquired from any of the other properties. It was, incidentally, also more than the priory received from another of its townships, South Shields. In addition, unlike Fulwell and Monkwearmouth, Southwick possessed a mill that provided a revenue of 100 shillings.[29]

Later on, in the early 1320s the priory apparently acquired the rest of Silksworth though the exact course of events is unclear. In 1323–4, Edward II granted the remaining part of the estate to Richard de Emeldon (also spelt 'Embleton'), a prominent Newcastle merchant who held the mayoralty of that town on several occasions, 'and it was at this point that the monks subsequently reckoned that they had acquired their title to the manor and lordship of the vill, but on what grounds remains to be established.'[30] Of Emeldon, Christine Newman comments: 'He seems to have held the whole manor from the priory at a rent of 13s. 4d.'[31]

To regulate various matters on its property, Durham Cathedral Priory held halmote courts: the circuit would begin in the summer, and further halmotes would then be held in the autumn and the following spring. The courts, presided over by senior members of the monastic community, dealt with matters such as the granting of vacant land to new tenants, the settling of disputes, and punishing wayward behaviour and breaches of manorial custom.[32]

Fortunately, halmote records shed light on the local scene. In 1296, for instance, some of the prior's tenants at Monkwearmouth were fined for ploughing land without permission. Furthermore, several Southwick tenants, Robert the miller, William Etteben, Alexander son of Henry, John Ros, and Thomas son of Ralph, were called to account and fined for sowing the land of Laurence son of Patrick without permission, and for carrying away the resultant corn.[33] Early the next year, a certain William Maye became the tenant of a toft and land at Fulwell. However, at the halmote provision was made for the previous tenant, Alan son of Peter. It was stipulated that for the rest of his life he should have lodging on the toft as well as three roods of the aforesaid land, namely one rood in each of the township's fields.[34]

We also read of a dramatic incident dealt with at a halmote in the autumn of 1365. John Reid, Hugh Rainaldson and other tenants from Southwick, carrying 'staves and other weapons', had forcibly entered the manor of Fulwell by breaking down gates in order to retrieve draught animals that had been impounded there. Consequently each of the wrongdoers was fined 40d.[35]

Moreover, an halmote entry on Fulwell from the summer of 1368 notes that John Gray and a woman named Agnes were fined over the theft of three loaves of white bread by their servants. White bread was a luxury (peasants' bread was of inferior quality) and the loaves were en route to Westoe where, presumably, they were intended to be consumed at the table of the Prior of Durham who possessed a manor house there.[36]

Farming and Mills

A substantial proportion of the land at Fulwell and the other local townships would have contained ploughed areas known as furlongs or flatts. Each flatt, (the preferred term in the North East) consisted of long narrow curving strips known as rigs, which normally followed the lie of the land to facilitate drainage: ploughed areas too small for full-length rigs were known as butts. Each rig consisted of a central raised area flanked by furrows. Consequently, flatts and butts had a corrugated aspect. Ploughing was done using teams of oxen that drew ploughs with iron cutting edges that turned the soil inward, thereby forming the central ridge in each rig as the team moved back and forth. In Sunderland, traces of 'ridge and furrow' can be seen at the east end of Backhouse Park.

The individual holdings of villagers were not compact. Instead, they consisted of scattered strips within the flatts and butts, and when engaged in farming the members of a community acted in concert: few villagers, for example, would have owned enough oxen to make their own plough team.

Likely, there was an approximately threefold division in the use of the arable land, with one third being sown with spring crops such as oats and barley, the other third used for autumn-sown crops such as wheat and rye, and the remainder left to lie fallow so that it could regain its fertility, a process aided by the use of manure.

Vital to the well-being of a community was its meadowland, usually low-lying ground along the banks of a stream or river. Meadows produced hay for winter fodder (presumably some livestock was slaughtered in the autumn and the meat salted for winter consumption) and provided grazing for animals once the hay had been gathered.

In addition to the arable fields and meadowland was pasture, whose primary function was to support the villagers' oxen during the grass-growing months of spring, summer and autumn. Every township also had moorland, which could be a source of resources such as wood, but whose main function was to serve as rough grazing for livestock belonging to members of the community.

Animals were sometimes disruptive and in early 1381 a halmote court conducted by officers of Durham Cathedral Priory, instructed the tenants of Fulwell that none of them were to allow horses, pigs, cows and oxen to leave the township without supervision (*'quod nullus eorum permittant equos, porcos, vaccas, boves, exire villam sine custodia'*) and that pigs were not to go across the 'Marlpots.'[37]

A number of local townships had a mill (most mills in medieval England were water-driven) which was built and owned by the lord, for whom it was a source of revenue. His tenants were obligated to have their corn ground there and a fraction of the ground flour went to the lord as payment. Unless stated otherwise, such as in Hugh du Puiset's charter to the burgesses of the port of Wearmouth, grinding corn at home using querns was prohibited though it no doubt occurred from time to time. The tenants also had to play a part in maintaining the mill in good order.

Some of the mills belonged to the Bishop of Durham, as was of course true of the mill mentioned in *Boldon Book's* entry for Bishopwearmouth and Tunstall. This was also the case with a windmill extant at Millfield (west of Bishopwearmouth) by the late 14th century. On the other hand, as noted, the mill at Southwick belonged to Durham Priory and in early 1370 its tenants at Fulwell, Monkwearmouth and Southwick, were reminded of their obligation to have their corn ground at the prior's mill and not elsewhere—*'ad molend. de Suthwyk et non alibi.'*[38] By 1383, if not earlier, the mill in question was a windmill and in the summer of that year two men, Robert and William, became lessees of the mill and of a Southwick fishery—*'ceperunt molend. ventriticum de Suthwyk ac piscariam pertin. ejusdem villae'*—assets last held by a tenant named John Reid.[39]

Most peasants on Wearside, in common with others elsewhere, were not fortunate enough to have a mill in their own village and were therefore obligated to transport their corn to one elsewhere. For example, the tenants of the Prior of Durham resident at Fulwell and Monkwearmouth had to make their way to the mill at Southwick. In the early 16th century, the Prior and monks of Durham were still taking an interest in such matters, as is revealed by records dating from 1505–6, when the tenants of Monkwearmouth and Fulwell were reminded of their obligation to grind their corn at Southwick and one of their number, a Fulwell tenant, was fined for not doing so. The miller's behaviour may have been a contributory factor—he was accused of swapping good grain for bad. The use of querns was however now permitted by the Durham monks but only if a licence had been bought from the lessee of the mill.

Religious Life

At a local level, the centre of religious life was the parish church and most of the people in the vicinity of Sunderland lived in the parishes of Monkwearmouth and Bishopwearmouth.

While some parishes in the North East comprised just one or two townships, many contained several and covered a significant amount of territory. This was certainly true of Bishopwearmouth, an extensive parish in excess of 20 square miles that embraced Sunderland and communities such as Burdon, Ryhope, Tunstall, Ford (a township first mentioned in 1361) and Silksworth. It has been suggested that such large parishes came about in Anglo-Saxon times when the Church, engaged in the process of establishing a system of territorial parishes, likely simply based their size on existing secular administrative units cum estates known as 'shires', units that were widespread in the region.

Monkwearmouth, although smaller than Bishopwearmouth, was likewise substantial and within its boundaries lay the townships of Monkwearmouth, Fulwell, Southwick and Hylton.[40] Other local parishes included Washington and the larger and more important parish of Houghton-le-Spring, which possessed one of the finest churches in County Durham, a structure that includes Norman fabric but mostly dates from the 13th century.[41]

In the early years of that century, religious life on Wearside must have been disrupted during the troubled reign of King John, one of England's most colourful monarchs, for the king quarrelled with the pope over who should be appointed Archbishop of Canterbury. As a result, in 1208, the pope placed England under an Interdict. Consequently, the clergy of England withdrew their priestly ministry in almost its entirety: for instance, marriages did not take place and the dead did not receive a Christian burial. The Interdict was finally lifted in 1214, after John had reluctantly submitted.

An artist's impression of life in England during the Interdict (John Kenney)

The parish of Bishopwearmouth was a rich living, and the parish church was imposing. St Michael's probably began its existence as a timber structure before the Norman Conquest. If so, evidence such as 18th century illustrations, suggests that the church was rebuilt in stone in the 12th century. Apparently, at this date the building comprised a Norman west tower, a nave with round arches opening to aisles, and a chancel. Significant alterations were made in around 1300—among other things, the aisles were widened and the chancel rebuilt. The church appears to have experienced further changes later in the medieval period, work that included heightening the tower and providing the nave with a clerestory. Sadly, owing to rebuilding in more recent times, almost none of the medieval fabric survives. The east end of the chancel is the most notable feature dating from the Middle Ages.

The rectorship of Bishopwearmouth was held by some very able men. One such was Adam Marsh (born c.1200 in the diocese of Bath) who was evidently appointed to the parish by his uncle, who became the Bishop of Durham in 1217. Marsh held the rectorship until 1232 and later became the first Franciscan friar to hold a chair of theology at Oxford. Plurality, the holding of several benefices simultaneously, was common during the Middle Ages and thus many of the rectors only visited the parish occasionally, if indeed they appeared at all. Hence the day-to-day ministry was left to subordinates.

The wills of some of the rectors express a desire to be laid to rest in St Michael's. That of Richard Holme, who from time to time had been called upon to play a role in diplomatic relations with the Scots on behalf of the state, is a case in point. He died in April 1424, having stated in his will that he wished to be buried 'in my Parish Church of Wearmouth.'[42]

And what of the parish of Monkwearmouth? Here, the rector was not an individual but an ecclesiastical corporation, Durham Cathedral Priory, and pastoral duties were entrusted to a vicar.

Medieval fabric at St Peter's includes these windows, dating from the mid 14th century, in the south wall of the chancel

The parish church was, of course, St Peter's, which had been repaired by Aldwin in the late 11th century. Subsequently, during the course of the 13th century the church was enlarged by the construction of a broad north aisle, delimited from the nave by three arches forming an arcade. However, the present north aisle (and much of the other fabric) only date from the mid 1870s.

Within the parish, Durham Priory had a daughter house or cell at Monkwearmouth, a site often referred to in the Middle Ages as Wearmouth and, less frequently, as North Wearmouth. Evidently the cell post-dated the departure of Aldwin and his monks in 1083 and our earliest date for its existence is the year 1235. The cell was presided over by a master, who usually only had one or two fellow monks under his charge, and was required to render a yearly account at Durham of the receipts and expenses of the cell.

The cell's principal buildings were evidently located to the south of St Peter's and the small complex included a cloister. In 1321 and thereafter, it was recorded that the cell possessed a master's chamber, as well as a hall, kitchen, bakehouse, pantry, and other structures including a brewhouse.

The cell was one of several that belonged to the Benedictine priory and was never well endowed—its sources of income included tithes from the parish of Monkwearmouth, payments for burial at St Peter's Church, and a home farm at Monkwearmouth.[43] Financial difficulties were thus not uncommon. According to R.B. Dobson, in the 15th century the cell was frequently on the brink of insolvency, for the masters 'regularly failed to balance their income and their expenditure', as is shown for example by the annual account for the year 1427–8, in which 'the master of Wearmouth recorded an excess expenditure of £14 over an annual income of £52.'[44]

Those present at Monkwearmouth were sent to Wearside by the Prior of Durham who was in overall control of the cells. Personnel at these daughter houses frequently changed. It was generally rare for monks to stay at one for a long time. To illustrate the point: on 19 May 1431 a monk named John Gateshead was sent to Monkwearmouth from a cell on Holy Island, but on 6 June 1432 he was transferred to Durham itself.

Evidently, some Durham monks found serving in daughter houses appealing. Finchale Priory, for instance, was a popular posting. But it is apparent that most cells, including Monkwearmouth, had less attraction. Indeed, Priors of Durham sometimes used dependent houses as dumping grounds for troublesome monks whom they wished to remove from the scene, effectively sending them into 'unofficial exile'.

From time to time the monks at Monkwearmouth were presumably visited by a monastic official from Durham known as the cellarer. The priory's records show

Finchale Priory, several miles upstream from Sunderland. The priory owned land in Sunderland and was a place of pilgrimage to which some locals journeyed to visit the grave of St Godric, (1065–1170)

that Sunderland was one of the places that holders of that office visited to purchase fish for the monastery and its many guests. In August 1307, for example, fish and eels were acquired at Sunderland, whereas in 1333–4 five loads of whiting and other fish were bought.[45]

Whilst here some cellarers doubtless popped across the river by ferry (there was no bridge until 1796) to have a chat with their fellow Durham monks. The ferry, operated by the monastic cell, crossed the river from a point at the foot of what later became known as Bodlewell Lane.[46] Prior to a great flood in 1400, at low tide one could also cross the river on foot via a ford that existed further downstream at the river mouth.

Years of Fear and Uncertainty

In 1296, during the reign of Edward I, an event occurred that was to affect the lives of the inhabitants of this locality—the commencement of a war between England and Scotland. The Bishop of Durham at this date was Antony Bek, 'the most valiant clerk in Christendom.' At the subsequent Battle of Falkirk in 1298—when an army under the command of the ardent Scottish nationalist, William Wallace, the hero of the dramatic but woefully inaccurate film *Braveheart* was soundly defeated—the bishop led a division that included Wearside's leading laymen, Sir Robert de Hylton (of whose family something will be said later) and Sir John FitzMarmaduke, whose seat was at Silksworth.[47]

In 1307 Edward I died. He was succeeded by his ineffectual son Edward II, a man cast from a very different mould, a man more fond of pursuits such as digging and thatching than he was of war, a point touched on in later years by his biographer who observed: 'He has achieved nothing laudable or memorable, save that he has married royally and has begotten an heir…. If he had devoted to arms the labour that he expended on rustic pursuits, he would have raised England aloft: his name would have resounded throughout the land.'[48]

Edward showed his incapacity in the military field in 1314. At Bannockburn, near Stirling, he led a formidable army (drawn largely from the North) to defeat at the hands of a smaller Scottish force under Scotland's monarch, Robert the Bruce. During the war, and especially after Bannockburn, northern England was subjected to repeated Scottish raids. Within weeks of the battle, raiders were at large in Northumberland and County Durham and some even pressed on into Yorkshire. The policy pursued by Bruce and his lieutenants was to collect as much plunder as possible and to induce communities into avoiding the destruction or loss of property by agreeing to pay blackmail. In June 1315, for instance, when Bruce was at Chester-le-Street, County Durham offered the sum of 800 marks for a truce until Christmas. Indeed, on at least eight occasions in the years 1311–27, Durham bought peace from the Scots. 'As far south as Ripon and Richmond', comments Jean Scammell, such agreements 'decided the extent to which life continued in the threatened counties and gave a pattern to what otherwise appears wholesale, wanton destruction.' She continues by stating that of the northern counties, 'Durham alone endeavoured to make block payments for the county as a whole, and as a result largely escaped damage although owing to the intervals between truces it did not gain total immunity.'[49]

Apparently, Scottish raiders did not plunder the settlements on Wearside. Nevertheless, their inhabitants would have been affected by the fear and uncertainty that prevailed in the region during these years, and were called upon to contribute to the sums handed over to the Scots to purchase truces. A key figure in collecting the money, was a leading member of County Durham's baronage, John FitzMarmaduke's son and successor, Richard, whose property included part of the township of Silksworth. FitzMarmaduke's life ended violently in 1318 when he was murdered on Framwellgate Bridge at Durham by one of his relatives, Robert Neville, the eldest son of the lord of Raby.

As part of England's war effort during this unhappy period, supplies were carried north by sea. One of the vessels involved was the *Falcon* of King's Lynn, Norfolk. In the winter of 1315–6 it did so laden with a cargo of wheat destined for the garrison of Berwick upon Tweed. The ship never arrived. It was driven ashore at Whitburn, and although the crew survived, locals stripped the vessel of tackle and cargo to the value of £200.[50]

To add to the problems caused by the conflict with Scotland, matters were made worse by the fact that the war coincided with natural disasters, at least some of which likely affected Wearside. In 1313–7 sheep murrain blighted flocks, while three successive wet summers, beginning in 1315, ruined hay and corn harvests, causing deaths from starvation and disease. According to the *Lanercost Chronicle* (written in Cumbria), 1316 witnessed 'such a mortality of men in England and Scotland through famine and pestilence

English soldiers fleeing from the Battle of Bannockburn (John Kenney). The defeat had serious repercussions for the inhabitants of the northern counties of England

as had not been heard of in our time.' Furthermore, history repeated itself in 1321 when the harvests failed again.

An indication of the impact the troubled years of the early 14th century had on Wearside can be gained from valuations made of Bishopwearmouth parish church. In 1292, when St Michael's was assessed for papal taxation, its revenues were deemed to be worth £100, a significant sum. By the time of another assessment, in 1318, the value had been reduced by almost 50 per cent.

Fear and uncertainty remained part of life in the North East in subsequent years, partly owing to further conflict with the Scots, and one of the fatalities was Richard de Emeldon, the prosperous Newcastle merchant and politician who rented the manor of Silksworth from Durham Priory.[51] He was killed at the Battle of Halidon Hill near Berwick upon Tweed in 1333. In 1346, moreover, a large Scottish army under Bruce's son and successor David II, invaded the North East and ravaged much of County Durham before being crushed in October at Neville's Cross near Durham City.

Turning to other matters, it is interesting to note that 1346 is regarded as the year in which Sunderland's shipbuilding history commences. This is because according to a 1697 copy of a document dated 1346, Thomas Menvill, possibly a younger son of a Durham landholder of some consequence, paid Bishop Hatfield an annual rent of 2s. to build ships at Hendon.[52]

The Black Death and its Consequences

In the middle of the 14th century the people of England could have been forgiven for thinking that the Fourth Horseman of the Apocalypse was riding by, for the country was struck by a dreadful pestilence that had swept across Europe from the steppes of central Asia. The plague arrived on the south coast in the summer of 1348 and began spreading along the roads, lanes and waterways of England, 'following the course of the sun,' as Henry Knighton wrote, 'into every part of the kingdom.'[53]

Three types of pestilence were involved: bubonic, pneumonic and septicaemic plague. The former was spread by rats. Its symptoms were a high fever and the buboes (inflamed swellings) that appeared in the groin and armpits of its victims, before putrefying and bursting. Pneumonic plague, on the other hand, another strand of the disease, spread by direct contagion and affected the lungs. It was more virulent—death was certain—and often killed within a couple of days. Rarer, but more deadly still, was septicaemic plague that resulted in death within hours. It has been estimated that the Black Death killed off at least 20 per cent (the figure was probably significantly higher) of England's population of approximately 5 million during 1348–50, and the inhabitants of Wearside did not escape its wrath.

The plague arrived in County Durham in 1349 during the episcopate of Thomas Hatfield. In mid July of that year the bishop's steward, Sir Thomas Gray (also spelt 'Grey') began his summer visitation of various places in the county in order to preside over the episcopal halmote courts, a task he performed on two other occasions each year. The bishop's halmotes were held in ten places in County Durham and each served tenants from nearby villages.

At his first port of call, Chester-le-Street, Gray conducted business as usual. He then proceeded to Houghton-le-Spring, where the nearest of the halmotes to Sunderland was held. After the steward arrived at Houghton-le-Spring (probably on the evening of Tuesday 14th), he found that people had lost interest in the future owing to fear of the approaching plague. As a result, there was a marked reluctance to pay entry fines to become tenants of vacant land in the bishop's hands. Moreover, Gray was informed that four inhabitants of Bishopwearmouth had recently died wretchedly, a possible reference to the Black Death.

This possibility is strengthened by what Sir Thomas encountered at Easington, not far from Houghton-le-Spring and Bishopwearmouth. The tenants were in a desperate state 'because of the pestilence', which, apparently, had just arrived. Later in the month, when Gray visited places in the south of County Durham such as Stockton and Darlington, he found conditions normal. Hence, as Frederick Bradshaw has suggested, 'it is perhaps safe to assume that' the Black Death entered Durham 'by way of Sunderland' and radiated out from it to Bishopwearmouth, Easington, and elsewhere.[54]

What is certain is that the plague struck Wearside, and struck hard. Among the places hit were the townships of Fulwell, Southwick and Monkwearmouth, where four, eight and 11, of the Prior of Durham's tenants perished. Richard Lomas has studied the plague's impact on 28 townships belonging to Durham Cathedral Priory and the number of tenants, both servile and free, who died: we should bear in mind, of course, that other folk such as wives and children would have also succumbed. According to Lomas, the average death rate for Fulwell, Monkwearmouth and Southwick was 60 per cent.[55] Of these townships, Fulwell had the lowest death rate, 56 per cent. Lomas does not give the exact percentages for Southwick and Monkwearmouth but places the former among townships that had a tenant death rate of between 50 and 59 per cent, whereas Monkwearmouth is listed among eight places where the percentage of deaths exceeded 60 per cent. Hence the three communities were among the 16 most badly affected townships, the worst of which, Jarrow, had a death rate of 78 per cent.

Bishopwearmouth evidently also experienced fatalities, for it was subsequently recorded that 'a very large number of the houses' had become ruinous 'for want of tenants.'[56] In view of the above, it is reasonable to conclude that Sunderland also suffered, and this is suggested by the fact that Nicholas de Skelton—who leased the borough from the bishop—had to obtain remission of four marks (£2 13s. 4d.) on the year's rent. (Lessees of the borough had to pay an annual sum to the bishop and any profits accrued from the borough over that figure went into their own pocket).

The Black Death inevitably affected England's economy, and for a variety of reasons hastened the change from the economic system in which a predominantly unfree peasantry held land primarily in return for labour services, to one in which land was principally held in return for money rents by an increasingly free peasantry. Ambitious peasants now had greater opportunities to advance themselves, by for example acquiring vacant land, than had been the case (population levels remained low for several generations partly due to further outbreaks) and this resulted in a more diverse society.[57]

Diversity had of course always existed to some degree, as has been seen when mentioning tenants of the Bishop of Durham in the late 12th century. Various types of tenancy also existed on the lands of the Prior of Durham, as is evident, for example, from rentals and other material dating from the decade before the Black Death. For one thing, freeholds existed at Monkwearmouth and Southwick but not at Fulwell. Although the holders of such land were free tenants some were required, among other things, to perform tasks normally associated with servile tenure such as labour services, albeit of a limited nature. Other tenants were the holders of husbandlands, of which there were four at Monkwearmouth in 1340–1, each of 48 acres.[58] The holders of such land paid a money rent instead of performing labour services. Other tenancies included bondlands—bondmen were the equivalent of the villeins mentioned in *Boldon Book*. Although no bondlands existed at Fulwell and Monkwearmouth, 10 were located at Southwick. Each was likewise 48 acres in extent and thus larger than was the norm for bondlands elsewhere belonging to the priory. For this land, the tenants rendered labour services. On this point, Lomas has commented: 'Although the stock of evidence is meagre, it justifies the belief that the prior's bondmen were equally and similarly burdened to those of the Bishop of Durham.'[59] To render such labour, the prior's local bond tenants journeyed to Fulwell, where the priory had demesne land. Other tenants held smaller holdings. Among such were peasants at Fulwell and Monkwearmouth who held a toft (homestead) and 16 acres.

In the disrupted conditions that existed following the Black Death, a number of neifs—a term used for unfree peasants—absconded from the villages to which they belonged (such flights had sometimes occurred before the plague) and, for one reason or another, some managed to remain at large even when their whereabouts was known to the authorities. For example, according to Richard Britnell, in June 1353 two of Hatfield's neifs from Bishopwearmouth were reported to be living at Southwick, which was of course the property of Durham Cathedral Priory, and they were still there in March 1360.[60]

We can obtain an insight into the changing nature of the local scene from a survey ordered by Bishop Hatfield towards the end of his episcopate, which ended in 1381. For one thing, the survey highlights that there was more variety of tenure at Bishopwearmouth than had once been the case—there were demesne tenants, bond tenants, cottagers and exchequer tenants. Exchequer land had been won from waste ground since the days of Hugh du Puiset's survey. It was so called because rents were initially obtained centrally by the episcopal exchequer rather than by the manorial organisation, although by Hatfield's day the revenue was collected by coroners appointed by the bishop.

The survey ordered by Bishop Hatfield shows that some individuals belonged to more than one category of tenant. A notable case in point is Cecilia, 'formerly the wife of John Nowell.'[61] At Bishopwearmouth, she was a tenant in all the categories. For instance, she held more of the demesne land than anyone else, 40 acres, of which 10 were held jointly with another female tenant. Almost all the other demesne tenants held 10 acres, for which most paid a rent of 18s. 4d, while others, like Emma, the widow of William Robinson, paid less, 15s. 8d. The money was not paid in a lump sum but was collected at intervals four times a year, as was also true of the other types of tenancy.

As far as bondland is concerned, most of the tenants in this category, all of whom also held other tenancies, each held a messuage (a house and adjacent land) and two oxgangs, both 15 acres in extent. The bond tenants, who used to perform the services contained in *Boldon Book*, now each paid a total of just over 31s. and six bushels of oats to their lord, or a proportionate sum depending on the size of their stake. William Wearmouth, for example, had two messuages and four oxgangs and so paid just over 62s. and 12 bushels of oats. Among other requirements, each of the bond tenants also gave two hens at Christmas and 10 eggs at Easter.

And what of cottagers and exchequer tenants? One of the former was Thomas Shepherd, who had a cottage and 12 acres (the same amount of acres as the cottagers of *Boldon Book*) and rendered 10s. 4d., as did some other tenants in the same category: others held a cottage and six acres, mostly for 5s. 6d. Each cottager also gave eight hens and 40 eggs at Christmas and Easter. John of

The seal of Thomas Hatfield, Bishop of Durham, 1345–81

Sunderland was one of the exchequer tenants. He held a toft and one acre, for which he paid 2s., and worked for the bishop four days at harvest time; the latter requirement was shared by several, but not all, of the other holders of exchequer land.[62]

Before mentioning what the survey says about the borough of Sunderland, it is interesting to note that evidence from a court roll dealing with the period from 10 June to 8 July, 1381, shows that discord existed between the tenants of Bishopwearmouth. They were all told not to quarrel, and evidently to prevent them from fighting among themselves, were ordered not to draw their knives and strike with them on pain of forfeiting 40d.

Of Sunderland, *Hatfield's Survey* records that it was leased from the bishop by Thomas Menvill for an annual rent of £6. This figure indicates to what extent the borough had been affected by adverse factors, including further outbreaks of plague, in the preceding decades for in 1358 Richard de Hedworth of Southwick, the Prior of Durham's senior tenant in that township, had leased the borough of Sunderland for a period of 20 years at an annual sum of £20.[63]

The survey records that Menvill held Sunderland,

> with the free rent of the borough worth 32s. 8d. a year, and with the fishery in the River Wear, together with the Borough Court, the tolls and stallages [the latter being payment for the right to erect market-stalls], with eight yares [artificial weirs thrown across the river to funnel fish swimming upstream into traps: the aim was to catch salmon and trout], belonging to the Lord Bishop, and with 8s. of rent from the Prior of Durham for a yare called Ebyare, and with 8s. of rent from John Hedworth for one yare called Onnesyare, and with a net set up in the harbour of the said borough.[64]

Furthermore, we read that Menvill occupied 'a certain place called Hynden [Hendon], for the mooring of vessels', for which he paid 2s. per annum.[65]

Records of Durham Cathedral Priory likewise show that changes occurred in the nature of land tenure on its property. For one thing, immediately after the dreadful days of 1349, the phasing out of labour services commenced. Moreover, prior to the plague the norm was for a tenant to have only one holding. Following the pestilence, however, while some tenants continued in the traditional mode, multiple holdings became widespread. Thomas Egermond of Fulwell provides an example of a local man on the make. Between 1397 and 1409 he increased his stake in that township, with the result that he held ten tenements and 60 per cent of all the tenant arable land: following Egermond's death in the late 1420s the agglomeration he had built up was dispersed. In the meantime, Robert Wake of Monkwearmouth had commenced building up a farm. This process began in 1422 when he acquired a messuage and 48 acres, and concluded in 1450 by which time he held 141 acres.

Shortly thereafter, a new arrangement—the syndication of land—was put into effect at Fulwell and Monkwearmouth. This occurred in 1470 and before 1491 respectively and included the demesne at Fulwell. In each case, the township was leased to a group of four men. Every member of the group held the same amount of the township's land as his colleagues and paid an equal share of the joint rent. This development also occurred at Southwick between 1516 and 1538, where the syndicate was three-strong. Doubtless the syndicates sub-let part of the land to other tenants.

The Hyltons and Hylton Castle

As the 14th century drew to a close, a local landowner, Sir William Hylton, whose family had been prominent on Wearside for generations, evidently commenced building a castle on his estate at Hylton, part of the parish of Monkwearmouth.

Although several tales have gathered around the history of the Hylton family (also spelt 'Hilton'), including legendary accounts of its origin, the first authentic reference to a member of the line dates from 1157 when 'Romanus de Helton' made an agreement with the Prior and Chapter of Durham whereby he and his descendants could have a chaplain at Hylton.[66]

In 1166 Henry II asked his lords, both lay and ecclesiastical, how many enfeoffed knights they had as their vassals and it was thus recorded that Hylton possessed three knights' fees of land. A knight's fee was enough territory to support and equip a knight, and three fees was quite a substantial feudal holding, one that placed Roman de Hylton among Hugh du Puiset's more important vassals. The fees in question, comprising adjacent manors on both sides of the river, were held of 'old enfeoffment.' In other words, they had been granted between the Conquest and 1135. This most likely occurred during the days of Bishop Ranulf Flambard (1099–1128) when the majority of such fees in the county were granted.

Sir Alexander de Hylton, who appears to have been the next head of the family—he was such by 1172—was one of the individuals who witnessed Puiset's charter to the port of Wearmouth. Alexander and his successors ranked as barons of the bishopric and had a close relationship with the Bishop of Durham. They attended his councils, had a say in the administration of the bishopric, and spent some of their time as members of his retinue.[67]

It is sometimes maintained that from 1295, when Sir Robert de Hylton received a personal writ of summons to parliament, heads of the line were also peers of the realm. But this view is not tenable for Hyltons were seldom called upon to attend parliament.[68] Nonetheless, the fact they did receive such writs is a further indication that the Hyltons were a family of some consequence.

Sir William Hylton, the man responsible for constructing Hylton Castle, was born in Northumberland. He first saw the light of day at Alnwick Castle, a stronghold of the Percys—Northumberland's most powerful family—and was baptised at Alnwick on 7 November 1355. His parents were Sir Robert Hylton and Eleanor, the daughter of a prominent Northumbrian, Sir William Felton of Edlingham Castle (located in a valley southwest of Alnwick) who had served, among other things, as Constable of Bamburgh Castle and had taken part in the Crécy campaign.

William Hylton was still a minor when his father died shortly before 27 May 1370 (the date is sometimes wrongly given as 1376) and he remained such until 1376 when he came of age upon reaching 21.[69]

It has been said of the Hyltons that they poured out their blood in warfare as though 'it were water.' The evidence does not support such a claim. Nevertheless, many members of the family did participate in military ventures and Sir William himself is a case in point. In 1383, for example, during the Hundred Years' War, he volunteered to take part in what proved an ill-fated expedition to Flanders. Moreover, according to the French chronicler Jean Froissart (who was well acquainted with the engagement), in 1388 Hylton was captured while fighting against the Scots at Otterburn in Northumberland, a battle that ended disastrously for the English. In addition, in 1402, by which time he had regularly served under the Earl of Northumberland's command at the frontier garrison town of Berwick upon Tweed, Hylton was present at the Battle of Homildon Hill near Wooler when the English avenged Otterburn.

The imposing west front of Hylton Castle, built c.1400

At the time of Homildon Hill, England was ruled by Henry IV. In late 1399 he had overthrown his kinsman Richard II (an unstable and increasingly tyrannical figure) and William, styled 'le Baron de Hilton' on Parliamentary Rolls dating from late that year, was one of those who had assented to Richard's imprisonment.

Evidently, work on constructing Hylton Castle was underway when Richard's reign ended. Hylton is often ascribed to a category of generally small castles known as tower-houses, which were popular in the North during the late Middle Ages. It measures about 75ft from north to south, and is approximately 45ft wide. The west front is the principal one, and its appearance is enhanced by a splendid heraldic display. This includes two banners. One bears Hylton's arms and the other has modified arms that Henry IV adopted in 1405. There are also many shields sporting the devices of families and individuals connected to the Hyltons for one reason or another. For instance, one of the shields bears the arms of Henry Percy, first Earl of Northumberland. Also represented are Ralph, Lord Lumley (who was killed in 1400 while attempting to overthrow Henry IV), and Sir William Washington.[70] A much more modest heraldic display adorns the exterior of a substantial turret projecting from the rear of the tower. This includes the White Hart, the emblem of Richard II, and its presence suggests that the castle was under construction by 1399.

Sadly, the tower is little more than a shell (three rooms survive in the turret projecting from the east face) but the original internal layout can be largely determined. There were four rooms on the ground floor, two on either side of a central passage leading through the structure. Those to the north were probably cellars. Of those to the south, the one closest to the entrance had a well and was evidently a guardroom. The other chamber appears to have accommodated one of the castle's officials. As one would expect, the principal room, a hall, was on the first floor. It was reached by a still extant spiral stair in the east turret, was centrally located, and rose all the way to the roof. The portcullis was situated on the west side of the hall, in front of the principal window, unless lowered to protect the entrance. Other chambers lay on either side of the hall, some of them at second-floor level. The spiral stair ascended even higher, giving access to a room at the top of the east turret (the highest chamber in the castle) and to the battlements. The latter were provided with machicolation, openings through which scalding liquid and other missiles could be dropped on assailants.

The imposing tower did not stand alone. For one thing, just to the northeast are the remains of the chapel of St Catherine (the earliest substantial amount of fabric dates from the early 15th century), in which some members of the Hylton family were buried. Other structures, including a hall and barns are known to have existed and were assumed to lie to the east of the castle, presumably around a courtyard. Interestingly, brief exploratory work, including a geophysical survey, undertaken in June 1994 under the direction of the archaeologist Stephen Speak and members of Channel 4's popular programme on archaeology, 'Time Team', uncovered evidence of a high status masonry range. Possibly a survival of Hylton's pre-existing manorial complex, it was located east of the tower and appears to have marked the far end of a courtyard that extended from the tower. Based on documentary evidence and analogy with other sites, the architectural historian Beric Morley has suggested that the range contained a grander hall than that in the tower. Furthermore, he suggests that structures along the north side of the courtyard comprised accommodation and that a barn-like building perhaps defined the south side of the courtyard.[71]

It is reasonable to conclude that the tower, described in the mid 15th century as a 'house constructed of stone, called gatehouse', served as the main residential quarters of the Hylton family. Certainly, examples are known of strongholds (Dunstanburgh and Bywell in Northumberland, respectively built in the 14th and 15th centuries come to mind), where the gatehouse not only served as an entrance but, unusually, also contained the principal accommodation.

For their part, Speak and Morley cite other parallels, such as Warkworth Castle where the Earl of Northumberland erected a splendid new keep (likely in the 1390s) that served as a private suite for himself and his family, whereas more substantial facilities for entertaining on a grand scale existed elsewhere on the site. Hylton

can be seen in the same light,
albeit on a more modest scale and
different in form.

At times, members of the
Hylton family threw their weight
around on Wearside. This was certainly the case in May 1411 when
William's heir, a knight named
Robert, rode into Sunderland at
the head of a strong following 'in
warlike manner' and insulted a
certain John Duckett. On Robert's
orders, an archer then shot Duckett in the throat, before another
retainer finished him off with the
pommel of a sword. The following year, Sir Robert and his father
(both of whom had made bind-
ing agreements with Thomas Langley, the Bishop of Durham, that
they would not attack any other
residents of Sunderland) were pardoned by the prelate for their part
in Duckett's death.

Sir William died on 25 May
1435 after a long and eventful life.

The stairway in the tower's east turret

He was succeeded by his son Robert, whose mother Dionisia was a daughter of a
junior branch of the family, the Hyltons of Swine, based in Holderness in the East
Riding of Yorkshire since the late 13th century.[72]

When Robert was head of the family a dramatic clash occurred with the monastic
cell at Monkwearmouth. The incident happened in 1439 and among those involved
was one of Hylton's men named John Potts. According to William Lyham (or Lyam),
who had been appointed Master of Monkwearmouth four years earlier, Potts had
frequently stolen corn and hay from the 'Celle of Monkwermouth' (with which
Sir Robert was at odds), and had 'somtym sett his horse in a place callid ye ald
kirke…defilying ye sam place and destroying hay agayns ye will…of ye keper of
ye said Celle.' Matters came to a head when Potts and other armed servants of the
Hyltons (they were carrying 'lang pykid staves and lang dagers') threatened and
assaulted Lyham and 'John Both monke his felowe.'[73]

Soon after this, on the same day, which was 'Seterday a next befor palmesonday
[i.e., 28th March]…Will'm of Hilton son and hayr to ye Baron of Hilton' arrived on
the scene, and angrily entered the chancel of the 'kirke of Wermouth wt outyn ony
prayer or reuerence…made or shewid to ye blessid sacrament.' Among other things,

he insulted Lyham before laying 'haund apon ye mastre of Wermouth vnlawfully and iniurously wtin ye qwer [chancel] of ye kirke' so that he dared 'noght abide in his plas for fere of bodely harme.'[74] Lyham and John Booth thus abandoned the cell, and in June the former was sent from Durham to one of the priory's other cells, that on Farne Island.

William Hylton, who dramatically features in the foregoing episode, succeeded his father in August 1448. William himself died in 1457, shortly after the commencement of the civil war known as the Wars of the Roses, and was succeeded by a son of the same name, a boy of around six. During this youngster's minority—in 1459 to be precise—the family chaplain, Robert Stainton, was excommunicated by the monks of Monkwearmouth who accused him of misappropriating tithes. Stung by their action, Stainton began a legal battle with their superior the Prior of Durham. The case eventually went to Rome, where it was decided that Stainton's excommunication was invalid. The decision was an unpalatable one for the chaplain's most obdurate enemy, the Master of Monkwearmouth, John Bradbury. In fact, an interesting letter exists which shows that he suggested to the prior that they should plan an ambush in order to waylay the messenger carrying the papal bulls from Hylton Castle to Wilton in Cleveland, where Stainton was then resident. The ambush, proposed to take place at or near Grindon Field, never occurred for the suggestion was not followed. Hence the young messenger, wearing a mulberry-coloured gown and white hose, made his journey in peace on a grey mare.

Coal, the Dissolution, and Salt

At about the time when work on Hylton Castle commenced, coal was shipped from Sunderland to Whitby Abbey. The enterprise is recorded in the account rolls of that Benedictine monastery for the years 1394–6 which include the following entry: '*Item de Willielmo Rede de Sundirland 4 celdr 13s. 4d*'. Little did William imagine when he set sail for Whitby carrying the four chaldrons of coal (the size of chaldrons at this date is uncertain) that centuries later he would be remembered as the person involved in the earliest known shipment of coal from the Wear.

In the 15th century, the exportation of coal—brought downstream from places such as Harraton and Biddick—continued, though the amount shipped to various destinations from the Wear was small and vastly outstripped by that exported from the Tyne. A number of yares that were deemed to interfere with river traffic, were removed following an order to that effect by Bishop Neville in 1440.

The monastic cell at Monkwearmouth derived income (doubtless intermittently) from the coal trade, for it received rents for a staithe named Thrylstanhugh. In 1415–7, for example, the monks obtained 3s. 4d. per annum, whereas in the years 1472–6 a staithe (possibly the same one) was leased out for a rent of 2s. 6d. The lessee then was William Lambton, a member of the gentry whose estate lay on the south bank of the River Wear a short distance downstream of Chester-le-Street and where coalmining was likely taking place.

In the 1440s, moreover, a saltpan makes an appearance in records of the monastic cell. It was located near the river mouth and the monks received salt as a tithe payment for its use. Shortly after the turn of the 16th century, another saltpan belonging to the cell was erected at an unspecified site. It operated at a modest level of production over a number of years and was possibly operative until the closure of the cell in the 1530s.

During the 15th century, the North East had experienced a major economic crisis. According to Anthony Pollard, overall in 'the first half of the century rents and other revenues from land fell by approximately one-third.'[75] In mid century, when County Durham's population was likely less than half it had been in 1348, the region was in deep depression, and although the second half of the century generally witnessed respite and partial recovery in the countryside, apparently urban areas fared less well.

Nonetheless, laymen still found it worthwhile to lease the borough of Sunderland. For much of the first half of the century the borough was evidently leased by Robert Jackson, who paid the bishop an annual rent of £6. Jackson, who died in 1440, possessed numerous properties in the borough and further afield, including at Ryhope. He also had a residence at Farringdon. Much grander owners of burgages in Sunderland at this date were the Nevilles of Raby, Earls of Westmorland since 1397.

Later, in 1463 Edward IV, who had seized the temporalities of the bishopric of Durham, leased *Sunderland juxta Mare* (Sunderland-near-the-Sea) to Robert Bertram. However, this arrangement soon ended when the bishop, Laurence Booth, regained control of the bishopric and leased the borough to someone else instead.

In the mid 1470s, the lease of the borough was granted to Ralph Bowes, who had recently become the head of one of County Durham's leading families, and he 'continued to hold the borough lease intermittently until his death in 1512.'[76] From the early 16th century, the bailiffs (formerly known as reeves) were paid a salary.

Although Sir Ralph's ancestral seat lay at Streatlam, roughly midway between Staindrop and Barnard Castle in southwest Durham, since the late 14th century his family had also been prominent figures in the vicinity of Sunderland. Through marriage to an heiress named Maud de Dalden, they had acquired the lordship of Dalden near Seaham—Dalden Tower became a popular residence for the Bowes—as well as the manor of Humbledon. The latter, sometimes spelt 'Homildon', comprised an extensive tract of land in the parish of Bishopwearmouth, including Pallion (beside the River Wear) and Barnes.

At the start of the 16th century, Sunderland remained a place of no great consequence in the diocese of Durham which was described, somewhat unfairly by the Cumbrian, Lord Dacre, as 'an economic backwater, a savage and infertile country' in which Newcastle's merchants alone 'constituted a single element of civilization.'[77] Sunderland was certainly outclassed by Tyneside's capital and although some ships visited Wearside from places like King's Lynn and Rochester, the level of activity was decidedly modest.[78]

During the course of the century some developments of great significance occurred. One of these resulted in the removal of an institution that had dominated the lives of many Wearsiders for centuries—Durham Cathedral Priory. This event occurred during the momentous reign of Henry VIII (1509–47). Dire financial straits were primarily responsible for his government's decision to close monastic houses and seize much of their wealth. Consequently, in 1536, under an Act of Parliament passed that year, the cell of Monkwearmouth was dissolved along with many other religious establishments whose annual incomes were less than £200: at the time of its dissolution, the cell had a small income of £25 8s. 4d. per annum.

Angered by the commencement of monastic closures, many people in Lincoln-shire and the North rose in revolt in late 1536. The rising, known as the Pilgrimage of Grace, was intended to compel Henry's government to halt the process of dissolu-tion. Among those who participated in the rebellion was Wearside's most important secular figure, Sir Thomas Hylton, a reluctant rebel. Thomas, like a number of the county's other grandees, including his relative Lord Lumley (Hylton's mother was a Lumley) was compelled to throw in his lot with the 'pilgrims' after they had threat-ened his property. In the event, Hylton played a notable role in negotiations held in Yorkshire that led to the peaceful conclusion of the revolt and a general pardon for those involved.

Although the cell of Monkwearmouth ceased to exist in 1536, St Peter's Church remained to serve the needs of the parish. Following the cell's suppres-sion, its inmates travelled to Durham Priory, which in common with other great religious houses, would soon share the same fate as the lesser establishments. Its end came on 31 December 1539 when the prior surrendered the monastery to royal commissioners.

Subsequently, in 1542 the site of Monkwearmouth's former cell was granted to a gentleman named Thomas Whitehead. Soon after this, in the summer of 1545 Henry VIII granted Whitehead 'the whole house and site lately of the Cell of Wear-mouth…which previously belonged to the monastery of Durham, now dissolved, and all messuages, houses, buildings, barns, stables, dovecots, ponds, vineries, gardens, orchards and lands within the bounds and precincts of the [former] Cell and belonging to it.'[79] Thomas did not receive this (and other property in Darlington) as a gift. On the contrary, he paid over £161 into the royal coffers to obtain the grant.

Monkwearmouth remained in the hands of his family for several decades, and in 1579 Bishop Richard Barnes enhanced their standing when he appointed Thomas Whitehead's son, William, not only bailiff of the borough of Sunderland but also vice admiral of the palatinate. The latter role entailed looking after the bishop's maritime interests, such as the right of wreck along Durham's coast and regulating ports. In 1598 William conveyed the manor of Monkwearmouth, centred on a hall that incorporated former monastic buildings, to Robert Widdrington (sometimes spelt 'Woodrington'), a member of a prominent gentry family based in Northumberland.

Henry VIII's reign had not only witnessed the Dissolution of the Monasteries. It also saw the passing of legislation that broke England away from the jurisdiction of the pope and resulted in the king becoming the Supreme Head of the Church in England. Henry's theological stance remained orthodox, nevertheless. But early in the reign of his daughter Elizabeth I (1558–1603), matters went further and resulted in the establishment of the Anglican Church, a Protestant institution.[80]

Protestantism thus became the state religion. A backlash occurred in 1569 when the Catholic Earls of Northumberland and Westmorland rose in an unsuccessful revolt. The rising made its presence felt on Wearside. For one thing, the head of the Hylton family, a knight named William (he was a nephew of Sir Thomas Hylton) rallied to the side of the Crown.

So too did another major landowner in Sunderland's vicinity, namely Robert Bowes, 'the Sheryffe of thys Countye of Durham, laytlye returned into theys parts, and redye with hys whole power and delygence to serve the Quene's Majestie.'[81] Born in around 1530, Bowes (who had attended Cambridge University but had left without taking a degree), was a grandson of the Sir Ralph Bowes who had leased the borough of Sunderland in the late 15th and early 16th centuries.[82] Robert had acquired property on Wearside through his marriage to a cousin named Anne Bowes, a co-heiress, through whom he obtained the manor of Humbledon, or Barnes as it had become increasingly known. At the start of the rebellion, Robert made his way to Barnard Castle, a royal stronghold whose steward was his elder brother George, and he was part of the garrison that was besieged and captured by the rebels.[83]

Although Catholics had been initially treated with a fair degree of toleration by Queen Elizabeth and her ministers, in the early 1570s a stronger line began to be taken. Even more repressive measures followed in the 1580s, a decade that witnessed the Spanish Armada, an attempt by the Catholic King of Spain to overthrow Elizabeth. Catholics were thus subjected to bitter persecution. Government spies endeavoured to keep a close eye on their activity and priests—who infiltrated the country from abroad—operated clandestinely, courageously risking their lives in order to serve the needs of fellow Catholics.

This was true of John Boste, an Englishman who had been ordained to the priesthood at Rheims, France, in 1581. He travelled to the North East and preached extensively. Of Boste, John Myerscough comments, 'there was scarcely any Catholic house or centre [in the region] where Father Boste had not stayed and ministered to the Catholics of the neighbourhood.' He continues: 'It is now certain that he had said Mass and given the Sacraments to Sunderland Catholics at Hylton Castle.'[84] Doubtless, Myerscough is referring to an incident in 1593 when Lady Anne Hylton was reported to the government for celebrating Mass, presumably at the castle. In a report addressed to Secretary Cecil, and dated 24 October, a spy named Anthony Atkinson stated as follows: 'The ladie Hilton did much use Boste's services and has often been at Mass.' Like many other priests, Boste met a martyr's death after falling into the hands of the authorities. He was brutally executed at Durham on 24 July 1594, having first been severely tortured during his period of incarceration.

Turning to other matters, in 1559 a royal commission reported that Sunderland was 'little frequented' by shipping in contrast to some other northern ports such as Hartlepool and, most notably, Newcastle. It was still a backwater in 1565 when another commission dealing with the ports in the bishopric reported that:

St Catherine's Chapel, Hylton Castle

> There is a fishing town and landing place called Sunderland which has thirty householders and is governed by Robert Bowes [of Barnes] under the Bishop of Durham, and ships and boats are there loaded and unloaded by licence of the bishop, but there are neither ships nor boats and only seven cobbles that belong to the town, occupying twenty fishermen. The town is in great decay of buildings and inhabitants.[85]

Sunderland's population may only have comprised around 150 people at this date and was perhaps even smaller. Other communities in the parishes of Bishopwearmouth and Monkwearmouth were likewise small. In effect, the borough of Sunderland was dead on its feet and positively Lilliputian when compared with some other places in the region. Gateshead's population in the mid 1560s is estimated to have been approximately 1,500 strong, whereas at Durham the figure was around 3,300. Newcastle was home to at least 6,000 people and the number may indeed have approached 8,000.

Sunderland was still nondescript in 1590 when Ralph Bowes (the heir of Robert Bowes of Barnes) acquired the lease of the borough for an annual rent of £4, a paltry sum.

However, in the closing years of the century Sunderland's fortunes took a decisive turn for the better. This followed the commencement of salt production on the south bank of the river in the late 1580s by a consortium intent on producing a commodity that was increasingly in demand. Robert Bowes of Barnes was one of the business partners, as were John Smith, a merchant of King's Lynn, and a prominent figure on Tyneside named Robert Anderson. They produced salt from seawater boiled in ten large iron salt pans and 'according to Bowes's partner, John Smith, more than 300 workmen had been brought in to Sunderland by 1587.'[86] The furnaces used to provide the necessary heat were fuelled by coal brought downstream from various places, including Offerton (which Bowes had acquired in the early 1570s) where a pit was especially sunk for the purpose.

The strip of land upon which production occurred lay between Sunderland and Bishopwearmouth, and ran eastward from the site of the present Wearmouth Bridge almost as far as Beggars' Bank (the future Russell Street) and the area was linked to Sunderland by Low Street. In the Elizabethan period, the location witnessed the development of a small township known as Bishopwearmouth Panns. Usually this is said to have developed as a result of the consortium's venture. However, other individuals had already started salt production at the site and as Christine Newman notes 'a number of children from the "Panns" were baptised during the 1570s.'[87]

Bowes and Smith invested several thousand pounds on their business undertakings on Wearside. The former alone had expended £4,000 by 1589. Indeed, financial difficulties ensued and by 1591 the salt pans were rusting and buildings associated with them were abandoned and becoming dilapidated. In 1593, however, a lessee of three of the salt pans, valued at £100, was a member of the gentry named Ralph Lambton, whose business activities also involved bringing coal downstream for shipment.

Indeed, shipments of coal from the Wear witnessed a marked upturn in the 1590s when an average of 2/3,000 tons annually left the river. For example, 36 ships carrying coal did so in less than three months during the spring and summer of 1594. Vessels involved in conveying the mineral from the port included ships from abroad, most notably the Netherlands.

Furthermore, in around 1601 Ralph Bowes of Barnes (who had succeeded his father in 1597) erected a quay at Sunderland from which salt could be loaded for export. In addition, as coarse, low-grade coal was suitable for salt production, Bowes was also able to export higher quality coal, thereby adding another string to his bow.

Hence, largely due to the business enterprise of figures such as the Bowes family, Sunderland and its environs had entered an exciting new phase as increasing quantities of salt and coal were shipped from the Wear. As H. L. Robson has commented: 'By 1600 the port had come to life … the commercial town of Sunderland had started its career.'[88]

CONFLICT AND GROWTH –
Wearside in the 17th Century

On 4 March 1640 the Rector of Whitburn, Thomas Triplet, wrote a letter to the Archbishop of Canterbury in which he referred to a local man as 'the great factotum, that rules both the religion and wealth of the town.'[1] George Lilburne of Sunderland was the man, and Triplet disapproved of him, a stance primarily due to their different religious views. But before dealing with the subject of religion, let us say something about Lilburne's background and career for he was a dynamic figure and undoubtedly the dominant individual in Sunderland in the mid 17th century.

George Lilburne was born at Thickley Punchardon near Bishop Auckland, the second son of a minor landowner of ancient family. When he settled in Sunderland is unclear. The earliest evidence of his presence locally dates from 1620 for in November of that year Lilburne, who was middle-aged, married Isabel Chamber of Cleadon, the daughter of a landowner. The marriage occurred at Whitburn Church. The couple's first child, Thomas, was baptised at Bishopwearmouth in 1622 by which time George was a local coal merchant.

Lilburne was no doubt eager to make a name for himself, and unlike Newcastle, Sunderland did not have merchant and trade guilds and was thus a place where a spirit of free enterprise prevailed, a place, as Pauline Gregg has commented, where Lilburne's 'expansive energies had more scope.' Here, 'by investing in collieries, obtaining leases of others, and selling them at a profit, as well as by trade in general, he prospered and became wealthy.'[2]

Sunderland at this date was vibrant, a far cry from the state of affairs that had existed only a few decades before. As noted in the preceding chapter, it had been transformed from little more than a fishing village into a scene of industrial endeavour, and its character was changed permanently. An indication of this transformation can be gained from the fact that in 1627 the town was deemed of sufficient importance for the title Earl of Sunderland to be bestowed on a baron named Emanuel Scrope, lord of Bolton Castle in Wensleydale. The earldom proved of short duration, for the title became extinct upon Scrope's death without legitimate offspring in 1630.

Another indication of Sunderland's rise is the amount of coal that left the Wear. According to John Hatcher, in 1608–9 (from Michaelmas to Michaelmas) some 14,700 tons were shipped from the river, over 3,000 tons of which went abroad, and in subsequent years the quantity continued rising significantly.[3] The coal was brought downstream from mines inland at Harraton and elsewhere by flat-bottomed keels, crewed by two or three people. The coal was then mostly shipped from the Wear by vessels belonging to other ports and the peak period for shipments was summer:

since the late 16th century beacons located at the river's mouth had warned crews about hazardous sandbanks.

Not surprisingly, developments on Wearside alarmed Newcastle's coal merchants—the Hostmen—who enjoyed a monopoly on the exportation of coal from the Tyne. Coal had been shipped from that river since the 13th century and the amount had risen dramatically during the late 16th century, owing to the increasing use of coal as a fuel due to depleting stocks of timber. In 1600 Queen Elizabeth had recognized the Hostmen's monopoly in return for a tax of 1s. per chaldron shipped.[4] The growing exportation of coal from the Wear angered them. Although the amount shipped was only a fraction of that from the Tyne, they were determined to ensure that the growth of the trade on Wearside was curbed.

Hence the Hostmen petitioned for the imposition of a duty on coal from Sunderland and James I (a Scot who succeeded Elizabeth in 1603) did as they wished in 1608. So, much against the will of those involved in the shipment of coal from the Wear, officials were established in the port to collect the levy. In late 1610, however, parliament compelled James to cease collecting a levy of 1s. per chaldron on the Wear's domestic sales. A larger duty (initially of 5s. a chaldron) likewise introduced in 1608, on coal shipped from Sunderland to foreign destinations, remained until the early 1640s.

Of Sunderland's coal trade during the early decades of the 17th century, Maureen Meikle comments: 'Before 1630, coal shipments from the Wear fluctuated year by year, averaging perhaps 30,000 tons. The highest recorded annual sale, of almost 40,000 tons, was in 1617.'[5] In the first half of the 1630s shipments peaked. According to Hatcher, the amount of coal shipped from the Wear in 1633–4 (from Christmas to Christmas) totalled almost 72,000 tons, of which over 8,000 tons were destined for foreign ports.[6] But for a variety of reasons, a sharp decline ensued in the second half of the decade.

London, not surprisingly, ranked among the markets for Sunderland coal, albeit not to as great an extent as was the case of shipments from the Tyne, and on this point B. Deitz states: 'Although the port's strength lay in supplying provincial and foreign markets, the capital played a key role in the first stage of growth. In 1615 London imported 313 tons of Wear coals. Twenty years later the city was Sunderland's largest market.'[7]

In the mid 1630s the levy on domestic coal sales lifted by James I, was reintroduced by his son Charles I (whose government was suffering pecuniary embarrassment) and it continued until the realm was disrupted by the Civil War.

By the 1630s, moreover, Sunderland's salt pans produced approximately 50,000 bushels of salt annually. Although not negligible, Wearside's salt industry was nevertheless completely outclassed by production at the mouth of the Tyne. In the 1640s, for instance, approximately 300 tons of coal were required annually for salt-making at Sunderland whereas around 3,600 tons were used by salt manufacturers at South Shields and as Meikle further notes, Sunderland 'never merited its own salt inspector.'[8]

Washington Old Hall, a fine example of a Jacobean manor house. Although it incorporates part of the medieval hall of the Washington family, it was built after William James, the Bishop of Durham, acquired the manor in 1613

A number of quays existed near the harbour. They were also constructed along the lower reaches of the river. One such, namely Bowes Quay, has already been referred to in the preceding chapter and was located on the south bank of the River Wear at Sunderland. Others included one erected further upstream at Deptford by Robert Ayres in 1629, and a ballast quay constructed at Monkwearmouth in 1632 (an earlier ballast quay had been built there in the 1590s) by Robert Widdrington, the grandson of the gentleman who had acquired the Monkwearmouth estate in the late 16th century.

By the time Widdrington constructed the quay—part of an expensive programme of expenditure on improving his local property—the river channel at Sunderland had shifted northward to some degree. In part, this resulted from a flood that had swept down the river in or about 1627. Increasing man-made encroachment, such as quays on the south side, was also deemed a factor.

Large quantities of ballast were brought to Wearside by ships visiting the river and were deposited on both sides of the Wear. This was especially true at Monkwearmouth where, owing to the lie of the land, discharging the ballast was easier and numerous ballast hills thus developed.

Some vessels that put in at Sunderland carried cargoes such as flax, malt and rye, as well as sawn timber from Norway. Other imports included tar, playing cards, apples, cider, raisins, cinammon and French wine.

Sooner or later during this period, George Lilburne prospered and took up residence in a fine stone house he had constructed near quays on the riverside. It was located at the far end of King's Street (now High Street East) on a site beside which Burleigh Street would be developed in the middle of the following century. The house was one of a number of substantial dwellings for the expanding well-to-do stratum of Sunderland's population, whose homes were grander and more well-appointed than ever before. The fine homes also included a residence for the Lambtons, a gentry family whose town house was located at Bishopwearmouth Panns.

In 1630 Lilburne's resources were such that he bought an estate at Offerton in the parish of Houghton-le-Spring (he retained his town house) from a gentleman called William Wycliffe who moved to Sunderland and whose home here evidently also served as a meeting place for official business. Of Lilburne, Gregg aptly comments that he was 'certainly "rising gentry," ... flourishing through his own astuteness and his ability to keep going a variety of concerns, letting money make money in all of them.'[9]

Morton's Charter

In March 1634, at the behest of Sunderland's inhabitants, Thomas Morton, the Bishop of Durham, granted the town (whose population included a growing number of migrants) a new charter which strengthened and extended the town's privileges. The charter's preamble states that 'Sunderland-near-the-sea' contains a port 'from which, in which, and through which, very many ships and other vessels' from England and 'foreign parts come and ply, introducing and importing merchandise, goods, and other saleable articles, and exporting from the said port sea-coals [i.e., coal] and grindstones, rubstones and whetstones, and other merchandise ... to the great profit and advantage of the kingdom.'[10] The charter provided for a mayor, 12 aldermen and 24 councillors, and stated that this 'body corporate and politic' was 'to endure for ever.' The bishop chose the first members of the corporation and not surprisingly a substantial percentage were men of substance.

The first mayor was Sir William Bellasis of Morton House (between Houghton-le-Spring and Chester-le-Street), High Sheriff of County Durham since 1625. In addition to holding the mayoralty, Bellasis, whom Triplet described as a 'scholarly gentleman', retained his position of high sheriff. He was also heavily involved in business, such as mining coal on his Morton estate and, from the mid 1630s, manufacturing salt at South Shields. In addition, in 1633 he was one of several gentlemen who had leased the borough of Sunderland from Bishop Morton for a period of 21 years.

Most of the aldermen were not local men. Sir William Lambton, for instance, had his main residence several miles away where his estate lay on the opposite side of the Wear to Harraton, a short distance downstream of Chester-le-Street. Lambton was one of Bellasis' fellow lessees of Sunderland and proceeded to lease the ten Bowes salt pans in the neighbourhood from 1635 onward. Apart from Lilburne, the only locally based aldermen were George Burgoyne (of either Sunderland or Bishopwearmouth) and George Grey of Southwick. The latter was a prosperous Yorkshireman who had bought the Southwick estate in 1630, after residing at Great Lumley in County Durham, from the Hedworth family who were based at Harraton.[11]

Morton's charter decreed that every year the mayor was to be elected from among the ranks of the aldermen. Elections were held in October, and it is not surprising that Lilburne was one of those elected to the mayoralty. He first became mayor in 1637 (in the spring of which numerous deaths occurred due to an outbreak of plague),[12] and retained the post the following year. He would become mayor once again in 1641. Lilburne proved an energetic holder of the office: for example, he was instrumental in bringing about a decision to build a 'house' to serve as a council chamber.

The charter also stipulated that Sunderland's borough court would be held every three weeks before a Recorder and would, amongst other things, 'have cognizance for ever of all pleas, below and amounting to the sum of forty pounds.' Furthermore, the charter decreed that the borough could have a market every Friday, and a fair on the Feast of St Philip and St James (1 May) and on the feast of St Michael the Archangel (29 September).[13]

The man whose family had been the principal lay landowners on Wearside for centuries was not one of those incorporated under Morton's charter. Henry Hylton, who succeeded to the family's estates in 1600 upon the death of his grandfather Sir William, had forsaken living in his ancestral home, Hylton Castle, in preference for residing at Michelgrove in Sussex.

Shortly before his death there in 1641, he drew up an unusual will in which he conveyed the whole of his estate (including land in Wiltshire) to the 'lord Maior of the Cittie of London … and to foure of the senior aldermen of the said Cittie'. They were to administer the properties for a period of 99 years—whereupon they would return to his legal heirs—and 'rents … and profits of the said mannors' were to be distributed for charitable purposes to the poor on Wearside and further afield.[14] Among the townships in question (the will terms them 'parishes') were Hylton, Fulwell and Sunderland.

Not surprisingly, the will was disliked by subsequent heads of the family, to whom Henry left a modest annuity. He was succeeded by a brother named Robert who soon followed him to the grave, whereupon headship of the family passed to another brother, John, who became involved in a lengthy legal battle in which he contested the validity of the will. The matter was still under dispute when he died in 1655.[15]

Prelude to Civil War

Morton's charter dates from a period when Charles I ruled without parliament, for he had abolished the national assembly in 1629 after it had repeatedly censured some of his policies. Charles ruled without parliament for eleven years (this is not quite as unusual as it may seem for in previous reigns, including that of James I, several years had sometimes elapsed between parliaments), and this period is known as the 'Personal Rule' or the 'Eleven Years' Tyranny.' The former expression is preferable: the latter likely conveys the impression of an utterly arbitrary monarch grinding down his hapless subjects. Charles did indeed sometimes behave high-handedly and was prone to duplicity. Nonetheless, he was an essentially decent man with a high sense of duty to God, his family and people, and the lives of the vast majority of his subjects were not rendered intolerable during these years.[16]

Without parliament to grant him subsidies, Charles resorted to raising money by various means. Ship money was one such. This was an annual charge, first raised in Elizabethan times for the refitting and enhancement of the navy, which the king reintroduced in 1634 and extended from coastal to inland counties the following year. Initially, opposition to ship money was not pronounced (one of those involved in its collection was Bellasis) and the requisite sums required from Sunderland were paid. However, by the close of the decade it had become increasingly hard to collect. Among those who refused to pay was Lilburne, the chief source of opposition in the borough.

Charles' religious policies also caused dissension. Soon after his accession in 1625 he aligned himself with the right wing of the Church of England, a faction—known as the Arminians—that wished, among other things, to introduce more ritual into services and beautify places of worship. Its adherents also rejected the notion of predestination, central to the views of Calvinistic Protestants.

The behaviour of Arminians could arouse strong passions. In 1628, for example, the puritanical Rector of Boldon, Peter Smart, preached a vitriolic sermon in Durham Cathedral in which he denounced fellow prebendaries who were introducing more ritual into services in the cathedral and beautifying it. He said that they were 'the whore of Babylon's dastardly brood, doting upon their mother's beauty, that painted harlot of the Church of Rome' and were 'whores and whoremongers' who committed 'spiritual fornication.'[17]

Among those whose views Smart found abhorrent was Francis Burgoyne, Rector of Bishopwearmouth since the spring of 1595.[18] Burgoyne was a zealous Arminian (as was Augustine Lindsell, who had become Rector of Houghton-le-Spring in 1623), and made his views manifest in his parish. For instance, he replaced the communion table in St Michael's Church with an altar located at the east end of the chancel. He also bowed to the altar in such an emphatic manner that his nose struck the ground and reportedly bled. Moreover, as part of his programme of introducing more ritualistic worship, Burgoyne installed new pews in 1632. As only 21 of the seats were allocated to merchants and mariners from Sunderland, the majority of worshippers from the borough were required to stand at the back of the church, as were other parishioners of lower social standing than the seat holders. For his part, Lilburne held two seats in the first pew in the north aisle, as did Wycliffe.

Francis Burgoyne died in 1633. In the same year, Charles I appointed William Laud to the archbishopric of Canterbury. Laud shared the king's reactionary opinions and under the new primate like-minded clergy were promoted, Puritans persecuted, and steps taken to restore the power and authority of the episcopate. Hence an increasing number of people decided that the king and archbishop were crypto-Catholics intent on undermining the Reformation.

A man who watched developments closely was Whitburn's rector, Thomas Triplet, who supported Laud and was irritated by the growth of Puritanism on Wearside. For example, in a letter to the archbishop written on 4 March 1640, he lamented that about three weeks earlier a mendicant preacher had arrived on the scene, 'who got leave to preach at Monkwearmouth, both forenoon and afternoon', and that George Lilburne and 'all the pack' of Sunderland's Puritans had crossed the river to listen to him, thereby forsaking the Rector of Bishopwearmouth, John Johnson, 'a honester man and a better preacher.'[19]

Lilburne was Sunderland's foremost Puritan and Triplet relates that in an argument with Johnson (Burgoyne's successor), Lilburne had the Magnificat quoted to him, whereupon he retorted: 'Prove it out of Scripture, or you say nothing!'[20] Lilburne was certainly outspoken on religious matters and his condemnation of the changes wrought by right-wing Anglicans led to his appearance before the Durham High Commission on a number of occasions to answer for his anticlericalism.[21] Indeed, on account of his disdain for Arminianism and his refusal to pay ship money, Lilburne suffered short terms of imprisonment and the seizure of goods.

Other people were also prepared to challenge the authority of the Church and the Crown: society at large was probably becoming less deferential. Triplet evidently believed that this was so, at least in urban areas. When writing to Laud on 4 March, Triplet thus declared that while it was profitable and honourable for the realm 'to have such towns as Sunderland was … come up and flourish

The attractive (and largely medieval) church at Whitburn

from small beginnings,' on the other hand, such places were centres of insubordination. 'So I think,' he continued, 'that the King's Majesty had better for a while despise that honour and profit that accrues to him … than to suffer little towns to grow big and anti-monarchy to boot; for where all these pestilent nests of Puritans hatched, but in corporations, where they swarm and breed like hornets in a dead horse's head.'[22]

By this date Charles was at odds with the majority of his Scottish subjects owing to an ill-fated attempt to introduce religious reforms in Scotland similar to those implemented in England. The Bishops' Wars were the result, and when Triplet wrote the letter referred to above—he corresponded with Laud on several occasions— the First Bishops' War had occurred and Charles was preparing a second campaign against his recalcitrant Scottish subjects.

In the summer of 1640 the Second Bishops' War broke out. Charles' lack of resources and widespread sympathy in England for his opponents, meant that things went badly for him. In fact, a Scottish army occupied Northumberland and County Durham and on 7 September Scottish troops seized over £800 from Sunderland's custom house. Days later, soldiers took up quarters in the town unopposed and so the inhabitants of Sunderland, like fellow North-Easterners, found themselves subsidizing the invaders.

To buy off the Scots, Charles was forced to summon the 'Long Parliament.' This moved against his 'evil counsellors' such as Laud (who found himself in the Tower and was later executed), introduced reforms, and in due course provided the disgruntled king with money to pay the Scots to return home. They did so late in the summer of 1641.

Shortly thereafter, as 1641 drew to a close, lurid reports from Ireland began arriving in England and Wearsiders no doubt became well acquainted with them. Ulster's Catholics—who falsely claimed to be acting in Charles' name—had revolted against Protestant British settlers and had slaughtered many of them. The revolt spread across Ireland and dramatically raised the political temperature in England.

Mistrust between Charles and his parliamentary opponents became extreme. He believed that they were intent on undermining the authority of the Crown; they, that he had absolutist and papalistic designs. Alarmed by rumours that the queen, who was a Catholic, was about to be impeached by the Commons for supposedly encouraging the Irish rebellion, Charles tried to arrest his five principal opponents in the Commons on 4 January 1642. Warned of his intent, however, they fled and following the king's unprecedented breach of parliamentary privilege both sides began preparing for civil war.

Later that same month, parliament printed copies of the 'Protestation', an oath (drawn up by the House of Commons in May 1641) in defence of 'the true reformed Protestant religion,' the king, parliament, and 'the lawful rights and liberties of the subject.'[23] All males aged over 18 were required to sign copies of it.

Hence in February, of Sunderland's 279 males over that age, 262 signed the Protestation—the other 17 were at sea.[24] In the rest of Bishopwearmouth parish, 495 parishioners also did so. Only two men refused to toe the line, Robert Hutcheson of Bishopwearmouth and Richard Huntley of East Burdon, both of whom were Catholics, valiant souls in a staunchly Protestant environment. Across the river, 171 men in Monkwearmouth parish complied, whereas three parishioners were at sea, and four Catholics refused to sign.[25]

By the Sword Divided

On 22 August 1642, Charles I unfurled his standard at Nottingham thereby commencing the Civil War, although two months would elapse before the first major engagement occurred at Edgehill in Warwickshire.

In June the king had appointed William Cavendish, the Earl of Newcastle ('a very fine gentleman') to prepare the Royalist war effort in the five northernmost counties of England, a region that was generally sympathetic to the monarch, as was true of most of County Durham.[26] Inevitably, of course, loyalties were divided on Wearside for while some locals favoured the Royalist cause others supported parliament.

Sunderland's mayor, George Lilburne, was emphatically one of the latter and he thus soon experienced the wrath of the king's supporters. Shortly after Newcastle arrived in the region, Lilburne was removed from one of his positions, that of a magistrate—his last appearance at the Durham Quarter Sessions was on 20 April 1642. In addition, he was arrested at Newcastle because he had tried to raise forces for parliament in the region. He managed to escape to Edinburgh in September but returned the following month (in which Edward Lee was elected Sunderland's mayor) under the protection of a prominent local Royalist, Sir William Lambton, one of his business associates.

However continued opposition from Lilburne, who spoke out against measures to raise Royalist forces in the county, soon meant that he was apprehended by the Earl of Newcastle. He was seized while fleeing from the wrath of local Royalists towards Yorkshire to join a prominent supporter of parliament. After being made captive, Lilburne was taken to Durham from where, in November, 'he was dragged on foot, through mire and dirt…to York Castle, where he was barbarously used till the end of 1643.' After remaining in custody for 14 months, he was exchanged for a Royalist prisoner. In the meantime 'his house…was plundered and scarce bread enough left for his twelve small children.'[27]

During his absence a trade embargo was placed on Sunderland under an ordinance issued by parliament on 14 January 1643. This stated that 'since the beginning of the present Troubles…Newcastle hath been the Principall In-let of Forreine Ayde' etc. for the king, and that to prevent this and to bring about the reduction of 'Newcastle, and the Parts Adjacent…no Shippe, Shippes, or Barques, shall henceforwards, make any Voyage for the fetching of Coales, or Salt, from Newcastle, Sunderland, or Blyth, or carrying of Corne, or other provision of Victuall, Vntill that Towne of Newcastle shall be freed…from the forces there now raised.'[28] Vessels that ignored the ordinance were to be seized.

For most of the Civil War, the North East saw little major military activity, which was concentrated in the South and Midlands. Certainly, for many Wearsiders their lives were far less affected by the conflict than was the fate of fellow countrymen in, say, the Thames Valley, which witnessed the coming and going of opposing armies. For instance, two major engagements were fought nearby at Newbury, in the first of which (on 20 September 1643) Henry Spencer of Althorp, whom Charles I had recently created Earl of Sunderland, was killed. Nevertheless, Wearsiders must have followed the course of the war with keen interest. Moreover some of them took up arms, as was true of John, the head of the Hylton family, who became an officer in the Earl of Newcastle's army.

It was only in 1644 that the North East witnessed significant conflict. In January of that year a large Scottish army over 21,000 strong under the Earl of Leven crossed the border to aid parliament's faltering war effort. The Marquis of Newcastle (Cavendish's earldom had been raised to a marquisate) was campaigning in Yorkshire when he heard of the invasion. He dashed north with part of his forces and entered Newcastle just before the Scots arrived outside its walls. Finding the town too tough a nut to crack, Leven crossed into County Durham on 28 February. He then proceeded toward Sunderland, which, according to a letter written here on 12 March 1644 in the tract *The Late Proceedings of the Scottish Army*, was deemed 'the fittest place for receiving of Intelligence, and supplying our army.'[29]

Henry Spencer (1620–43), Earl of Sunderland

Progress was slow, owing to inclement weather. The Scots crossed the Wear 'at the new bridge near Lumley' on Saturday 2 March, and after resting to observe the Sabbath at Herrington on the 3rd, entered Sunderland unopposed on the 4th.[30] The same source relates:

> All that day, and the day following, was spent in taking care to supply the Army with Provisions; which we obtained with no small difficulty, being the enemies Countrey…the greatest part of the whole Countrey being either willingly or forcedly in Arms against the Parliament, and afford us no manner of supply, but what they part with against their wills.[31]

Leven's army encamped between Bishopwearmouth and Sunderland where they 'dug in, creating a fort with trenches and mounds on the three landward sides, while the steep bank leading to the Panns sand shoal provided a natural riverside defence.'[32] In addition, from the 5th, other Scottish soldiers were garrisoned at Monkwearmouth. The total number of Scots far outstripped the combined populations of the local communities.

The Marquis of Newcastle, at the head of a smaller army, followed Leven and, according to the letter cited above, crossed the Wear via the 'new bridge' on the 6th and advanced towards Sunderland: a confrontation was in the offing. This is sometimes said to have occurred at Boldon, on the north side of the river, but our most reliable sources state that the encounter took place south of the Wear. *The Life of the Duke of Newcastle*—written at Cavendish's dictation in the 1660s—gives the location as 'Pensher Hills.' In his diary, a Scot named Robert Douglas located the scene of the fighting as rough terrain south of Offerton and notes that the Scots had awaited the enemy, who deployed at Penshaw Hill, by taking up a position on Humbledon Hill.[33] In short, it seems most likely that the fighting took place in the intervening ground, somewhere between West Herrington and Offerton and particularly in the vicinity of the latter.

Of the encounter, we read in *The Late Proceedings*: 'Both Armies were drawn up in Battell [on Thursday the 7th], the enemy having the advantage of the ground…we could not without very great disadvantage engage our Armie, in regard of the unpassable ditches and hedges betwixt us. Both armies faced other till the setting of the Sun.'[34]

The following day, which dawned after a bitterly cold night, skirmishing ensued between 'some small parties of Horse', by which time Newcastle and the bulk of his army had commenced falling back towards Durham City. The onset of a 'great storm of Snow' prevented the Scots from giving pursuit and so they returned to Sunderland. The number of casualties in the skirmishes that had occurred were presumably low (the claims of the opposing sides differ significantly on the matter) and the bitter weather reportedly caused some Royalist deaths by exposure.

At some time prior to 12 March, two ships with meal from Scotland and a ship from London carrying cheese and butter arrived at the port. Nonetheless, Leven was desperately short of supplies.

New Bridge, a 14th century structure over the Wear near Chester–le–Street. It was crossed by the armies of Leven and the Marquis of Newcastle in March 1644

On the 12th he marched towards Durham, leaving two regiments to hold Sunderland. He arrived at the city on the 13th. There was no sign of the enemy, though, and after the horses' fodder ran out the Scots retraced their steps to Sunderland, 'a place of so great consequence to us' as the writer of the letter quoted from above noted subsequently in *A True Relation of the Proceedings of the Scottish Army*.[35] This time, however, they encamped north of the river and large quantities of supplies, including 10,000 musket balls to augment the munitions of Leven and his men, soon arrived after being shipped from Scotland.

Newcastle moved against them on the 23rd, shortly after being joined by a dashing Scottish Cavalier, the Marquis of Montrose. According to *A True Relation*, on Sunday the 24th Newcastle drew up his army 'at a place called Hilton, two miles and a halfe from Sunderland, the same distance as when [he] faced us before, only this is on the north side Ware, the other on the south.'[36] Other sources agree that the Royalists took up a position in the Hylton/Boldon area.

To confront Newcastle, Leven deployed on high ground in the vicinity of Southwick, and other Scottish troops (including Robert Douglas) were stationed to the north on elevated terrain around Boldon.

Of proceedings we read in *A True Relation*:

> Our cannon were at Sunderland…but by the help of the Sea-men lying in the haven, wee conveyed one great peece over the water, who themselves drew itt up to the field where it was to be planted. After the Armies had faced each other most part of that day, toward five aclock the Cannon began to play, which they [the Royalists] bestowed freely though to little purpose, and withall the commanded Foot fell to it to drive one another from their hedges, and continued shooting till eleven at night, in which time we gained some ground.[37]

Another contemporary source, *The Taking of the Fort at South Shields*, (the fort had been captured by a detachment of Leven's army on the 20th), agrees that the fighting was conducted by the infantry: the presence of many hedges and ditches prevented the effective involvement of horse, and unfortunately for Newcastle, he was strong in cavalry and weak in foot. Hostilities, we are told, 'continued very hot, till after twelve of the clock at night. Many officers, who have been old Souldiers did affirm they had never seen so long and hot service in the night time; there was divers killed on both sides, but the number of their slane [Royalists] did very farre exceed ours, as wee understood by the dead bodies we found the next day.'[38]

Late on the 25th, Newcastle withdrew to Durham following further clashes, including hand-to-hand fighting in the vicinity of Boldon Hills. The 30 March issue of the influential Royalist news-sheet *Mercurius Aulicus*, relates that as he did so the Scots assailed his 500 strong cavalry rearguard 'with all the Horse they had' (about 3,000 troopers) and were beaten off following the intervention of Sir Charles Lucas and his cavalry brigade.

In mid April, Newcastle dashed south into Yorkshire following the defeat of the soldiers he had left there. He was pursued by Leven (who had left Sunderland on 30 March and taken up a position near Durham City), and their forces were part of

A re-enactment at Hylton Castle, in August 2010,
of the battle fought in the vicinity in 1644

larger armies that clashed near York on 2 July in the greatest battle of the Civil War—Marston Moor—which ended in defeat for the Royalists. Newcastle fought bravely in the encounter, an engagement in which Sir William Lambton, one of his officers, the commander of a tough regiment raised on Tyneside and in northern Durham, was killed.[39]

In the interim, in May, Royalists led by Montrose endeavoured to recapture Sunderland but were fought off on the 26th by the combined efforts of the town's garrison and local seamen and townsfolk who fought alongside them.

Relations between the garrison and some members of the local population were certainly amicable. In fact, marriages occurred, as is evidenced by the Bishopwearmouth Parish Registers. For example, Adam Thompson, a 'souldier of the garrison,' married Ursula Bee on 27 August 1644.

After Marston Moor, Leven returned north and in mid August laid siege to Newcastle again. As the entrance to the Tyne was commanded by a Royalist garrison at Tynemouth Castle, supplies were transported to Leven's army via Sunderland. On 16 September, for instance, the House of Commons ordered that 200 barrels of powder destined for the besieging force should be shipped to the port en route to Newcastle. Furthermore, on 24 September, authorisation was given for the shipment of 82 packs of clothes, 28 of linen, 100 barrels of powder, shot, match etc. aboard a vessel named the *Samuel Justina* for Scottish troops at Sunderland.

Newcastle was bloodily stormed by Leven that October and days later the garrison of Tynemouth Castle capitulated. The Royalists' ascendancy in the region was well and truly over.

Since March, Sunderland had been the headquarters of a parliamentary commissioner in control of the county's affairs. He was a baronet from Lincolnshire, Sir William Armine (also spelt 'Armyne'), and Sunderland remained his base until the late autumn when he moved to Newcastle.

It has been suggested that Sunderland's 'puritanically minded corporation' was suppressed by the Royalists shortly after the Civil War commenced, and was thus a casualty of the conflict. Recent research by Maureen Meikle has shown that the corporation continued to exist, albeit overshadowed for part of the war by the presence of parliament's commissioner, Armine.[40]

At this time, as in the Tudor period, adherence to Catholicism could result in death, as occurred on 7 September 1644 when priests named John Duckett and Ralph Corby were savagely executed at Tyburn in London. They had been arrested separately in July while engaged in travelling about County Durham to minister to the needs of Catholic laity. Duckett was thus brought to Sunderland and imprisoned, where he was soon joined by Corby. They were then shipped to the capital to be tried and condemned.

Meanwhile, towards the end of March 1644 parliament had allowed ships to trade at Sunderland once again. Shortly after the Scots occupied the town, parliament revoked part of the ordinance passed in January 1643; an ordinance that had caused great hardship in London owing to the shortage of coal supplies. Hence many colliers now hastened north to engage in the vital trade. Some however, were captured by Royalist vessels operating from Scarborough. On the other hand, between March and the fall of Newcastle, Sunderland served as a naval base used by ships belonging to parliament's fleet and these captured a number of Royalist vessels.

When Sunderland's coal trade resumed in the early months of 1644, parliament hoped that revenue derived from customs could go towards paying the Scottish troops campaigning in England. In the event, less money was acquired from the borough's custom house than expected. Corruption was blamed. But in November 1644, an official named James Sword was appointed collector of customs and a marked impovement occurred. Indeed, following discussions in parliament, in 1645 a levy of 4s. per Sunderland chaldron was imposed on all coal shipped from the Wear. Among troops whose salaries benefited as a result were soldiers stationed at Sunderland. It was not until early 1647 that the Scottish soldiers in the North East left for home, by which time large quantities of supplies had been landed at Sunderland to be consumed by troops in the region.

In June 1646 the Civil War had ended with parliament and its Scottish allies triumphant. Overall, Sunderland fared well during the conflict and enjoyed a higher public profile than ever before. It had also witnessed far less destruction than some other communities. At Newcastle, for example, during the siege of August–October 1644 the inhabitants were subjected to repeated artillery fire and as a result of this, and the breaching of its walls by cannon and mines, a significant amount of damage had been done. When the town's indomitable mayor finally surrendered, he had to be protected by Scottish soldiers from irate townsfolk.

Following the Civil War, King Charles was a prisoner (he spent part of his captivity on Tyneside) and, after a brief resumption of bloodshed in 1648 in which Royalists once again came off worst, Charles was put on trial and executed in London in January 1649. News of his trial and death caused widespread dismay, even among the ranks of former opponents. However George Lilburne and his eldest son, Thomas Lilburne of Offerton, felt otherwise and had supported the king's demise.

Changing Fortunes

During the course of 1644, a policy had commenced of seizing property of men in County Durham who supported Charles I. Fines were also imposed on people believed to have Royalist sympathies. Royalists continued to be fined, and forced to hand over money in order to retain possessions, into the 1650s.

George Lilburne played a part in imposing punitive measures on Wearside (and further afield) for he served as one of the sequestrators in County Durham. He did so as a prominent figure in a new body, namely the County Committee, of which his elder brother was also a member.

One of the Wearsiders affected was George Middleton of Silksworth, a member of the gentry of modest estate who was head of a junior branch of the Middleton family of Belsay in Northumberland. He retained his property after agreeing to pay a fine of £120. Middleton was one of a number of people who compounded with a leading Parliamentarian Sir Henry Vane of Raby Castle and the County Committee, in November and December 1645. John Harrison of Sunderland, described as a yeoman, was another. In his case, the figure involved was £20. Even more, £50, was required from Ralph Holmes of Bishopwearmouth, yeoman, a member of a family that had farmed in that locality for several generations. A much smaller sum, £5, was imposed on each of two Sunderland yeomen, Thomas Clarke and Thomas Caldwell.

Later, though, in November 1651 following a petition, it was resolved by the authorities 'That all such inhabitants of the County of Durham named in the title of the said petition who did compound with Sir Henry Vane [etc]…be absolutely discharged from sequestration and pardoned.'[41] Among the individuals so named were Middleton, Harrison, Holmes and Caldwell.

The Bowes family of Barnes also found itself embroiled in troubles. In 1650 William Bowes (whose paternal grandfather Robert had acquired land on Wearside in the mid 16th century) died in London. William had been a Royalist and so his property at Ryhope and Barnes was 'sequestered for delinquency.' As a result, the guardians of his young son, also named William, requested 'a reasonable composition.' In the event, the family paid a hefty fine of over £900 in 1651 and an even greater sum exceeding £1,200 a few years later.

North of the River Wear, Monkwearmouth Hall and its estate of 240 acres and ballast quay, were confiscated because a Catholic gentleman, Ralph Pudsey of Stapleton in Richmondshire, had died fighting for the king at the Battle of Naseby in June 1645. Pudsey had acquired the Monkwearmouth estate earlier in the decade by marrying Elizabeth, the widow of Robert Widdrington. Subsequently, after challenging the seizure of the estate, Elizabeth was granted a widow's third of the property in the early 1650s.

Meanwhile, one of the measures parliament had instituted after winning the Civil War was the abolition of episcopacy in 1646. With the bishopric of Durham thus dissolved, the sale of its possessions commenced and among the purchasers was Colonel George Fenwick of Brinkburn, Northumberland, who acquired the borough of Sunderland in 1649 for over £2,851. Born into Northumberland's gentry in 1603, Fenwick was a graduate of Cambridge and a lawyer by training who had made his mark in New England in the late 1630s and early 1640s. He was for instance a key figure in the development of what would become Connecticut. Fenwick had returned to England in 1645 shortly after the death of his wife. He became a staunch Parliamentarian army officer, and was appointed Governor of Berwick upon Tweed in the same year that he bought Sunderland.

In addition, in 1652 Fenwick (who was still Berwick's governor) purchased Elizabeth Pudsey's share of the Monkwearmouth estate. His involvement there was not problem free. Indeed, in 1654 Fenwick declared that 'He has been at great charges in removing the ballast, repairing the quay, and employing keels to take the ballast from ships, whereby the profits are almost lost.'[42]

Despite their mutual background as former adversaries of King Charles I, Fenwick's arrival as a major player in local affairs struck a discordant note with Sunderland's hitherto 'great factotum' George Lilburne, and they were not on good terms. Much of the bad blood resulted because Fenwick was an ally of Sir Arthur Haslerig, whom parliament had appointed Governor of Newcastle in late 1647 and one of whose daughters Fenwick, a widower, married.[43]

Haslerig clashed with Lilburne on various matters, including control of the highly important colliery at Harraton. Since 1644, Lilburne and George Grey of Southwick had been lessees of the colliery, now under state ownership. But Haslerig opposed this situation and in October 1649 his ally, Fenwick, commenced the violent transfer of the colliery into different hands. Hence the mine was duly leased by army officers favourable to Haslerig.

In short, questionable behaviour occurred among the victors of the Civil War. As William Dumble comments, 'despite the real commitment of both Haslerig and the Lilburnes to the Parliamentary cause since 1642 both parties showed an acquisitive interest in the valuable properties within the county and especially along the middle and lower reaches of the Wear, for the gain of themselves or their associates.'[44]

In the 1650s during the Protectorate of Oliver Cromwell, which commenced in late 1653, Lilburne's fortunes improved and his influence reached its height. For one thing, in the middle of the decade Haslerig was removed from office by Cromwell. In contrast, the Lord Protector was on amicable terms with Lilburne, who became one of County Durham's first MPs in 1654—under the bishops the county had sent no representatives to parliament. Two years later, Lilburne became High Sheriff of County Durham, the first Sunderland man to do so, whereupon his son Thomas replaced him as a Durham MP. Furthermore, in 1657 Colonel George Fenwick died.[45]

During the years when the bishopric of Durham no longer existed, the spiritual needs of Sunderland's Protestant population were entrusted by the victorious Parliamentarians to Puritan clergymen. The first such 'intruder', William Johnson, was appointed to Bishopwearmouth in 1646 following the removal of his predecessor, a Royalist named Christian Sherwood. It is said that the rectory had been badly damaged by troops and Johnson thus spent over £41 (a fairly substantial sum) on repairs over the next few years.[46]

Turning to other matters, in this period local agriculture experienced significant changes. A move away from arable cultivation towards increased animal husbandry occurred and in 1649 or thereabouts a process of enclosure transformed Bishopwearmouth's large common fields into much smaller parcels of ground. Consequently fewer people were

A statue of Oliver Cromwell (1599–1658) at Westminster

employed in farming and some of those who had derived their livelihoods in such a way, moved to urban areas like Sunderland.[47]

On the whole, the town's economy was buoyant during the Republican period. Salt manufacture continued (salt was the Wear's second most important export) but was harmed to some extent by competition from Scotland. Needless to say, coal remained by far the main cargo shipped from the Wear. However, shipments of coal were adversely affected in the years 1652–4 during an Anglo-Dutch war, and the enemy captured a number of colliers as they sailed down the east coast. Hence some of Wearside's seafarers were held captive. In fact, as late as the summer of 1656 a number of local sailors had still not been repatriated.

In addition, the activity of press gangs intent on gaining 'recruits' for Cromwell's navy caused alarm on Wearside. In the years that followed the end of the Anglo-Dutch War, privateers also threatened shipping and armed vessels based at Dunkirk and Ostend struck fear into the crews of the collier fleet.

Increasing religious diversity was also evident during these years. For example, some Puritans were Presbyterians. Locally, a small Presbyterian congregation came into existence in the mid 17th century and met in a house 'in the West end' of Sunderland. The town's most prominent Presbyterian was George Lilburne, and his son Thomas shared his religious outlook.

The Quakers, a branch of Christianity that appeared in the mid 17th century, soon had local adherents for Quakers were present in Sunderland from 1653. Nationally, the Society of Friends encountered a great deal of hostility, much of it self-induced. Quakers sometimes disrupted church services, denounced ministers as false shepherds, or harangued passersby whom they viewed as ungodly. One of Sunderland's first Quakers was George Humble, a well-to-do skinner and glover who had been made a member of Sunderland's corporation by Bishop Morton in 1634. It is recorded that initially the local Quakers met 'at ye house of George Humble at ye beginning, who was a faithful man, and died a Prisoner for his Testimony' in September 1658.[48] He had been incarcerated for his beliefs after clashing with George Lilburne, who had no time for Quaker views.

Lilburne was also hostile to Baptists and on a Sunday in August 1657 he stopped the wife of a Parliamentarian army officer, and seized her horse, as she was en route to a Baptist meeting in Sunderland. Her mount was held until a fine of 20 shillings was paid.[49]

The Restoration and Beyond

Oliver Cromwell died in September 1658. His well-meant but dictatorial rule had been widely unpopular, but George and Thomas Lilburne had remained faithful to the cause.[50] Thomas in particular, proved an energetic supporter of the Lord Protector in County Durham. Moreover, following Cromwell's death he gave his support to his son and successor Richard, who briefly held the reins of power. 'I am so settled upon this government', Thomas wrote in October, 'that I am ready to part with anything for the maintaining of it.'[51]

In the event, national sentiment was moving very strongly in favour of a restoration of the monarchy. Consequently, in the spring of 1660 Charles I's eldest son returned from exile and was duly crowned at Westminster Abbey the following year.

In line with developments nationwide, Charles II sent a commissioner to Sunderland charged with obtaining oaths of supremacy and allegiance from the mayor, four senior aldermen and the town's customs officer.

1660 not only witnessed the return of the monarchy, it also saw the restoration of episcopacy. The man appointed to the see of Durham was John Cosin, who had been a prominent member of Durham's Arminian clergy before the Civil War. Of his reception into his diocese, he enthusiastically wrote, 'at my first entrance through the river of Tease there was scarce any water to be seene for the multitude of horse and men that filled it.'[52]

Naturally, not everyone was pleased with the return of the old order. For instance, after the Restoration the minister at Bishopwearmouth since 1654, William Graves (the 'third intruder')[53] who styled himself 'Parson of the Parish', was ejected to make way for a committed Royalist of longstanding, Robert Grey.[54]

On 'April ye 22 day 1661', Grey presided over a group of local men known as 'Ye gentlemen and twelve' (the parish vestry) who had gathered to discuss the election and choosing of churchwardens and overseers of the highways. Later that year, it was resolved to call upon the parishioners who possessed seats in the church to contribute financially towards carrying out repairs to St Michael's, which had experienced some neglect or damage in the preceding years. Among other things, the refurbishment programme entailed altering the pews, bringing lead from Wolsingham to re-lead the roof, and acquiring items such as service books. In addition, Grey also carried out restoration work on the rectory.

Also affected by the Restoration were people who possessed episcopal property, such as Sunderland, for this reverted to the bishop. Consequently, the heirs of the late George Fenwick lost out. Instead, Cosin leased the borough to a gentleman named Robert Adamson.

Not surprisingly, George Lilburne was unenthusiastic about the Restoration, following which his influence waned significantly. Indeed, in 1662 he was apprehended for a while on the instructions of the Bishop of Durham and his house searched for arms. He was barred from holding public office in County Durham and the same penalty applied to his son Thomas. As Cosin declared: 'They are now looked upon … as men below all public employment.'[55]

For the last years of his life, which ended in 1665, Thomas lived at Offerton, and was associated with his father in founding a hospital at Houghton-le-Spring. For his part, although his best years were certainly behind him, George Lilburne was nevertheless a figure of some importance on Wearside. In early 1666, for example, he was entrusted with distributing £50 from a county fund to inhabitants of Sunderland affected by the plague.[56]

London is, of course, the place usually associated with the outbreak of 1665–6: 'It is a sad noise to hear the bell to toll so often,' lamented the diarist Samuel Pepys, but lives were destroyed elsewhere. Bishopwearmouth Parish Register contains an entry that is a reminder of this fact. It reads: 'Jeremy Reed, of Billingham, Kent, bringer of the plague of which died thirty persons out of Sunderland in three months, was buried on 5th July, 1665.'[57]

By this date, the government had introduced a new tax based on the number of hearths in a home, and although the poorest members of society were exempt from paying, some people of limited means did pay. The hearth tax returns show that (under an assessment on Lady Day, 1666) the majority of people within the parishes of Bishopwearmouth and Monkwearmouth had humble homes that only possessed one fireplace, a state of affairs in line with County Durham as a whole.

At Bishopwearmouth, for instance, out of a total of 235 homes, 202 were single-hearth dwellings, residences that contrasted starkly with the finest home, the rectory, which had nine hearths.

In Sunderland, the number of houses that paid the tax was 115. In this case,

Sir Thomas Williamson (1636–1703) second baronet, by Gerard Soest. Through his marriage to Dorothy Fenwick he acquired the manor of Monkwearmouth

the number of homes that did not do so is unrecorded but probably exceeded those that did pay. A pronounced difference existed between the borough (and to a lesser degree its satellite of Bishopwearmouth Panns) on the one hand, and the parish of Bishopwearmouth in general. The proportion of more prosperous dwellings was far greater. For example, whereas 23 of Sunderland's taxpayers had homes with only one fireplace, 17 had dwellings with four hearths. Even larger homes existed, including George Lilburne's with no less than nine, the same number as in the biggest residence in Bishopwearmouth Panns.

Among the more substantial homes in outlying districts was William Haddock's at Barnes, which had five hearths. Haddock had acquired the property by marrying into the Bowes family. William, the last male member of the line of Bowes long connected with Wearside, had died in the summer of 1661 at the early age of 20.

The 1660s witnessed a change of fortune for the Hylton family, now headed by John Hylton, who had succeeded his father (also John) in 1655. John had control of the family estates restored to him following a prolonged legal battle with the City of London involving his uncle's will drawn up shortly before the Civil War.[58] Inevitably, the litigation had been costly, and presumably it was in order to improve his finances that John proceeded to sell one of his properties, the manor of Barmston, to George Lilburne in 1669 for £2,750. Lilburne was now of advanced age, and died in 1676. Though not as well known as his nephew, 'Free-Born John' (whose connection with Sunderland is unclear)[59], he was nonetheless an able, resourceful and formidable character who deserves to be remembered with respect.

By the time of Lilburne's death, the Williamsons—a gentry family who first appear as landowners in 15th-century Nottinghamshire—had arrived on Wearside.[60] The head of the line, Sir Thomas, had inherited a baronetcy bestowed upon his father in 1642, on the eve of the Civil War. Thomas, who had succeeded to the title as a young man in 1657, inherited little else for his father was a Royalist and had incurred a hefty fine of £3,400 imposed by the victors of the war.

The impoverished second baronet was thus compelled to sell the bulk of the family's land. His fortunes, however, revived through his marriage to Dorothy Fenwick (born at Saybrook in New England in 1645) whose father was the late

Colonel George Fenwick of Brinkburn. When the colonel had died in 1657, Dorothy was one of his co-heirs and her inheritance included part of the Monkwearmouth estate. Consequently, by the late 1660s Dame Dorothy, as she became known as a result of her marriage to a baronet, was living at Monkwearmouth Hall with her husband, Sir Thomas. The residence, also known as 'North Wearmouth Hall', adjoined St Peter's and was later described as a 'large, noble old mansion, built about the age of James I.'[61] This may have been the case, but some of the fabric was of more recent date. In 1689, moreover, Dorothy proceeded to buy her elder sister's share of the Monkwearmouth estate, a share that had passed to Dorothy's nephew.[62]

In 1661 an interesting figure named Walter Ettrick (born in Dorset in 1628 and a Royalist during the Civil War) had become Sunderland's customs officer. The customs house, erected earlier in the 17th century, was located at the east end of Low Street and overlooked one of the quays. Ettrick retained the post until his death at Bath in 1700, during which period he and his staff came under the direction of a Board of Customs, a state of affairs that existed from 1671.

In addition to serving as customs officer, Walter Ettrick had obtained property on Sunderland's riverfront and, in 1673, purchased half the manor of Barnes. Walter's interests also included the collection of tolls for using the bishop's ferry between Sunderland and Monkwearmouth. In 1661, Bishop Cosin granted the lease to Ettrick—for several generations, the ferry had been leased to members of the Bowes family—and Walter's descendants continued to hold the lease into the late 18th century. Passengers using the service were charged additional fees on Friday (market day) and for the two annual fairs.[63]

During the second half of the 17th century, British warships and armed merchantmen were often in action as is depicted in this scene

Further Anglo-Dutch Conflict

From March 1665 until July 1667, England was again at war with Holland. Nationally, there was a fear of invasion and steps were thus taken to prevent an enemy landing. At Sunderland, in July 1666 a small number of soldiers arrived and were stationed in the borough and at Monkwearmouth. In addition, during the hostilities some of the town's sailors were impressed into the Royal Navy. The reality of the war was also brought home to Wearsiders when they heard gunfire from naval vessels at sea, and when Dutch warships, intent on disrupting the coal trade, appeared off Sunderland, whereupon warning beacons were lit. Although the enemy seized some colliers, thanks to the efforts of the Royal Navy many others did manage to sail successfully—among foreign vessels that carried Wear coal during this period were ships from the German ports of Emden and Hamburg, both of which had long-established trading links with the Wear.[64] Even so, for several weeks in the spring of 1667 Sunderland's seaborne trade was brought to a standstill because of the presence offshore of over 20 Dutch men-of-war.

Subsequently, on 7 June as the war was drawing to a close, a letter to Bishop Cosin was written by four gentlemen in Sunderland, one of whom was John Tempest, an appropriate name in view of the letter's contents. They informed Cosin as follows:

> We did according to your Lordship's orders draw our companyes and troops to this place on tusday last, the same night and the next day we were *entertained* wth a most violent storme, wch had a lamentable effect upon a fleet of 100 light colliers coming from the Southward and being in sight of the port when the storms began, we heare of many being cast away on this coast and by the judgement of able seamen it is doubted that at the least one half of them is lost…but we are in hopes that if the dutch fleet were out they would run the same risque and secure us for some time from any attempt from them; we shall be circumspect and diligent in our stations.[65]

In early 1672, after a lull in hostilities, the third Anglo-Dutch War commenced. The conflict lasted two years and once again the North East collier fleet was subjected to significant disruption. In August of that year, for instance, 23 colliers carrying coal from Sunderland were forced to enter the River Tees to shelter after sighting hostile ships. Nevertheless, according to John Hatcher, in 1673–4 (Christmas to Christmas) over 125,000 tons of coal left the Wear, of which more than 8,000 tons went to foreign ports.[66]

The River Wear

During the 17th century, water bailiffs appointed by the Bishop of Durham (John Rand was granted the post as early as 1609) and Crown-appointed bodies of local worthies known as the Commissioners of Sewers, were charged with managing the river. The Attorney General, John Banckes, declared in 1628 that the commissioners were responsible for acting against 'all offences and offenders in building staithes, casting rubbish into the river at Sunderland' etc. Moreover, records from the 1660s show that a vice-admiralty court, answerable to Bishop Cosin, operated in Sunderland. Among other things, the court imposed penalties on those who impeded navigation of the river in one way or another, by for example constructing quays that jutted too far into the river channel.

But as Stuart Miller has commented, the water bailiffs, commissioners and vice admiralty court 'were limited to essentially negative action' owing in part to 'their lack of earmarked finances.'[67] Hence the increasing use of the river was accompanied by worsening conditions. In September 1645, during the Civil War, officials at Westminster stated that they had received information that the 'river of Wier wch. falls into the sea at Sunderland' was 'much annoyed' owing to the deposition of ballast in the water and that the 'comittee for the admiraltie, have given order, to the water bailiff there, to take care, yt. no such abuse be hereafter comitted, or suffered in the said river.'[68] Furthermore, the subsequent preamble to royal letters patent granted by Charles II to a certain Edward Andrew in 1669 authorizing him to raise contributions to build piers and lighthouses, and to cleanse the harbour, states that owing to the sandbanks 'and rubbish daily increasing,' the river had been rendered almost unnavigable.

Even allowing for exaggeration, there can be no doubt that the situation was far from ideal. Nature was principally to blame for the state of the river. The banks constantly eroded and the soil, combined with silt carried downstream from the Wear's upper reaches, gathered about the numerous man-made projections such as jetties, or was deposited on the bar at the harbour entrance. Also, large sandbanks such as the Stell Canch divided the river mouth into narrow and shallow channels, the Stell and the Sledway. To make matters worse, colliers sometimes deposited their ballast of sand indiscriminately as they entered the harbour or lay at anchor, and keels travelling downstream were frequently overloaded and at times jettisoned coal into the river in order to avoid sinking.

Just what Edward Andrew achieved is uncertain and little if any improvement may have occurred. The situation was certainly not trouble free in 1675 when the harbour was inspected by a member of the peerage, Richard Lumley, one of the Wear's greatest coalowners. The viscount thus issued instructions for the entrance to be made deeper to facilitate navigation and as a result a shoal was removed thereby improving matters to some degree. Nonetheless, problems continued. Owing to the limited depth of water, large ships that sailed to the port were either only partially loaded within the harbour and received the rest of their cargo from keels that ventured beyond the harbour entrance, or acquired their whole load by the latter method.[69]

In 1693 an eminent hydrographer, Captain Greenville Collins, published a thorough survey of the British coast that he had undertaken in the 1680s, in which he noted that on Wearside two beacons existed at the entrance of the harbour to aid navigation.

Industry and Recreation

In about 1682 a well known ironmonger named Ambrose Crowley, a young man in his mid twenties who had an iron manufactory in the Midlands, transferred the works to Sunderland where he opened a factory at the west end of Low Street, one of the town's main thoroughfares. One of the advantages of being located on Wearside was its coastal situation. Crowley could bring in iron shipped from Sweden, or places along the English coast, and could export his products more easily than if he were based in a landlocked area. In 1688, according to the *Privy Council Register*, Crowley's substantial workforce numbered about 100 men, some of whom were foreigners—Catholics from Liège in what is now Belgium—and further expansion was planned. The register also states, 'the Persons already imployed by [Crowley] have taught the English workmen there to work better and swifter than formerly and to make such nailes as are used in Holland for sheathing of Shipps.'[70] But there was a problem. The foreign workmen encountered hostility from locals. Crowley had thus petitioned James II for protection, hence the record of events in the *Privy Council Register*. As a result, on 6 July 1688 Nathaniel Crewe, Cosin's successor as Bishop of Durham, was ordered to ensure that such molestation ceased. In the event, the problems continued and in 1691 Crowley moved the works to Winlaton, a short distance west of Gateshead.

A more long lasting venture on Wearside was the lime industry, in existence from at least the mid 17th century. Limestone was quarried in Bishopwearmouth parish and burnt in kilns along the river using low-grade coal as fuel. The output from the kilns was primarily used to de-acidify land used for cultivation. Lime was also used to make an 'hydraulic' mortar that was highly water resistant.

In contrast, the glass trade was of more recent development. Glass manufacture was taking place by 1685, when the first recorded shipment of glass bottles from the Wear occurred. Later, in around 1696 the Sunderland Company of Glassmakers (a ten-strong syndicate) was formed and proceeded to establish works at Bishopwearmouth Panns and Ayre's Quay, east and northwest of Bishopwearmouth respectively, as well as further upstream at Southwick: the firm imported trained men from elsewhere.

Sunderland's trade was still overwhelmingly dominated by the shipment of coal, which peaked in the 1680s. In the middle of the decade, almost 165,000 tons probably left the Wear in a single year.[71] Other cargoes conveyed from the river included lead, butter and short cloth. Salt also ranked among produce that left the port, but the heyday of local salt manufacture was over.

In turn, a wide variety of materials and goods were imported. For example, Maureen Meikle comments that by 1670 shipments arriving at the port included items such as 'thread from Ostend, earthenware and Rhine wine from Rotterdam, Silesian broadcloth and damask for tabling and linen drapery from Ostend, as well as Norwegian timber, French canvas, pantiles from Rotterdam, aquavitae from Dunkirk and iron from Flushing.'[72]

Some of the imports (such as timber from Norway) were required by the Wear's shipbuilding industry, whose scale of production was modest. In the 1640s, local shipbuilders had included Francis Redhead and Roger Thornton at Bishopwearmouth Panns. From mid century onward, members of the Nicholson family were also involved in building ships, whereas from about 1672 if not earlier a local landowning family, the Goodchilds of Pallion, constructed small ships to transport lime produced by their kilns.[73]

Ropemaking also occurred, as was true for example on the Town Moor. In addition, fishermen laid out their nets there to dry and housewives gathered on the moor to perform various tasks, such as bleaching and drying linen.

The Town Moor also served as pasturage. Grazing rights were controlled by a group of men composed of freemen and stallingers. The body numbered 12 freemen and 18 stallingers and the former were allowed more stints on the moor than their less privileged colleagues.[74] When necessary, the ranks of the freemen were filled from those of the stallingers, who were burgesses of inferior status.

Turning to other matters, in their spare time many Wearsiders derived pleasure from sport. Sunderland's Town Moor was a major focal point for recreation, including the game of football, an activity that could be pretty rough and ready. Indeed, in 1667 an ill-fated individual named Richard Watson was killed while playing the game in Sunderland. Other sports conducted here (and doubtless elsewhere in the neighbourhood) included wrestling, bowls, and shooting pistols. Brutal entertainment was also provided such as bull-baiting, a practice in which a tethered bull was set upon by bull mastiffs or terriers. Eventually, the tormented animal, exhausted after attempting to repel the dogs, was led away to be slaughtered. Bull-baiting not only provided a gory spectacle but was also thought to enhance the quality of the meat, so much so that in 1681 a fine was imposed on butchers in the borough who sold unbaited meat.

The Glorious Revolution and its Aftermath

In 1685 Charles II died and was succeeded by his brother, James II. By this date, the Quakers were not as unpopular as had been the case in the 1650s and a prominent local Quaker was William Maude, a wealthy Sunderland merchant and a longstanding member of the Society of Friends. In 1657 he had granted some of his land on the western fringe of the borough to serve as a Quaker burial ground. In 1661, moreover, he had been imprisoned for his beliefs. After holding meetings in a succession of private homes, the Quakers were permitted to build themselves a meeting-house in 1688. It was located near the west end of the borough on ground immediately to the south of their cemetery, and fronted onto High Street.

James II was a staunch Catholic, whose promotion of fellow adherents of Rome caused widespread resentment. In December 1686, for instance, he appointed 15 co-religionists as JPs in County Durham. One such was John Lamb, 'a popish Justice of the Peace' who exchanged insults with Dr Robert Grey, the Rector of Bishopwearmouth, when both met while en route to Durham City. Lamb 'overtook the Doctor, sneered at him, and told him he wondered he would ride upon so fine a palfrey when his Saviour was content to ride upon a colt, the foal of an ass; the Doctor replied "tis true, sir, but the king has made so many asses justices of the peace, he has not left me one to ride upon."'[75]

In 1688 resentment at the rule of King James came to a head, and 'seven persons of quality' (one of whom was the Wear coal magnate Lord Lumley) invited the king's Protestant son-in-law, William of Orange, to invade England. At the beginning of November, William duly landed in Devon at the head of an army, whereupon the king, whose support was evaporating, fled to France.

Lumley was the most influential of James II's opponents in the North East, and during November and December he played a key role in securing the region for William. On 5 December, he moved towards Durham City at the head of armed horsemen and, having been joined by a large number of local Protestant gentry, proceeded to take the city unopposed. By the third week of December the North East was controlled by Lumley and other supporters of the Dutch prince, a state of affairs that was in line with the overwhelming weight of public opinion.

A marble wall-tablet in St Peter's Church, commemorating Dame Dorothy Williamson, (1645–99)

During these weeks, some mobs vented their anger on Catholics and others deemed sympathetic to King James. Locally, ugly events occurred when Sunderland's Quaker meeting-house and other property was attacked. On the evening of 20 December, a group broke into the house but left, only to return at around 1am with 'a rabble of boys and dissolute men of the baser sort' and spent the remaining hours of darkness ransacking the place of worship, burning its fittings, and damaging the building itself. Indeed, the structure was so badly affected that it needed to be rebuilt. In addition, at around 8 o'clock a mob, reportedly several hundred strong, attacked some Quaker homes by smashing their windows. Among the ringleaders during the night's activities were local men of stature such as shipmasters. John Miller has stated that the attack on the Quakers' meeting place was perhaps 'a case of mistaken identity at a time of anti-popish panic' or due to resentment at the support some Quakers in the country had given to James II.[76]

As a result of the 'Glorious Revolution', William and his wife Mary ascended the throne in February 1689 and during the course of that year parliament passed the Toleration Act which granted freedom of worship to Quakers and other nonconformists except Catholics.

In the same year, England became embroiled in conflict with Louis XIV of

France, and hostilities continued until 1697. Consequently Walter Ettrick, Sunderland's customs official, was ordered to seize any French ships that entered the River Wear. Protection was also provided to the collier fleet by both the Royal Navy and Dutch warships. In 1693, moreover, 'great guns' and gunpowder were despatched to Sunderland from Scarborough.

By this date one of Wearside's society figures, Dame Dorothy Williamson, was in her late forties. In the event, she only had a few more years to live for she died in 1699 and was buried at Monkwearmouth in St Peter's Church. In her will, she left in perpetuity the sum of £1 each per annum to 'North Weremouth Town' (Monkwearmouth), Hilton, 'Suddick' (Southwick), Fulwell, and 'Bishopweremouth.' 'North Weremouth Shore' (Monkwearmouth Shore) was to receive £3. For its part, Sunderland, which had been described in 1695 as 'a handsome populous town,' [77] would receive the annual sum of £2.

Dame Dorothy predeceased her spouse, Sir Thomas Williamson, who followed her to the grave in 1703. Wearside lost another of its 'bigwigs' when Robert Grey's long rectorship of Bishopwearmouth came to an end shortly thereafter. He was found dead in his study in July 1704.

By now, Sunderland was on the eve of significant changes that would enhance its status, prospects and sense of self-importance. A new era was at hand.

A LARGE & POPULOUS TOWN – Sunderland during the 18th Century

During the reign of George I (1714–27) a vivid depiction of Wearside was made by an interesting visitor, the topographer Samuel Buck, who engraved a view of Sunderland (as seen from rising ground on the north side of the river) in around 1720. Among other things, Buck's work depicts smoke rising from glasshouses, shipbuilding in progress, and cannon deployed on high ground on the south bank of the Wear to protect the harbour.

Buck's engraving also contains an extravagant depiction of Sunderland's new pride and joy—Holy Trinity Church. By the second decade of the 18th century, the parish church at Bishopwearmouth was far too small to accommodate the majority of parishioners. Thus Sunderland's residents waged a successful campaign to transform their township into a parish in its own right and built Holy Trinity.

The church was consecrated on 5 September 1719, several months after an Act of Parliament had created the parish of Sunderland. The act, which came into effect on 1 May of that year, states that Sunderland was 'a large and populous Town, containing six thousand souls, and upwards,' and had 'become a place of great trade and commerce' whose inhabitants had 'built a beautiful Church, and a Vestry-

Holy Trinity Church from the southwest

room ... and ... dwelling House for a Minister ... being desirous to be a Parish of themselves, distinct and separate from the Parish of Bishopwearmouth.'[1]

Holy Trinity was undoubtedly erected in a thriving town, and was constructed on a piece of land known as the Intake, located off the southern end of a street laid at the eastern fringe of the borough in around 1710. The road, subsequently known as Church Street, was fashionable and contained substantial homes, three storeys high and five bays wide.[2] Moreover, from around 1720 this part of the town witnessed further urban expansion to the northeast of Church Street, work that included the construction of Fitters Row by Edward Browne (d. 1730) who built himself 'a commodious mansion' at the southern end of the street.[3]

An impressive merchant's home (now a public house) built in Church Street c.1710

The first Rector of Sunderland was Daniel Newcome (sometimes wrongly spelt 'Newcombe') who was inducted in July 1719 and perhaps played a key role in designing Holy Trinity. On this point, Geoffrey Milburn noted: 'We do not know who designed the church. One source says that the first rector ... was also its "principal architect." He certainly was one of the chief promoters of the scheme to found the new parish and church and this may be what the phrase implies; but it could well be that he also had a hand in the design.'[4]

Newcome, whose rectory was located just to the north of the church, retained the post until his death in 1738 and enhanced Holy Trinity in various ways. For instance, he added an apsidal chancel to the east end in 1735.

In addition to serving as a place of worship, the building also contained a parish library and reading room, and the vestry room. The latter, located beneath the library in the southwest corner of the structure, served as an administrative centre.

Select Vestries and Almshouses

Local government on Wearside, as elsewhere, was administered by parochial select vestries, committees of respectable inhabitants elected periodically by the ratepayers.

In the case of Sunderland, its first vestry was elected in June 1719 and vestrymen continued to run the parish for the rest of the century and beyond.

The Act of Parliament which established Sunderland parish, states that a meeting was to be held in the vestry room of Holy Trinity to 'chuse twenty-four substantial and creditable inhabitants of the said parish…each of which shall have a freehold estate, or other estate of inheritance of the yearly value of ten pounds, to be Vestry-men for the parish for the space of three years.' The vestry was authorized 'from time to time…to rate, tax, and assess all tenants, occupiers, and farmers of all houses, keys, lands, tenements, hereditaments and estates whatsoever in the…parish…with…sums of money as they or the major part of them' thought 'just and reasonable.' Of the sum raised, £80 was to serve as the rector's stipend. Furthermore, the select vestry was authorized to appoint churchwardens, overseers of the poor, and other parish officers. One such was the scavenger, who had 'to cleane the streets from dirt or mire.'[5]

Select vestries were legally obligated by an Act of Parliament of 1704 to provide fire-fighting equipment for their parishes. For its part, Sunderland parish had two engines that were kept in the porch of Holy Trinity. A keeper of the engines was appointed annually, and when a fire occurred he was assisted by volunteers taken from the ranks of bystanders or passersby.

In 1740 Sunderland's select vestry constructed a workhouse (the money was raised by public subscription) less than a stone's throw from Holy Trinity and its rectory. The 'poor house', located on Church Lane, was enlarged in 1779.

Almost 20 years later, Sir Francis Eden observed of Sunderland:

> The Poor are supported partly in a Workhouse, partly at home. There are at present 176 persons in the house. There are 36 children, two-thirds of them bastards, who are employed in a pin factory. The boys are generally bound apprentices to the sea service. The remaining inmates are mainly old women and prostitutes. Few old men are found here, being mostly employed as scavengers or picking oakum…. About 279 poor families are supported at their own homes.[6]

Bishopwearmouth also had a workhouse. It was founded in 1750 when the local vestry bought a house at the junction of Low Row and Durham Road and converted it to serve the needs of some of the poor of the parish. On the other hand, of Monkwearmouth parish Eden observed: 'The Poor in many of the townships are in a miserable condition; nor has any judicious plan yet been adopted for administering relief to them in a beneficial manner.'[7]

Supplementing the aid given to the poor by the select vestries was that provided by almshouses. Among such, were dwellings erected in 1727 beside St Michael's Church, Bishopwearmouth. They were established through the generosity of a widow named Jane Gibson. In her will she left a substantial sum of money to a friend who was entrusted with buying ground for the building of 'twelve decent rooms…firmly with stone' for the benefit of 'twelve poor persons that shall from time to time be chosen to inhabit in the said rooms.'[8]

Among other almshouses were some established through the Muster Roll Fund.

This was created by an Act of Parliament of 1747 aimed at raising money for the support of 'maimed and disabled' merchant seamen and the widows and children of sailors lost at sea. The act stipulated that 6d. a month was to be deducted from the wage of every merchant seaman aged over 14. Locally the fund resulted in the founding of the Assembly Garth almshouses when the Trustees of the Port of Sunderland bought nine houses and about an acre of land for that purpose in 1750. The almshouses were erected just to the southwest of Holy Trinity Church and were cheek-by-jowl with the town's venue for meetings and theatrical events, the assembly hall.[9]

The Town Moor and Legal Matters

As noted above, Holy Trinity Church was erected on land known as the Intake. The plot in question was formed in 1718 when stone walls were constructed to divide the Town Moor into three sections, the Intake, and the Great Moor and North Moor.

Early in the 1700s, some members of the body of freemen and stallingers claimed that their group owned the Town Moor, but were overruled by their fellows who 'declared that ye Freemen were not Owners of the Soyl of ye Said Common but had only a right of herbage thereof.'[10] As the century progressed, however, the latter changed their tune and thus became embroiled in a number of disputes. In 1731, for example, a lawsuit was brought against them by Sir Edward Milbanke and William Ettrick. The plaintiffs claimed to be the owners of a quay on the edge of the Town Moor under a grant from the bishop, while the freemen and stallingers maintained that the quay was their own property.[11] However, in this and other lawsuits, the freemen and stallingers were unable to validate their claim.

It was commonplace during this era for members of the clergy to serve as magistrates and one such was Edmund Tew, Rector of Boldon from 1735 until his death in 1770. Tew was born in Northamptonshire and was a graduate of Cambridge University. He became a magistrate in 1750 and dealt with numerous cases over an area that included Sunderland and other communities on Wearside. Magistrates frequently heard cases at their own homes or conducted hearings at inns, and one of Tew's fellow magistrates was Teasdale Mowbray of Bishopwearmouth (d. 1785) whose family was well-known on Wearside.

Among wrongdoers who came to Tew's attention was John Green, a thuggish Sunderland attorney. On 13 April 1752, Tew recorded that he had granted a 'general warrant against…John Green upon oath of Jane Carr of Sunderland Pans, for breaking head, and giving her many visible bruises on the eye, arm, back etc. for asking him for a debt due to her.'[12] Green's violent behaviour was not a solitary offence. Days earlier, the lawyer had also assaulted Thomas Carre of Monkwearmouth Shore, whom he knocked to the ground. The latter pursued the matter. As a result, Green had to answer a charge of assault and battery when the next quarter sessions were held at Durham and was fined 1s. Other cases against him were also held at the quarter sessions, most notably one in which he incurred the hefty fine of £5 for assaulting a magistrate, namely George Baker of Elemore Hall (near Pittington), one of the county's gentry. Green was sentenced to remain in gaol until the sum was paid.

In an even more serious case, Tew heard that the accused was a Sunderland shoe-maker named William Neessham (or Neesham). On 22 July 1754, Tew thus granted a general warrant against him 'for a rape and giving the foul distemper to Sarah Turner an infant of 10 years of age.'[13] The rape reportedly took place in Sunderland workhouse, but Neessham was subsequently acquitted at the assizes.

Religion and Education

At the beginning of the 18th century there were two parish churches in the imme-diate vicinity of the borough of Sunderland, namely St Peter's, Monkwearmouth, and St Michael's, Bishopwearmouth. Both were Anglican. As noted, these were soon joined by Sunderland's Holy Trinity. In 1769, moreover, St John's also opened its doors for worship. The latter stood right at the southeast end of the built-up area of Sunderland and was not a parish church—no baptisms, marrriages etc. were performed there until its status changed over a century later. Rather, it was a daughter chapel of Holy Trinity and was erected to help cope with the increasing population of Sunderland parish. The man primarily responsible for its construc-tion was John Thornhill, born c.1720, a prosperous coal exporter and freemason.[14] Indeed, he largely financed the project and is said to have designed the building, which resembled Holy Trinity. Thornhill held the right of choosing curates to serve the chapel for the first 21 years of its existence.

St Peter's Church, Monkwearmouth, in 1785

The elegant interior of Holy Trinity Church

In contrast, the Rector of Bishopwearmouth—the wealthiest clergyman on Wearside—was appointed by the Bishop of Durham, as was the Rector of Sunderland parish, a far poorer living. The incumbent of St Peter's, Monkwearmouth (another poor living), owed his position to the heads of the Hylton family, and from mid century onward the Williamsons.[15]

One of those who held the lucrative rectorship of Bishopwearmouth was John Laurence, a Cambridge graduate from Northamptonshire who had a penchant for gardening. So much so that during his years as rector, 1722–32, he published a massive five-volume work entitled *A New System of Agriculture being a Complete Study of Husbandry and Gardening*. His posthumous reputation was such that he was deemed worthy of inclusion in the *Dictionary of National Biography*.[16]

Throughout the Georgian era state persecution of Catholics continued, primarily through legal restraints and disabilities. However, it eased somewhat from 1778 onward. Furthermore, though the Act of Toleration of 1689 had made the lot of other nonconformists easier, they too suffered from disabilities during this period. In addition, at times mob action occurred. In 1746, for example, when feelings were running high as a result of the Jacobite rebellion of the Catholic Bonnie Prince

Charlie, the Catholic chapel in Sunderland (located in a house in Warren Street, at the foot of High Street), was attacked and destroyed by a mob mainly consisting of sailors.[17] In the 1780s, after an interlude in which they worshipped at nearby Vine Street, local Catholics moved west to meet for worship in a new chapel in Chapel Street—the future Dunning Street—in Bishopwearmouth.

Other denominations included the Quakers and some of Sunderland's most important families, such as the Maudes and Ogdens, ranked among their number. Baptists also lived on Wearside and had several chapels, including one erected on Sans Street in 1798.

What was probably Sunderland's first purpose-built chapel, the Corn Market Chapel, was constructed in the heart of the town in 1711 between High Street and Low Street, roads running parallel to each other on an east-west axis.[18] The Calvinistic congregation, which included many Scottish immigrants, was large and the chapel's first minister was the Presbyterian, George Wilson, already an established figure in the town. In the 1730s, part of the congregation (the Presbyterian element) seceded following the introduction of hymns that were not to their liking, and duly founded a Presbyterian chapel in Robinson's Lane in 1739.[19] Some members of this congregation, who lived on the north side of the Wear, found crossing the river a hindrance—one had to cross by ferry at this date—and so a congregation was formed in Monkwearmouth in 1777. This occurred with the assistance of the Robinson's Lane Chapel.

During the mid 18th century Unitarian views were held by some of those who attended the Corn Market Chapel, including one or two of its ministers. Such worshippers rejected the Trinity doctrine, an unorthodox stance for the doctrine was, and is, central to the beliefs of most Christian denominations although the *New Catholic Encyclopedia* acknowledges that: 'The formulation "one God in three persons" was…not fully assimilated into Christian life and its profession of faith, prior to the end of the 4th century…. Among the Apostolic Fathers, there had been nothing even remotely approaching such a mentality or perspective.'[20] At the Corn Market Chapel orthodoxy was duly restored, and Unitarianism only reappeared in Sunderland in the early 19th century.

A significant development during the 18th century was the introduction of Methodism. This movement was founded by John Wesley and his brother, Charles, whilst at Oxford University. Both belonged to the Church of England but thought that it had failed in its duty to enlighten the people and so became travelling evangelists, boldly taking the Word of God far and wide.

Charles was the first to visit Sunderland. He did so on 16 June 1743 and preached to a large crowd, no doubt in High Street, the main thoroughfare. 'Never', he recorded, 'have I seen greater attention in any at their first hearing.'[21] John first visited Sunderland the following month. He was to do so again on 31 occasions, and during some of these he also preached at Monkwearmouth, including in St Peter's Church.

Methodism struck a chord in Sunderland. As Geoffrey Milburn has commented, one reason for this was that the town, in common with many other ports, generally had 'an open, tolerant community, with a frank, outspoken and democratic air about it. It wasn't dominated by parsons and squires.'[22] A society (a local unit of Methodists) soon formed and met in a succession of temporary meeting houses. In 1752 John Wesley noted that it was 'one of the liveliest Societies in the north of England.'[23] Later in the decade some of its members who were unwilling to desist from smuggling, a common practice in coastal towns, were 'cut off' from membership of the society at Wesley's command.

In 1759 he opened Sunderland's first purpose-built Methodist chapel in Numbers Garth, off High Street. This in turn was replaced by an elegant chapel built in Sans Street in 1793—three years after Wesley's final visit to Wearside—by which time the congregation included several people of means.

Societies formed larger units called circuits, and one such was the Sunderland Circuit founded in 1782. This consisted of northeast Durham and part of Northumberland (it was subdivided in the early 19th century), and its name testifies to the importance of Sunderland in the Methodist movement in the region. In 1791, the year of John Wesley's death, the circuit had 1,301 members (staunchly committed individuals), 300 of whom belonged to the Sunderland society, and 135 of whom belonged to that of Monkwearmouth, whose chapel in Whitburn Street dated from 1761.

During the mid 18th century Jews settled in Britain from Holland and Germany, and a small number of them came to Sunderland, thus adding another dimension to the town's religious life—the first known Jewish resident was a silversmith and jeweller named Abraham Samuel, who died in 1794. The Jews worshipped in the home of their rabbi. In 1781, though, Jews from Poland who had recently arrived on Wearside, parted company with the established Jewish congregation and converted part of a house on Vine Street into their own synagogue.

There was no state system of education during this period. Educational possibilities were thus limited or non-existent, depending on one's social position or good fortune. However, a fine grammar school existed at Houghton-le-Spring, namely the Kepier School founded in 1574. One of the 'old boys' was the Durham country gentleman and historian, Robert Surtees, who was born in 1779 and went to Kepier when he was seven years old. While at the school (which he attended until he was 14) he made friends with the sons of a Herrington gentleman whose daughter he was to marry.[24]

Humbler schools existed on Wearside. For example, the freemen and stallingers successfully petitioned Bishop Crewe for permission to found a school on the Town Moor in 1705. Another school was operated by Sunderland Workhouse (which opened in 1740). Among other establishments was the Donnison School, built near Holy Trinity in 1798. It was founded through the generosity of an Anglican widow, Elizabeth Donnison, who left money for such a purpose in her will of 1764. The school offered free education to girls between the ages of 7 and 16 who were taught several subjects, including reading, knitting, sewing and spinning. Another Charity

The Donnison School

school was founded through the generosity of a Quaker named Edward Walton who made provision for its establishment in his will of 1768. The school, located in Bishopwearmouth, provided a free education to a small number of youngsters whose parents were Quakers, as well as children who were disadvantaged in some way.

Not to be overlooked are Sunday Schools. Michael Longridge, a prosperous Wesleyan Methodist mercer, was chiefly responsible for the founding of the first of the town's Sunday Schools in 1786. Another man interested in their provision was John Hampson. In 1788, while curate of St John's, the much-travelled Hampson bemoaned the behaviour of the local youngsters, 'never have I beheld children so rude and uncultivated,' he said.[25] He believed that Sunday Schools were the answer.

Finally, it is interesting to note that in the 1730s the highly gifted and devout young scientist, Thomas Wright of Durham, taught mathematics and navigation to sailors in Sunderland during the winter months when shipping virtually ceased owing to the inclement weather.

The Harbour and River Improvement

In the early years of the 18th century the state of the river and harbour was so poor that in 1705–6 Sunderland coal merchants and coalowners, dissatisfied with existing arrangements for governing the river, attempted to gain legislation for the establishment of a body mandated to improve matters. Owing to opposition from the Tyne interest, the attempt failed.

In 1716, however, Thomas Conyers and John Hedworth promoted a bill with the purpose of improving Sunderland harbour and rendering the River Wear navigable as far as Newbridge, 11 miles upstream near Chester-le-Street. Conyers was MP for Durham City. Hedworth had represented County Durham in parliament since 1713 and owned a large colliery on 'Chester Waists' from where coal was carried by a long wooden wagonway to the Wear at Biddick ford (near Fatfield) en route to be shipped at Sunderland.

A committee of the House of Commons appointed to examine the bill met on 28 March 1717, coincidentally the year Handel's *Water Music* was premiered. According to a leading London lawyer, Charles Sanderson of the Inner Temple (who favoured the Tyne interest), it was biased in favour of the bill. 'Mr Hedworth gott all friends there', he informed a friend named William Cotesworth, a major figure on Tyneside.[26]

When the bill passed to the House of Lords several petitions were made against it, including one from the Common Council of Newcastle: the Tyne interest had already presented a petition against the bill at committee stage. Nonetheless, the bill was passed by the Lords without any substantial amendments. Hence on

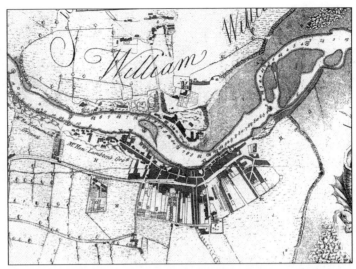

A section of the map by Burleigh and Thompson drawn in 1737

22 June 1717, an Act of Parliament established a body known as 'The Commissioners of the River Wear and Port and Haven of Sunderland', a body whose members included local gentry, Anglican clergy, coalowners, professional men and coalfitters—the latter were middlemen between the coalowners and the colliers.

Thus the River Wear Commission was born. It was granted powers for 21 years and its jurisdiction initially extended as far upstream as Durham City. The commission was authorised to raise necessary funds for carrying out and maintaining improvements to the harbour by a levy on all coal shipped from the Wear.

The first engineer to make a report for the RWC was James Fawcett. In his report, dated Sunderland, 19 August 1718, Fawcett referred to endeavours that had been made to improve navigation by tackling the problem of the Stell Canch, 'one of the principal impediments to Navigation.' Such attempts, he declared, 'were never yet able to gain above 18 or 20 inches more water than at present wch was Effected about 35 years agoe; but neglecting to keep the Channels open—'tis now grown worse than ever.' In short, he concluded gloomily, if nothing were done 'in a little time the Haven will be Intirely ruined.'[27] The first major undertaking of the RWC—whose most active members were usually local merchants and coalfitters—was the construction of a south pier. Work began on this project in or shortly before 1723 (the commission had to borrow money to help finance the undertaking) and was completed by 1730. The pier was 1,000ft long, 30ft wide, and curved inwards. It was constructed to drive the full force of the river against the bar and to shelter the harbour, and was probably designed by a harbour engineer named William Lellam.

In 1748 the pier was described by the eminent Swiss engineer, Charles Labelye, as 'one of the Most Magnificent and best built in the whole world.'[28] Labelye had been invited to Sunderland by the RWC, which had been reborn through an act passed on 17 June 1747 after being in abeyance for a number of years—the upper limit of its jurisdiction of the river which initially extended as far as Durham City, was reduced to Newbridge.

Labelye had travelled up from London and arrived in Sunderland in July. Here, he conducted himself with his usual thoroughness and, following his return to Westminster, provided the RWC with a detailed report on measures to undertake. The construction of a north pier was one recommendation. Large-scale dredging was another, as was the consolidation of the river into a single channel. As a result, in the early 1750s William Vincent, in his capacity as resident harbour engineer, a post he held in the years 1752–4, blocked the north channel (the Stell) and began dredging to deepen the remaining channel.[29] The RWC owned manually operated dredging equipment and the work was contracted out by the commission to local entrepreneurs, a state of affairs that lasted until 1796: thereafter, it was done directly by a department of the RWC.

Work on a north pier, sorely needed to protect the harbour from north winds that sometimes wrought havoc, finally commenced in 1786. It began shortly after the south pier had been extended and re-routed to direct ebb tides more effectively than had been the case: it was believed that the original alignment was responsible for the development of a large sandbank in the river mouth. By 1795, a 700ft long north pier had been erected, but it was soon extended by Jonathan Pickernell, who became harbour engineer that year.

The routine activities of the RWC were concerned with ensuring that use of the river was not rendered difficult or dangerous owing to the actions of man. Fines were imposed on the owners of jetties and quays which fell below the standard required by bylaws, and on those responsible for dumping ballast etc. into the water.[30] Additionally the RWC ensured that keels were not overloaded.

Trade and Industry

In the early 18th century Sunderland was a vibrant, bustling town, and the Act of Parliament of 1717 that established the River Wear Commission refers to some of the sources of this prosperity, foremost of which was the coal trade.

By 1704–10, for example, an annual average of around 174,260 tons of coal was being shipped from the Wear, significantly more than a third of Newcastle's average for the same period. As Joyce Ellis aptly states of the regional capital, 'competition from alternative sources of supply, notably from the rapidly-developing port of Sunderland, was cutting into Newcastle's provincial and export markets, leaving it dangerously dependent on demand from the metropolis.'[31]

Consequently, London's share of Newcastle's shipments rose. Whereas 67 per cent of the Tyne's coal was bound for the capital in 1682–3, by 1710 the proportion had risen to 83.7 per cent. In marked contrast, M.W. Flinn notes that Sunderland's coal trade 'was more evenly distributed between London and the "coast." In 1710 London was the destination of only twenty-eight per cent of Sunderland's shipments, Yarmouth taking thirteen per cent, King's Lynn eight per cent, Boston seven per cent and Whitby six per cent.'[32]

Understandably, in view of the growing competition from the Wear, the Tyne interest was not pleased by the subsequent improvements made by the RWC. In 1725 the Earl of Oxford visited Newcastle upon Tyne and noted: 'They [the persons involved in the coal trade], seem at present a little jealous of Sunderland which has of late shared with it pretty considerably in this trade and as I am told is likely to gain more and more upon it every day.'[33]

Such fears were justified. Coal sales from the Wear destined for London and coastal markets approached 40 per cent of such sales from the Tyne in the 1730s, around 50 per cent in the 1750s, and 60 per cent in the 1790s. The quantity of coal involved was considerable. In 1790, for instance, some 763,000 tons were shipped from the Wear.

None of the coal that left the river was mined in the immediate vicinity of Sunderland. It was still extracted at collieries located further inland, and during the course of the century a network of horse-powered wagonways developed to carry the coal to the Wear. By 1788 pits linked to the river by this means included Lambton Main and collieries at Harraton, Newbottle, Usworth and Washington.

A directory of the 1790s notes that, as in the past, large sea-bound vessels frequently lay just beyond the bar at the mouth of the harbour at Sunderland to receive part of their cargoes. At times this rendered the task of keelmen dangerous for they were 'often lost in venturing off to the ships.' But when contrary winds prevented vessels from leaving the Tyne 'ships at Sunderland, riding in the open sea,' were able to sail as soon as they had received their full cargoes.[34]

Like the coal industry (and in marked contrast to the Wear's salt industry) the local glasshouses evidently witnessed an increase in output in the early years of the 18th century. An indication of the scale of production can be gleaned from the fact that in 1715, a ship named the *Prosperity* left the Wear partly laden with over 18,000 glass bottles. During the course of the century, several new glasshouses were founded, such as the Bishopwearmouth Glass House established near the Panns Ferry in about 1765. In short, Wearside and Tyneside were the principal suppliers of glass to the capital and bottles and broad window glass were prominent items produced.

Sunderland was the only significant exporter of lime between the Humber and the Forth during the 18th century (more limited production occurred at places like Beadnell and Holy Island) and limestone was quarried and burnt on both sides of the Wear. There were lime kilns at Pallion and on the Town Moor, whereas across the river they existed in the vicinity of Southwick and at Fulwell.

Another industry that was more than a passing phase was manufacturing pottery. Sunderland's first record of a pottery is to be found in the *Newcastle Journal* of 23 June 1753, where an advertisement states that it was 'situate nigh the pier.' It appears to have developed into what was known as the Sunderland or Garrison Pottery, operative by the close of the century.[35] Among other such establishments was the North

Hylton Pottery founded in 1762 by William Maling of Hendon Lodge[36] (a wealthy landowner who hailed from Scarborough) as a business interest for his two young sons: Maling had settled in Sunderland in 1723 when in his mid 20s. The pottery was located close to a site where clay could be extracted, and had ready access to the river to ship its products. The firm printed pictures onto its wares using copper plates and in the mid 1770s the renowned Northumbrian engraver Thomas Bewick—or one of his partners—produced designs for the firm whose output included creamware tea and dinner services decorated with a variety of patterns.

Other businesses included a pottery set up at Southwick in the summer of 1788. The firm, which produced brown and creamware, was formed by a partnership that included a young man named Anthony Scott (previously the manager of a pottery at Newbottle) and a payroll dating from August of the following year lists 27 employees.[37] In around 1794, another pottery commenced production at Low Ford, South Hylton, a venture owned five years later by John Dawson, who had trained at Maling's North Hylton Pottery.

Some Wearsiders were engaged in the copperas industry. The first works were established in the mid 18th century at South Hylton by a surgeon named William Scurfield. In about 1772, if not before, a copperas works was set up closer to home by Messrs Biss and Ogden at Deptford, which developed into an industrial suburb in the late 18th century. The works used pyrites from Lyme, Dorset, from which sulphur products were extracted for various purposes, such as the making of dyes and for paper manufacture.

Much more significant were shipbuilding and the construction of other craft. According to Joe Clarke, over 150 vessels can be identified as having been built on the Wear before 1776, the largest of which was the 500-ton *Duke William*, built in 1748. *Lloyds' Register* of 1776 includes 63 Sunderland-built vessels totalling 12,222 tons (it must not, of course, be assumed that these represent that year's shipbuilding output on the Wear) and as Clarke comments, the register shows that 'the port was already capable of building large vessels, and of a quality comparable to other places.'[38] Nevertheless, it shows too that the tonnage of ships built in ten other ports exceeded that of Sunderland.

As the 18th century drew to a close enterprising individuals, such as the Laing family from Fife who founded a shipyard at Monkwearmouth Shore in 1793, seized the opportunity presented to them by increasing demand for ships. Certainly, it was during the closing decades of the period that the industry began the expansion locally which transformed it from one of nondescript status to Sunderland's foremost industry. For example, according to William Hutchinson, during the 1780s several shipyards were 'constantly employed' on Wearside, and some of these are depicted on the *Eye Plan*—a contemporary map by John Rain.[39] One such was the yard of a prosperous shipbuilder, Thomas Nicholson, which was located on the riverside in Bishopwearmouth Panns. Moreover along its northern edge, the *Eye Plan* includes a partial depiction of events on the north side of the Wear and has a fine scene portraying shipbuilders at work close to the harbour entrance.

Most of the ships built were merchantmen. However, the occasional warship was constructed, such as the *Achilles* and the *Bucephalus*, by Messrs. Thomas Dixon and James Stafford of Monkwearmouth Shore in 1781–2. The largest vessel constructed on the Wear prior to the 19th century was the 925-ton *Lord Duncan*, launched at Southwick on 2 March 1798. Whereas most of the ships were intended for the coastal trade, the *Lord Duncan* was destined for the Mediterranean and West India trade.

Allied to shipbuilding were the ancillary industries of sail-, rope-, and block-making. The most notable ropeworks was founded when Webster and Grimshaw established the world's first factory for machine-made rope at Deptford in c.1794, and where production thus differed from the traditional method of rope manufacture. The latter entailed the use of a rope walk, along which strands were laid out

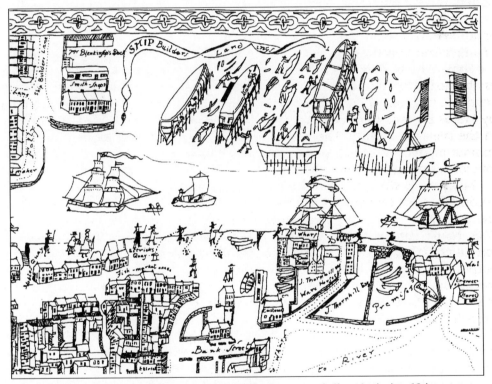

A scene by John Rain depicting shipbuilding at Monkwearmouth Shore in the late 18th century

and then twisted together. Of course, timber was also required by the shipyards, and Rain records the presence of a number of 'raff' (timber) yards on his *Eye Plan*. One such is 'Mr Bonner's raff yard' (now Bonner's Field), on the north side of the river.

Of Sunderland, the *Universal British Directory* states: 'The trade and shipping of this port are become very considerable…A great revenue arises from its exports.'[40] Salt, grindstones and copperas are some of the exports mentioned: imports included corn, flour, wines and timber. According to the directory, 4,905 and 705 ships were cleared from the port in 1790 for coastal and overseas trade respectively, and the principal foreign markets were France, Holland and the Baltic ports.

Prominent Families and Imposing Houses.

In 1737 a map of the River Wear from Sunderland to Newbridge was produced by Mark Burleigh and Isaac Thompson.[41] Among other things, this fascinating work notes the property of gentry like the Williamson family who, as mentioned in the preceding chapter, had arrived on Wearside in the reign of Charles II as a result of the marriage of Sir Thomas Williamson to Dorothy Fenwick. Sir Thomas died in 1703, whereupon the title and estate passed to a brother, who was in turn succeeded in 1707 by his son, Sir William, the fourth baronet, High Sheriff of County Durham from 1723 until his death in 1747. Sir William had married into the Hedworth family of Harraton.[42] His estate included Monkwearmouth Shore, which was developing more rapidly than neighbouring Monkwearmouth. Moreover, Sir William had purchased Whitburn Hall (he did so in 1719) a more secluded residence than the family home, Monkwearmouth Hall, which was abandoned in favour of Whitburn.[43]

Burleigh and Thompson also note the property of the Grey family of Southwick, beyond whose land lay the substantial estate of John Hylton, which straddled both sides of the River Wear. Hylton Castle—over a mile west of Southwick—was of course his ancestral seat and extensive alterations had been made to the former stronghold. In the first decade of the 18th century, a previous head of the family had gutted the interior so that a regular three-storey arrangement of rooms could be inserted. Furthermore, a Classical north wing of three storeys was added. At some stage after 1728—when an engraving of the castle was made by Samuel and Nathaniel Buck—John Hylton also made his mark on the imposing residence. The most notable addition, was the construction of a south wing to match that to the north. He also adorned the main rooms with elaborate plasterwork.

John was the last of his line. Upon his death on 25 September 1746 his property passed to his nephew Sir Richard Musgrave, who subsequently assumed the name of Hylton but nevertheless sold Hylton Castle to Mrs Bowes of Streatlam and Gibside in 1750.[44]

Burleigh and Thompson show that further upstream, much of the land along the Wear between North Hylton and Washington was owned by one of the river's leading coalowners, Richard Lumley, the second Earl of Scarborough.

Another family prominent in the coal trade were the Lambtons, whose ancestral seat, Lambton Hall, lay on the south side of the Wear a short distance downstream from Newbridge.[45] In 1737 the family was headed by a gentleman named Henry.[46] His property included land east of South Biddick. He also possessed ground in Bishopwearmouth parish and had a town house in Sunderland. The three storey brick home, five bays wide, stood in an isolated position at the east end of High Street and faced south.[47]

Other large residences on Wearside during the Georgian period included Ford Hall, a dignified two-storey structure with an elegant central porch, erected south of

West view of Hylton Castle. The Classical wings added in the 18th century can just be seen

the river on land that had belonged to the Hyltons. It was built in 1785 by a prominent local figure named George Mowbray whose family owned extensive property on Wearside—including land that would become Mowbray Park in Victorian times. Several years later, he sold Ford to John Goodchild for £14,500. Goodchild let the property to a local shipbuilder named William Havelock and in 1795 William's son Henry (who was to achieve fame by helping to quell the Indian Mutiny in 1857) was born in the hall.

Recreation

Blood sports were a popular form of entertainment during this period. Bull, bear and badger baiting drew large crowds and took place on Bishopwearmouth Green and on the Town Moor. Cock fighting was also popular and was usually conducted in the yards of public houses. Moreover, fox hunting had come into vogue—it was introduced into County Durham in 1738—and by the time of John Rain's *Eye Plan* some local gentlemen were members of the Bishopwearmouth Independent Hunt whose hounds were kept in a kennel in Hind Street.

In addition to serving as a venue for baiting animals and cock fighting, the Town Moor was also the setting for horseracing and other communal events such as festivals and fairs. Bowling, a popular pastime, also took place on the moor and elsewhere for that matter.

There were numerous alehouses on Wearside and many people no doubt spent much of their leisure time in these establishments for heavy drinking was a feature of 18th century life: Rain shows the existence of several local breweries, such as the Stafford Abbs brewery in Monkwearmouth. Furthermore, some would have visited local taverns which can be likened to licensed restaurants. There were also several inns that catered for travellers, including Bishopwearmouth's *Peacock Inn.* Another noteworthy inn was the *Golden Lion* in Sunderland. It stood at the junction of Queen Street and the High Street and was a favourite venue for meetings of the RWC.

By the late 18th century, Sunderland possessed a theatre, namely the Theatre Royal situated in Playhouse Lane (the future Drury Lane) off the south side of High Street, and not far from the boundary with the parish of Bishopwearmouth.

The theatre was founded in the 1760s by Thomas Bates who established a circuit of theatres in a number of locations such as Stockton, Darlington and Durham. Bates and his company would perform at one of these venues for part of the year before moving to another. The Sunderland theatre, one of the earliest in the circuit, was housed in a building that had served as a Methodist chapel and the first performance occurred on Christmas Eve, 1768.

Among the plays performed in subsequent years were works by Congreve and Sheridan. The latter's comedy, *School for Scandal* (which was premiered in London in May 1777) received its first performance in Sunderland's theatre, which had recently been enlarged, on Friday, 4 December 1778. A bill advertising the performance states that the 'Doors will be open'd at Five and the Curtain drawn up Exactly at Six o'clock' and that tickets were available from 'Mrs Seymours near the Theatre and the Usual Places.'[48]

Bates' colourful nephew James Cawdell, who was born in Hertfordshire in 1750, played a major role in the activities of the Sunderland theatre. For example, he was 'Mr Surface' in *School for Scandal* and, on Wednesday 17 January 1781, acted in a comedy entitled *Provoked Husband, or a Journey to London*, one of whose authors was Sir John Vanbrugh. The bill advertising this event notes that tickets could again be acquired from Mrs Seymour's premises located in the adjoining street, Spring Garden Lane.

In 1782 Cawdell eloped to Gretna Green with the 15-year-old daughter of a Sunderland publican (James Martin of the *Golden Lion*) but returned to the town and, from 1788 onward, ran the theatre business. Cawdell died at Durham in 1800 and was buried in Sunderland, whereupon the circuit passed into the management of Stephen Kemble, a member of 'the most distinguished theatrical family in the land.'[49]

A Subscription Library was founded in Sunderland in 1795 by a group of gentlemen of literary interests that included some of the leading figures in the town. The annual subscription of two guineas meant that membership was confined to persons of some means. The library was situated in High Street in a room above the bookshop of one of its members, the first librarian William Dobson, but in 1801–2 premises were purpose-built in the same street.

Those with the inclination and money to do so, could also find entertainment and enlightenment further afield. For example, in the mid 18th century a Novocastrian named Charles Avison, whom the *New Grove Dictionary of Music and Musicians* describes as 'the most important English concerto composer of the 18th century', held regular subscription concerts in Newcastle.[50] The concert programmes included material by various composers and Avison's own melodious compositions.

Among musicians who participated in the concerts was an interesting figure who settled in Sunderland in 1761, namely William Herschel. Born in Hanover in 1738, as a young man he had made his way to England in the belief that it would further his career. Upon being disappointed because music in London was dominated by Italians, Herschel headed north and, after a brief spell at Richmond, settled on Wearside where he became a music teacher and wrote his Symphony no.8 in C minor in the spring of 1761. He proved popular among the town's well-to-do who sent their offspring for instruction. In addition, he became the musical director of garden concerts in Newcastle (a rival venture to Avison's concerts) and also played in Avison's orchestra. Consequently, Herschel frequently travelled to and fro from Sunderland and Newcastle. He left Wearside in the early 1760s, later turned his attention to astronomy, and discovered the existence of the planet Uranus in 1781.

Another musician linked to Sunderland was William Shield, who was born at Swalwell in County Durham in 1748 and studied music with Avison. Shield became a friend of John Thornhill, the prominent Sunderland businessman and freemason and composed music for the foundation ceremony of St John's Church in 1769. He also composed a piece for the building's consecration. The music was performed by a choir from Durham Cathedral. Subsequently, Shield was again called upon to write music for another notable local event, the dedication of the masonic base, Phoenix Lodge, on 5 April 1785. The music was set to an ode by Dr Tippin Brown and was likewise performed by musicians from Durham Cathedral. In addition, Shield performed at the Theatre Royal.

Rain's 'Eye Plan' — Wearside in the Late 18th Century

Between 1785 and 1790 John Rain, the parish surveyor of Bishopwearmouth, drew an *Eye Plan of Sunderland and Bishop Wearmouth from the South*, a detailed work that is an important source of information for the local historian. It testifies, for instance, to the expansion which Bishopwearmouth and Sunderland experienced during the 18th century, a point readily apparent when the *Eye Plan* is compared with the map of 1737 by Burleigh and Thompson. For one thing, it shows that a new suburb had developed to the northeast of Bishopwearmouth. However, before discussing this, we shall first concern ourselves with the old village, which did not extend far in any direction from St Michael's Church and was a nodal point in the area's road network—a fact that indicates its antiquity—for the major roads leading to Wearside from Durham, Stockton and elsewhere converged on the place.

Not surprisingly, Bishopwearmouth's population was not uniform. It ranged from poor folk such as the inhabitants of the workhouse to persons of consequence like George Mowbray, a wealthy coalfitter whose grand house was located to the southeast of the green. It faced south towards Back Lane (today's Vine Place) and had spacious grounds extending to Back Lane and to Crowtree Lane (Crowtree Road) to the east.

Presumably, the green was the ancient centre of the village, and just to the north of it Rain depicts St Michael's, essentially a medieval structure whose tower had been provided with a clock. Just to the east of St Michael's, Rain notes the Hospital House. This comprised Jane Gibson's almshouses founded in 1727. North of the church, he portrays the rectory whose grounds included an ornamental garden. As

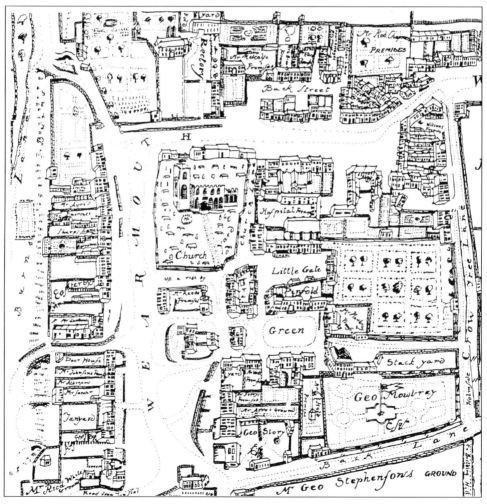

Rain's *Eye Plan*: Bishopwearmouth

the parish of Bishopwearmouth was large and important, the living was usually given to well-connected gentlemen and the rector at this date was Henry Egerton, a member of an aristocratic family and a man noted for entertaining on a lavish scale.

When progressing east from the rectory down what is now part of High Street West, one came to the *Peacock Inn*, the village's principal inn, to which many travellers resorted. It stood where the *Londonderry Arms* now stands and on Rain's map is referred to as 'Mr Wilson's Premises.'

Continuing eastward down the Sunderland Lonnin, as High Street West was called, en route to Bishopwearmouth's larger neighbour, there was, to one's right, a block of land extending south to Back Lane and eastward from Crowtree Lane to the northern continuation of Back Lane, today's Sans Street. This block mainly comprised the ornamental grounds and residences of wealthy individuals. One such was Christopher Fawcett, who had served as Recorder of Newcastle upon Tyne and belonged to a landowning family of some consequence in the North East. His estate in Bishopwearmouth parish totalled 19 acres. It was adjoined to the east, in part, by the hamlet of Sunniside, immediately to the south of Sunderland Lonnin and near the east end of the block of land in question.

To one's left, when heading down Sunderland Lonnin from the *Peacock Inn*, was the new suburb referred to earlier. This consisted of, from west to east, Hopper Lane (which became Castle Street), Chapel Street (now Dunning Street), Queen Street, Factory Street (Cumberland Street), Green Street, and Pan[n] Lane. On Burleigh and Thompson's map, the only part of this area developed consisted of houses along the east side of Pan Lane and those at its southern end facing onto Sunderland Lonnin, the latter dwellings being known as the 'Half-way Houses.' Rain shows that this suburb—erected on the land of Ralph Robinson of Middle Herrington—chiefly consisted of the homes of artisans and well-to-do folk.

East of this suburb, and opposite Fawcett's property, was open land belonging to Major-General Lambton, one of County Durham's leading gentry, which extended to just beyond where the Panns Ferry crossed the Wear at the point now occupied by Wearmouth Bridge.[51] Beyond this ground, was more built-up land running eastward to Russell Street, which formed part of the west boundary of Sunderland parish. Hence this area, Bishopwearmouth Panns, was within the parish of Bishopwearmouth. It was semi-industrial and also contained Sunderland's bank, operative since at least 1768.[52]

South of this area, and thus on the opposite side of Sunderland Lonnin, were Sunniside and some of the ornamental grounds referred to earlier, which extended as far east as the part of Back Lane that became Sans Street and formed the southern half of Sunderland parish's west boundary. Change was at hand, however. Around 1800, new middle-class streets—of which Villiers Street was the grandest—would be laid out here, aligned north-south.[53]

East of the parish boundary, the continuation of Sunderland Lonnin was known as the High Street. Along the street, Sunderland's main thoroughfare, Rain depicts houses and businesses, as well as the market cross at the junction of High Street and Union Lane. Next to the cross he shows two of the town's markets, those of the bakers and butchers.

North of High Street, the land was built up, virtually without break, to the vicinity of the south pier and was partly bisected by Low Street, Sunderland's second major thoroughfare.[54] In 1737, much of the land to the south of the High Street still consisted of burgage garths. By Rain's day, the transformation of this area (which

Rain's *Eye Plan*: Sunderland, with Holy Trinity in the foreground

extended south to a lane that was to become Coronation Street and Prospect Row) into an urban one was virtually complete.

At the top of Queen Street, which ran south from High Street, Rain depicts an unnamed inn, none other than the *Golden Lion*. Some of its competitors are identified on the plan, as is true of the *George Inn* further up High Street. A stone's throw from the *Golden Lion*, Rain also notes Phoenix Lodge, the headquarters of Sunderland's freemasons, occupying ground between Queen Street and Pewters Lane, which likewise ran southward from the High Street. Freemasonry had been established in the town since 1755 and in the early days the lodge met at a house in Church Street, a short distance to the east.[55] Several other venues followed before a purpose-built lodge was erected in Vine Street in the late 1770s. In 1783, though, it was destroyed by fire and Phoenix Lodge was built as a replacement in 1784–5.

Phoenix Lodge, which is still in use by freemasons

Further down High Street from the *Golden Lion* were Sunderland's finest streets, Church Street, Vine Street, Silver Street, and Fitters Row, the homes of professionals, coalfitters and other prosperous individuals.

Pressing further east, one came to the harbour. Along the seafront, in close proximity to the south pier, Rain drew two of the gun batteries established during the course of the 18th century to protect Sunderland from privateers such as John Paul Jones, or from the French with whom Britain was at war more than once during the century. The batteries were manned by local volunteers and militiamen.

After High Street, Sunderland's next main thoroughfare was of course Low Street, running parallel to it closer to the river. A number of streets linked the two roads. One such was Bodlewell Lane, which led down to the point where the Sunderland ferry crossed the River Wear. Several wharfs were located off Low Street and the ferry operated from the east side of one these, since known as Wylam Wharf after an early 19th century owner, Edward Wylam.

In 1994 the wharf was excavated by archaeologists and their findings, states W.B. Griffiths, 'revealed that the area was reclaimed from the river by ballast dumping in the sixteenth and seventeenth centuries'.[56] The excavations also uncovered the existence of a sequence of structures dating from the late 17th century into the early years of the 19th. One of the structures was mostly built of well-dressed sandstone blocks bonded with mortar. Probably in the mid 18th century, it was incorporated in a cellar predominantly built of sandstone. The cellar was duly modified—perhaps over a period of time—and this included building a brick partition wall on an east-west axis that divided a large room in two: part of the space to the south of the partition evidently served as a coal bunker.

Over 200 sherds of stratified pottery were found, the earliest dating from the

16th century. Some of the sherds were from pots of English manufacture. Others came from wares made in the Low Countries and Germany. These included fragments of two Lower Rhine Slipware dishes datable to the early to mid 18th century and comparatively rare in Britain. Moreover, over 300 clay tobacco pipe fragments were uncovered, dating from the mid 17th century onward. Most of the pipes were manufactured in the North East, where the main centre of production was Tyneside, but pipes were also produced on Wearside during the 18th century.

Excavations in progress at Wylam Wharf
in the summer of 1994

Wearmouth Bridge, Impressment, and Sunderland Barracks

When John Rain drew his *Eye Plan*, no bridge crossed the Wear at, or near, Sunderland.[57] As crossing the river by ferry could be time consuming and dangerous, agitation for the construction of a bridge occurred and in 1788 Robert Shout, the port of Sunderland's engineer, put forward a design which failed to become reality. Then, in 1790, Rowland Burdon and Ralph Milbanke were elected MPs for County Durham having promised, among other things, to improve local communications. Burdon was interested in providing Sunderland with a bridge and was chiefly responsible for the legislation necessary for its construction being passed by parliament in June 1792.

On 24 September 1793, the foundation stone was laid and work on erecting stone bridge abutments soon commenced. It was not until the spring of 1795 that construction work reached the level from which iron ribs would be assembled between the abutments: iron was chosen to span the river because it was cheaper and lighter than stone. Timber scaffolding was erected in the river during the course of the summer, to support the ribs as they were assembled and put into place that September. Additional work, such as the construction of a roadway, ensued. Finally, on 9 August 1796 the bridge was opened. The structure was 236ft long, 32ft wide, and had a low-water clearance height of 100ft. It was the largest single-arch cast iron bridge in the world, and in time would transform the axis of development on Wearside from an east-west to a north-south one.[58]

The bridge's fame soon spread far and wide. Sunderland's pottery industry played a part in this development. Pots illustrated with transfers showing views of the bridge appeared. Indeed, even before construction of the bridge had commenced pots were produced bearing the design of the bridge 'to be erected.' Such pots were bought as souvenirs by visiting sailors, or were taken to various ports of call and sold by colliers operating from Wearside.

By this date Britain was at war—it had become embroiled in the French Revolutionary War in 1793—and it was a conflict in which a young Wearside sailor, Jack Crawford, achieved national prominence. He was born in Sunderland in 1775, the son of a keelman of Scottish extraction, and entered the Royal Navy in 1796 having previously worked on keels and in the merchant navy. The war was going badly for Britain and there was fear of an imminent invasion. The outlook improved in February 1797 when a Spanish fleet, allied to France, was defeated at Cape St Vincent, an action in which a young officer named Horatio Nelson first greatly distinguished himself.

Wearmouth Bridge. Opened in 1796, it was a marvel of engineering

Later in the year, the battle that brought Crawford to prominence occurred. He was serving on HMS *Venerable*, the flagship of Admiral Duncan, who was charged with blockading the Dutch coast to prevent the Dutch Navy from putting to sea from the Texel. On 11 October, Duncan (who had briefly returned to British waters) intercepted the Dutch fleet, which had sailed in his absence, and both sides fought with customary valour. In fact, the Battle of Camperdown—fought a few miles off the coastal village of Camperduin—was one of the fiercest battles of the war. At one point in the fighting, Duncan's flagship was surrounded and attacked by several enemy vessels before assistance was rendered. The battle ended with the surrender of the Dutch admiral after HMS *Director*, commanded by Captain William Bligh (of mutiny on the *Bounty* fame) administered the *coup de grâce* to his flagship.

During the bloody encounter, Duncan's colours were shot away from HMS *Venerable's* topgallant masthead on several occasions, and on the final occasion part of the masthead itself was shot away. Crawford now stepped into the limelight.

Either of his own accord, or with orders to do so from Duncan, he scaled the mast under fire and nailed the flag to it, receiving a wound to the cheek in the process.

News of the battle's victorious outcome was enthusiastically received in Britain. There were widespread celebrations and Admiral Duncan was rapidly elevated to the peerage. Crawford also received recognition. He was rewarded by his hometown, for in March 1798 he was presented with an elegant silver medal commemorating his action. Furthermore, at the victory celebrations in London, Jack was presented to George III, and in 1806 he attended Nelson's funeral and walked in the procession wearing the medal he had been presented by the people of Sunderland.

It is said that Crawford volunteered to serve in the Royal Navy. Perhaps this was so. But he may have been pressed into service instead, for in time of war the Royal Navy always resorted to the unpopular but necessary task of using press gangs in coastal towns to gain 'recruits', and Sunderland was inevitably a target for the Impress Service because it had a large population of sailors. Not for nothing does the *Universal British Directory* note that the town's coal trade, 'a capital nursery for seamen,' generally furnished 'a very liberal quota for … manning his majesty's fleet' in time of war.[59]

A statue of Jack Crawford (1775–1831) in Mowbray Park

Press gangs often encountered hostility. On 19 April 1803, for instance, on the eve of renewed conflict with France following a brief period of peace, Captain Adam MacKenzie informed the Admiralty that a press gang led by one of his subordinates, a Sunderland resident, had received a hostile reception on Wearside: 'Lieutenant Bounton has this instant come away from Sunderland to inform me, that he durst not attempt to impress at that place last night, as Mobs of hundreds of Seamen, Soldiers and Women … threatened the lives of himself and People, whether they acted or not.'[60] MacKenzie himself thus made his way to Sunderland with a stronger force and, despite further opposition, seized 22 men, only five of whom were however deemed fit for the service and were thus sent to fight for their king and country.

Some years earlier, as part of

the war effort, the government had commenced a programme of founding barracks nationwide. In February 1795 a committee representing the town and port of Sunderland complained to the government that only one company of militia was present to defend Sunderland's five hundred sail of ships in supplying the capital with coal, and land on the Town Moor was offered as a site for the construction of barracks.

The government responded swiftly. The Barracks Department contracted a London builder, Thomas Neill, to build wooden barracks in Sunderland to the east of High Street on the part of the Town Moor nearest the harbour. By July 1795 the barracks were completed. They were to house infantry, and could accommodate 1,528 rank and file plus officers, and cost £20,754. Consequently, the congregation of nearby St John's Church was swollen by soldiers stationed at the barracks.

In addition, in March six warehouses were hired in Sunderland to serve as temporary barracks and property was also hired elsewhere in the locality for the same purpose, at for example, Monkwearmouth, Fulwell and Whitburn. Upon the return of peace in 1802, the rented barracks were given up (though property was re-rented following the renewal of hostilities in 1803), but Neill's barracks survived beyond the Napoleonic Wars well into the 19th century: a century that witnessed continuing expansion on Wearside, and the development of Sunderland into the foremost shipbuilding town in the world.

'THE PLACE IS ALL LIFE AND BUSTLE'

S o wrote the Reverend Thomas Dibdin following a visit to Sunderland in 1837. He continued:

> Trade is prodigiously upon the increase; attested by extending wharfs, and increasing manufactories, which vomit forth their black, broad, and long extended columns of trailing smoke....Houses, windows, walls, pillars, posts, and posterns, were all more or less veiled in what may be delicately designated as black crepe. Even the human countenance seemed to partake of it; and for one pure intermingling of the lily and the rose, you shall see a score of carbonated physiognomies.[1]

Dibdin was greatly impressed by the enterprising and industrious spirit he encountered. He wrote: 'the lads of Sunderland are wide awake to their calling, and to a sense of what tends as much to their profit as their credit. You see these "lads" bustling and squeezing about in the narrow streets, which branch from the main (and nobly-wide) streets from morning till night.'[2]

Essentially, Dibdin viewed Sunderland as a thriving town with a productive population. He was not the only visitor in the first half of the 19th century who was of this opinion. For example, at the end of the Napoleonic Wars, Robert Surtees came here while working on his monumental history of County Durham and wrote as follows:

> Since the rapid increase of the commerce and population of Sunderland within the last fifty years, a proportionate improvement has taken place in the general appearance of the town. The High-Street exhibits a line of handsome shops; the streets have been paved and lighted, a Theatre, Assembly-rooms, and some other public buildings, have been erected; a handsome Subscription Library was founded in 1801, & lastly, in 1814, a very noble Exchange, including an Auction-Mart, Committee-Room, Post Office, News-Room, and Merchants'-Walk, was built in the High-Street, at an expense of 8000 [pounds] subscribed by individuals in 50 [pound] shares.[3]

The population growth referred to by Surtees continued in subsequent decades, primarily due to the influx of people in search of employment. In 1801 Sunderland's population had numbered 12,412, but by 1831 it had risen to 17,060. Growth also occurred in neighbouring communities such as Bishopwearmouth and Monkwearmouth Shore (which were to be incorporated in the Municipal Borough of Sunderland in 1835), for in the same period their populations grew from 6,126 to 14,462, and from 4,239 to 6,051 people respectively. Furthermore, this process continued in the two succeeding decades. Hence by 1851 Sunderland's population totalled 63,897. In regional terms, only Newcastle upon Tyne was more populous, with 33,003 inhabitants in 1801 and 72,131 in 1851.

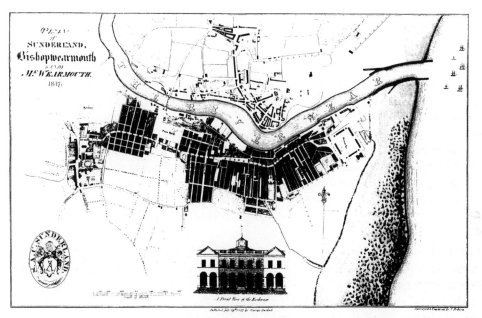

Map of Wearside in 1817

Sunderland's appearance thus changed greatly. At the beginning of 1850 an article in the local press observed:

> With the growth of the population the town has expanded in a corresponding ratio. Whole streets have been rapidly thrown up, mainly in Bishopwearmouth and Monkwearmouth....A great change for the better has taken place also in High Street. Whilst old places of business have undergone a thorough renovation so as to be scarcely identical with their former selves...new, and, in many cases, magnificent shops have sprung up in great numbers, on the sites of the shrubbery and flower plots in front of the dwelling-houses, formerly so pleasing and picturesque a feature of the main street in Bishopwearmouth.[4]

Many of the migrants who flocked to Sunderland during this period were born in the vicinity of the town, as was true of a substantial percentage of the workforce of Monkwearmouth Colliery—a pit that commenced production in 1835 and where the bulk of the workforce lived in a colliery village that developed in part of the township of Monkwearmouth Shore. Of 362 men resident in the pit village by 1851, over 40 per cent had been born within ten miles of the place.

Newcomers from further afield included many Scots and Irish. By 1851, just over 3 per cent of Sunderland's population had been born north of the border and an even larger number, almost 6 per cent, first saw the light of day across the Irish Sea.

Elsewhere on Wearside, communities also grew to some degree. At Tunstall, for example, in 1851 the number of inhabitants was 70, only 17 more than had been the case at the beginning of the century. At Fulwell, the increase was more significant. The population almost doubled in the period 1801–51. Even so, the township was hardly overcrowded. The residents in the latter year only numbered 169.

Some of Sunderland's other neighbours experienced more substantial demographic changes during the same decades. Ford township is a case in point. Residents more than trebled in number, rising from 602 to 1,922. Even more noteworthy is Southwick. According to the census of 1801, the township had a population of 554 people but fifty years later this had increased almost fivefold to 2,721. Immigration, of course, was the decisive factor. Peter Gibson thus comments that 'according to the 1851 census, two thirds of Southwick's residents were immigrants.' These included many people from Ireland—no less than 8.5 per cent of the village's population. Consequently, 'one person in twelve in Southwick was Irish born.'[5]

The 1830s, in particular, witnessed rapid demographic changes on Wearside as a whole. Indeed, the decade beheld the fastest rate of growth the area experienced during the entire century, with an annual average increase of 3 per cent.

The fast increase in population during the first half of the 19th century inevitably caused, or at least worsened, certain social problems, a point mentioned below.

Housing and Social Conditions

A government report of 1836 noted:

> Sunderland and Bishop Wearmouth at no distant time were two distinct Towns…but…the intervening space had been gradually curtailed and at last filled up by buildings, so that at present the two form only one Town. With the exception of one street, in which there are some respectable houses and shops, Sunderland presents the appearance of one mass of small houses crowded together, with interstices of narrow lanes, rather than streets. The population in them is so dense as to give the appearance of unhealthiness as well as absence of cleanliness. This is not the case in Bishop Wearmouth; in the new part of the Town, that adjoining Sunderland, there are some good streets and excellent houses, and it is in this part that the higher classes of inhabitants reside.[6]

The greatest concentration of housing for members of Wearside's middle-class community ran westward from Villiers Street, and included even newer homes (likewise on a north-south axis) erected on the Fawcett estate, where construction was in progress by 1820 and would continue into the 1850s. This resulted in the straight terraces of Fawcett Street, John Street, Frederick Street and Foyle Street. The earliest of the four, Fawcett Street, was the most prestigious for it was the widest and contained the largest houses. An advertisement in the *Sunderland Herald* of 25 July 1845, duly stated that one such had three reception rooms, two kitchens, and eight bedrooms.[7]

In contrast, the most characteristic houses built for members of the working class were single-storey terraces known as Sunderland Cottages: the first such appear to have been built around 1840 near a newly sunk pit, Monkwearmouth Colliery. Of Sunderland Cottages an authority on housing, S. Muthesius, has written: 'With the exception of some streets in Darlington and Jarrow, other urban concentrations of one-storeyed houses are unknown in England.'[8] In contrast to working-class housing elsewhere on Wearside such as in the parish of Sunderland—the East End, where overcrowding in old tenements was the norm—Sunderland Cottages were generally occupied by single families. Of many such residences, Angela Long has aptly observed: 'these scaled-down dwellings had one magic ingredient—privacy. The tenant, or owner, had his own front door and his own yard.'[9]

Foyle Street, built to house well-to-do families

Of the homes of many Wearsiders, we read:

> The dwellings of the poor, as regards their structure, may be divided into three classes. The first, including the modern built houses of two storeys, occupied in tenements, which are comfortable and cleanly. The second, including cottages generally of modern structure, occupied by one or at most by two families, likewise comfortable and cleanly, and furnished with small yards and other conveniences. The third, large dwellings consisting of three or more stories each, with dark cellars occupied in tenements, in which reside from six to twelve families, having in most cases a single room for each family, ranging from 12 feet by 8 feet to 14 feet by 10 feet. The houses are ill-ventilated, in consequence partly of the windows being built up to evade the window-tax, partly on account of the houses being built in rows back to back, without any passages or yards between them.[10]

As the report of 1836 mentioned earlier makes clear, the parish of Sunderland was certainly more densely populated and less prosperous than Bishopwearmouth and other parts of the municipal borough for that matter. Some years later, after visiting the town, Dr Augustus Granville made the following observation which adds weight to the above:

> The approach to the pier from the upper part of the town, unfortunately, is through a long dirty street, the prolongation or tail of High-street, inhabited by the lowest class of people, principally mechanics and sailors, and from which branch off, to the right and to the left, very many narrow passages or alleys, those of the latter leading down to the water-side, and all presenting...the very sink of gloom and filth—an apt nest or rendezvous for typhus and cholera.[11]

Indeed, several years before Granville's visit, Sunderland had become notorious as a result of an Asiatic Cholera outbreak that occurred in late 1831. It was the first such outbreak in the nation's history, and the town was ridiculed for the way in which it handled the crisis. The well-known diarist, Charles Greville, wrote that 'The conduct of the people of Sunderland' was 'more suitable to the barbarism of the interior of Africa than to a town in a civilised country.'[12]

Although the disease had evidently already claimed victims, the first person to display the classic symptoms, severe diarrhoea, vomiting and cramp, was a 12-year-old girl called Isabella Hazard who died on 17 October. At the beginning of November, on the recommendation of James Butler Kell, the surgeon of the 82nd Regiment, contact between troops based in Sunderland's barracks and the townsfolk was greatly restricted. Shortly thereafter, the harbour was placed under quarantine by the Privy Council in London (there was no embargo on travel by road however), and this greatly angered the business community which pressured local doctors to state that such a measure was unnecessary in order to have the ban lifted. Consequently, the *London Medical Gazette* made the following observation about Sunderland's leading figures, 'it seems very clear that the public safety is in their estimation a very secondary object when brought into competition with the sale of coals.'[13]

Dr William Clanny (1776–1850). He invented the Clanny Lamp (a miners' safety lamp) and was the chief consultant at the Infirmary at the time of the cholera outbreak during which he behaved honourably. He wrote a number of articles for the *Lancet*, and the first scientific treatise on cholera

There were 534 cases of cholera on Wearside in 1831 and early 1832, of which 215 ended in death, and some of the cases were treated in the Infirmary, a hospital built a decade earlier in Bishopwearmouth.[14] Understandably, the problem was most acute in the parish of Sunderland. 156 of those who perished were residents of the parish including Jack Crawford, the 'hero of Camperdown.'[15]

As has been noted, the squalor of the East End which accounted for the high rate of cholera cases was still a marked feature of the parish of Sunderland in 1836 and when Dr Granville visited the locality. It was, moreover, to remain so.

In 1845, for example, Dr D.B. Reid visited Wearside whilst conducting an inquiry for the government into conditions here, a task in which he was ably assisted by a local committee. The resulting report listed several factors that caused the 'comparative unhealthiness' of the East End. Overcrowding was inevitably one such. The number of people inhabiting the closely packed houses was too high, a point stressed by a sub-committee:

> many of the streets are built so that the backs of the houses in one row come immediately in contact with those of another, leaving no intervening space for ventilation or necessary conveniences. The number of persons inhabiting these houses is too great to admit of their living in a state of health, one room generally contained a whole family, consisting, in many cases, of seven, or even more, individuals, and not unfrequently pigs are admitted within the houses.[16]

Another factor was 'the want of cleanly habits in the people.' We read:

> In Fitter's-row, there is a narrow confined place, called the Hat Case…. In No.10, there is a yard in which there is a most offensive midden, rented to a man for 9d. a-week, and cleaned out, he says, every 8 or 10 weeks, but to all appearance never entirely emptied, being, as we afterwards found out, the chief depository for all the abomination in this neighbourhood…. Stinking stagnant water has no outlet from this row, in which human ordure and other disgusting objects are so thickly deposited that one can hardly step clear of them; with respect to the streets there is little excuse for their being so filthy in this part of the town where the Directors of the [Durham and Sunderland] railway have improved the sewerage by forming deep subterraneous drains, all that is required of individuals is to sweep their refuse…into the proper channels, but this they neglect to do, and the consequence is, the gutters are never clear, and the pathways are always dirty.[17]

That some inhabitants of Sunderland parish were in 'want of cleanly habits' cannot be doubted. Nonetheless it would be grossly unfair to simply write off the problems of the East End as the result of ignorance and failings of character on the part of the locals. Many of them no doubt fought hard to keep themselves and their families clean and healthy in circumstances which, as the report itself notes, were far from ideal.

One of the circumstances that made life more trying in the parish than it was in, say, Bishopwearmouth, was inadequate lavatory facilities, a factor mentioned in the report. Hence it made the following recommendation:

> The committee are of the opinion that the health and comfort of the public would be promoted by the erection of some more public necessaries especially in the parish of Sunderland, in which not one-seventh part of the houses are furnished with a necessary. These necessaries should be placed under proper regulations to ensure as great a degree of cleanliness as possible, and the committee feel assured, that until some such course is adopted, the very disgraceful and indecent practice at present so prevalent for children and even adults, to resort to the public streets and lanes, for the purposes which nature requires, cannot be put to a stop, and the public must thus continue to be offended by the most indecent and unseemly exposures.[18]

Of course, it was not just the East End that had squalid conditions. They could be found elsewhere in the town and further afield. North Shields and Newcastle illustrate the point. Of the former, we read: 'There are not any public necessaries, or any public urinals…the want of which is much felt by the poorer inhabitants, and proves a fertile source of street nuisance, and outrage against common decency', whereas of Newcastle it was observed:

> In this populous city…parts of the borough…are in an extremely neglected condition, many new streets are unpaved and in a dangerous state; such house and private drains that exist in the houses of the middle and higher classes are generally defective and offensive; the dwellings of the poor are very deficient in all conveniences and necessaries…[and] there are large public depôts for refuse in objectionable places.[19]

And what of Sunderland's water supply? On this point, Reid differed from the committee for he wrote: 'In Sunderland, as in other places, the supply of water and mode of distribution is far short of that which is essential for health and comfort…places were pointed out to me…where wells, which had been in use by the public, were removed and had not been replaced.'[20]

The principal supplier was the Bishopwearmouth Water Company, established in 1824. It supplied piped water to 670 houses out of a total of 6,086 at an annual rate ranging from 10 to 30 shillings depending on the class of house. The company also had 29 standpipes supplying its 'pure and good' water to less fortunate individuals. Water could also be obtained from the 92 private pumps on the south side of the river, while to the north the inhabitants of Monkwearmouth Shore could use a well belonging to Sir Hedworth Williamson 'open to his tenantry, and others who may choose to avail themselves of its advantages, at the charge of 6d. per quarter, or 2s. per annum for each family, without reference to number.'[21] But some of Monkwearmouth Shore's residents preferred to buy water transported by cart from two wells in neighbouring Monkwearmouth.

Despite recommendations in Reid's report, and attempts to make improvements by local bodies such as the town council, conditions did not greatly improve. In fact, in the latter half of the 1840s they worsened in the East End due to an influx of labourers who came to work on the creation of a large dock. Hence when Robert Rawlinson visited the town in 1849 to inspect the state of public health, he concluded that 'the borough of Sunderland is not so healthy as it may be.'[22]

Several things contributed to this judgement. One was the state of the drainage system. Rawlinson's report includes the following statement by two local engineers:

> There are very few private drains communicating with the sewers. The ordure and offensive matter from the houses are generally…thrown into the streets…where it remains, giving forth unhealthy effluvia…until removed by the scavenger or a shower of rain. Indeed, it is difficult to say where the refuse water from some of even the better class of houses finds an outlet.[23]

Furthermore, in concluding his report, Rawlinson stated that many streets were unpaved 'and in a very filthy and even dangerous condition,' and that the lighting was not as 'general and extensive' as it needed to be 'for safety and comfort.'[24]

A major factor that contributed to the state of affairs in the town was the existence of several local bodies exercising authority, a situation that resulted in conflicts of interest and confusion. These included the Improvement Commissioners of Sunderland and Bishopwearmouth, established by Acts of Parliament in 1810, who were empowered, among other things, to clean and light the streets. Rawlinson accepted that the commissioners' lack of funds contributed to their failure to provide a truly effective service. In connection with Sunderland's commissioners, for instance, his report includes the following

> the amount of rate which the Commissioners are authorized to levy in Sunderland is but 2s. 6d. in the pound on the rateable value of property, the sum raised has been found insufficient to maintain and keep up the streets efficiently, and to enable the Commissioners to remove nuisances and obstructions in the manner and to the extent they wish.[25]

Nevertheless, though Sunderland was not as 'healthy' as Rawlinson desired, it was not in a state of terminal decline. There were positive developments occurring. One such was the establishment of the Sunderland Water Company in 1846 following the passing of the Sunderland Water Act: the bill had been put forward by the council and had been opposed by the Improvement Commissioners, several of whom belonged to the board of the Bishopwearmouth Water Company. As a result of the act the new company took over the assets and equipment of the old one. The defunct firm had only produced 80,000 gallons of water a day, and the mains were usually turned off at night and from Saturday night till Monday morning.

Sunderland Water Company set about improving the situation. The company proved highly successful from the outset and its first chairman (who served in that capacity until 1863) was one of Sunderland's leading doctors, William Mordey.

The company soon began erecting waterworks at Humbledon Hill. Subsequently, at the firm's annual general meeting held at its offices at 7 Fawcett Street on 31 January 1850, the following report noted that William Whittle had been engaged to serve as the 'master sinker' responsible for sinking the shaft and that the work had been 'done in a most substantial and satisfactory manner.' In addition a reservoir, built by Messrs Winship and Nesbitt, with a capacity of one million gallons had been completed, as had the engine house, the latter erected by Messrs Tone and Son. Other work had included laying the main pipe from the reservoir to the town. Furthermore, the report declared that the

> necessary alterations to connect the pipeage of the old and new works have been carried out in the greater part of the borough, and the remainder will be done as soon as the days are long enough for the men to work their regular hours ... [and] that within a month's time, water can be furnished equal to all the demands which can be required in the town and neighbourhood.[26]

1846 also witnessed the passing of another corporation-sponsored bill. The aim was to improve the town's gas supply for the quality of street lighting had been criticised in Reid's report—streets in Sunderland had first been illuminated by gas in March

1824. The bill had been strenuously opposed by the Improvement Commissioners who had established the Sunderland Gas Light Company in 1823 with its works in Low Street. Their opposition now continued, for they took steps to hinder the activities of the Sunderland Gas Company which came into being as a result of the act (its works were at Ayre's Quay) and whose first chairman was the councillor, Anthony John Moore. For instance, they refused to let it use existing mains for its gas: the rival firms were to amalgamate in 1854.

Finally, mention must be made of those members of society who were unable to care for themselves owing to misfortune, age or illness. For much of this period, as in the past, care of many of these people was the responsibility of the parishes, which accommodated at least some of those to whom they rendered assistance in their respective workhouses. In 1836, however, the Sunderland Poor Law Union was established under the Poor Law Amendment Act of 1834. The union consisted of the parishes of Monkwearmouth, Sunderland and Bishopwearmouth—save for the villages of Burdon and Silksworth, which were in different unions—and the elected Board of Guardians, whose first chairman was the mayor, Andrew White, was henceforth responsible for continuing the work previously undertaken by the parishes.

In 1827 Bishopwearmouth parish had replaced its small workhouse at the junction of Low Row and Durham Road with one at Gill Bridge Avenue, opposite Crowtree Road. This workhouse was now taken over by the Board of Guardians, enlarged, and opened as the first Sunderland Union workhouse on 20 April 1838. The town's other workhouses ceased to exist.

The work of the parishes and of the subsequent Board of Guardians was supplemented by charity. In addition, there was the seamen's fund (which had financed the establishment of the Assembly Garth almshouses in 1750). To help accommodate at least some of the many members of the town's seafaring community reliant on the fund for assistance,

Trafalgar Square almshouses

the Trafalgar Square almshouses were constructed in 1840 to supplement Assembly Garth.[27] They were built in the grounds of the former Sunderland parish workhouse and cost about £3,000, most of which came from the fund, the remainder came from charitable donations. Trafalgar Square's 104 rooms were each occupied by a man and wife, widow or widower.

Religion and Education

At the commencement of the 19th century the Church of England had two places of worship in Sunderland, namely the parish church of Holy Trinity and its daughter church of St John's. In addition, in the immediate vicinity were the parish churches of St Peter's at Monkwearmouth and St Michael's, Bishopwearmouth.[28]

During the first half of the century, the Church made an attempt to meet the needs of the locality's expanding population. St Michael's (whose fabric was in a sorry state) was substantially rebuilt in 1806–8: the construction programme included rebuilding the tower, enlarging the nave—a task that partly entailed shortening the chancel—and installing galleries. George Garbutt later described the church as 'a neat substantial edifice, built of free-stone.'[29] Later, still, in 1849 the prominent Newcastle architect John Dobson added galleried transepts in order to provide extra seating.

In addition, daughter places of worship were established in the vast parish of Bishopwearmouth, as was true of St Thomas' on John Street, a building erected in the heart of the town in 1829. Other dependent places of worship in the parish included St Paul's at Ryhope in 1827, and St Andrew's, Deptford, in 1841. The latter soon ceased to be a daughter of St Michael for it was elevated to the status of a parish church in 1844, as was St Thomas' on John Street.

The Church of England also erected new places of worship north of the river, namely Holy Trinity, Southwick, in the years 1842–3 and All Saints, Monkwearmouth, in 1844–9. The former served as a chapel within Monkwearmouth parish until it gained parish status of its own in 1847, whereas All Saints was made a parish in 1844.

Nonetheless, despite this and the zealous ministry of clergymen like Robert Gray, Rector of Sunderland parish

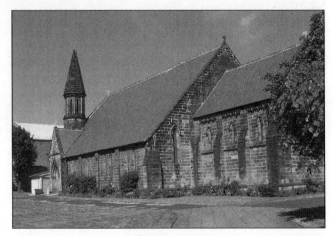

All Saints Church

(1819–38), the Church's response was inadequate. Consequently, Anglicanism was not the dominant religious force on Wearside.

It was the nonconformists who held the upper hand. The evangelicalism of the Methodists in particular bore fruit and by the middle of the century Methodism was the foremost religious force in Sunderland. Several branches of Methodism existed and were represented locally, such as the Wesleyan Methodists and the Primitive Methodists. The latter, present from the early 1820s, were strongly committed to proselytizing among the poor. Other denominations, including the Quakers and

Baptists, likewise engaged in evangelical work and thereby experienced growth whereas in 1841 a new group, the Mormons, made its first convert in Sunderland.

Not surprisingly, non-Anglican places of worship became increasingly common. For example, the United Presbyterians opened a chapel in Coronation Street in 1822, while in the same year the Quakers moved westward, from their old meeting house on High Street, to worship in Nile Street. Two years later, the Primitive Methodists began worshipping in a humble chapel in Flag Lane, a narrow alley deep in the East End. In 1829, a section of the expanding Jewish community ceased worshipping in Vine Street—where a place of worship was established in the late 18th century—and converted a house in High Street into a synagogue.

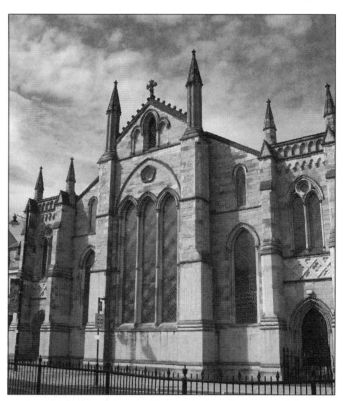

St Mary's Church, Bridge Street. Opened in 1835, it was designed by Durham's foremost architect Ignatius Bonomi

Furthermore, in 1831 Unitarians—who rejected the Trinity doctrine—opened a chapel on Bridge Street. Of them, Geoffrey Milburn has commented: 'Unitarianism appealed to thoughtful people who liked to reason about matters of faith, and was perhaps the most intellectual of the dissenting groups.'[30] In 1835, moreover, St Mary's Roman Catholic Church opened on the opposite side of the road, and the following year Wesleyan Methodists began meeting in a chapel in Fawcett Street which served wealthy members of that branch of Methodism.

Finally, in the 1840s a disenchanted young Welsh curate named Arthur Augustus Rees left the Church of England and built the Bethesda Free Chapel on Tatham Street in 1844–5. Rees, a very lively character, attracted a large congregation to Bethesda and many members of this very evangelical community were likewise former Anglicans.

The above gives some idea of the variety and vitality of religious life locally during this era, and the list could easily be extended.

At the opening of the period dealt with by this chapter, the Rector of Bishopwearmouth was a celebrated author, Dr William Paley, who had held the living since 1795. While on Wearside, he wrote one of the most influential books of the 19th century—*Natural Theology*—which was published in 1802 and proved an instant success. Central to Paley's argument in this famous book, which argues in favour of God's existence, is the analogy of a watch and a watchmaker. Of a watch, Paley comments, 'when we...inspect the watch, we perceive...that its several parts are framed and put together for a purpose.... This mechanism being observed...the inference, we think, is inevitable; that the watch must have had a maker.'[31] He continues, 'every indication of contrivance, every manifestation of design, which existed in the watch, exists in the works of nature; with the difference, on the side of nature, of being greater and more, and that in a degree which exceeds all computation.'[32] Paley argues his case at great length and in considerable detail, and *Natural Theology* has justly been described by the *Encyclopaedia Britannica* as 'the standard exposition in English theology of the teleological argument for the existence of God.'[33]

One of Paley's successors was Dr Gerald Wellesley (a brother of the Duke of Wellington) who became Rector of Bishopwearmouth in 1827. Wellesley was a notable pluralist. He held numerous ecclesiastical appointments at the same time and was thus often away from Wearside for long periods. This angered some people. The *Durham Chronicle* of 9 April 1831 contains the following:

> The Hon. and Rev. G.V. Wellesley, Rector of Bishopwearmouth...is expected to arrive at the Rectory, Bishopwearmouth, from the continent, in June, after an absence of 15 months during which period he will have received the enormous sum of £4,000 and upwards, for the latter Rectory alone!!! How long will this corruption be tolerated? [34]

A clergyman held in much higher regard on Wearside was Robert Gray, who succeeded John Hampson as Rector of Sunderland in 1819. Born in 1787, the son of a prosperous London jeweller, Gray was educated at Oxford University and from 1816 until Hampson's death, served as a curate for his own uncle and namesake, the Rector of Bishopwearmouth. Although Gray came from a far more elevated social background than his parishioners, as Rector of Sunderland he cared intensely about their spirituality and general welfare and was prepared to dip into his own pockets to help finance local causes that were close to his heart, such as providing schooling. Gray combined compassion with courage, qualities that he displayed to the full when his parish was struck by disease. During the cholera outbreak of 1831–2 he frequently visited the sick, and he died of typhus in February 1838 contracted while tending parishioners afflicted during another epidemic. Huge crowds attended his funeral, and the *Sunderland Herald* of 24 February lamented: 'no town in the Empire ever sustained a heavier loss by the death of an individual than Sunderland has now to deplore on the removal of so holy and zealous a pastor.'

To a considerable extent, education was linked to religion for Anglican clergymen and leading nonconformists were involved in establishing schools and Sunday Schools with the intention of educating the children of the lower classes so that they could lead more productive lives based on Christian values. To cite an example: in 1808 the Rector of Bishopwearmouth, Robert Gray (the uncle of the Rector of

Sunderland just mentioned), played a major part in founding an elementary school next to St Michael's. In 1812, the school was provided with a new building in Low Row, and some years later Garbutt commented as follows: 'The building consists of two storeys, the lower one appropriated to the use of the boys, and the upper one to that of the girls.... The number of children under tuition at present is upwards of 500.'[35] In a history of Sunderland published in 1830, James Burnett refers to another school—Sunderland Parochial School—which originated from a parish school for boys established near the workhouse in 1808. According to Burnett, the school, which had moved to Vine Street in 1823 (by which date girls had been admitted) was generally attended by 400 boys and 150 girls. An infants' school was added in 1835. Both establishments were liberally endowed by the Rector of Sunderland, Robert Gray, and following his death in 1838 they were named the Gray Schools in his honour.

The pupils referred to by Garbutt and Burnett, and those who attended other Church schools founded in this period, received an education strongly Anglican in character. Some nonconformist parents were prepared to send their offspring to these schools, whereas others were not and thus some non-Anglican schools were founded. One such was a Catholic school established in Pann Lane (behind St Mary's Church) in the mid 1830s. Its staff included members of religious orders. Among such were the Sisters of Mercy, nuns who settled in Sunderland from Ireland in 1843 at the behest of the parish priest and proved good teachers.

The fees for attending the schools mentioned above were generally low (a penny a week for instance), but there were other schools attended by children from more prosperous backgrounds.

From 1830 the most notable private school was the Grange. This was situated near the present Civic Centre and was founded by a Scot, Dr James Cowan. The school was attended by local boys as day scholars, and by others from further afield who were boarders, for under Cowan's headmastership (he retired in 1846) the Grange acquired a national reputation.

Initially, Cowan had opened a modest private school in William Street in 1822. This soon moved to Green Terrace and, in the summer of 1830, the school transferred to the Grange, a mansion in approximately 12 acres of ground. Progress was rapid after this relocation, a point noted by C.S. Collingwood:

> The Grange School soon began to take a very leading position, and...stood on something like a level with the great public schools of England.... The fact was, before railways were made and when travelling was a very difficult and tedious operation, the Grange met a very real want, especially for boys living in the North, and beyond the Scottish borders.[36]

The quality of instruction is also noteworthy: 'Latin and Greek occupied a prominent place among the subjects taught...but ample room was found for French, German, and English language and literature, mathematics, drawing, etc, and one characteristic of the school was the attention bestowed on all boys whether clever or not.'[37]

Among the school's admirers was Daniel Sandford, Professor of Greek at Glasgow University, who sent his three sons to the Grange. Some of the pupils also belonged to landed families, especially from north of the border.

Joseph Wilson Swan

One of the boys who received his education locally during this period was Joseph Wilson Swan, who would become one of Britain's leading inventors, best known for his invention of a successful incandescent electric lamp.

Swan was born at Pallion Hall on 31 October 1828. The house, in a predominantly rural setting and with a garden sloping down to the River Wear, belonged to Addison Fenwick and Swan's father was employed as the manager of Fenwick's lime kilns in the vicinity.

As a child, Swan found much to fascinate him in the locality. In later years he recalled that in addition to watching shipbuilding occurring across the river at Southwick, or vessels making their way up and down the Wear, he explored the local countryside and 'a great limestone quarry with its alpine precipices, as they seemed to me.'[38] He also visited the industrial suburb of Deptford—located between Pallion and Bishopwearmouth—where, for instance, at least three glassworks existed in the 1830s. Then, in the middle of that decade, the Swan family left Pallion Hall and moved to a modest house in Olive Street, Bishopwearmouth.

Swan attended 'dame' schools before becoming a pupil at another private school, one run by a Scottish clergyman named John Wood, and recalled that it was attended by about 200 boys, some of whom were boarders. He became a pupil at the school in about 1838, at which time it was based at Hendon Lodge. Around 1840, it moved to new premises, Hylton Castle. Joseph left the school at some point after his twelfth birthday and proceeded to enjoy country life by staying with a relative at Elwick.

In late 1842, by which time the Swan family had moved to Derwent Street, Joseph returned to Sunderland to enter an apprenticeship with one of the town's numerous pharmacies, that of Messrs Hudson and Osbaldiston based at 9 High Street. He remained with the firm until 1846, when he moved to Newcastle to work in the chemist shop of a relation, and it was on Tyneside that Swan subsequently made the inventions in the fields of electricity and photography which made him famous.

Nonetheless, it was during his years on Wearside that he became keenly interested in science. As a child he had been intrigued by experiments performed by a family friend named John Ridley, who was fascinated by electricity. Moreover, of the period when he was apprenticed to Hudson and Osbaldiston, Swan commented, 'all my spare time was spent in chemical and electrical experiments, carried out for the most part by means of home-made apparatus and appliances.'[39]

In addition, while on Wearside, Swan had his 'imagination kindled in a new direction.' He recalled:

> As I passed the shop window of Thomas Robson, a well-known engraver in Bridge
> Street, Sunderland, I had there my first glimpse of a photographic portrait. It was

a most excellent daguerreotype portrait of Mr. Robson. I paid repeated visits to that window, while it hung there, with constantly increasing wonder at this astounding scientific achievement.[40]

Swan also attended lectures that enhanced his interest in scientific matters, including ones delivered by a pioneering figure in the study of electricity, W.E. Staite. At one such, held at the Athenaeum on Fawcett Street in October 1847 during the annual soiree of Sunderland's Literary and Philosophical Society—by which date of course Swan was resident in Newcastle—he watched Staite demonstrate an incandescent lamp. According to the *Sunderland Herald* of 29 October, it produced 'a fine, white, piercing light, too bright for common vision to cope with.'

Swan was profoundly affected by what he saw and heard on Wearside, and as one of his children later wrote in connection with his scientific achievements: 'It was in Sunderland that the impulse was given and the inspiration came.'[41]

Industry and Commerce

We shall begin with the industry for which Sunderland became chiefly associated—shipbuilding—an industry that, as noted in the previous chapter, began to flourish on Wearside in the last quarter of the 18th century.

In 1800, the Wear launched 12,662 tons, thereby exceeding the output of the Tyne. Although in the next few years the latter river's output was usually greater, the expansion of the industry on Wearside continued and by the close of the first decade of the century the Wear was beginning to enjoy more sustained dominance. Indeed, in 1816 Robert Surtees stated that: 'In ship-building the Port of Sunderland stands at present the highest of any in the United Kingdom.'[42] This view was soon corroborated by Garbutt, who also observed: 'The township of Monkwearmouth-shore...owes its present consequence to the extensive ship-building yards which during the war [against France] were established there, and the increasing commerce upon the river.'[43]

Shipbuilding inevitably experienced the fluctuating fortunes that affected yards elsewhere. In 1825, for instance, output was nearly 21,000 tons but during the next five years it was lower, averaging almost 15,000. Output then increased during the 1830s. So much so, that 251 ships (totalling 64,446 tons) were constructed in 1840, a number of ships built on the river in a single year that 'has never been exceeded.'[44] In 1840 there were 76 shipyards. However, Wearside's shipbuilders then experienced a brief but sharp depression, one most acute in the years 1842–3, and many yards failed. By 1843 only 31 remained. The total tonnage built on Wearside in that year was a mere 21,377 tons. Inevitably, the number of people employed in the shipyards fell dramatically. Whereas in 1841 there had been 3,100 shipwrights, the number had dropped to 1,000 by the following year. Wage rates likewise plummeted, falling from 31s. 6d. to 19s. 6d. Of course, shipyard workers were not the only ones affected. Numerous shops closed and these included many businesses in the main thorough-fare, High Street.[45]

Fortunately a revival began in 1845, and over 51,000 tons were launched in 1850, by which time Sunderland's economy was much healthier. Of the town, an article in the *Sunderland Herald* declared: 'The shops and dwelling houses then shut up [in the years 1842–3] and placarded "to let" are not only, at this moment, all occupied, but the same is to be said of large numbers since built.' In addition, the article mentions the 'improved condition of our working classes' who 'generally, enjoy, at present, a fair day's wage for a fair day's work.'[46]

During the first half of the 19th century, many shipyards founded on Wearside (often by humble groups of craftsmen eager to capitalise on increasing demand for vessels, most notably colliers), were short-lived affairs, lasting less than a year or two. Several, though, were to become famous in the world of shipbuilding. For example, in 1807 Luke Crown commenced building at Monkwearmouth Shore. Peter Austin did likewise in 1826—twenty years later the firm crossed to the south side of the river—and in 1837 George Bartram and John Lister set up a yard at South Hylton and proceeded to launch their first ship the following year.

Meanwhile, in 1818 John and Philip Laing (brothers who had commenced shipbuilding at Monkwearmouth Shore in the 1790s) moved their yard across the river to Deptford. Later that year, their partnership ended and Philip continued to run the business himself until 1843 when it passed into the hands of his 20-year-old son, James.

Furthermore, in the late 1830s William Doxford commenced shipbuilding upstream at Cox Green near Washington. Although he went bankrupt in 1841, he resumed construction four years later. In 1846, moreover, Robert Thompson, a shipwright in his late forties who had worked at yards on both the Tyne and Wear and had intermittently constructed vessels on his own account or with partners, founded a yard at North Sands that would become well known.

The census for 1851 records that there were 653 shipwrights under 20 years of age in Sunderland, and 1,372 who were 20 years and over. When one bears in mind that the town's male population at this date aged 21 to 60 was 12,153, it becomes clear that, despite the reverses experienced in the early 1840s, a substantial percentage was still employed in shipbuilding. Of course, it has to be noted that in addition to individuals working in the shipyards, were people employed in related industries such as sail- and ropemaking.

Timber was the material used for the construction of ships on Wearside throughout the first half of the 19th century, and was often purchased on credit from timber merchants. During this period, as in past years, many vessels were constructed here (and elsewhere) 'on spec', with the hope that the finished product would

Robert Thompson's shipyard in 1846

find a buyer. As Joe Clarke has commented, several factors enabled 'Sunderland ship-wrights to build ships at prices other ports could not match.'[47] One was the economical use of timber, a fact highlighted by Joshua Wilson who wrote in 1848, 'if a Twelve Years Ship is built at Sunderland…you will generally find a small vessel built next to it…the refuse timber [from] the Twelve Years ship is put into the lower class vessel.'[48]

Sunderland's yards undoubtedly produced lower class vessels, cheaper to purchase, than did ports elsewhere in Britain. But what of their quality? In 1835 Henry Woodroffe (the South Shields' seamen's leader) told a Select Committee dealing with shipping disasters that he believed Sunderland's vessels were 'the worst-built ships in the world.'[49] This was certainly an extreme view, but other individuals also voiced criticism of the output from the town's shipyards. For instance, an article in the first issue of *The Northern Tribune*, published in 1851, claimed that 'Until about 10 or 12 years ago…the character of the vessels built on the Wear was considered "sloppy"', while in connection with the same period William Fordyce said: 'The degree of perfection in construction would seem to have been regulated according to price. Hence it came to be derisively said that the Sunderland ship-yards could "either build a ship or make one."'[50] That some 'cowboy' shipbuilders operated on Wearside can hardly be doubted. On the other hand, it would be wrong to conclude that all were either incompetent or downright unscrupulous. Fordyce noted that a vessel constructed at Southwick in 1810 by Mr. B. Howard 'was considered of so fine a model that the builder was presented with a piece of plate as a testimonial of high appreciation.'[51] Furthermore, 11 Sunderland shipbuilders subscribed to *A Treatise on Marine Architecture* published in Edinburgh in 1830, thereby evincing a desire to further their knowledge of the 'Theory and Practise of Shipbuilding.'

In 1846 Sunderland's shipwrights formed themselves into a trade union, and as Clarke has observed, 'Probably very nearly a 100 per cent membership was achieved.' He also states that the union 'quickly established a solidarity which many would envy and their employers could rarely match.'[52]

Although fatalities sometimes occurred in the shipyards, obviously the industry was much safer than coalmining, which took a heavy toll. For example, on 25 May 1812 disaster occurred at Felling Colliery between Gateshead and Jarrow when a lighted candle ignited gas, thereby causing an explosion that wrought havoc and claimed 92 lives.

The following year, as a result of the tragedy, a body known as The Society for Preventing Accidents in Coal-Mines was founded in Sunderland. One of its members was Dr William Reid Clanny (an Ulsterman who had settled in Bishopwearmouth in 1805) who proceeded to invent the first miners' safety lamp. On 20 May 1813 he presented his invention to a meeting of the Royal Society of Arts in London. Clanny subsequently modified the design and experimented in person with the lamp at Herrington Mill Pit (at Penshaw) on 16 October 1815: his lamp comprised a metal case, fitted with a semicircular glass, and contained a candle that was fed air by bellows.

In August of that year, the eminent scientist Sir Humphry Davy had visited

Wearside as a guest of the Rector of Bishopwearmouth, Robert Gray, and while doing so was shown Clanny's lamp. Davy was impressed by the invention and shortly after returning to London, constructed his own celebrated safety lamp. However, he acknowledged Clanny's work, for at a meeting of the Royal Society on 9 November he described Clanny's lamp as an 'ingenious arrangement.' Davy's lamp was used in mines from 1816 onward. Moreover, on Tyneside George Stephenson (best remembered for his achievements as a railway engineer) likewise devised a safety lamp but also acknowledged the debt he owed to the pioneering work of Clanny.

The first half of the 19th century witnessed a great increase in the exploitation of the northern coalfields owing to growing demand for coal and technological advances which enabled this demand to be met, and Sunderland was involved in this process. Sunderland is located on clay and permian magnesian limestone, and it was the advances in technology which allowed the coal beneath the limestone to be reached. In May 1826 work commenced on sinking Monkwearmouth Colliery, work which followed closely on the heels of that at Hetton, the first pit sunk through the limestone covering much of the Durham coalfield.[53] At Hetton, the shaft was sunk to 891ft. At Monkwearmouth the shaft had to be sunk more than 1,500ft before the first worthwhile coal seam was reached in October 1834, making Monkwearmouth the deepest pit in the world at the time.

Production began in the following year, and it was not long before some 40,000 to 50,000 tons annually were mined. Moreover, the shaft was sunk even deeper, reaching 1,722ft in April 1846, and the census of 1851 indicates that by that date 178 youths and 630 men over twenty years of age were engaged in mining at Monkwearmouth.

In early 1841 John Leifchild visited the colliery while collecting information for a Royal Commission Report dealing with the employment of children. He was informed by George Elliot, the manager, that parents entreated him to employ their children 'from five years and upwards.' One such child at the pit was Robert Pattison, 'now six years of age' who had worked in the mine for four months.[54] Like other boys under thirteen at Monkwearmouth, Pattison was employed as a trapper, earning about 5s. a week. The youngsters had to open and close the doors along the underground passageways for the trains of coal wagons and in so doing ventilate the colliery.

At about twenty, after passing through some intermediate grades, an employee became a hewer. An anonymous visitor to Monkwearmouth in the middle of the century wrote as follows: 'The "hewers" are the key of the pit, the centre of the mining system.'[55] In 1841 such men were guaranteed enough work to enable them to earn at least £1.50 each a fortnight, and concerning them George Patterson has written: 'The hewer's normal day was much shorter than that of his ancillary workers. The bond [a yearly contract between the miner and his employer], set the maximum at eight hours and in fact most hewers worked six or seven hours, although the long winding times at Monkwearmouth could mean another hour underground.'[56]

Miners underground in the mid 19th century

In late 1849 the Scottish publisher, William Chambers, visited the colliery and of his visit he wrote the following:

> There are two entrances to the mine—one called the downcast, and the other the upcast shaft; the former being employed for admitting fresh air, and the latter for bringing up the used air, along with the smoke of a fire which attracts it from the various parts of the pit. These two orifices of the mine, however, are each employed at the same time for raising coal, and around them respectively are mechanical appliances, with all the bustle of rising and sinking wagons, and turning out the coal which is every moment arriving at the surface.[57]

Chambers proceeded to descend into the depths of the colliery. He did so via the downcast shaft—the less deep of the two—and recalled:

> we were speedily at the bottom of the shaft, where we were received and disengaged by the dusky figures in attendance.... We were at the end of a long gallery, which was whitewashed and lighted with gas—a sort of Thames Tunnel on a rude scale, stretching away into the bowels of the earth.... We now proceeded along the gallery or tunnel... encountering as we advanced trains of coal wagons, drawn on a railway by horses under the guidance of boys, on their way to the

> shaft…. The spectacle of horses at work in such a situation inspired sorrowful feelings [however]…. Fresh provender and water are brought regularly down to them; and to give me an idea of their comforts, I was taken into their stable, which is a large excavation in the side of the tunnel, fitted up with stalls and other conveniences.[58]

Chambers then travelled onward, down an inclined plane, into the deepest part of the mine:

> On arriving at the foot of the incline, which is at the full depth of 1800 feet, I found things a little bit more rude than in the stage above. There was here no gas, and the galleries branching out in different directions, were apparently more confined. We had got to the level of the great seam of coal…. About five feet thick, it glittered a continuous mass like a wall on each side…. Along the principal route towards the workings we bent our way and walked altogether a distance of perhaps the third of a mile, the channel always getting more confined [and upon arriving]…. at the spot where the wagons were being filled, we found two parties of men…the next thing to naked…engaged in digging the coal from the seam…. The temperature, as shown by a thermometer, was 86.5 degrees …. We were in the heart of the great seam, which stretches for many miles, and is, apparently, inexhaustible…. The seam is not difficult to work. By means of a pick, the colliers brought down great masses.[59]

Among other industries on Wearside during the first half of the 19th century were glassmaking, ropemaking and the manufacturing of pottery. There were three branches of glassmaking—bottles, tableware and window glass–and during this period the industry continued the process of expansion here which it had enjoyed in the 18th century. It was during these years that there was an increase in the demand for bottles, and among the works producing these were that at Ayre's Quay, Bishopwearmouth Panns Bottleworks (both dating from the late 17th century), Ballast Hill Bottleworks and Deptford Bottlehouse founded in c.1800 and 1807 respectively. By 1833 Sunderland produced more bottles than anywhere else in the North East. Not surprisingly, in view of this and other developments in local glass-making, the Reverend Dibdin subsequently observed that Sunderland did 'a great stroke of business in the glass-way.'[60]

In 1836, the year before Dibdin visited the town, James Hartley established the Wear Glassworks in association with his brother, John. They arrived in Sunderland after travelling up from Smethwick near Birmingham, where they had been members of a glassmaking partnership that had just dissolved. Two years later, the works were extended at a cost of some £50,000. John Hartley left the business shortly thereafter—he moved to Staffordshire—whereas James remained in charge of the firm, which was to become one of national importance, manufacturing window glass, stained glass and tableware.

The bulk of the tableware produced in Sunderland during this period was intended for the general public, but some exceptional work was created, the finest being the dessert and wine service of almost 200 pieces made for the third Marquess of Londonderry in 1824.[61] It cost nearly 2,000 guineas and was the work of the Wear Flint Glass Company, established in about 1805.

The ropemaking industry was also well established on Wearside by the commencement of the 19th century, and likewise experienced growth during the first half of the century, with collieries and railways providing new markets for rope. The largest rope works was Webster's at Deptford, founded in c.1794. Dibdin visited the factory and wrote: 'The ordinary vulgar phrase is, to "give a man rope enough and he will hang himself." Such an unfortunate creature never be in need of "rope enough" at Sunderland—for at the manu-factory of Mr. Webster, one rope was manufactured nearly three miles and a half long:—without a single splice! This was for the great neighbouring railroad.'[62] At the time of Dibdin's visit, hemp was the principal material used in ropemaking. But in 1840 Webster's began producing wire ropes, in imitation of recent developments elsewhere.

Webster's Ropery

In the years 1800–50, there were several potteries on Wearside. Some dated from the late 18th century, as was true for instance of Scott's Pottery at Southwick and Dawson's Pottery at South Hylton, both of which produced items of high quality. New firms included the Bridge or 'Jericho' Pottery Company and the Sheepfold or Rickaby's Pottery, founded in c.1829 and 1840 respectively.

Children were among those employed in the potteries. They worked a twelve hour day (including an hour and a half for meals) and overtime was common. In certain localities, potteries were a major facet of the economy. This was certainly the case of Dawson's, where the pottery gave employment to a significant proportion of the village's workforce.

Much of the pottery manufactured on Wearside was exported to Europe. In 1819, for example, 145,092 pieces of earthenware were shipped to Holland. The output from the potteries was solely earthenware, primarily aimed at people with moderate incomes. The range of articles produced was considerable, but dinner services and tea-sets comprised the bulk of the pottery manufactured. The best-known pottery made here during this era was white earthenware decorated with pink or purple lustre. This pottery—known as Sunderland Ware—is ornamented with a variety of designs, the most common are views of Wearmouth Bridge, and is now eagerly collected. As

Neil Sinclair has written, the fame of Sunderland Ware is such that 'pottery making, although it was certainly an industry of importance, is sometimes given a greater significance [in the town's history] than it merits on economic grounds.'[63]

Papermaking also took place. Sunderland's first paper mill was the Wearmouth Mill at Ayre's Quay, Deptford, founded in about 1826 by Vint, Hutton and Co who used old sails and other material to produce various types of paper. A fire halted production during a strike in early 1846. Early on the morning of 6 February passing workmen saw that the premises were alight and despite efforts to combat the flames by Bishopwearmouth parish fire engine and a floating fire engine belonging to a ropery, the building collapsed as 'flames shot up into the air with prodigious fury.'[64] Production at the site resumed in August 1848, under Robert Hutton and W.H. Richardson.

Vint, Hutton & Co also started Ford Mill at Claxheugh, about two miles upriver from Deptford, Production got under way in the summer of 1838 but the mill soon passed into other hands, and by 1850 the business was operating as J. Blackwell & Co.

Breweries also existed. In addition to small-scale production carried out by publican-brewers, several more ambitious enterprises were conducted. One such was a firm founded by Cuthbert Vaux near Wearmouth Bridge in 1837. When he set up the business, Cuthbert was in his mid-twenties and had recently ended a partnership with another local brewer to whom he was related by marriage. Initially, the scale of activity was modest but the firm made progress and in 1843 moved to new premises in Union Street where it remained well into the second half of the century.

Early in the period, Robert Surtees wrote as follows: 'The coal-trade, it may readily be conceded, is the staple trade of the Port. Nearly 530 vessels are entirely employed in it. The chief vend is to the Metropolis and the South-West of England; but in Peace, large quantities are exported to the Baltic, France, Holland, and Flanders.'[65]

The amount of coal shipped from the port increased between 1800 and 1850, though not continuously. 624,804 tons were shipped in 1801, whereas in 1830 the figure was 1,387,420 tons. The trade was then affected by the opening of Seaham Harbour (a few miles to the south) and in 1832 coal shipments from the Wear were 183,618 tons less than they had been two years before, and they did not exceed the 1830 figure until 1845. In 1850 shipments totalled 1,718,427 tons.

Surtees also noted that:

> The lime-trade is another very principal branch of the commerce of Sunderland. The chief works are at Pallion, where there are 15 kilns, which burn annually nearly 30,000 tons of limestone, affording 10,000 Winchester chaldrons of lime. From 25 to 30 vessels, of from 40 to 100 tons each, are employed in the trade. The exportation is chiefly to the Yorkshire Ports, and to all the Ports on the eastern coast of Scotland.[66]

Of the town's trade, John Brough made the following observation in Garbutt's *History*: 'A want of spirit seems to prevail on the part of our merchants, who, rather than purchase their cargoes abroad...prefer having them from the neighbouring ports,

Fulwell Mill, an eye-catching part of Sunderland's
industrial heritage. It was built in 1806–8

at second-hand rate.'[67] However, according to Burnett, by 1830 this had changed. The merchants now imported 'many articles direct to this port.'[68] Among the imports listed by Burnett were timber, tar, flax, iron, corn, flour, and spirituous liqours.

In view of the above, the Port of Sunderland was inevitably a busy one. In fact, in 1829 Sunderland was ranked as the fourth port in the kingdom. Some of the shipping statistics are as follows. In 1800, 5,835 and 119 vessels were cleared from the port for coastal and foreign trade (the latter figure was low owing to Britain's involvement in a war against France and its allies), whereas in 1850 the figures were respectively 8,856 and 1,408 ships.

More than once, the Wear was disrupted by strike action on the part of seamen, as was the case when a major strike occurred in 1825. Low wages was one of the bones of contention. Sunderland's magistrates, anxious to maintain order, obtained a force of dragoons from Newcastle and requested that they be provided with a permanent military force by the Home Office, a request that was not fulfilled. On 3 August, striking sailors boarded ships whose crews were not party to the strike and overpowered guards placed on the vessels by the magistrates. In response, John Davison, a magistrate and himself a shipowner, arrived on the scene with a detachment of dragoons and recaptured the seized ships. As one of the vessels on the Wear, the *Busy*, which had been loaded under armed guard, was making for the sea, those on board were pelted with stones and other missiles by strikers and their sympathizers on the river bank, whereupon Davison, 'for the preservation of the lives of himself, and the Constables and Soldiers, directed the latter to fire, and four men were unfortunately killed in consequence.'[69] A few vessels proceeded to leave the Wear. But on 11 August, shipowners informed Sunderland's magistrates that the 'trade of the port, [was] if possible, in a worse state than before the late unhappy events' owing to the lawless conduct of striking seamen, lawlessness that still included intimidating other seafarers into not sailing.

Sunderland harbour from the south pier c.1830, showing a collier making for the sea

At last, though, on the 17th, a settlement was reached and a wage increase was part of the deal.

More of Sunderland's male population was engaged in seafaring than in any other occupation—during the Napoleonic Wars many local sailors were seized by the enemy and endured long periods of captivity[70]—and it was inevitably a tough and dangerous livelihood. In the years 1827–9 alone, 107 ships from the port were lost. M. A. Richardson records the following account of the fate of a number of light colliers which sailed from Sunderland in October 1829. The vessels sailed

> with a fine north-west wind and a smooth sea; but during the night, the wind having shifted to the north-east, a most tremendous sea came on, and morning presented one of the most awful spectacles witnessed [in Sunderland] for many years. Day-light discovered four vessels lying on their broad-sides on the south rocks, and by three o'clock P.M. there were fifteen vessels on shore and wrecked between the south pier and Hendon. About four o'clock, the Eleanor of Monkwearmouth, which had sailed the day before for the northward, in putting back, sunk off the mouth of the harbour, and all on board perished…in sight of some thousands of spectators, unable to render the slightest assistance.[71]

Railways, the River and Docks

During the first half of the 19th century much of the coal shipped from the Wear was brought downstream by keels loaded with coal mined inland. The process of transporting the coal to the waiting colliers, and loading them, employed many people. According to Taylor Potts, in 1810–1, 25 per cent of the total population of Sunderland and the other communities at the mouth of the Wear was employed in this process or was dependent on those so engaged.

It is understandable, therefore, that great anger resulted when, probably in the summer of 1812, Nesham and Co. commenced moving coal by wagonway from its collieries in the vicinity of Newbottle to staithes just above Wearmouth Bridge, thereby avoiding the use of keels. This led to a riot on 20 March 1815 by the keelmen and their supporters who vandalized the wagonway before a troop of cavalry arrived from Newcastle and restored order.

The wagonway soon became known as the Lambton Railway, following its purchase by John George Lambton in 1822.[72] In that year, moreover, another railway began transporting coal to staithes just upstream from those already referred to. As Neil Sinclair has written, the Hetton Colliery Railway 'occupies a place in railway history since it was the first complete line to be engineered by George Stephenson and used locomotives as well as stationary steam engines and self-acting inclines to move coal.'[73] By 1830, 53 per cent of the coal shipped from the Wear arrived here via this line and the Lambton Railway.

In 1836 the Durham and Sunderland Railway opened. As Tom Corfe has commented, owing to the undulating nature of the terrain over which the railway would operate, the engineer involved, T.E. Forster

> had doubts about the expensive work that would be involved in producing a line level enough for locomotives, and no great faith in those cumbersome and unreliable machines for coal haulage; so he opted instead for fixed engines, and it was by these that the Durham and Sunderland was worked for the first twenty years of its existence, save when in emergency horses and (on one remarkable occasion) sails were used.[74]

Unlike the other railways mentioned above, the Durham and Sunderland—which approached via Ryhope—carried passengers, who alighted at a station on the Town Moor. But as one such, Dr Augustus Granville noted, to the detriment of the passengers the owners of the railway looked 'for remuneration chiefly from the conveyance of coals and merchandise, which are neither in haste nor prone to murmur' (the coal was carried to staithes on the south side of the Wear) and thus adhered to their own 'cumbersome mode of managing the railroad.'[75]

In 1839 another passenger carrying line, The Brandling Junction Railway, from Gateshead and South Shields, was opened to Monkwearmouth and so people could travel to Sunderland by rail from both north and south of the Wear. The initial station was replaced within a decade by a much more imposing one.

As seen in the previous chapter, the River Wear Commissioners were respon-

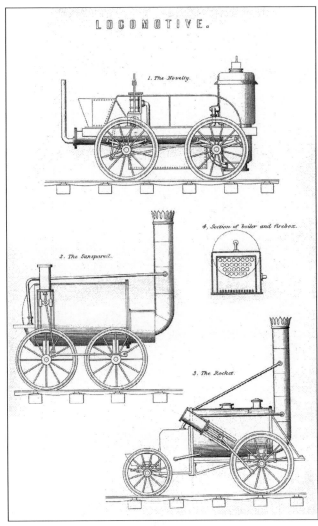

Early locomotives

sible for the maintenance and improvement of the river. Initially, the commission's operations were funded by a duty on coal exports and by loans, but from 1809 onwards this income was supplemented by a duty payable by every ship per voyage which used the harbour.

One of the RWC's duties was to ensure that the river was free of man-made obstacles that would hinder navigation. Keel skippers and the masters of colliers were thus fined for mooring in prohibited areas, or for dumping ballast into the river. Moreover, businessmen whose wharfs and jetties were hazards to traffic were prosecuted. The most celebrated case of this occurred in the years 1818–24 when the RWC engaged in a bitter dispute with the powerful Pemberton family, which had among other things built a loading jetty out into the channel. The case resulted in the establishment of a legal quay line beyond which no structure could project.

The RWC also engaged in dredging. In the early years of the century a steam-powered dredger was used (it had come into service in 1798), but this was not very successful and so in 1804 there was a return to manually operated equipment, before steam dredging restarted in 1811. Stuart Miller has noted: 'By the mid-nineteenth century more was being dredged in one year than had been raised in the whole of the period between 1748 and 1804.'[76]

The RWC was, of course, also concerned with the harbour. In 1801–2 the resident engineer, Jonathan Pickernell (who was soon to be dismissed for the theft of RWC property), constructed an elegant 76ft high stone octagonal lighthouse at the end of the north pier. Then, in the 1830s, one of Pickernell's successors, John Murray,

Monkwearmouth Railway Station. Designed by a local architect Thomas Moore, it was built in 1848. Of it Sir Nikolaus Pevsner commented: 'If one does not mind a railway station looking like a Literary and Scientific Institution or Provincial Athenæum … Monkwearmouth is one of the most handsome stations in existence.'

extended the pier and in 1841 moved the lighthouse along it to a new resting place. As Miller comments, the lighthouse 'was undercut, and a wheeled cradle on rails was inserted. The unstable structure was corsetted in planking and iron straps and braced with huge timber uprights. It was then moved along the rails using forcing screws and winches at a rate of 33 feet per hour over a distance of 475 feet.'[77]

By this date the Port of Sunderland had been adversely affected by the opening of Seaham Harbour in 1831 (work on which had begun in 1828), and contemporaneous harbour developments further south on Teesside. In order to meet the challenge, the RWC had commissioned a consultant, Robert Stevenson, to determine the best options for the construction of a dock. In a report of 28 September 1829, Stevenson declared his preference for a 30-acre dock on the south side of the river. The bulk of the RWC's members supported the proposal, as did a group of Sunderland businessmen.

However, Sir Hedworth Williamson, one of County Durham's MPs, objected to the scheme. He favoured the construction of a dock on the north side of the river on his own property at Monkwearmouth Shore and, even though most of the coal shipped from the Wear came from collieries to the south, mustered enough support to defeat a bill for the alternative. He then proceeded to sponsor the development of a 9-acre site near the north pier. In 1837 the dock, designed by Isambard Kingdom Brunel, was opened but, owing to its small size, soon became known as 'Sir Hedworth's bathtub.' In 1839, it was linked to the Brandling Junction Railway and witnessed its first shipment of coal in August of that year. The baronet suffered severe financial difficulties as a result of the dock's construction, for the original estimate of £30,000 became £120,000.

In view of the North Dock's limitations, it is not surprising that the desire for a south dock remained. In fact, it was the dominant political issue locally. As Tom Corfe has noted, when the 'Railway King' George Hudson was elected as one of the town's MPs in 1845

> it was on the understanding that he would press the issue in Parliament and apply his well-known financial wizardry to produce the necessary capital. In return Hudson saw Sunderland as both a base for his political ambitions and an outlet for the extensive railway empire that he was, by dint of various dubious financial transactions, rapidly assembling.[78]

Consequently, in 1846 work commenced on a south dock, designed by Murray. Thousands of men were employed on the task, many of whom had flocked to Sunderland to obtain work, among them individuals who had emigrated from Ireland as a result of the Great Famine. The work resulted in the creation of a 47-acre dock, which was opened on Thursday, 20 June 1850, by Hudson amid great pageantry. Nationally, Hudson's reputation was now in ruins—his unsavoury transactions had come to light and his railway kingdom had collapsed. In Sunderland, though, his popu-

Harbour scene in 1841. The lighthouse on the
north pier is being moved to a new position

larity was still marked and the opening of the dock was witnessed by approximately 50,000 spectators, many of whom viewed him as a hero.

One eyewitness was John William Campbell, a resident of Church Street who recorded in his diary that by 10.30am the 'river was covered with boats and people in great expectation of the procession.' He continues by stating that although the weather was 'Oppressively hot, yet it could not be a finer day to look down the Docks and see the people and all the colours; was the finest sight ever beheld, people dressed in their Sunday attire and a number of carriages, carts drawn up the eastern side of the Dock.' Moreover, though the proceedings culminated at around midday when the dock was opened, a festive spirit prevailed for many hours, a fact recorded by Campbell. He notes that 'during the night hundreds of squibs and crackers were let off. Tar barrels were rolled, besoms dipped in tar and set fire were kicking about all over the High Street.'[79]

The following day, the *Sunderland Herald* declared: 'In no one incident in the history of this borough.... has its future prosperity been so bound up as in the formation of the Sea-Dock.... It is a great attempt successfully carried to completion, to obviate the disadvantage of a shallow and narrow river.'[80]

The same paper continues:

> Great commercial towns, like individuals and nations, have their great epochs and eras, they have some days of such paramount interest and importance that all the rest of the history is, comparatively, tame and poor.... Such a day...in the annals of Sunderland, was Thursday June the 20th, 1850, the Great Holiday as we must emphatically term it. When, after toils and exertions, mental and physical...the Great Dock...was at last fairly opened.[81]

As hoped, the dock proved a success. The first shipment of coal occurred the following month and it was not long before the dock was a scene of vibrant activity that resulted in a marked upturn in the town's economic fortunes.

Recreation and Entertainment

From the foregoing it is obvious that society on Wearside was very diverse. This was also true of the recreational activities in which the people engaged, activities determined by the taste, disposition and circumstances of the individuals in question.

Entertainment included rustic events such as bull baiting, which had however passed its heyday and was made illegal in 1835, as were some other blood sports. Two years later, the town council passed a bylaw to the effect that anyone guilty of causing or abetting dog fights and the baiting of bulls, bears, badgers or any other animals, was to be fined 2s. 6d.

A newer form of recreation was cricket, and the first recorded local match (mentioned in the *Newcastle Chronicle* of 25 July 1801) witnessed the defeat, by a team based at Monkwearmouth Shore, of visitors from Sunderland. Furthermore, a few years later the *Tyne Mercury* of 14 June 1808 stated that Sunderland Cricket Club had played a 'grand match' on the Town Moor.

The team later became known as the Gentlemen's Club. Subsequently, in 1834 it changed its name to the Bishopwearmouth Cricket Club, and away games included matches on Newcastle's Town Moor. In 1850 the club merged with Hendon Terrace Cricket Club—whose ground was the Blue House Field in Hendon—to become the Sunderland Cricket Club and the aforementioned ground served as its home.

Some Wearsiders belonged to the Subscription Library in High Street, whose annual fee of two guineas restricted membership to persons who were relatively prosperous. Of the library, one of its founders, George Wilson Meadley states in a work of local history published in 1819, that it comprised: 'A valuable collection of books, in almost every branch of literature…. The number of volumes according to the present catalogue, amounts to 4355, exclusive of periodical works, whilst an income of about £230 a year affords the means of progressive additions.'[82]

The quotation is taken from the first history of Sunderland ever published, George Garbutt's *A Historical and Descriptive View of the Parishes of Monkwearmouth and Bishopwearmouth, and the Port and Borough of Sunderland*. Garbutt, a printer by trade, had settled in Sunderland in 1812, and some of the material in his book—a mine of information—was contributed by other writers.

On occasion, cultured people grouped together to form various societies. One such was the Sunderland Literary and Philosophical Society, established in 1834, largely at the instigation of Dr William Clanny. Initially, it met in rooms on Villiers Street before moving to a new home, the recently built Athenaeum on Fawcett Street, in the 1840s.

Of the society, Corfe has commented:

> The story of the Lit. and Phil's twenty-year life was not entirely an easy one. There appears to have been a good deal of internal dispute, and several attempts were made to establish breakaway or rival societies…. But in its early days the members shared a commendable enthusiasm for spreading enlightenment amongst their fellow citizens.[83]

Hence in addition to providing concerts and balls, the society organised classes to teach languages such as French or to provide instruction in other fields such as science. In late 1849, the Scottish publisher William Chambers visited Sunderland in order to preside at one of its meetings and of his visit to the town recalled: 'My visit to Sunderland opened up a fresh scene of industry, brought me in contact with many intelligent minds, and revealed to me much kindliness of feeling'.[84]

Another body was the Sunderland Natural History and Antiquarian Society. This was founded in late 1836 and, to begin with, used the rooms in Villiers Street of the above-mentioned society. The Natural History and Antiquarian Society assumed responsibility for a museum collection that had been in the hands of the Subscription Library since 1821; a collection that had been formed by a short-lived venture, the Subscription Museum founded in 1810. In the early 1840s, the society moved to the Athenaeum. Shortly thereafter, following talks between the two parties, in 1846 Sunderland town council took over the society's collections and in so doing established the first provincial municipal museum in the country.

Towards the end of the period, the Athenaeum certainly played an important role in the town's cultural life. An article in the *Sunderland Herald* observed:

> Of Fawcett Street—the principal and most imposing street in the town … the chief ornament is the Athenaeum. This building contains a spacious and beautiful assembly hall, with saloon, ante-rooms, etc, and a lecture-room. One portion of it is occupied by the Literary and Philosophical Institution and newsrooms, and another by the Borough Museum. The exterior is an original Ionic design, with portico and columns. The effect is massive and imposing, though perhaps not quite so grand as it would have been had the elevation been a little higher than the adjoining houses.[85]

Pleasure could also be derived from attending performances at the Theatre Royal founded in the 1760s. It was located in Playhouse Lane, which had become known as Drury Lane by the early 1820s. Of the theatre, Garbutt claimed that 'there is no respectable provincial stage throughout the kingdom, where the exhibitions are produced with more attention as to correct representation, or with more liberality, as to appropriate decoration and display, than that of Sunderland.'[86]

Not everyone approved of the moral worth of theatrical performances. This was true of Robert Gray, the Rector of Sunderland. On 16 March 1828 he preached a sermon entitled 'The Sin and Danger of Frequenting the Theatre', in which he told his congregation that 'Probably not a single piece could be found, in the whole compass of plays now acted upon the stage, which even a moral character and much less a man of piety could entirely approve of .' Theatres misrepresented real life and excited 'wishes and desires' that could not 'be gratified.'[87]

In the same year, the theatre was demolished and rebuilt. A few years later, in 1831, it passed into the hands of Henry Roxby (a native of Hull who used the stage name 'Harry Beverly') and, following his death in 1843, his widow and son managed the venture.

A popular form of recreation was drinking. A commercial directory for the years 1820–2, lists 70 taverns and public houses, while *Parson and White's Directory* of 1827 lists 258 establishments (including a few hotels). One of the public houses mentioned was the *Half Moon Inn*, in High Street East. It dated from the 18th century, and in March 1801 it was one of three such places whose windows were smashed during a riot over the price of corn.

During the 19th century the seaside became increasingly popular as a place of resort. It was believed that bathing in seawater was of great benefit to the health and that sea breezes were likewise very beneficial.

One of the localities in Sunderland's vicinity that attracted bathers was Ryhope, a point noted by Garbutt:

> The village of Ryhope has for some years past been frequented by several respectable families during the summer season, in order to enjoy the delightful exercise of sea-bathing; for which purpose the beach, a little to the east of the village, is admirably adapted, on account of the hardness of the sands, and the absence of rocks.[88]

Hendon likwise appealed to bathers, as James Burnett observed:

> As a bathing place, Sunderland, in the summer season, is a place of great resort. Numbers from the interior of the country embrace the opportunity of enjoying the benefit of sea-bathing. Lodgings are not dear, and easily obtained. A set of metallic and hot baths were established in the year 1821, near the moor: and at Hendon, there are most excellent hot baths, and a number of machines for sea-bathing, conducted and attended by Smith Graham.[89]

In 1842 a hotel overlooking the sea was built at Roker to a design by the celebrated northern architect, John Dobson, on land owned by the Abbs family. The establishment was called *Roker Baths Hotel*—it is now simply *Roker Hotel*—and sea water was pumped into the building to provide hot and cold baths, showers and steam vapour baths.

Pollution spoilt some visits to the seafront. Of this, we hear:

> The inhabitants of, and the visitors to, many of our sea-side watering places are often exposed to annoyance and sometimes to injury from the discharge of the town drainage upon the much-frequented sea-beach.... many a family returns inland from the sea-side fevered with the stench at the sea-beach, rather than invigorated with the sea breezes.[90]

Inevitably, outings to the seaside occasionally ended in tragedy, as occurred on Wednesday 15 October 1845 when three pupils and a master of the Grange School—Sunderland's premier place of education—lost their lives at Hendon Beach when bathing conditions suddenly became treacherous. Two of the fatalities were sons of the Scottish baronet, Sir David Baird.

Local Government

The parochial administrative structure survived into the first half of the 19th century. From time to time the ratepayers of the parishes of Sunderland, Bishopwearmouth and Monkwearmouth, elected vestries which would attend to matters such as the upkeep of the parish churches and, for example, appoint overseers of the poor and scavengers to clean the streets.

However, owing to the growth of population, this arrangement became inadequate to deal with the resultant problems and so here, as in many other towns, it was supplemented by Improvement Commissioners, bodies of local worthies appointed by Acts of Parliament. As noted earlier, two such acts were passed in 1810, one for Sunderland and the other for Bishopwearmouth and its small satellite, Bishopwearmouth Panns. Both authorized, among other things, the paving, lighting, watching, and cleaning of streets. Moreover, the act for Sunderland provided for the construction of a town hall or market house. Hence the Exchange of 1814 was erected to serve as a commercial, social and administrative centre. Over the years the commissioners undoubtedly made some improvements to the local scene but it is worth noting that in 1847 government inspectors concluded that, on the whole, they had failed the ratepayers.[91]

In 1835 during the Tory administration of Sir Robert Peel, the Municipal Corporations Act was passed by parliament and Sunderland was among the corporate boroughs listed in the legislation intended to reform municipal government in England and Wales. Sunderland's inclusion in the list of corporate boroughs had been a close run thing. Although the community had been granted borough charters in the 12th and 17th centuries, the commissioners who visited the town in 1833 while collecting information for the proposed legislation, did not find a body exercising 'municipal authority.' Bishop Morton's charter of 1634 authorizing the appointment of a mayor, aldermen and common councilmen had fallen into disuse. Instead, the commissioners found a small body calling themselves 'the freemen and stallingers of the Borough of Sunderland,' who claimed that they were an ancient corporation, though they were not involved in local government, save for exercising authority over rights of pasturage and usage on the Town Moor.

In view of the above, it is not surprising that the commissioners decided that Sunderland's status as a corporate borough was very dubious. Nonetheless they subsequently decided to rank the town in the list of corporations 'possessing or exercising municipal functions', anyway.[92] They were no doubt swayed by the fact that Sunderland was populous and had recently received parliamentary representation.

Norman Gash has commented of the Municipal Corporations Act that administratively it 'did little more than impose a uniform structure of democratically elected councils on the 178 old corporate boroughs found to exist in England and Wales,'[93] councils that would be elected by male ratepayers of three years standing. Some of Sunderland's citizens objected to the establishment of a town council fearing that this would result in party political disputes and be a drain on their finances. On 17 December 1835, a meeting of those opposed to such a move was held at the Exchange. Leadership of the opposition movement was provided by Dr Gerald Wellesley, the Rector of Bishopwearmouth. A substantial number of those who favoured a town council (which they hoped would bring about better services) were likewise present. So much so that one of them, Andrew White, was chosen to chair the meeting and resolutions approving the founding of a town council were passed.

But as John Pearson has written: 'A practical difficulty arose concerning the election of a town council. There was no mayor to act as presiding officer as required by the Municipal Corporations Act.'[94] Consequently, the Attorney General advised that the senior freeman of the body referred to above should officiate. If he declined, the most senior freeman willing to do so was to preside. So, on 26 December, an election was held (presided over by Richard Spoor, the fifth most senior freeman), and six councillors were chosen for each of the borough's seven wards. Shortly after this two aldermen were elected for each ward and, on New Year's Day, 1836, Andrew White was elected mayor.

Nevertheless, the opponents of the establishment of a town council had not given up and proceedings were commenced in the Court of King's Bench. There it was maintained that the election on the 26th was invalid, for there had been no

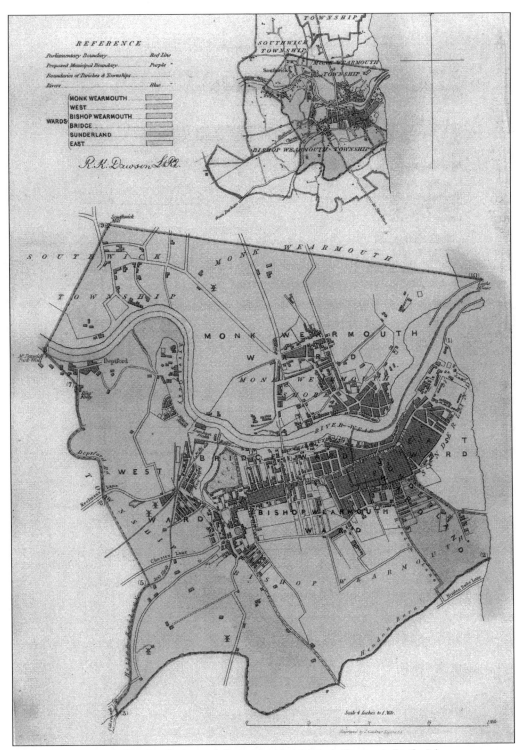

A map showing the proposed municipal boundary. In the event, Southwick
was excluded and the number of wards increased to seven

mayor to act as presiding officer and because the solicitor for the 'corporation' of freemen and stallingers had had to compile and distribute the electoral roll as there had been no Town Clerk to do so. Additional legislation was therefore deemed necessary to legitimize the corporation. This received the royal assent on 17 July 1837 shortly after the accession of Queen Victoria.

Inevitably, the Mayors of Sunderland were prominent figures in the social and political life of the town. Andrew White, for instance, was a leading local businessman—*inter alia* he was Chairman of the Directors of the Sunderland Joint Stock Bank, a partner in the Bishopwearmouth Ironworks, and a director of the Durham and Sunderland Railway. In July 1837 he resigned from the mayoralty to stand for parliament, (he duly became a Liberal MP representing Sunderland), whereupon Richard Spoor was elected

Queen Victoria

as his successor. A prominent Freemason, Spoor had strong commercial interests: he was among other things a Director of the York, Newcastle and Berwick Railway, and had been heavily involved in the establishment of the Sunderland Chamber of Commerce in 1832.

While the majority of the men who served as Mayors of Sunderland were born on Wearside this was not universally the case, although all the mayors up to the year 1850 were native to the North East. Spoor is a case in point. He was born in Newcastle in 1794, but moved to Sunderland in the late 1790s when his father settled in the town where he duly became a wholesale draper and a wine merchant. So, too, is Joseph Brown, who held the mayoralty in 1839. He was born at North Shields in 1784, the son of a draper. After studying medicine in Edinburgh and London, he joined the army medical service and served in the Peninsula and elsewhere. In 1818 he returned to Britain, gained an M.D. the following year, and moved to Sunderland, where he was appointed a member of the staff of the infirmary in 1822. A deeply religious and compassionate man, Brown was very sympathetic to the poor and as a member of the town council was particularly concerned with improving their living conditions.

The grandest of Sunderland's mayors was Sir Hedworth Williamson, who held the mayoralty in 1841–2 and again (briefly) in 1847: he resigned to stand for parliament. Born at the family seat, Whitburn Hall in 1797, he succeeded his father as seventh baronet in 1810 and married the daughter of the first Lord Ravensworth in 1826. Williamson was far from being a parochial figure—he had for example spent much of his time in Italy, where two of his children were born. Moreover, in the years 1831 to 1837 he was a member of parliament, representing County Durham. Locally, his political powerbase was Monkwearmouth Shore, of which he was the landlord.

In 1837 following the additional legislation necessary to legitimize the council, the corporation commenced drafting bylaws and established a police force for the municipal borough, (which comprised Sunderland, Monkwearmouth, Monkwearmouth Shore, and as much of Bishopwearmouth as lay within a radius of a mile of the centre of Wearmouth Bridge). An advertisement for recruits stated: 'No Person will be employed who is above 35 Years of Age, or under 5 feet 9 inches in height, and preference will be given to unmarried Men.'[95] The new force numbered 53 men, and its head, Superintendent William Brown, was a former London policeman—upon its establishment, the Improvement Commissioners ceased appointing watchmen, whose performance as law enforcers had come in for some censure. Reduced income from rates during the depressed years of the mid 1840s led to a temporary reduction in the police's manpower and rates of pay.

Other undertakings of the council during this period included the founding of England's first provincial municipal museum in 1846 and the acquisition of land along Hendon Road for public baths and wash houses. These opened in 1851, the year in which the powers of the corporation were increased by an Act of Parliament. The powers of other local bodies, such as the Improvement Commissioners and Bishopwearmouth Highways Board (the latter, founded in 1836, was responsible for the maintenance and improvement of Bishopwearmouth's streets) were vested in the council thereby ending the disputes and uncertainty about jurisdiction that had hitherto prevailed.

Parliamentary Representation

Since 1673 when County Durham's freeholders were enfranchised, Sunderland had been represented by MPs for the county. One such was John George Lambton—who owned property on Wearside and served as an MP from 1813 until 1828. In that year he was made a baron, and in 1833 he became the first Earl of Durham. He died in 1840 and Penshaw Monument, a prominent landmark in the vicinity of Sunderland, was erected to his memory four years later.

In 1832 parliament passed the Reform Act, which changed the structure of parliamentary representation. Some towns, for instance, which did not have MPs of their own were given seats in parliament and Sunderland was one such. The fact that it would now have its own representatives was a cause of great rejoicing among the townsfolk, who had pressed for such representation by petitioning parliament and by supporting candidates in favour of parliamentary reform.

Sunderland parliamentary borough created by the Reform Act was a constituency comprising Sunderland, Bishopwearmouth, Bishopwearmouth Panns, Monkwearmouth, Monkwearmouth Shore and Southwick. It was to have two MPs. The act gave the vote to owners of houses worth £10 per annum, and thus here, as elsewhere, the majority of the populace was disqualified from voting. Some 2,500 people were entitled to vote in a constituency whose population totalled about 41,000.

Three titled men were to play a major part in the political life of the new constituency. They were the third Marquess of Londonderry, the Earl of Durham, and Sir Hedworth Williamson, one of the county MPs. The first was a Tory, while the others were Liberals, and all had financial reasons for taking an interest in Sunderland's affairs. The former were leading figures in the exploitation of the Durham coalfield whereas Sir Hedworth was involved in the lime trade (he had a quarry at Fulwell) and was the principal landlord on the north side of the river.

On 14 December 1832, the constituency's first MPs were elected by an enthusiastic turnout, at which time (according to the *Durham Advertiser*) the returning officer, Addison Fenwick, told Sunderland's voters from the hustings: 'You have been placed in a situation of political importance, which, from the extent of your trade, wealth, and population, you are justly entitled to.'

Andrew White (1792–1856). Sunderland's first modern mayor. He later represented Sunderland as a Liberal MP in 1837–41

The victorious candidates were Durham's relative and nominee, Captain George Barrington, and Sir William Chaytor, another Liberal.[96] However, it soon became apparent that Barrington was mentally ill and so a by-election was held the following year. This was won by the Tory businessman, William Thompson, a man 'intimately conversant with commercial and shipping subjects', who enjoyed the backing of Londonderry. He retained his seat in the general election of 1835, at which time Williamson's brother-in-law and nominee David Barclay (who was also supported by Durham) likewise emerged victorious.

Barclay had had to compromise over the docks issue, a subject at the heart of local politics in the 1830s and 1840s and one that cost his relation, Williamson, a good deal of popularity owing to the part he had played in thwarting plans for a south dock in the 1830s. As noted earlier, Williamson favoured the construction of a dock on his own land at Monkwearmouth Shore; a stance that led to his being called a traitor who wished to profit at the town's expense. Nonetheless, the issue of a south dock did not die and Barclay had agreed to support the idea of such a dock, whilst declaring that he would 'hail the event' if north docks were constructed.

It will be recalled that when Williamson's north dock opened in 1837, it was too small for the town's needs. Hence in 1845 Londonderry and Sunderland's Tories persuaded the great entrepreneur, George Hudson—then at the height of his success—to be their candidate in a by-election in the belief that he could triumph at the polls and improve Sunderland's languishing economy by bringing about the creation of the necessary dock facilities.

Hudson arrived by train on 28 July, and received a very favourable welcome. A reporter for a national newspaper, *The Times*, observed that 'the public enthusiasm was altogether in Mr Hudson's favour, and a more brilliant reception was perhaps never given to any candidate in any part of England.'[97]

From the balcony of the *George Inn*, Hudson duly addressed prospective electors gathered in High Street. According to the *Sunderland Herald* of 1 August, he declared, 'it is because I have made a fortune, and am independent, that I come here to ask for your suffrages to send me to Parliament, that there I may crown all.' Hudson promised that he would do everything he could for Sunderland. The promise struck a chord, and on 14 August 1845 he became one of the town's MPs, gaining 627 votes, 130 more than his rival.

Hudson was re-elected at a general election held in August 1847, and in the following November he was again present in Sunderland to lay the foundation stone of the South Dock, then under construction. It is interesting to note that as a result of a by-election held the following month Hudson was joined as one of Sunderland's MPs by Sir Hedworth Williamson, who stood as a Liberal candidate. As Alan Heesom has observed, his election 'owed not a little to the fact that the docks crisis was, at last, on its way to solution.'[98]

Elections sometimes witnessed unruly behaviour. To illustrate the point: in 1841 stones were thrown by vagabonds at the victory procession of Lord Howick—the heir of the second Earl Grey—a Liberal who had just won a by-election in Sunderland.[99] Electioneering was also expensive, for among other things money was spent on bribing the electorate. For instance, owing to costs occurred on his behalf by members of his campaign team, Howick's victory proved more expensive than he had anticipated. When approached to become the Liberal candidate he had been informed that the election would cost him under £1000. This proved not to be the case, however. Heesom comments that the 'total demand on Howick and his [campaign] committee was finally in the region of £5,000', of which Howick 'had to find £1,500 in addition to £500 he had paid before the campaign began.'[100] Thus, in a letter of 12 September 1842, Howick duly lamented to his father: 'I was certainly very ill used by those who assured me so positively that the whole expense wd. not exceed £800 & I am very sorry indeed that I ever went near the place.'[101] Nonetheless, we should bear in mind that electoral violence and bribery were not confined to Sunderland. They were characteristic of politics nationally during this period.

Radicals made their presence felt from the 1830s onward. Sunderland's leading Radicals were the young businessmen, James Williams and George Binns, who ran a bookshop in Bridge Street, Bishopwearmouth, a shop that was the centre of local Chartist activity. Like their fellows, they wished among other matters, to see the suffrage greatly extended from that allowed by the Reform Act and warned that violence would otherwise ensue from disgruntled members of the working class. Consequently, on 15 July 1839 following a meeting on Sunderland Town Moor, they were arrested for sedition and, the following year, were imprisoned in Durham Gaol for six months. They returned to Sunderland as heroes and continued working for the cause they had espoused.

The strength of Radicalism in Sunderland during this period can be gauged by the results of the by-election of 1845 won by the Tory, George Hudson. Even so, Colonel Thomas Perronet Thompson (a 'Chartist of the wildest school' according to the *Manchester Guardian*) gained a significant proportion of the votes. On this point, Heesom comments, 'the result…showed that, in a straight fight between a Radical and a Tory, 44 per cent of Sunderland's electorate were prepared to cast a Radical vote—a higher figure than could be found in contemporary Gateshead or Newcastle.'[102] Although no Radical was elected to represent Sunderland in parliament during this period, their day would come.

Sunderland's press was openly partisan. The *Sunderland Herald*, which first appeared on 28 May 1831 (a few months after the advent of the town's first newspaper, the short-lived *Sunderland General Shipping Gazette and Advertiser*), was strongly pro-Liberal and dismissed the local Tories as 'an unintelligent set.' In January 1838 the *Sunderland Beacon* made its appearance—financially backed by Lord Londonderry and his friends—and returned fire on behalf of the Conservatives with equal vigour. For example, it described Sunderland's Liberal MP, Andrew White, as 'wandering, weak, and garrulous.'[103] It was soon incorporated with the *Northern Times*, which became the *Sunderland Times* in 1844. In the late 1840s the *Sunderland Times'* circulation was such that it was averaging 15,000 copies a year, whereas the *Sunderland Herald* reached the 100,000 mark in 1848. Both papers were published on a weekly basis and survived well into the second half of the century.

MIXED FORTUNES 1851–1918

I n a handbook for travellers published in 1864, John Murray observed as follows:

> Sunderland ranks high among British seaports, but the whole town is black and
> gloomy in the extreme, and the atmosphere is so filled with smoke, that blue sky
> is seldom seen, especially in the lower part of the town, which consists for the
> most part of a maze of small dingy houses crowded together, intersected by lanes
> rather than streets; dirt is the distinctive feature; earth, air, and water are alike
> black and filthy…. There are no fine buildings in Sunderland.[1]

Though Murray was impressed by the thriving port and the 'famous Cast Iron
Bridge over the Wear,' one wonders how many would-be visitors were put off by
his evocative, but essentially condemnatory description of Sunderland. That much
of the town was depressing has been highlighted in the previous chapter. Poverty
was deep-rooted, whilst Sunderland's industries certainly made their mark on the
sounds and atmosphere of what Henry Irving described in 1856 as 'a very large shipbuilding, coaly town.'[2]

On the other hand, Sunderland's population was not uniform. The statement
by a character in one of Disraeli's novels (published in the 1830s), that the country's population was divided
into two nations, the 'Rich' and
the 'Poor', was paralleled on
Wearside. Furthermore, the situation was more complex. Society
was not simply comprised of two
nations: there were many grada-
tions. Some of Sunderland's
population were emphatically
poor but others were better off,
in some cases only marginally
so, while the town's leading
businessmen and professional
figures belonged to echelons of
society that lived well by the
standards of the day.

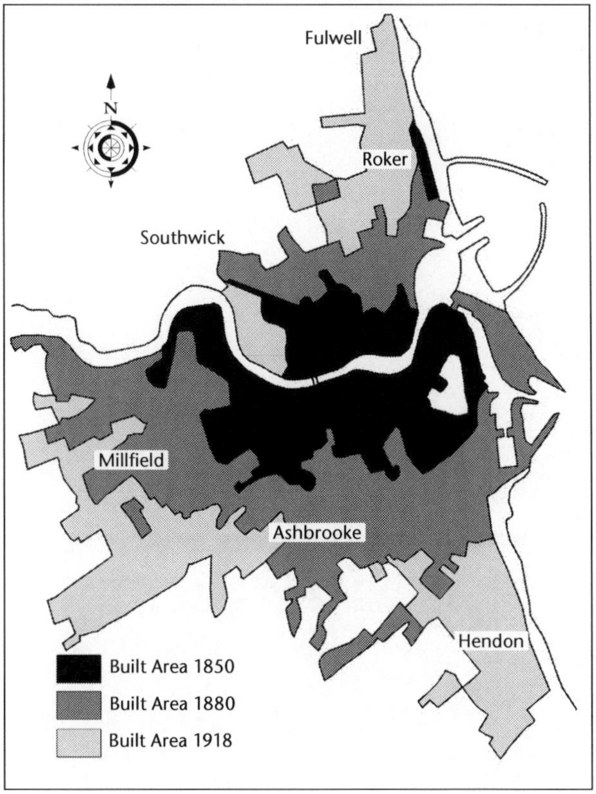

During the period dealt with
by this chapter, Sunderland's
economy generally continued
expanding and this resulted in
further population growth. In
1851 the municipal borough's

Map showing the growth of Sunderland

population stood at 63,897 people. In the decades that followed the figure increased and by 1881 numbered 116,542. The total climbed to 151,159 inhabitants by 1911, by which time Sunderland was a county borough.[3] Inevitably, this upward trend resulted in the physical expansion of the town, and the extension of the borough's boundaries in 1867 and 1895. Hence in both terms of population and physical extent, by 1918 Sunderland was significantly different to what it had been in 1851.

This was also true of some of the town's neighbours. A case in point is Southwick, which had witnessed a rapid phase of growth in the first half of the century, and continued to develop. This was especially so in the years from 1851 to 1881 when the population rose from 2,721 to 8,178. Marked growth also occurred at Tunstall. In 1851, it was a quiet township whose population was only 70 strong. Twenty years later, though, the figure was approaching the 400 mark and a meteoric rise then ensued. By 1881, in fact, Tunstall's population had soared to 4,306. In both places, industry was the driving force behind growth. Southwick's development was partly due to shipbuilding, whereas at Tunstall it was the sinking of Silksworth Colliery (which commenced in 1869) that brought about such a transformation in part of the township. The area in question became known as New Tunstall and, from 1884 onward, New Silksworth.

Housing and Social Conditions

As noted in the previous chapter, from about 1820 onward the Fawcett estate had been transformed into the principal middle-class residential neighbourhood. However, this situation did not last. Retailers moved their premises westward along High Street to attract the custom of the area's well-heeled inhabitants and during the third quarter of the century shops and offices began to encroach into Fawcett Street itself. By the mid 1880s, when Binns, one of the town's leading stores, moved

Fawcett Street from the south c.1880

from High Street to the southern end of Fawcett Street, the residential character of the latter had largely become a thing of the past. John, Frederick and Foyle Streets, likewise experienced this process of infiltration and by 1891 the former was 'sometimes termed the local Chancery Lane, from the number of solicitors' offices in it.'[4] But the change happened at a slower rate and the streets retained a semi-residential character into the 20th century.

Thus, sooner or later, the inhabitants of the streets in question moved elsewhere, most notably south to Ashbrooke and its environs, half a mile and more from the town centre. As Graham Potts has commented: 'Here was land raised above the town, away from the pollution of the river, offering the possibility of a healthy rural situation and yet within convenient walking or carriage distance of the business centre. It was ideally situated for middle class suburban development.'[5]

Although access to this area was facilitated by the construction of Burdon Road in the latter half of the 1830s (in order to link the town centre directly with Ryhope Road), residential development commenced in the middle of the century. Some of

Langham Tower on Ryhope Road. It is now part of Sunderland High School

the houses were very substantial detached properties, homes of the town's most affluent figures. Bede Tower, on Ryhope Road, was one of the first such mansions and was constructed in 1851 for the solicitor, Anthony John Moore, who was to serve as Sunderland's mayor in 1854–5. Among those that followed was neighbouring Langham Tower, completed in 1891. It was built for the shipbuilder William Adamson, and the design owes much to Norman Shaw's Cragside in Northumberland.

Many terraces were also constructed, and though less grand, some of these nevertheless provided other well-to-do families with fine homes. This was true, for example, of St George's Place built on the Grange Estate in 1855–6.[6] Measures were taken to ensure that the quality of life in such places remained high. It was, for instance, stipulated in the ground deeds of the 24 houses of St George's Place that the residents would pay towards keeping it 'in order, as a Promenade, Shrubbery, or Pleasure Ground.' In addition, at a general meeting of residents it was agreed, among other things, that the 'appointed gardeners and keepers' were 'to prevent children from swinging on the gates and trees, from trampling on the flower beds, or plucking the flowers, from injuring the trees…or playing any rough games.' Residents were also 'to instruct all tradesmen and especially milk purveyors not to allow their conveyances to be brought into the Square as the drive is only intended for carriages.'[7]

Middle-class houses were also erected north of the Wear, most notably in the Roker area. In the mid 1850s Fordyce wrote that 'the north-eastern portion of Monkwearmouth [land owned by the Abbs family]…has been much improved within the last twenty years, by the erection of the baths at Roker, with an elegant hotel and a handsome row of dwelling houses, overlooking the sea to the north of the harbour mouth.'[8] Fordyce was referring to Roker Terrace, which included *Roker Baths Hotel* and was built in the early 1840s. For many years the properties mentioned by Fordyce remained rather isolated. This continued to be the case even after the establishment of Roker Park in 1880 on 17 acres of land granted to the town by Sir Hedworth Williamson (who had succeeded his father as eighth baronet in 1861) and the Ecclesiastical Commissioners. But as the century drew to a close significant development began. Fine late Victorian and Edwardian terraces were thus built around the park and Roker became a popular suburb, described in 1904 as 'Probably the most pleasant part of Sunderland, whether from a resident's or a visitor's point of view.'[9] No doubt many of Ashbrooke's residents would not have agreed.

Numerous dwellings for working-class members of Sunderland's population were built on both sides of the river. The Williamsons played a part in this development. Fordyce relates that in Monkwearmouth during the first half of the 1850s several streets, including Dame Dorothy Street and Dock Street, were constructed 'comprising upwards of 400 houses, and affording accommodation for a considerable proportion of the increasing population of the parish.' The layout and the mostly two-storey houses, were designed by the region's foremost architect, John Dobson, and Fordyce states that the dwellings were a 'decided improvement in the domestic architecture of the neighbourhood.'[10] Later in the century, the eighth baronet followed in his father's footsteps by developing land, this time to the north of a new street, Roker Avenue. His land agent drew up an estate plan and plots were then sold to builders who proceeded to construct homes that were mostly Sunderland Cottages. One of the streets was named after the Liberal premier, Gladstone, and others were named after prominent figures, Bright, Cardwell, Forster, Hartington, Ripon, Selbourne and Stansfield, who served in his cabinet in the years 1868–74: Elsewhere, Sunderland Cottages were also constructed north of the river, at Fulwell, for example, which throughout this period lay outside the municipal boundary.

On the opposite side of the Wear, such cottages were erected to the south of Sunderland parish in New Hendon and elsewhere like Grangetown. Others were built in Millfield in the 1870s and 1880s. A significant number of Sunderland Cottages were also erected along Chester Road—formerly Chester Lane—and at High Barnes in the late Victorian and Edwardian eras (as were fine middle-class homes such as the Westlands) by which time some of the cottages were double-fronted.

As Angela Long notes,

> There was undoubtedly a hierachy within the cottages themselves, with the better built houses occupied by skilled workers [including some holders of lower middle-class occupations] on sites further away from the river—next to fields and farms—while older, smaller, less well constructed cottages were occupied by a mix of lower group workers on sites nearer the river. The estates of Pallion and Millfield were never viewed by locals as quite as 'up-market' as Barnes and Chester Road.[11]

Not surprisingly, a large proportion of the houses built for working-class folk were situated close to industrial sites like Hartley's Glassworks and the Hendon Paperworks, founded in the 1830s and 1870s respectively. Furthermore, many of the houses constructed for working-class people were owner-occupied. Indeed, owner occupancy was evidently more marked here than in most towns (this was also true of middle-class areas of Sunderland), and as Potts has commented: 'This was in part the result of the high wage rates enjoyed by skilled men in the town and in part the result of the multiplicity of small building societies that encouraged regular saving and which permitted repayments over long periods at low weekly sums that might hardly exceed normal rents.'[12]

Some inhabitants of the houses referred to above had grown up in the East End. Although they had left that part of the town, other working-class people continued to reside there and were joined by newcomers forced to settle in the neighbourhood by economic necessity.

A report on St John's parish in 1896 states that many of the small parish's large population of nearly 10,000 people had been compelled to move there for financial reasons:

> Low rents are an irresistible inducement to those who have been routed in the struggle for daily bread, or who have not sufficient energy to work regularly for a living…. Anyone familiar with their lives can feel nothing but an aching pity for these victims of misfortune…. Ill-housed, ill-fed, ill-clad, void of any purpose reaching beyond the present moment—surely the sad story of their lives must blister God's book with the recording angel's bitter tears.[13]

The same report states that the parish (formed in 1875 when St John's Church was granted parish status) was 'practically one really dismal wilderness of tenemented property' in which the houses were 'not only built back to back, but the yard spaces were also so covered with buildings as seriously to interfere with the ventilation and lighting of the dreary dwellings and to make the provision of needful sanitary conveniences a practical impossibility.'[14]

In view of such conditions here and elsewhere in the East End—and other factors such as heavy drinking—it is not surprising that the health of eastenders was not good. This can be demonstrated by reference to the infant mortality rate. According to another report of 1896, the *Report of the East End Commission to the Ruridecanal Conference*, the infant mortality rate over the last six years was 239.2 per thousand live births compared to 168.3 for the borough as a whole and 150 in the large towns of England generally! Overcrowding, poverty, and consequent ill health were not new to the East End. Nonetheless, the commissioners were of the opinion that in general the condition of the inhabitants was worse than had been the case a quarter of a century earlier.

Of the children, the report notes that they were

> generous, open to impression, but not industrious, and given to falsehood, the girls especially being dirty and untidy in person. Indeed, it appears that in personal habits and moral characteristics the girls are worse than the boys. Their character largely reflects the influence of home, where they are too often habituated to untidiness, foul language, lying, brawling, thriftlessness, idleness, taste for drink, etc.[15]

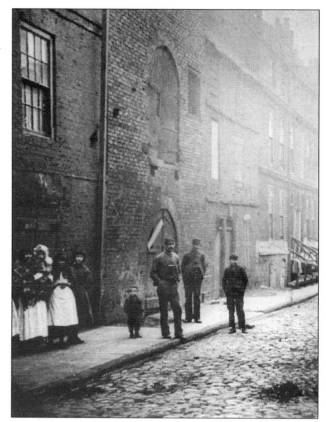

Fitters Row in the East End in 1893

Heavy drinking was, understandably, a major problem. There were 144 public houses and the report states that 'it was difficult to find at what age boys and girls do not drink, and that, though the girls do not drink so much as the boys, the case is reversed with regard to the adults, the women drinking harder than the men.'[16] Gambling was also rife: 90 per cent of the residents betted on horses. So too, was prostitution. There were 51 brothels and the ratio of convictions for prostitution was 1 in 22 in contrast to an average borough figure of 1 in 50.

Conditions in much of the East End undoubtedly shocked middle-class people, such as the commissioners, who familiarized themselves with the area. Many working-class folk likewise found the neighbourhood unsavoury. It is significant that the report on St John's parish states that 'it is not at all unusual for families who have been ministered to by St John's to leave the Parish at the first opportunity as soon as their worldly circumstances permit.'[17]

Clearly, then, some eastenders found conditions intolerable and made their escape. Others would have done the same if good fortune or ability had enabled them to leave. On the other hand, it would be wrong to assume that everyone found life grim and depressing. For one thing, some eastenders would have known little or nothing else and thus have been accustomed to their lot in life. Furthermore, there was reportedly a strong sense of community spirit.

Steps were taken by the council to improve conditions in the East End, and elsewhere in the town for that matter. For one thing, public baths and wash houses were constructed. The first opened in Hendon Road on 7 April 1851. It included 'separate departments for male and female bathers' and a spacious wash-house, of which Fordyce noted: 'The washing room is fitted up with 34 stalls, and the drying room with a corresponding set of apparatus heated by steam.'[18] Moreover, according to Fordyce, by the end of the year 15,806 bathers had used the baths and 3,914 people the wash tubs.

Baths and a washing hall were subsequently built at Monkwearmouth on land given to the corporation by Sir Hedworth Williamson, the seventh baronet. They opened in February 1854. Further baths, including a swimming bath, duly opened on the site of the former workhouse in Bishopwearmouth closed by the Board of Guardians in 1855. They did so in March 1859.

By this date Sunderland's workhouse was located on a site—now occupied by Sunderland Royal Hospital—just outside the town. The workhouse, designed by the York architect, John Oates, opened on 13 October 1855 and had accommodation for 500 people. It had its own hospital, schools, farm and mortuary, and was extensively enlarged in subsequent years.

The 1850s also witnessed the commencement of the installation of an adequate sewerage system. In October 1855 the corporation's surveyor, William Crozier, produced a comprehensive scheme for 55 miles of drains intended to improve Sunderland's unsatisfactory sewerage facilities. It was estimated that doing so would cost £83,802. His plans were adopted by the council, and in the next six years the scheme came into being.

Of the sewerage system, it was noted in 1871: 'The sewers of the town, judging from the contour of the ground, must have, for the greater part, excellent fall. They are discharged into the tidal Wear or the sea, the water within them and the pressure constantly varying with the ebb and flow of the tide'. However, the same report continues:

> The ventilation of the sewers is not satisfactory: writing from our own inspection, there is an almost entire absence of it.... The pernicious effects of non-ventilation to sewers cannot be too well known nor too strongly denounced...Gases foul and dangerous will generate within the sewers, and if exits for the gas do not exist at the *summits* of each, will find a way into the houses, out-houses, or yards.... Not alone the sewer gases may enter these improper places for their reception, but what is of greater consequence and danger, also the contagium of any communicable disease that may happen to be rife in any part of the town wheresoever, provided there is a connexion with the sewers of each locality.'[19]

Indeed, the authors of the report were of the opinion that the inadequacies of

Sunderland's sewers had contributed to the death toll in an epidemic of smallpox that had struck the town earlier that year.

Meanwhile, in 1867 the infirmary—run by a private body—had moved from the foot of Chester Road to a site on New Durham Road where the facilities comprised an administrative block, two pavilions containing seventy beds, and an operating theatre. By 1892, following additions, the premises could accommodate 214 patients. The hospital (known as the Royal Infirmary from 1911 onward) was supplemented by others, such as the Havelock Hospital for Infectious Diseases which opened on Hylton Road in 1892.

The growth of Sunderland resulted in areas such as Hendon Valley, which had been frequented for recreational purposes, being swallowed up. To offset this loss, public parks were established. Work on Sunderland's first public park commenced in 1854 when the corporation purchased Building Hill, hitherto part of the Mowbray estate, and proceeded to landscape the site, plant trees and make meandering gravel paths. Mowbray Park duly opened in 1857.

Nine years later, following the purchase of land just to the north from the North Eastern Railway, it was supplemented by the opening of the Extension Park on 10 July 1866. An iron footbridge was constructed over the railway cutting that separated the sites, thereby linking them. The parks totalled 18 acres and by 1902, at the latest, the whole area had become known as Mowbray Park. The north side of the river gained its first park when, as noted earlier, the council was given land for such a purpose at Roker in 1880. Almost thirty years later, the town gained another park when the corporation opened Barnes Park in 1909.

Mowbray Park in 2011. The area shown was formerly the Extension Park

During this period, steps were also taken to remove slums and improve the quality of housing in areas such as the East End. The Sunderland Extension and Improvement Act of 1867 empowered the corporation to 'erect improved Dwelling Houses for Mechanics, Labourers and other Persons of the Working and Poorer Classes' to rent and sell, and authorized the demolition of slum property.[20] The scale of the work that followed was not great. Among the developments which occurred was the replacement of two narrow lanes in the East End with James Williams Street in the early 1870s. The street, with homes for artisans, was named after a late member of the council who had been a leading sanitary reformer and had led the fight that resulted in the 1867 act.

Subsequently, the Housing of the Working Classes Act of 1890 obligated local authorities to inspect their old housing, and, if need be, respond to what they found. At a meeting of January 1892, it was decided that the corporation should (under Part I of the act) acquire blocks of slum property and clear them in order to make way for better housing. A report followed. In July the Corporation Health Committee resolved that this should be done with the Hat Case and Fitters Row areas, and the Flag Lane area, all in the East End—the latter was the biggest of the blocks and was dropped from the plan that developed.

Events moved slowly, for a variety of reasons, and it was not until 1903 that the first flats were ready to be occupied. The rent for a three-room flat was 5s. 6d. a week, and 4s. 6d. for a two-room flat, which it was said were the same as for comparable accommodation in the locality. Evidently, the corporation had some difficulty in letting the properties. Frequent rent reductions ensued in the next two years, thereby attracting other tenants. The flats (designed by a London firm, Angell and Berry, and constructed by a leading local builder John Brown Stott), were called Harrison's Buildings in honour of Alderman J. Harrison. They provided accommodation for about 350 people and as George Patterson has commented, 'Sunderland's first council-housing' was 'an island of good housing in a sea of slums and squalor.'[21]

Among those who took a keen interest in the poor during this period was Frank Caws—born on the Isle of Wight in 1846—who settled in Sunderland in 1867. An architect by profession, Caws was also a religious man with a strong desire to help those in need. His most well known charitable venture, aimed at helping boys compelled to beg or sell items on the town's streets, was the Waifs Rescue Agency and Street Vendors' Club.

Caws remained committed to such charitable activity until his death in the spring of 1905 at his home in Belle Vue Crescent. Posthumous tributes honouring his memory included the following:

> His was a most genial sunny, disposition, and a quiet calm, unostentatious exterior concealed a warm heart that was ever moved with sympathy with the poor.... In the ragged tattered, forlorn little street urchin, whose condition seemed positively hopeless, Mr Caws saw material from which might be molded good men and women.[22]

Religion and Education

The growth of Sunderland inevitably resulted in the continued construction of places of worship and the creation of new parishes. Under the leadership of a succession of dynamic Bishops of Durham this process happened on a notable scale following the Bishopwearmouth Rectory Act of 1867. This resulted in a number of parishes, such as St Mark's in Millfield (1872) and St Luke's, Pallion (1874), being carved out of the huge ancient parish, and in time these were themselves subdivided to create others. New parishes were also carved out of the parishes of Monkwearmouth and Sunderland, as was true of St John's (1875) in the East End and St Cuthbert's, Monkwearmouth, in 1880.

So far we have been dealing with the Church of England. Nonconformity was, however, dominant in the town and thus not surprisingly a considerable percentage of the places of worship founded were built to serve non-Anglican congregations. Owing to limited space, only some of these can be referred to. For example, in 1851–2 the Ebenezer Congregational Chapel was erected on the corner of Fawcett Street and St Thomas' Street, whereas St Patrick's in the East End (1860–1) and St Joseph's, Millfield, 1872–3 (the latter was rebuilt in 1906–7), were provided to serve members of Sunderland's Catholic community.[23] There were several Methodist groups in the town and one such, the Primitive Methodists, built a chapel in Tatham Street in 1875. During the course of this period nonconformity became increasingly respectable and consequently a number of nonconformist places of worship were built in affluent areas. Among such were Park Road Church, built by the Methodist New Connexion in Ashbrooke in 1887, and St John's erected in the same area the following year to serve the town's wealthiest Wesleyan Methodists.

Many of the new places of worship were nondescript, and this was especially the case in working-class areas. However, notable churches were constructed. This is true of the Methodist churches in Ashbrooke referred to above. It is also true of Christ Church (built in 1862–4 to serve an Anglican congregation in Ashbrooke) and of the 'New Scotch Church' on North Bridge Street, Monkwearmouth, which was erected in 1892 to accommodate Presbyterian worshippers and replaced an earlier 'Scotch' church on the same site. However, pride of place belongs to St Andrew's, Roker, built in 1906–7 for Anglicans. The church, which skilfully combines tradition with bold experimentation and a sense of grandeur with human proportions, was largely paid for

An early photograph of Christ Church

by the local shipbuilder John Priestman. It was designed by Edward Schroeder Prior (a member of the Arts and Crafts movement) and has been described by the famous architectural historian Sir Nikolaus Pevsner as: 'One of the architecturally most interesting and successful churches of its date in England.'[24] Of St Andrews, Sir John Betjeman commented, it is a '20th century building that may reasonably lay claim to greatness...a bold and imaginative

St Andrew's Church, Roker. It is Edward Prior's greatest building and 'the Cathedral of the Arts and Crafts Movement'

experiment which has triumphantly succeeded.'[25]

During the 1870s many Lithuanian Jews settled in the town, having escaped persecution. Sunderland already had a long-established Jewish community (which since 1862 had been worshipping at a new synagogue in Moor Street) and, in time, the arrival of the newcomers resulted in the establishment of another synagogue, on Villiers Street South, in 1899.

The 1870s also witnessed the arrival of the Salvation Army. This occurred in 1878. The army's work struck a favourable chord among the town's poorer classes and by 1884 four Corps had been established.

As Rosemary Sharpe has commented, it was perhaps in response to the activities of the Salvation Army that Orders of Lay Evangelists were established in Sunderland in the 1880s by the Church of England.[26] The evangelists in question were working-class men enjoined to preach to other working-class men. What is clear is that during the late 19th century the Church of England experienced a revival of its fortunes in Sunderland, as a determined, zealous, effort was made to regain ground it had lost to nonconformity. For instance, teams of visiting missioners were sent by the Church to Sunderland in 1874 and 1890 to work alongside the parish clergy, while the closing decades of the century saw active lay involvement in Anglican worship in various capacities.

It would be wrong to ignore the contribution made by women. Some, for example, held Bible classes for adults or Sunday Schools for children, or served as Church of England district visitors taking provisions such as soup, soap and jelly to the homes of the poor in their respective parishes. Two notable ladies involved in the religious life of Sunderland and its environs were Priscilla Maria Beckwith (1806–1877) and Emily Marshall (1832–1915). The former, a member of the gentry, lived in Silksworth House—since renamed Doxford Park—and was described as 'the kindest and best of women.'[27] She became an ardent Catholic and was responsible for founding a substantial church, St Leonard's, in 1872–3 at New Silksworth. The latter was the sister-in-law of two local vicars, and among other things, wrote *A Suggestion For Our Times* in which she advocated a greater role in the Christian ministry for women.

A census of worship taken on 30 March 1851 indicates that about a third of Sunderland's population attended at least one service at church or chapel that day. But as the years passed organized religion's attraction declined, despite the endeavours of the various denominations to stem the tide. The decline was most marked in poor areas. A report on St John's parish, in the East End, records that: 'The people do not attend church in large numbers. Several reasons may be given for this, lack of inclination and lack of clothing account for a percentage of absentees, but the main reason seems to be that it is not customary to go.'[28] The report, though, does note that the people did 'welcome pastoral visitation' and were anxious to have the ministration of the clergy in times of sickness or sorrow. Moreover, it states 'the parents make a special effort to send their children to the School on the day fixed for the examination in Religious Knowledge.'[29]

The religious denominations were heavily involved in education. According to an educational census of March 1851 the number of children under 15 in the municipal borough was 13,815, and of these 8,516 were on the town's school registers. There were 144 schools. Twenty-four were 'public' schools, i.e., voluntary schools provided by the various denominations with aid from educational societies and the state. On the day of the census they were attended by 3,360 children. The remaining 120 schools were private and were attended by 3,983 pupils that day.

Among the former category was the Gray School, Vine Street, which, as was customary, had separate rooms for the boys and girls. It was visited in 1853 and 1854 by the Reverend D.J. Stewart, a government inspector of schools who wrote: 'Whenever I have visited this institution at least one half of the children, both on account of age and attainments, would have been more profitably employed in an infant school.'[30] We are told that the average attendance was 392, of whom 218 were boys. In 1857 the school moved to new premises near Trinity Place on the dwindling Town Moor. Since 1838 the freemen and stallingers had had the right of placing 42 children in the school to be educated free of charge—the rate for the other pupils was 1d. a week—and this remained the case after the freemen and stallingers ceased to exist in 1853. In that year they became, by an Act of Parliament, the Principals and Guardians of Sunderland Orphan Asylum, although the asylum itself was only built in 1861.

The Gray School was an Anglican establishment and was just one of a number of Church schools. Another was the Rectory Park School, built adjacent to the old burial ground in Bishopwearmouth in 1854. The school could accommodate 600 boys and girls and was described by Fordyce as 'after the manor house style.'[31] It was

Sunderland Orphan Asylum

designed by John Dobson, and cost about £2,300, of which £777 was provided by the state. As new parishes were created, so new Church schools were founded. In 1870 the number of Church schools was 15. Among those which followed, was that in St John's parish referred to above, established in Prospect Row in 1884.

Other schools catered for children from non-Anglican backgrounds. The British School was one such. It found its permanent home adjacent to the Nile Street meeting house of the Quakers in 1856, and was attended in the main by boys from upper working-class backgrounds. For 47 years the school's head-master was Robert Cameron, an able Scot whose native tongue was Gaelic (he only learned English in his late teens) and under whom the school acquired a fine reputa-tion. Among the other denominations that had their own schools were the Catho-lics. St Patrick's c.1860 and St Benet's, 1865, were two of the schools in question, while among Methodist schools were several belonging to the Wesleyans. They had five by 1873.

This era also witnessed the opening of more private schools. Archdeacon Robert Long, who moved to Sunderland in 1883 as the new Rector of Bishopwearmouth, played a part in this process for through his initiative meetings were held which resulted in the opening of the Sunderland Church High School for Girls on 29 April 1884. The school's premises were initially 10 and 11 Park Terrace, but in February 1887 it moved to a purpose-built site on Mowbray Road. The first headmistress was an experienced teacher, Miss Mary Gilliat, who had obtained an Honours Certificate from Newnham College, Cambridge. The same meetings initiated by Long led to the contemporaneous establishment of a high school for boys. This was initially housed at 2 Park Terrace and subsequently moved to Bede Tower. Unlike the girls' school, it only survived into the early 20th century. On the other hand, another boys' private school, Argyle House (founded by James Hanna in 1884), is still in existence.

An Education Act of 1870 resulted in the election of the Sunderland School Board the following year, whose first chairman was the glass manufacturer James Hartley. Religious affiliation was a determinant in this, and subsequent, elections. In general, small nonconformist denominations with few or no schools of their own were in favour of non-sectarian education, whereas denominations such as the Catholics and the Anglican Church which already possessed a number of schools, wished to see an expansion of the existing system of voluntary schools. In its early years the board was dominated by those who favoured the latter: disunity among their opponents played into their hands. In January 1877, however, the Unsectarians finally triumphed. They dominated the board almost permanently thereafter until 1903 when, under an Education Act of the previous year, the board's duties passed to the council.

Following its establishment in 1871, the board—which covered the area of the municipal borough—carried out an assessment of the town's existing schools and found that there were 11,853 places available, while the number of children of school age was 18,169. The board thus set to work providing new schools. The first was on James Williams Street. It was built in 1874 and had accommodation for 1,000 pupils. Among the 17 Sunderland Board Schools that followed were Diamond Hall, Millfield (1878), and two in Monkwearmouth, namely Stansfield Street (1883) and Redby School (1899). Meanwhile, in the mid 1870s school boards had been established elsewhere in the vicinity, including at Fulwell, Hylton, Ford and Southwick.[32]

In 1880 elementary education was made compulsory, and in 1891 the education provided by Board Schools became free—hitherto small fees had been charged. In addition to providing elementary schools, the board also opened a 'higher-grade school' for older children—the Bede. This opened on 28 April 1890 and was situated in Grange Terrace. 321 boys and 261 girls enrolled on the first day, and the school soon attracted pupils from well beyond the borough's boundaries. The fee was 10s. 6d. a quarter, though there were some free places. The school, which had separate departments for the sexes, was enlarged and reorganized in 1905, becoming the Bede Collegiate School.

There were several avenues by which adults could enhance their knowledge. By the close of the century the vast majority of churches and chapels had institutes that included lecture halls and reading rooms. The Sunderland Mechanics' Institute (founded 1825), which moved from the Athenaeum to the Lyceum in the early 1850s, also promoted learning. The institute's secretary at this date was a remarkable young man born in 1831, Thomas Dixon, a cork cutter by trade who had a real thirst for knowledge and love of culture. He contributed to the institute's fine library and, eager to extend the cultural opportunities open to fellow working-class folk, played a part in the agitation which resulted in the opening of the Public Library in 1858. Moreover, he corresponded with many of the leading literary and cultural figures of his day, such as John Ruskin and Charles Dickens.

As Geoffrey Milburn notes, grants from the Science and Art Department of the Board of Trade helped 'educational ventures promoted by local voluntary initiative.'[33] This led to the establishment of institutions such as a School of Science and Art in Bishopwearmouth in 1869 which, after several changes of location, was housed in the Town Hall on Fawcett Street.[34] By 1897 the total number of evening students attending schools in receipt of Science and Arts grants in Sunderland was 1,430.

Mention must also be made of the Technical College, founded by the council. This opened in 1901 in Green Terrace, Bishopwearmouth. 671 people enrolled as students on the first day, 30 of them full-time. The college had four departments:

Physics and Electrical Engineering, Chemistry, Mechanical and Civil Engineering, and Commerce and Languages. In 1903 'sandwich' courses were introduced for local engineering apprentices and the college was the first in England to introduce such a scheme. Over a period of three or four years such apprentices would spend six months of each year in full-time attendance at the college, time that would count as part of their apprenticeships.

Finally, in 1908 the Sunderland Training College was founded in Westfield House (opposite the Technical College) to train teachers.

Commerce and Trade

'Sunderland is essentially a commercial town, its inhabitants being almost all engaged in business of one kind or another.' So wrote James Patterson in 1891.[35] 'The main business street' he tells us, 'is still the High Street, although it now no longer enjoys the monopoly which it has held so long, as Fawcett Street, and the Borough Road (and especially the former) ... are being altered so rapidly that these important arteries are rivalling it in handsome, well-appointed places of business.'[36] Indeed, Patterson further notes that Fawcett Street was 'decidedly the best business street in the town.'[37] For some years, since 1879 to be precise, visitors to Sunderland had had ready access to the street from the Central Station built that year in nearby Union Street.

On the west side of Fawcett Street, at the junction with St Thomas Street, were the 'handsome' banks of Messrs Woods and Co. and Lambton and Co. Both were in the Classical style, and were built in the mid 1870s and 1889–91 respectively—

High Street in the late 19th century. The domed Hutchinson's Buildings on the right (1850–1) and the exuberant Elephant Tea House diagonally opposite (1873–7), were respectively designed by George Middlemiss and Frank Caws who had successful practices in Sunderland

Fawcett Street from the south in the 1890s

the former had become Barclays Bank by 1900, and the latter Lloyds Bank by 1909. Some years after Patterson wrote his *Guide* another bank appeared in Fawcett Street. This was the York City and County Bank, built in 1902–5 (opposite Lambton & Co.) and again in the Classical style: until recently it was a branch of another bank, HSBC.

Among shops in Fawcett Street were Messrs Hills and Co., and Binns. The former was founded by William Hills in 1852 and was originally on the corner of Nile Street and High Street. It was sited at 19 Fawcett Street, and a guidebook published by the council in 1898 relates that Hills did 'an extensive business in the town and throughout the district generally.' Among other things, it had a 'choice selection of books of different kinds' and 'all branches of general stationery' were fully represented.[38]

Binns dated from 1807 when George Binns (the father of the Sunderland Chartist of the same name mentioned in the preceding chapter) founded a drapery business in High Street. By 1856, after a spell in Villiers Street, the firm had moved further west to another site in High Street. In the mid 1880s, Joseph John Binns, a grandson of the founder, moved to 38 and 39 Fawcett Street and in 1897 the business became a limited liability company, H. Binns, Son and Co. Ltd.

The shop was a fine one. The same guidebook states:

> On the first floor…are the elegant show saloons for the display of stylish milli-
> nery, in all the latest London and Paris confections, mantles, jackets, capes and
> other fashionable out-door wear, ladies' underclothing, lingerie and hosiery,
> and a comprehensive assortment of high-class out-fittings, blouses, skirts, and
> costumes, dressing and tea gowns, in all the most favourite materials and dain-
> tiest of trimmings…. The business throughout is of a good class influential order,
> the firm numbering on their books the names of many of the principal families
> resident in the district, and in addition they enjoy the general support of a wide-
> spread and increasing connection among all classes of the Sunderland public.[39]

Binns went from strength to strength and the premises were extended by the annexation of other shops to form a department store. By 1913 floor space totalled almost
two acres and there were nearly 400 staff.

Competition was provided by other local department stores, such as J.T. Calvert
& Co. Ltd, which occupied 122–9 on the north side of High Street West. The business
had been established in 1854 by J.S. Turnbull, but entered a period of significant
growth after it was acquired in 1883 by J.S. Calvert. Of the shop we read:

> Modern commercial enterprise
> in its most comprehensive form
> is embodied in the mammoth
> emporium of Messrs. J.T. Calvert &
> Co. Limited, which in the extent
> and diversity of its departments, no
> less than the magnitude of business
> transacted, is entitled to rank with
> the largest concerns devoted to the
> supply of every-day requirements
> in the North of England.[40]

Among specialist shops that also catered
for well-heeled customers were a branch
of Messrs Townsend & Co, and Messrs
Ferry & Foster. The former, which occupied 22 Holmeside from 1897 onward,
sold excellent glass and china whereas
the latter business, founded in mid century, was located at 3 Bridge Street by
1871. At that date it was run by Robert
Ferry but by 1886 he had gone into partnership with his son-in-law Frederick
Foster.[41] The business sold sheet music
and a wide range of instruments, including pianos by eminent manufacturers
like Bechstein and Steinway & Sons.

An advertisement from 1902 for Joplings, one of the
town's leading stores. The business dated from the
early 19th century

Numerous shops, of course, catered for less affluent customers and some of these were located in the enclosed Arcade, which opened in 1874 and extended south-ward from High Street West to St Thomas' Street. It was 'very much like a bazaar', comments Philip Curtis, 'and as much stock as possible was hung up outside the shops.'[42]

Shipbuilding and other employment

Turning to industry, we find that shipbuilding was still a major source of employ-ment. The census of 1851, for instance, records that there were 2,025 shipwrights in Sunderland whilst the total number of people involved in shipbuilding and related industries like sailmaking was 2,708, in other words 10.9 per cent of the town's workforce. A few years later, when the number of yards stood at, or around, 75, Fordyce wrote as follows:

> From the entrance of the harbour up to Hylton Ferry [i.e. South Hylton], the banks of the Wear, on both sides, are crowded with ship-building yards, docks, etc…scarcely an opening on the shore of the river, or a nook or crevice in the limestone rocks which overhang it, can be found, in which a ship, of large or small dimensions, is not in course of erection. Sunderland is emphatically the first shipbuilding port in the world.'[43]

In addition to well-established businesses, such as Doxford's, which moved from Cox Green (near Washington) to Pallion in 1857, and Laing's at Deptford, new yards along the riverside included William Pickersgill's at Southwick. The latter yard is sometimes said to have been founded in 1838, but actually launched its first ship in 1854.

Another new yard was Robert Thompson's, likewise at Southwick. Thompson was born in 1819 and was the son of Robert Thompson I, the shipwright who founded a yard at North Sands in the mid 1840s. Robert junior initially worked in his father's yard but, after briefly holding a partnership in the enterprise, left to found his own business in 1854.

The shipyards at Southwick lay outside Sunderland's municipal boundaries, as was thus also the case with yards further upstream like Bartrams at South Hylton. In 1871, though, that firm moved downriver to a new site at the South Docks from where it proceeded to launch ships into the sea, a unique feature among yards on Wearside. On the other hand, in the same year Osbourne, Graham and Company commenced iron shipbuilding at North Hylton, thereby starting what would become the most important of the yards to operate at Hylton.

In mid century, all the ships built on the Wear were of wood and were powered by sail, and this remained true of the majority for some time to come. The Wear's shipbuilders were slower at adopting the use of iron than yards elsewhere, such as on the Mersey and the Tyne where the North East's first iron ship was built at South Shields in 1839. In contrast, the Wear's first iron ship, the 77-ton *Loftus* was launched on 27 February 1852. It was constructed by George Clark (born at Fatfield in 1815) who had established an engineering works in Sunderland in 1848, and

The graceful *Torrens*

the shipbuilder, John Barkes. The following year, 1853, Laing's also built an iron ship, namely the 479-ton *Amity*. Subsequently the proportion of wooden ships built by Laing's fell sharply (nine of the ten vessels constructed in 1860 were of iron), and other yards likewise began making iron ships. Doxford's, to name one, did so in 1864. Consequently, by the 1870s iron was dominant. The river's last wooden ship, the *Coppermine*, was built in 1880 by William Pickersgill, who was killed in an accident at his yard in that year, by which time he had just commenced iron construction.

For a relatively short period, from the 1860s, the output of some of the ship-yards included 'composite' vessels which had iron frames and wooden hulls. These included the *City of Adelaide*, built at North Sands in 1863–4 by Pile, Hay and Co.[44] The ship was launched on 7 May 1864 and, in addition to carrying cargo, could also convey over 270 passengers. The vessel soon made its maiden journey from London to Adelaide in South Australia and over a period of years carried thousands of emigrants from Britain to Australia.

The yard that produced the largest number of composite ships on the Wear was Robert Thompson's at Southwick. It constructed 18 fine composite vessels in the years 1865–74, the first of which was aptly named *Southwick*.

In 1875 Laing's launched the *Torrens*, a composite ship that duly sailed from Plymouth to Adelaide in a record-breaking 64 days, thereby supplanting a record previously held by the *City of Adelaide*. Of the ship, the writer Joseph Conrad (who served on the *Torrens* as second mate in the early 1890s) recalled: 'The way that ship had of letting big seas slip under her did one's heart good to watch. It resembled so much an exhibition of intelligent grace and unerring skill that it could fascinate even the least seamanlike of our passengers.'[45]

In the 1880s, the steel hull was introduced locally. On the Wear, Doxford's pioneered the abandonment of iron by building four steel ships in 1883, and the transition was almost complete by 1888. The change from iron to steel was more rapid than had been the case from wood to iron. As Joe Clarke has commented: 'This was in large part due to similarities in working steel compared to iron in contrast to the profound technological change from wood to metal.'[46] Moreover, by the close of the decade hydraulic equipment—locally first used in J.L. Thompson's yard at North Sands in 1885—was in general use as a supplement to hand-riveting.

The fortunes of the industry, as always, fluctuated considerably. The mid 1880s is a case in point. In 1883 output stood at 212,313 tons. But the following year it was less than 100,000 tons, and in 1886 output was scarcely above a quarter of what it had been three years previously. The fact that Southwick's largest yard, Robert Thompson's, launched no vessel in 1887 illustrates how dire things became.

As Peter Gibson comments,

> Contemporary newspaper articles make sad reading on the distress that existed in Southwick and Sunderland among respectable working men. Acute poverty, caused solely by the want of work, resulted in families having to pledge everything in their homes to provide food and keep the rent up to date; and in many cases even clothes and bed linen were pawned to keep 'the wolf from the door.'[47]

Thankfully, as the 1880s drew to a close the situation improved dramatically. The subsequent Edwardian era, however, likewise witnessed a dramatic change in fortune. In 1906, output reached 365,951 tons. It fell to only 92,022 tons in 1908 but then began rising again. Consequently, whereas in September 1906 the Wear's yards employed 12,672 people, in 1908 this had fallen to 4,068, before climbing once again as demand for vessels increased.

When building in metal began the number of yards declined, and by the close of the 19th century there were only 13. One such was Laing's, a yard that had commenced building oil tankers (a new type of vessel pioneered on the Tyne) in the 1890s. Another survivor was Doxford's. The yard became the biggest on the Wear—by 1904 it was 36 acres in extent—and in 1905 and 1907 Doxford's headed the shipbuilding output for Britain.[48]

Inevitably, shipyards could be dangerous places in which to work. Indeed, according to unpublished work by Derek Haynes, in the years 1851–1918 at least 520 shipyards deaths occurred on the Wear, albeit 32 of these was attributed to natural causes and one was a suicide.

The second half of the 19th century witnessed the increasing use of steam propulsion for ships—the first steam propelled seagoing vessel built in Sunderland was the *Experiment* of 1845 by T. Rountree, whose engines came from South Shields. Steam-powered vessels remained very much in the minority, however, throughout the 1850s and for some years to come. The Wear's last sailing ship, the *Margarita*, was launched in 1893 by William Pickersgill junior.

In view of the gradual abandonment of sail, marine engineering became well established on Wearside and was pioneered by George Clark, who manufactured the Wear's first marine engine in 1854. One of the firms involved in such activity was John Dickinson and Son's engineering works, which had opened in 1852 at Palmer's Hill near Bonnersfield, Monkwearmouth. In addition, Doxford's opened engine works in 1878 to supply engines for their own vessels, by which time Wearside had witnessed an important engineers' strike that had reduced the working day to nine hours.[49] In the early 1900s, the Doxford works commenced a research programme aimed at developing a diesel engine, a project that was temporarily halted by the Great War but was shortly thereafter successfully completed.

Coalmining was another source of employment in the locality during this period, which saw the opening of Ryhope Colliery in 1859, Silksworth Colliery in 1873 and Hylton Colliery in 1900. Another local mine was Monkwearmouth. In May 1869 the men there went on strike following a reduction in their rates of pay, and their justifiable action resulted in contacts being made with miners from other collieries in the county where wages had likewise been cut. The upshot of this was the establishment of a union, the 'Durham Miners' Mutual Association', in November 1869. The first president and secretary of the association had both been leading figures in the Monkwearmouth strike and had lost their jobs as a result. Of the strike, Dr John Wilson, MP, the General Secretary of the Durham Miners' Association, wrote early in the 20th century, it 'was the real, although not formal, starting-point of our Union.'[50] One of the union's early undertakings was negotiating the abolition of the bond (the contract which legally bound a miner to his employer for a full year) which was generally viewed with hostility by miners.

At this date it was still the norm for boys employed in mines to work long hours. In 1872, though, the Mines Regulation Act was passed, in which the first restrictions on hours to be worked were made: henceforth boys' hours were reduced to 54 per week and limited to between the hours of 6am and 8pm.

Overall, the industry was becoming less hazardous, partly thanks to a qualified inspectorate. Nonetheless, disasters inevitably sometimes occurred as was true in Northumberland's New Hartley Colliery in 1862, when 204 lives were lost, and Seaham Colliery where 164 perished in an incident in 1880. Thankfully, none of the local pits was the scene of a comparable disaster, but tragedies certainly took place. For instance, an explosion at Washington Colliery on 19 August 1851 claimed 34 lives, whereas an explosion at Hetton Colliery on 20 December 1860 destroyed 22 men and boys as well as all the horses and ponies in the pit.

Shortly thereafter, Monkwearmouth Colliery experienced a tragic incident that happened while repair work was being done to one of the shafts. Just after midnight on Saturday 6 September 1862, men carrying out the maintenance were on a cradle (open-sided lift) suspended from a strong rope by six chains. However, a large section of scaffolding further down the shaft collapsed. It caused such a strong rush of air down the shaft as it hurtled into the depths of the pit, that four of the chains holding the cradle gave way. Hence it tipped to one side and the five men upon it (whose ages ranged from 21 to 38) were plunged to their deaths, and as Maureen Anderson comments:

> Recovery of the bodies was difficult as to reach them the shaft had to be cleared of debris and made safe. Also the bodies had come to rest in the Hutton seam where work had been temporarily abandoned because of an inundation of water. While this work was ongoing the colliery remained idle leaving nearly 600 men and boys with no work.[51]

For part of this period, Sunderland's glassmaking industry was dominated by James Hartley's Wear Glass Works, founded in 1836. The firm was important. Indeed, in the early 1860s it produced a third of the sheet glass in England. Hartley retired in 1869 and unfortunately the business subsequently declined, owing to squabbles between the partners running the firm, bad industrial relations, and strong competition from rivals at home and abroad. In fact, in 1894 the works ceased to exist. Interestingly, in the previous year James Hartley—a grandson of the firm's founder—went into partnership with Alfred Wood, manufacturing stained glass at works in Portobello Lane and this company continued in operation for the rest of this period and beyond. Among Sunderland's other glass works were Ayre's Quay Bottleworks (dating from the late 17th century) which continued production until 1880, and Diamond Hall Bottleworks founded in 1857. Three years later this firm was purchased by the politician and businessman John Candlish, who had started his working life as a child at Ayre's Quay Bottleworks.[52] Diamond Hall Bottleworks closed in 1877.

During the 1850s, Wearside's pottery industry flourished and included well established firms founded in the late 18th century such as Southwick or Scott's Pottery, Low Ford or Dawson's Pottery, and the Sunderland or Garrison Pottery. But as the 19th century progressed, the industry went into decline. Pottery from the continent began arriving in Britain in increasing quantities, aided by the lack of import duties, and by the close of World War I in 1918 the vast majority of Sunderland's potteries had ceased to exist. Of the aforementioned firms, Scott's was the last to go under. It did so in 1896 and the closure of this, the largest works, highlighted the plight of Wearside's pottery industry.

Among other industries were papermaking and ropemaking. Local firms included the Wearmouth Paper Company located at Ayre's Quay, Deptford, where paper production had commenced in around 1826. The business, whose premises were rebuilt following a fire in 1846, continued in operation until 1902 making types of brown paper.

A couple of miles upstream was Ford Mill, which had started producing paper in 1838 and was operating as J. Blackwell & Co. by 1850. Ten years later, the mill was purchased by Thomas Routledge and Company. Under Routledge (who had just arrived in Sunderland) new facilities were added and Ford became the world's first large-scale producer of paper from esparto, a type of grass with 'properties that enabled high grade printing paper to be made', and Routledge thus 'revolutionised the manufacture of fine papers in Great Britain.'[53] He died in September 1887, five months after a fire had caused serious damage to part of the plant. Production had thus ceased, but resumed in January of the following year and continued well into the 20th century. Over the years, an inadequate supply of water bedevilled the mill, which derived some of its water from an adjacent spring and the river (water from the latter had to be clarified) and so, to address the problem, the company sank a number of wells.

Meanwhile, in 1872 Routledge's stepson, Frederick Norton Miller—who had served as the manager at Ford—opened the Hendon Paper Works on Commercial Road, New Hendon. Although ownership soon passed into other hands, Miller served as the managing director for over a decade.

In 1873, the *Sunderland Times* noted that the new paper mill was 'admirably supplied with a magnificent well of pure water.' However, the plant's most notable feature was the fact that the 'manufacturing process [was] carried on in a continuous and progressive line of buildings, the locomotive taking in the raw material at one end, and the finished article being taken out at the other.'[54] The Hendon Paper Works developed into the largest mill in the North East and employed over 400 workers in the early 20th century.

There were several local ropemaking firms, including the well-known firm of Webster's, one of the leading ropemakers in the country. Webster's products were machine-made and in 1892 they produced a six-mile long steel wire rope weighing 25 tons for a colliery at Whitehaven. Other firms, though, used the traditional method of making ropes on walks, a laborious process. One such was Craven and Speeding of Roker Avenue, founded in 1860.

Breweries also existed in the town. Towards the close of the period one of the most important was Cuthbert Vaux & Sons, a business founded in the 1830s and which had been based in Union Street since 1843. In the 1870s the Union Street site was earmarked for redevelopment—the construction of the Central Railway Station—and so in the summer of 1875, under the direction of Cuthbert's eldest son John Story Vaux, the firm moved to a location in Castle Street/Gill Bridge Avenue.

Cuthbert Vaux died three years later, leaving his two sons to continue running the prosperous business. In the event, John followed his father to the grave in 1881, whereupon his young sons, Cuthbert and Ernest, became partners of their uncle. In 1896 the business became a private limited company. Two years later a young local chartered accountant called Frank Nicholson, who subsequently married into the Vaux family, was appointed manager of the brewery which now covered over two acres. Through his business acumen the firm (which employed 200 people by 1900) expanded to become a major force in the industry.

At the beginning of the 20th century, Ernest Vaux served with great distinction during the Boer War as a member of a Maxim detachment—the maxim was a machine gun—and in 1901, following his return from South Africa, the brewery issued a new product, Maxim Ale, to celebrate his homecoming. The beverage was potent. Reportedly, the ale was so strong that landlords complained that it had

VAUX'S
- STOUT.

"THE LANCET" says :

In the brewing of this Stout it is said that by paying greater attention to the operation of mashing an increased proportion of nutritive substances appears in the wort and hence in the Stout. The results of our examination confirmed this statement. At the same time the Stout is free from acidity and is yet of a ripe character. As is well known, Stout appears to be easier of digestion than beer, and doubtless in the present case this is particularly so, since the digestive action of malt has been pushed in the process of production to a maximum degree.

"THE LANCET,"

May 21st, 1898.

Analysis.

I have from time to time analysed the Stout brewed by **C. VAUX & SONS, Ltd.** I have found it to be uniformly sound and free from excessive acidity. It contains a large amount of nutritive matter, both as regards carbo-hydrate and nitrogenous food. **VAUX'S STOUT** is an extremely pure and wholesome drink.

(Signed)

LAWRENCE BRIANT, F.C.S., F.R.M.S., &c.,
LONDON.

C. VAUX & SONS.

An advertisement from the *Sunderland Yearbook* of 1902

an adverse affect on trade for patrons became slumberous after only one bottle. Hence it was duly reduced in strength.

Often overlooked, but an important source of employment, was domestic service. Indeed, census returns indicate that domestic service was the second most important source of employment for most of this period and, of course, the principal one for females. In 1881 the number of domestic servants stood at 5,293 (the figure includes charwomen and laundresses), 12.2 per cent of the employed persons returned, and in percentage terms the figure is the highest in this category. In fact, the figure for domestic service is higher than that for any other occupation in that year.

The building industry was also important and increased during this era. In 1851, 1,608 people were so employed, some 6.4 per cent of the town's workforce. In 1901 the figure was 4,299 (7.5 per cent), and by this date more people were employed in the industry than in any other in Sunderland save for shipbuilding.

A firm that expanded greatly during the years under discussion was the Sunderland and South Shields Water Company. Initially, this was simply the Sunderland Water Company (founded in 1846) but in 1852 it merged with its more northerly counterpart. The firm's commitments grew in subsequent years and by 1905 it was the monopoly supplier of an area of 115 square miles, supplying 58,374 houses and 406,282 people, a third of County Durham's population. By 1914 the company was the third largest private water company in England and Wales and had 13 pumping stations. Among these were the works at Fulwell and Cleadon, dating from 1852 and

The ornate facade of Frank Caws' Elephant Tea House built in the 1870s

1863 respectively. The company drew its supplies from deep wells. Consequently, it was able to maintain a good supply, unlike some other companies elsewhere whose surface supplies were adversely affected by drought. Moreover, the water was far less prone to pollution.

Seafaring and the Harbour

Census returns show that before 1871, more people were employed in seafaring than in anything else. In his article, *Occupations in Northumberland & Durham*, D.J. Rowe includes shipowners and barge and boatmen in this category, and the highest figure given is that for 1861 when the number of Sunderland's inhabitants in this group was 4,917, i.e., 16.2 per cent of the employed persons returned.[55] Seafaring was a harsh occupation, of which George Patterson comments:

> it could be argued that the sailor was the most exploited of all working-men. He lived in the vile conditions of an overcrowded, unventilated, leaky and verminous foc'sle, his food was often old, foul and inadequate, as owners, captains and suppliers all cheated to line their pockets. He worked harder and longer than the hardest working navvy ashore for wages less than those of most common labourers, and in every port pimps, prostitutes and publicans waited to strip him of the wages he had.[56]

It was also very hazardous. This point was made by Joseph Chamberlain, the Presi-

Ryhope Pumping Station. Designed by Thomas Hawksley, a nationally eminent waterworks engineer, it was built in the late 1860s. It was one of several pumping stations belonging to the Sunderland and South Shields Water Company. It is now preserved by the Ryhope Engines Trust

dent of the Board of Trade, in a speech at Newcastle upon Tyne in 1884—three years after losses nationwide had peaked at nearly 4,000 masters and men. 'We know,' he said, 'that the miner's is a dangerous and perilous trade, but the loss of life has never been, even in the heaviest year, more than one in 315 of the persons employed. In the case of British shipping…one in 60 of those engaged in it met with a violent death in a single year.'[57]

Well over a decade before Chamberlain's speech, Samuel Plimsoll set to work to improve the sailor's lot and much of the evidence he used in his campaign (which began following his election to parliament in 1868), came from the North East. Overloading was one of the evils he highlighted, an evil referred to in 1875 by an authority, Sir Digby Murray, as 'a disease on the East Coast', and it is evident that one of those guilty of this practice was the Sunderland shipbuilder and shipowner, James Laing.

Plimsoll's struggle was a lengthy one. In 1875 legislation introduced his concept, the load-line, but an amendment to the law gave the task of determining its position to the shipowners! It was years later, in 1890, that a new act stipulated that the position of the load-line should be fixed in accordance with rules decreed by the

Board of Trade. Even this act was not ideal: it made exceptions for small ships and vessels wholly engaged in the coastal trade.

It is interesting to note that in its latter stages Plimsoll's campaign was supported by the National Amalgamated Sailors' and Firemen's Union of Great Britain and Ireland, of which Plimsoll was the honorary president. The forerunner of the National Union of Seamen, it was founded in Sunderland in 1887 by a local man, Joseph Havelock Wilson, born in 1858, who ran a temperance hotel and coffee shop in High Street East. Wilson shared Plimsoll's desire to improve conditions for sailors and, unlike him, had first-hand knowledge of seafaring, an activity he had commenced when aged 14 and had since abandoned. The union expanded rapidly and in 1889 Wilson moved the headquarters to London.

Owing to the perilous nature of seafaring, a number of volunteer life brigades were established during the second half of the 19th century (the first was formed at Tynemouth in 1864) and Sunderland was no exception. For one thing, in the summer of 1866 the River Wear Commission set up a brigade and this shadowy body, known to have been extant four years later, was manned by its employees. Thereafter, in 1877 the current Sunderland Volunteer Life Brigade was formed. It was divided into five companies, three of which were based south of the river, and two watch houses were set up near the harbour entrance the following year. As Kathleen Gill aptly notes: 'In comparison to some other brigades, Sunderland was well funded and supported by businesses and prominent people within the town.'[58]

And what of the port? The exportation of coal, the staple export, still occurred on a major scale. In 1856, for example, 2,204,898 tons were shipped from the Wear. In

The ferry *Wear* in the late 1890s

subsequent years the amount rose—though the rise levelled off somewhat in the 1890s—and 5,117,230 tons were exported in 1904, a figure not surpassed during the period with which this chapter deals. In contrast, owing to its declining use in the shipyards, the amount of timber imported fell. On the other hand, the importation of iron, steel and ores naturally rose. In 1874, 26,561 tons were brought to Sunderland, and by 1912 the figure had risen to 132,511 tons.

To cope with demand and combat damage done by increasingly large vessels, changes were made to the harbour and docks. In the 1850s, under the direction of Thomas Meik (the RWC's resident engineer) the South Dock was expanded, thereby achieving a total water surface of 66 acres: the facilities included a southern sea outlet into Hendon Bay, completed in October 1855, thereby obviating the need for vessels using the dock to use the River Wear. Between 1864–8 the RWC supplemented the existing facilities by adding Hendon Dock to the system, whereupon the South Dock became known as Hudson Dock. Furthermore, in the next two decades all entrances to the docks were widened and, in the early 1870s, a dredging programme commenced to deepen the river and harbour and by 1914 the channel had been deepened to at least 18ft.

The RWC was also responsible for constructing breakwaters to the north and south of the piers. Work on Roker Pier commenced in 1885 under the direction of Henry Wake (born in Monkwearmouth in 1844 and an old boy of the Grange School) who had succeeded Meik in 1868. Goliath, a 290-ton hydraulic crane, lifted great blocks of masonry, some weighing as much as 56 tons, into place. The 2,800ft long breakwater, with a lighthouse containing the most powerful port light in the country, was completed in 1903—work on a comparable south breakwater, begun ten years earlier, was still in progress but in 1912 (the year after Wake's death) it was decided not to proceed any further.

Roker Pier was officially opened by John George Lambton, the third Earl of Durham, on 23 September 1903. Of the event, we read:

> The ceremony of completing Roker Pier took place this afternoon in the presence of a large and influential company. The approaches and the pier itself had been made gay with flags and banners.... At Roker large numbers of people assembled to witness the proceedings from the terraces. At the shore end of the pier was a stand upon which the band of the Northumberland Hussars rendered a programme of music.... The weather was gloriously fine.[59]

Grandees who witnessed the opening ceremony included the sixth Marquess and Marchioness of Londonderry and Sir Hedworth Williamson, the Mayor and Mayoress of Newcastle and Sunderland's MPs, Sir William Theodore Doxford and John Pemberton. These, and other persons of consequence, were conveyed along the pier by an engine and carriage to the lighthouse where Jenneson Taylor, the Chairman of the River Wear Commission, delivered a speech.

Among other things, he declared that although the construction programme had been undertaken in the face of the tremendous difficulties that hamper and retard work of such a kind in this exposed portion of the N.E. Coast…no serious mishap had occurred to this pier…and no life had been lost. The object of the scheme of building this and the South Pier, which was already far advanced, was to make the port of Sunderland available in all weather, and at all times of the tide, to all classes of vessels that traded to it or might seek it as a place of refuge.[60]

Railways, Bridges and Trams

During the period dealt with by this chapter, Sunderland's railway network expanded and new stations were built. For one thing, 1852–3 saw the advent of the Penshaw Branch.[61] The line approached from the west via South Hylton, Pallion and Millfield and then skirted the south side of the town centre (a section of its long-abandoned route can still be seen bisecting Mowbray Park) in order to link up with the Durham and Sunderland Railway at Hendon. Locally, small stations were erected along the line at South Hylton, Pallion, Millfield and to the north of the present-day Civic Centre: the latter was misleadingly known as Fawcett Street Station. The Penshaw line was opened by the York, Newcastle and Berwick Railway, soon to become part of the North Eastern Railway.

Another significant development happened in 1854 when the Marquess of Londonderry (whose dock facilities at Seaham could not cope with demand) opened the Seaham and Sunderland Railway to carry some of the coal mined in his pits to the South Dock. The line, which soon also carried passengers—it did so from the summer of 1855—was eventually taken over by NER at the turn of the twentieth century.

Meanwhile, the station that had been built on the Town Moor in the mid 1830s had been replaced in 1858 by Hendon Station, which was erected to the south and was likewise in close proximity to the South Dock complex. Just over twenty years later, this station was also superseded. Its successor, Sunderland Central Station, was constructed in the heart of the town in 1879. As part of the same scheme, a railway bridge designed by Thomas Harrison, one of the country's leading civil engineers, was built across the Wear thereby linking, for the first time, lines on both sides of the river.[62] As a result, Monkwearmouth Station (built in the late 1840s) experienced a sharp downturn in passenger use.

Sunderland's railway bridge was constructed cheek-by-jowl with a much older structure, Wearmouth Bridge. However, although erected in the 1790s and strengthened in 1804, the famous structure had received a very thorough overhaul at the hands of the renowned engineer Robert Stephenson in the late 1850s. The height of the masonry abutments was increased, most of the superstructure replaced, and a wider and more level deck provided. The original iron ribs were retained but were augmented by tubular wrought-iron arches inserted between them.

Subsequently, in the Edwardian era Charles Harrison (the nephew of Thomas Harrison) was called upon to design Queen Alexandra Bridge, which was named after Edward VII's Danish wife. The bridge was built in 1905–9 to span the river

A view of the river from about 1910, with staithes in the foreground

between Southwick and Pallion and was a joint venture by Sunderland Corporation, the North Eastern Railway, and Southwick Urban District Council.[63] The bridge was officially opened to great acclaim on 10 June 1909 by the Earl of Durham. It had road traffic at one level and a railway line above. The latter was provided to convey coal to the South Dock. Several million tons of coal were transported over the bridge annually in the early years, but by the end of the First World War the volume involved had shrunk considerably and the line was abandoned shortly thereafter.

By this date Sunderland had a well-established tram network, for 1878 had witnessed the establishment of the Sunderland Tramways Company, authorized to run trams to Roker, Christ Church, Tatham Street and the docks. The first service began running to Roker on 28 April 1879, and by 11 June routes totalling 3.54 miles had been completed. Further lines were soon added (at the council's expense) and were leased to the company. Initially, all the trams were drawn by horses. The company's first steam locomotive commenced operating on 15 September 1880 but frequent breakdowns resulted in this, and other locomotives, being discarded. Horse-drawn trams therefore continued in use. By the close of the century the council wished to take over the company, and on 1 August 1899 it received royal assent authorizing such action. The corporation soon introduced electric trams. On 31 July 1900, the first of these ran from the *Wheatsheaf* to Roker, and then to Christ Church before returning to the depot at the *Wheatsheaf.*

Recreation and Entertainment

Sunderland's inhabitants inevitably engaged in a wide range of entertainment and recreational activities.

Some well-to-do persons with literary tastes, for example, belonged to the Subscription Library. At the start of this period it was situated in High Street, but in 1878 the library moved to a fine new building in Fawcett Street. James Patterson states that the building was 'excellently adapted for giving every accommodation to members.'[64] The principal room was on the first floor, and in all, the library stocked about 20,000 volumes. The books were 'of all shades of opinion' and Patterson continues: 'When [it] is added that for the privilege of access to these thousands of books, the annual subscription is only one guinea, the advantages gained by the fortunate members can be readily understood.'[65]

From 1858 the Subscription Library, and other private libraries, were supplemented by the Public or Free Library located in the Athenaeum on Fawcett Street. Up to 1866 its books were for reference only. The Athenaeum also housed Sunderland Museum. According to Fordyce, this was 'rich in shells and other minerals besides many other curiosities.'[66] Evidently, it was well attended. The number of visitors between 1 January and 1 November 1855 exceeded 10,000.[67]

In the 1870s the corporation decided to build a more spacious library and museum just off Borough Road, in the Extension Park. The winning entry in the resultant architectural competition was that of a leading Sunderland firm, J. and T. Tillman, and the new building opened on 6 November 1879. The library was situated on the ground floor, and this was also true of the Museum Room, which primarily dealt with natural history. However, the latter was open to the roof but had an internal balcony at first-floor level. Admission was free, but prior to 1906 one had to pay to see the Antiquities Room and the Art Gallery on the first floor. Adjoining the rear of the building was a large conservatory—the Winter Garden—which housed tropical plants, several cages of foreign birds, and a pond well stocked with goldfish.

Before 1911 anyone wishing to borrow books from the library had to consult a list to see which titles were available, but in that year 'open access' to the shelves commenced. Patterson records that in 1891 the library had an average circulation of 400 books a day, and by 1902 its expanding collection numbered over 25,000 volumes.

During the Edwardian era, the library was supplemented by the opening of three branch libraries at Monkwearmouth, Hendon, and Kayll Road in 1908–9, and Hendon's was the first 'open access' library in the North East. The libraries were paid for by Andrew Carnegie, a philanthropic Scottish millionaire responsible for the founding of many libraries nationwide, and the open access policy was introduced by a colourful figure named Charlton Deas (the son of a Newcastle accountant) who had become director of Sunderland's museum, art gallery and library in 1904.

Meanwhile, in the Victorian period antiquarian societies had been founded in towns and cities nationwide and Sunderland was no exception. In response to a circular initiated by George Washington Bain (an Ulsterman who had settled in

The library and Winter Gardens viewed from Mowbray Park, c.1900

Sunderland in 1876), a meeting of gentlemen interested in forming such a society was held in the Board Room of the Industrial and Provident Building Society, Fawcett Street, on 21 November 1899. It was thus decided to form the Sunderland Antiquarian Society, and the inaugural meeting was held in the same building on Tuesday 1 February 1900. The Earl of Durham was elected the society's patron and Thomas Randell was elected its president. Randell, who had been born in Wiltshire in 1848, had become Rector of Sunderland in 1892. James Patterson, the author mentioned above, also ranked among the founder members.

In the preface of the first volume of their journal, Randell observed:

> They considered that Sunderland and its vicinity would furnish sufficient interests and abundant materials to occupy the attention of such a Society, and that the educated population of the County Borough and surrounding neighbourhood was large enough to ensure a constant supply of members whose numbers and zeal would justify and maintain the existence of such a Society.[68]

The group's first annual report proudly relates that the 'Society is in a flourishing condition, there having been 78 candidates elected and enrolled as members up to 31 December 1900.'[69] The membership was overwhelmingly middle class. Moreover, initially no women were permitted to join—the first to do so, Mrs C.H. Elliott, became a member in 1909, three years earlier than is usually stated. On the other hand, females could attend excursions to places of historic interest. For example, on 22 August 1906 ladies were present when the society visited Holy Island and had a rather hair-raising start to the return journey: 'After tea the party left the Island by brakes across the sand which proved a unique experience as the tide was up to the axles of the vehicles, thus creating some excitement.'[70]

Theatres and music halls played an important part in the life of the town. In 1851 the Theatre Royal was still operating in Dury Lane and was under the management of Sam Roxby. The theatre was located in Sunderland's East End, an area that had of course become increasingly squalid and sidelined, making patronising performances less appealing. An anonymous writer recalled in 1889: 'The Sunderland theatre appeared to have selected a hiding place where no-one could find it except the oldest inhabitants—up a narrow, dirty close, as if ashamed of itself.'[71]

The venue's prospects worsened in 1852, when the Lyceum opened in Lambton Street, closer to the heart of the town. The facilities of the new building included a concert hall, and in 1854 this was fitted up as a theatre. Although fire destroyed the Lyceum in late 1855, it was promptly rebuilt and opened again in the middle of the following year with a performance of Bulwer Lytton's *Richelieu*, in which a young Londoner, Henry Irving, who went on to become the most famous actor of the Victorian era, made his professional debut.

In the meantime, Roxby had responded to the challenge posed by the Lyceum by erecting a new Theatre Royal in an even better location than its rival. His new venue, which opened a week after the Lyceum went up in flames, was located in Bedford Street, the northern continuation of one of the town's premier residential roads, John Street, and replaced the theatre in Drury Lane.

Evidence, albeit scant, shows that in the mid 1850s music halls also operated in the town. They were located in the East End and patronised by working-class audiences. For instance, in 1859 one of the venues for music hall (also known as 'variety') included the former theatre in Drury Lane, which apparently briefly reopened thanks to a certain Mrs Ward, who was deeply involved in promoting music hall in the neighbourhood.

In 1863 the same venue (mostly shut since late 1855) entered an exciting new phase as the Wear Music Hall, whose founder was Stuart Henry Bell. His venture proved a success, so much so that in 1871 Bell replaced the building with a more comfortable and larger hall erected on the same site—while work was in progress, he briefly leased the Theatre Royal to stage variety shows. Following its reopening in October 1871, the Wear continued to flourish. As George Patterson comments: 'The Wear remained the most popular...and most financially successful venue in the town, open every night and all year round.'[72] However, in 1884 the Wear, which by then had come under pressure from tougher competition, such as the Avenue Theatre, closed down.

The Avenue Theatre, in Gill Bridge Avenue, a better part of town, opened in October 1882 and soon switched to variety. By this date the Lyceum had been

The Avenue Theatre, which opened in 1882

destroyed by fire in the summer of 1880, thereby ending its existence. On the other hand, the Theatre Royal was still operating. Its fortunes, which had sometimes languished, took a decided turn for the worse following the opening of the Avenue and in 1883 it likewise became a music hall.

Entertainment was also provided by the Victoria Hall in Toward Road, which opened in 1872 and was capable of seating 3,200 patrons. It was hired out for public meetings and entertainments by the Victoria Hall and Temperance Institute. In 1883 the building gained national notoriety. On 16 June, 183 children were crushed or suffocated to death after racing down from the gallery to gain their share of presents being distributed following a performance, only to have their progress fatally impeded by a partially bolted door. A happier event occurred at the same venue on 4 May 1896, when the visiting Tussaud Exhibition presented Sunderland's first 'moving picture' show, one of the first seen in the provinces, to an enchanted audience.

Yes, the age of the cinema was dawning, and from the early 1900s onward several venues (including the Theatre Royal) began showing moving pictures in addition to providing other entertainment. Sunderland got its first permanent cinema in the Edwardian era for in May 1906 the Monkwearmouth Picture Hall, situated in a former chapel, was opened by George Black senior at Bonnersfield. It was a great success and regularly filled to capacity, 750 people.

At this date the Avenue and Theatre Royal still ranked high among Sunderland's premier places of entertainment. In 1902 (when both houses were under the same management) the former was described as 'our local Savoy, and the most popular place of amusement in town' and the latter as 'a popular house amongst a very large portion of the populace, who throng it night after night.'[73]

For its part, in the years 1903–6, the Victoria Hall was modernised and extended before reopening on 7 November 1906 with a performance that featured Sunderland Philharmonic Society (founded in 1860) and the celebrated Halle Orchestra. Of subsequent events, Albert Anderson states: 'Under the guidance of the local authority a revitalized Victoria Hall continued for several years in its picture pioneering role, with only the very best in moving pictures being brought to the town.'[74]

In 1907 Sunderland gained another notable place of entertainment, namely the Empire, which opened in High Street West on Monday, 1 July, and was 'beautiful in every detail' and 'capable of seating over 3,000 people.'[75] Of events, we read:

> The public had their first taste of the new Empire last night, when two perform-
> ances were given. In each case the magnificent building was packed in every
> part, and the greatest enthusiasm was manifested. At a quarter to seven the first
> 'house' was full, and the audience sat expectant. Suddenly the lights were flashed
> on, the size and beauty of the interior was made evident, and there was a sponta-
> neous outburst of applause. As this subsided the orchestra struck up the National
> Anthem and the whole of those present rose. The curtains were drawn back and
> Miss Lilian Lea sang 'God Save the King.[76]

The opening night programme included Rossini's *William Tell Overture*, various comic acts and dancers. However, the star of the show was Vesta Tilley, a middle-aged music hall artist of international repute celebrated for amusing impersonations of males. According to the *Echo's* reporter, she 'had a reception the warmth of which must have been gratifying to her' and she proceeded to make 'the whole theatre ring with applause and laughter.' The critic declared: 'All her work was exquisitely artistic, and she has never done it better than last night.'[77]

The Empire, designed by Sunderland's leading firm of architects, that of William and Thomas Milburn, was owned by Richard Thornton who had been born in South Shields in 1839 and had established several places of entertainment in the North East. It proved a great success and was Thornton's favourite 'Hall of Fame.'

Another place of entertainment was the Olympia Exhibition Hall, which had opened in Borough Road in 1897. It was converted into a giant pleasuredrome two years later, with roundabouts, gondolas, and a free menagerie, and was a great attraction for several years whose shows included visiting circuses. But in 1910 the Olympia—which also showed some films—closed due to waning attendances by a public drawn to other forms of entertainment provided at venues like the King's Theatre (opened in Crowtree Road in 1906) and at a growing number of cinemas. One of the latter was the Wheafsheaf Hall at the bottom of Southwick Road, where films were shown from 1907 onward. In 1911, to mark the coronation of George V, it was renamed the Coronation Picture Palace but was soon popularly abbreviated to 'the Cora.'

In the following year, Sunderland's first purpose-built cinema, the Villiers Electric Theatre (a much grander affair than the humble Cora), opened and was soon joined by another significant cinema in Sunderland's history, namely the Havelock, which began operating at the end of 1915. Located at Mackie's Corner on Fawcett Street and High Street West, the Havelock was the town's plushest cinema and could seat 1,700 patrons, far more than some of its rivals, such as Fawcett Street's Theatre de Luxe (across the road from the Town Hall) and the Queen's Hall Kinema in Bridge

Street, the northern continuation of Fawcett Street. The arrival of the Havelock was a body blow to both of these cinemas, which had opened in 1912, and they went under in 1917.

Pleasure of a different sort could be gained by visiting Sunderland's tastefully laid-out parks. Of that at Roker, Patterson noted that there were 'Bowling Greens and Tennis Lawns, where anyone can find amusement for a small fee. The little lake

THE PARK LAKE ROKER

Roker Park c.1900

is used by the Sunderland Model Yacht Club for sailing their vessels on ... [the park] is only a few years old, and the trees are small as yet, but there is promise of considerable beauty of foliage for future years.'[78]

Of Roker itself, Patterson wrote:

> Roker is rapidly becoming a popular seaside resort in the north and it only wants better accommodation in the shape of a good hotel and more lodgings to make it the most popular one north of Scarborough. There is one hotel in the centre of the Terrace which enjoys for the present the monopoly of the little watering place. Most of the houses on the Terrace are occupied as private residences, but lodgings may be obtained at several. In the summer months excursion trains bring in visitors by the hundred, and then the sands are gay with the crowds of happy children. Boats are always in attendance for hire when the weather is at all suitable, and the bathing is decidedly good. The space between the piers is reserved for ladies.[79]

Children having fun at Roker c.1900

Although Roker was the town's main seaside resort, bathers still frequented Hendon beach. Moreover, by the early 20th century Sea Lane (or Seaburn as it would become known) was attracting a growing number of visitors and photographs of c.1910 show a promenade and facilities such as the substantial Seaburn Cafe. A finer promenade, with stone seats, was erected during the First World War.

In addition to the hotel at Roker, other hotels in Sunderland included the *Queen's Hotel*, located towards the north end of Fawcett Street, and the *Grand Hotel*, Bridge Street. The *Queen's* was established in the middle of the 19th century, and of it we read in another guide: 'This well-known and largely patronised family and commercial hotel deservedly holds a high rank among the various hostelries of Sunderland, the first place being assigned to it by numbers of the travelling public.' The hotel possessed a 'fine dining room with a capacity for over 110 guests' and the cuisine is said to have been excellent.[80] Over 40 people could be accommodated in the bedrooms and nearly all of these, like the public rooms, were lit by electricity. The *Grand Hotel*, a newer establishment erected in 1888, was likewise a fine hotel.

More numerous, of course, were the town's cafes and public houses. Notable among the latter, were the *Dun Cow* in High Street West and the *Mountain Daisy* on Hylton Road, both erected in 1901.

Sport was also very popular, both in terms of participation and spectatorship. Rowing was a favoured sport, and featured in the Wear Regatta, held between

THE

GRAND

⁕ HOTEL,

BRIDGE STREET.

Handsomely Furnished.
Electrically Lighted Throughout.
Well Lighted Stockroom.

National Telephone, 319.

An advertisement from 1902 for one
of Sunderland's finest hotels

1834 and 1914. Among local devotees were members of Southwick Rowing Club. The latter was formed in around 1890 and according to Peter Gibson soon 'developed into one of the most illustrious of its kind in the North of England.'[81] The club attracted support from figures such as the shipbuilder John Priestman and Major Ernest Vaux, as well as from numerous residents of Southwick.

Cycling, too, became popular both in terms of racing or simply for pleasure.[82] The 1870s witnessed the advent of a bicycle that became known as the 'penny-farthing', whose front wheel, above which was the saddle, was much larger than the rear wheel. Penny-farthings, used almost exclusively by well-to-do young males, were lighter and faster than previous cycles and were more suitable for racing.

On Wearside, the first of many local cycling clubs was the Sunderland Bicycle Club founded at the instigation of an enthusiast, the tailor T.H. Holding, at a meeting at the *Queen's Hotel* in May 1877. The annual membership fee was set at 7s. 6d. (beyond the pocket of many Wearsiders) and founder members included James Adamson, a shipowner and shipbuilder, and the tobacco merchant W.R. Ward. New members were chosen by ballot and one of the unsuccessful candidates was the son of a publican.

The club, whose members had to wear a uniform, held its first race meeting at Hendon in 1878 but bad weather ruined the event. Nonetheless the club continued to hold annual races into the mid 1880s, by which time Holding was no longer on the scene for he had left Sunderland in 1880.

In 1884 the club changed its name to the Sunderland Cycling Club, thereby permitting the use of tricycles, which were popular with females. In addition, at the same time it was stipulated that members had to be at least 18 years old.

Most rides took place in the evening, under the direction of the club's captain (Holding was the first) and popular destinations included Penshaw Monument and Finchale Priory. However, members were sometimes insulted by onlookers and other road users.

Some cyclists were primarily interested in racing, as was true of the members of Sunderland's Kensington Cycling Club, an all male enterprise founded in 1885 and which played a part (as did the Sunderland club) in establishing a permanent cycle track around the Blue House Football Ground at Hendon. The first race meeting there was held in the summer of 1889. The event rapidly became very popular and attracted amateur cyclists from numerous clubs in the region, including ones based at Houghton-le-Spring, Newcastle and Whitburn. In 1892, the Kensington Club had a membership of 220 and was thus the largest cycle club in the neighbourhood.

Meanwhile, in 1885 the death knell of the penny-farthing had been sounded by the introduction of the 'safety bicycle', whose wheels were of comparable size to each other. By the early 1890s, pneumatic tyres had also been introduced. Cycling thus became more comfortable and the decade witnessed an explosion in its popularity, with females taking

An illustration showing a variety of cycles

up bicycle riding in large numbers for the first time. This surge in popularity meant that the membership of Sunderland Cycle Club rose to approximately a hundred.

By the opening years of the 20th century, though, owing to the advent of motor-cars, some of the Sunderland Cycle Club's members were losing interest (as was also true of the Kensington club). The number of cycle trips dropped and a steep decline in membership occurred. The *coup de grâce* took place in 1910 following the death of the club's president, the shipbuilder George Bartram (the son of Robert Appleby Bartram) who had been the dominant figure since T.H. Holding's departure. At the Annual General Meeting in December of that year, the decision to dissolve the club was taken.

Cricket and rugby also had devotees. Initially, the Sunderland Cricket Club (founded in 1850) was located in Hendon but it later moved to Holmeside and then to a site on Chester Road.[83] Rugby, on the other hand, was a later arrival. The *Sunderland Times* of 30 December 1873 states that for a number of years it had 'been a matter of surprise' that no rugby club existed 'in a large town like Sunderland.'[84] The paper notes, however, that the situation had just been rectified by the formation of a club whose membership was almost 90 strong after only a week's existence. Many of the rugby club's members also belonged to the Sunderland Cricket Club and home matches were played at its Holmeside Ground.

Close ties between the two groups continued and in 1887 the clubs, which 'had been united in all but name for several years', amalgamated to become the Sunderland Cricket and Rugby Club.[85] The new entity began developing the Ashbrooke Sports Ground which opened in May of that year, and from the outset it was intended that other sports would also be played at the new location: provision was thus made, for instance, for lawn tennis, quoits and bowls. Ashbrooke became a sports venue of some importance and its members distinguished themselves collectively or individually. This is highlighted by the fact that between 1903 and 1912 Sunderland won the Durham Senior League Cricket Championship no less than seven times. In the latter year, moreover, the tennis player Helen Aitchison won a silver medal at the Olympics in Sweden.[86]

In the meantime, 1879 had witnessed the founding of the Sunderland and District Teachers' Association Football Club. The driving force responsible for the club's establishment was a Scot named James Allan, and in common with all the other members of the early team he was a schoolteacher by profession.

The club's first ground was at Blue House Field in Hendon, which served as its home for two years, This was followed by a succession of other grounds during the late 19th century, the longest lasting of which was on Newcastle Road, where the club was resident for over a decade from 1886.

Membership of the club had been opened to non-teachers in 1881, and its name had changed to Sunderland Association Football Club as a result. Two years later Sunderland AFC became one of the nine founder members of the Durham Football Association, and proceeded to win its first trophy on 3 May 1884 by beating Darlington 2-0 in the Durham Association Challenge Cup final. Sunderland went on to win the trophy on three other occasions, the last time was during the 1889–90 season. In the interim, on 8 November 1884, the club's first ever fixture in the FA Cup was played at Redcar where they lost 3-1.

In the early years, the team's colours were predominantly blue. These were supplanted by a shirt of red and white halves worn in conjunction with navy-blue knee-length trousers. Then, for the opening game of the 1886–7 season (by which time the club had moved to Newcastle Road), the team wore shirts with red-and-white stripes for the first time. By 1888 doing so was the norm.

In May 1890 Sunderland AFC, which had commenced paying its players a few years earlier, received a major boost when it gained admittance to the recently established Football League. The club had already notched up a number of victories in friendly matches against League sides. Indeed, on 5 April the team had thrashed one of the country's top teams, Aston Villa, 7-2, leading one of the Villa officials to declare that Sunderland had a 'talented man in every position', thereby giving rise to the tag, 'The Team of All The Talents.'[87]

Having been admitted to the Football League, Sunderland won the championship four times between 1892 and 1902, during which period football became the town's principal spectator sport. Subsequently, in 1913 (after experiencing a number of poor seasons) the club topped the League for the fifth time. Not only that, in the same year the team were the FA Cup runners-up in a match played at Crystal Palace.

By this date Sunderland AFC's home had long ceased to be on Newcastle Road, for it had moved to new premises, Roker Park, opened on 10 September 1898 by the sixth Marquess of Londonderry. The first game at the new ground was played the same day and was eagerly watched by a capacity crowd of 30,000. Various changes ensued, and by the outbreak of the First World War in 1914 Roker Park could hold 50,000 spectators.

Politics and Newspapers

In 1851 Sunderland's MPs were the Liberal baronet, Sir Hedworth Williamson, a Whig, and the Tory businessman, George Hudson. In the general election of the following year Williamson declined to stand (his seat went to a fellow Liberal, albeit a Radical, William Digby Seymour), while Hudson returned to parliament with the greatest number of votes, 866. Hudson told the electors: 'You have supported me in many trials.... When all had forsaken me, Sunderland has remained firm to me. My right hand shall forget her cunning before I forget the favours I have received at your hands.'[88]

By this time Hudson's reputation nationally had been seriously dented owing to his dishonourable business dealings. Here, though, many people were still willing to vote for him owing to the prominent part he had played in bringing about the construction of the South Dock. In-fighting among Sunderland's Liberals who, as noted, were divided into Whigs and Radicals, also helped him to retain his seat. Instead of giving both their votes to the Liberal candidates many gave their second vote to Hudson. These factors enabled him to do so again in the election of 1857, although on this occasion a Whig, Henry Fenwick, topped the poll.

Hudson's luck ran out in 1859. For several years his parliamentary attendance had been, to put it mildly, erratic and many people's patience and gratitude had finally evaporated. Moreover the Liberals were temporarily united, partly owing to their candidates' support for further parliamentary reform (unlike Hudson) and a strong desire to oust the Tory. Hence, Fenwick and William Schaw Lindsay, a Radical, were elected: Hudson finished a poor third.

The 1865 general election witnessed the victory of the Conservative businessman James Hartley (the other successful candidate was Fenwick), who just gained more votes than the Radical, John Candlish. The latter, who had been a Tory as a young man, was however to join Hartley in parliament following a by-election in 1866. Hartley retired at the next election, that of 1868, by which time Sunderland's registered electors had grown from 3,468 in 1866, to 11,364 as a result of the 1867 Parliamentary Reform Act. In the election, Candlish and another Radical, Edward

Temperley Gourley, triumphed and as Patricia Storey has commented: 'The 1868 election in Sunderland is most notable for deciding the power struggle within the Liberal Party in favour of the Radicals.'[89]

In subsequent contests the winning candidates were always Liberals, even when, in 1886, there was a strong swing to the Tories nationally. Then, in 1895, the shipbuilder William Theodore Doxford became the first successful Tory candidate since Hartley. He took the seat of the businessman Samuel Storey, one of the town's MPs since 1881, whose defeat was partly due to a an effective smear campaign waged against him by a local newspaper, *The Post*, which among other things made dubious allegations about his record as a local employer. Doxford topped the polls, a result in line with events nationwide. Five years later he retained his seat and was joined by a fellow Tory, the Etonian, John Pemberton.

On the eve of the 1900 election, Edward Temperley Gourley, who had

The politician and businessman,
John Candlish, (1816–74)

proved a good MP and had represented Sunderland continuously since 1868, resigned on the grounds of ill health: he died within two years. Before beginning his parliamentary career, Gourley had also served as a town councillor and had been Sunderland's mayor in 1864, 1865 and 1867.

By 1906 Conservative fortunes nationally were on the wane. This was also true in Sunderland for in the election of that year Pemberton and David Haggie were resoundingly defeated by the Liberal, James Stuart, and the Labour candidate, Thomas Summerbell, a member of a new political party who thus has the distinction of being Sunderland's first Labour MP.[90] A major issue by this date was whether Free Trade should be allowed to continue. Stuart and many other Liberals answered, 'yes', as did Labour's Summerbell. Others, Storey for one, agreed with many Conservatives that tariffs should be imposed on imported goods to safeguard British agriculture and industry. In the next general election, that of 1910, the victors were Storey (who stood as an Independent Tariff Reformer) and a like-minded Tory, the shipping magnate James Knott. The result is said to have been partly due to Storey's eloquent argumentation in favour of Tariff Reform. Another election was held later in the year, though. On this occasion, Storey and Knott declined to stand on grounds of poor health. Consequently, the seats were won by the Liberal, Hamar Greenwood, and the Labour candidate Frank Goldstone. They were to serve as Sunderland's MPs throughout the First World War.

Space does not permit more than a cursory discussion of the council. A prominent councillor in the mid 19th century was the former Chartist, James Williams, who was elected in 1847 and was keenly interested in 'moral and social reforms.' He played a part in bringing about the Sunderland Borough Act of 1851 (which vested the powers of other local bodies, such as the Improvement Commissioners, in the council) and later led the campaign to secure more powers for the corporation which resulted in the 1867 Sunderland Extension and Improvement Act. Among other things, as a result of the extension of the borough's boundaries, two new wards, Hendon and Pallion, were created. Moreover, the act authorised the council to borrow money to pay for the compulsory acquisition and demolition of specific blocks of slums within the next ten years.

In 1869, the year after Williams' death, another interesting individual, to whom reference has already been made, namely Samuel Storey, became a councillor. He was born at Sherburn near Durham City in 1841 and, in late 1864, settled in Monkwearmouth which was to serve as his political power base and whose condition he worked to improve by implementing clauses of the 1867 act. Storey was a Radical, and the 1870s witnessed the emergence of a dominant Radical group in the council under his able leadership. He became mayor in 1876 and held the office again on two occasions. The Radicals' ascendancy gradually waned during the 1880s. This was partly due to Storey's election to parliament in 1881, which deprived them of his strong leadership.

By this date an Act of Parliament had removed the property or rating qualifications required for town councillors, thereby allowing working-class men to stand for

Samuel Storey (1841–1925), a dynamic
newspaper-owner and politician

election. The first, locally, was Thomas Smith, a glass mould maker who was elected in 1882, two years after the act came into being. Smith was a Liberal. The first Labour councillor, Henry Friend, was elected in 1891. For many years Labour's strength on the council was weak. As Patricia Storey has commented, 'by the outbreak of World War I there was still only a handful of Labour councillors and it was not until 1935 that they became the majority party on the Council.'[91]

Since the corporation's inception in 1835, meetings had been held in the Exchange Building and a magistrates' court on East Cross Street. In 1873, the council decided to hold an architectural competition for a suitable town hall that would be built on land at the north end of the Extension Park, now part of Mowbray Park. One of the entrants was Frank Caws, an able and idiosyncratic architect who had settled in Sunderland in 1867 and had started his own practice in Fawcett Street in 1870. In the event, legal proceedings brought the scheme to nothing: only buildings of a recreational nature that would be freely open to the public could be built on the land in question. Several years elapsed before land was purchased for a town hall on Fawcett Street. Another architectural competition was announced in 1886 and was duly won by an architect based in East Anglia named Brightwen Binyon. The resulting town hall was officially opened on 6 November 1890 by the mayor, Robert Shadforth, a staunch Liberal who had first been elected to the council in 1875. Later, it was aptly noted: 'the Town Hall is a fine building, whose beauty is never fully appreciated owing to its cramped position.'[92]

The town's newspapers continued to play a part in local politics, as was true for example of the *Sunderland Herald*, which dated from 1831 and had always supported the Whigs. In contrast, the *Sunderland Times* (which first appeared in 1844) championed the Tories until it was purchased by James Williams in 1857, whereupon it became an effective mouthpiece for the Radicals who had earlier enjoyed some badly needed favourable press coverage in the pages of the *Sunderland News*, which existed in the years 1851 to 1855 and was set up by John Candlish to do just that. While Candlish's short-lived paper failed to attract enough advertisements and ran at a loss, the *Sunderland Times* continued in existence until 1878, although over the

Sunderland Town Hall. Designed by Brightwen Binyon
of Ipswich, it opened on 6 November 1890

years its political stance became increasingly moderate. The paper appeared twice-weekly from 1862 and, in 1876, changed to daily publication in the face of strong competition, most notably from the *Sunderland Daily Echo and Shipping Gazette*.[93]

Founded in 1873, the *Echo* was the town's first successful daily evening newspaper and its first issue, which numbered four pages, appeared on 22 December.

The first editorial declared:

> The present issue is a modest attempt to repair the disadvantage under which our borough labours, to supply the widely acknowledged want of a full daily report of local and general events.... One special feature...will be our shipping news. Those whose fortunes are embarked in shipping, and those who have friends and relatives...exposed to the dangers of the seas, alike will find in our columns the latest and most perfect intelligence obtainable.

One of the founders of the *Echo* was Samuel Storey, and the paper was staunchly pro-Radical. The *Sunderland Daily Post*, established in 1876, had a different stance. It was created by Tories to serve their cause. In the summer of 1881, the *Sunderland Herald* (which had recently gone over to daily publication) was sold to the *Post* and the papers were merged as the *Sunderland Herald and Daily Post*.

Of local papers, Maurice Milne has observed: 'A sense of humour was not a pronounced characteristic of the conductors of Sunderland journalism. The usual political confrontation was accompanied by a degree of personal rancour rarely approached in other newspapers centres of the North-East.'[94]

The War Years

In 1980, when reflecting on the start of the 20th century, the former prime minister Harold MacMillan declared: 'Everything would get better and better. This was the world I was born in....Suddenly, unexpectedly, one morning in 1914 the whole thing came to an end.'[95]

The onset of the First World War was indeed a turning point in history, and the lives of Sunderland's inhabitants were, to varying degrees, affected by the conflict. News of its commencement arrived shortly after midnight on 5 August and was related to a bellicose crowd gathered outside the *Echo* offices.

During the course of the next four years around 18,000 of the town's menfolk served in the armed forces and Philip Hall has stated: 'Probably about a third of them were killed or wounded.'[96] Wearsiders served in various regiments, most notably the formidable Durham Light Infantry that included units raised locally such as the 20th (Service) Battalion whose history has been admirably traced by John Sheen.[97]

The veteran of the Boer War, Colonel Ernest Vaux, likewise served in the DLI. He commanded the 7th battalion, fought in France and Belgium, and was among other things twice mentioned in despatches for his gallantry. It is certainly a malign myth that officers generally avoided exposing themselves to danger, for in percentage terms the British Army actually lost more junior officers than it did rank and file.[98]

Sunderland's shipyards made a fine contribution to the war effort. Not surprisingly, during these years (by which time pneumatic tools had just come into use) the yards were very busy and owing to the departure of many men to the front, women became part of the workforce in 1916. In addition to naval craft, such as 21 torpedo boat destroyers built by Doxford's, many merchant vessels were constructed. In 1915 the number was 31 (111,329 gross tons) and this steadily increased to 60 vessels totalling 267,759 tons in 1918. In short, during the war the yards mainly produced merchant ships and these totalled approximately 900,000 tons. King George V and Queen Mary visited the shipyards on 15 June 1917 in recognition of the services rendered.

The town's marine engineering firms likewise played their part. One such was Dickinson & Son, established in 1852. In addition to producing engines totalling 112,240 hp during the war years, the firm 'carried out repair work for torpedo boats and machining on Hotchkiss guns for the Admiralty.'[99] For its part, Doxford's wartime production included the making of boilers capable of providing over 400,000 shp for naval vessels.

In addition to serving in the shipyards, women were also drawn into other occupations normally performed by men. For instance, in June 1915 the first 10 female conductors began serving on the town's trams and by the close of the war all 87 conductors were women.

The war also affected Sunderland AFC. One of the greatest players in the history of the club, Charlie Buchan, stated that owing to the hostilities there was little interest in the game. At the end of the 1914–5 season, League football was suspended and remained such throughout the remainder of the conflict. The majority of the Sunderland team joined the Army and Buchan—who enlisted with the Grenadier Guards—was one of two members of the disbanded squad who won the Military Medal.

The enemy brought fear and bloodshed to the homefront, although on one occasion the attempt to inflict harm backfired for on 23 February 1917 a submarine, SM UC 32 commanded by Herbert Breyer, blew up a short distance from Roker Pier. The U-boat was laying mines and detonated one of its own devices. Three of the crew survived but 19 lost their lives.

Sunderland's worst experience of the war occurred on Saturday 1 April 1916 when a Zeppelin flew over Wearside in an easterly direction, heading down the river. As it did so, it dropped high explosive bombs and incendiaries on Monkwearmouth, causing death and destruction around the *Wheatsheaf* and further east in, for example, Whitburn and Victor Streets. Among the casualties were people sheltering in a tram at the *Wheatsheaf*. In all, the Zeppelin's deadly cargo killed 22 people and injured over 100.[100] One of the eyewitnesses of the raid was Richard Wake, who recalled years later:

> I was coming towards North Bridge Street and was close to the *Wheatsheaf* when
> the tram was blown up. I was about fourteen…and had never been so scared in
> my life. The noise was terrible. People were running all over the place. There was
> a lot of screaming and I could see bodies being pulled from the tram.[101]

A reminder of the Zeppelin threat still exists. At Fulwell there is a concrete acoustical mirror, principally comprising a 11ft high rear wall 18ft long, containing a 15ft mirror. The date of construction is uncertain: such dishes were built from 1917 into the post-war period. Designed to give warning of approaching airships, the mirror would reflect a signal to a collector head and then to a receiver. Noise of an approaching Zeppelin could be picked up some fifteen minutes away, its course plotted, and defensive measures taken.

Little over a year after the Zeppelin's deadly raid, other Wearsiders lost their lives late on the evening of Thursday, 24 May 1917, when a biplane that had taken off at a nearby aerodrome (founded the previous year and later known as RAF Usworth) flew over Southwick. It was piloted by Lieutenant Philip Thompson, who took to the air and headed towards the sea in order to test a newly fitted gun. Upon returning, he flew low over Southwick green, eagerly watched by a crowd that had gathered for an outdoor meeting. As Thompson did so, sunlight affected his vision and he hit a flagstaff located in the centre of the green. His plane came crashing to the ground at the west end of the green, killing two people, fatally wounding three others, and injuring eight less severely. Thompson was exonerated of any criminal negligence at an inquest.

The hapless outdoor meeting at Southwick had been held to discuss ways of

An acoustical mirror at Fulwell, designed to help counter Zeppelin activity

using food in an economic manner, for food shortages were experienced during the war. Indeed, in 1918 rationing was introduced. Fortunately, by this date the bloodshed was drawing to a close and the end of the conflict—which had made an indelible impression on the lives of countless Wearsiders—was announced on 11 November of that year.[102]

BETWEEN THE WARS

In the popular imagination, Britain between the wars was a land of mass unemployment and poverty, hardship and misery—the land of the Jarrow March—a land unfit for heroes. There is truth in this, but it is not the whole truth. It is only part of the picture, not the whole canvas. Inter-war Britain did witness positive developments and this is true of areas worst affected by the Depression such as Wearside. Hence the Sunderland of 1939 was, in large measure, a very different place to what it had been at the end of the Great War.

Nonetheless, the lives of countless thousands of Wearsiders were affected by unemployment during this period, a situation that caused untold despair and suffering. At first, however, in the years immediately following the war, it was a different story. The shipyards (the great powerhouses of the local economy) were buoyant as vessels were constructed to replace those lost during hostilities, and because of the high levels of world trade. Boom and slump have always characterised the industry and thus it is not surprising that the situation changed in the early 1920s as demand contracted.

It continued doing so until 1926, after which there was an improvement. Sadly, the upturn proved brief. Events far from Wearside were the cause. In October 1929 the Wall Street Crash happened and the collapse of the U.S. money market had a domino effect. Shares elsewhere likewise plummeted and stockbrokers took to jumping off high buildings in despair. Others fell too, figuratively speaking, including many Wearsiders for the collapse of the money markets resulted in a worldwide economic disaster—the Depression.

Unemployment therefore became a marked feature of life in Sunderland. It had, of course, already been a serious problem during the slump years of the 1920s, peaking at about 19,000 in 1926, the year in which the nationwide General Strike took place.[1] Now, though, it became even more acute. Just how many people were unemployed is uncertain for most women were not entitled to benefit and so do not appear in the statistics, while from 1931 onward the government stopped counting individuals deemed to have scant hope of ever working again. Nevertheless, the general course of events is clear. Figures for registered unemployment show that in February 1930, the number of people registered at the town's three labour exchanges totalled 11,339. The situation then worsened dramatically. In May of the following year the number had risen to 24,163. A year later it stood at 27,322. It continued rising, reaching a peak of 29,071 in May 1934.[2] However, as bad as things were they were not as bleak as in nearby Jarrow. There, in the previous year, unemployment reached 77.9 per cent.

Jarrow's plight was caused by the closure of the town's main employer, Palmer's shipyard, founded in 1851. Sunderland's mass unemployment was in large part also due to the disastrous effect the world economic collapse had had on the shipbuilding industry. This is highlighted by the census of 1931. Total male unemployment on Wearside was 36.6 per cent, of whom about two-thirds had worked in the yards or associated industries.

Unemployment would have been even greater if it had not been for migration. The areas hardest hit by the Depression were those, such as Wearside, heavily reliant on old industries like coalmining and shipbuilding and whose remoteness from markets made them unattractive to would-be employers. Most new factories opened elsewhere, particularly in London and the Home Counties. They had more appeal to industrialists who, owing to the development of electrical power, were no longer constrained in their choice of site by their reliance on coal. Consequently, migration from the most depressed areas occurred and occurred on a significant scale. This is illustrated by the fact that County Durham's population fell during the 1930s while that of England as a whole rose. Many of those who moved were from Wearside. As George Patterson notes, Sunderland's population fell from 185,903 in 1931 to 182,400 in 1938 and this was despite the fact that the birth rate always exceeded the death rate throughout this period.[3]

After 1934 unemployment did decline (though at a slower rate than the national average) until 1937 when the improvement ground to a halt. Thus, on the eve of the Second World War, the number of people without work in Sunderland was still high. In June 1939 the figure in receipt of unemployment relief was such that Sunderland was emphatically at the bottom of a league table of 47 large towns in England and Wales.

Most of the people who lost their jobs during the inter-war years had been insured against unemployment and were therefore entitled to benefit owing to the contributions they had made. Under the Unemployment Insurance Act of 1920 they were entitled to 15 weeks of benefit in any one year and this was subsequently extended to 26 weeks. From 1931 onward a stringent test was applied to those wishing to continue receiving benefit. This was the means test. It took into account savings, assets, and the incomes of any members of a household. Attempts at evasion were commonplace. Possessions, for instance, were spirited away temporarily so that they did not have to be sold in order for the family to qualify for benefit. Of the deeply unpopular means test (conducted by Public Assistance Committees), Charles Mowat has commented, it was 'an encouragement to the tattle-tale and the informer, the writer of anonymous letters and the local blackmailer; to all sorts of unneighbourliness.'[4]

And what of people such as civil servants and domestic servants who had been excluded when unemployment insurance was extended to the vast majority of workers in 1920? If they lost their jobs they had to go 'on the parish' where the payments came out of the local rates—unlike the benefit referred to above which came from the Treasury—and were even less generous. A means test also applied and prior to an Act of Parliament of 1929 this was conducted by the Poor Law Guardians. In that year the Guardians were replaced by Public Assistance Committees nationwide. The position of those 'on the parish' locally improved after Labour gained control of the PAC on 9 November 1934. Payments were immediately increased. A couple's income, for instance, rose from 20s. to 26s. a week.

By this date the bulk of the unemployed were the responsibility of a government-financed body, the Unemployment Assistance Board, formed as a result of legislation passed in 1934 and so the local PAC, like others elsewhere, lost much of its importance.

The Standard of Living

It must not be supposed that all families in receipt of unemployment benefit were worse off than had been the case before work was lost. Financial assistance was based on the individual needs of the members of a household—unlike, of course, a wage—and therefore some families were actually better off. For most, though, unemployment brought hardship. Inevitably people did what they could to supplement their income. Florie Kendray, whose husband was out of work, has recalled:

> Many's the time I've put two bairns in the pram and walked with them [from the East End], to the tip at Seaham Harbour. When I'd got as much in the sack as the pram would hold I'd take the elder bairn out, put the coal in then sit him on top of the sack.... Sometimes I'd go with my husband to Ryhope Beach and sit on the bank top in the middle of the night till the tide went out. We'd pick sea coal, he'd carry his sack home on his back, I'd carry mine on my head.[5]

The Old Arcade, an indoor market in the
East End photographed in 1930

It was not just in a financial sense that unemployment had an effect. Psychologically and physically, too, it made an impact and family life was often adversely affected by tension and despair. In a paper read to the British Assembly in 1936, a Dr R.D. Gillespie stated that it was his experience that 'among the working classes unemployment is more apt to affect the nervous condition of the mother of the family' than that of the spouse.[6]

Understandably, the burden of trying to care for loved ones with less money took its toll, as did depriving oneself for the children's benefit. Such self-sacrifice on the part of mothers was commonplace. A report based on findings in England and Wales in 1936 stated: 'All of us are agreed that in most unemployed families, the parents, and in particular the wives, bore the burden of want, and in many instances were literally starving themselves in order to feed and clothe the children reasonably well.'[7] Certainly unemployment affected them to a greater degree than it did the young men J.B. Priestley came across on his travels around England in the autumn of 1933, men whom he described as 'undisciplined and carefree, the dingy butterflies of the back streets.'[8]

Women in Sunderland undoubtedly put their families before themselves and suffered accordingly. One consequence was a rise in the rate of maternal mortality. Average maternal mortality in 1926–30 was 4.01 per thousand births, but this rose to 5.22 per thousand for 1931–5, a rise of 30 per cent—the average for England and Wales in the latter period was 4.3. Furthermore, in the same periods stillbirths rose from 36.6 to 39.8 per thousand.[9]

It was not just families affected by unemployment that experienced dire circumstances. For one reason or another, many others had to make do as best they could. Grace Daly (whose father worked in the shipyards) belonged to one such. Of her childhood in the early years of this period, she recalled:

> We slept five to a bed, top to toe. There were thirteen of us living in two rooms.... We never had cups. My father used to take these empty tins of condensed milk, smooth all round the jagged edges, and then he soldered metal handles onto them, fettled cups for us. We never thought there was owt to be ashamed of, only how clever he was to think of it.... My mother learned to make and mend, she could create a meal out of next to nothing. We learned to be frugal.

Though poverty existed throughout the period, it was not universal. Wages fell during much of the era, but they did not fall as far as the cost of living which, despite rising again from 1933, was 35 per cent below the 1920 average in the summer of 1939. Consequently, real incomes (people's spending power), increased, that of the average wage earner by about 18 per cent. The period also witnessed a reduction in the birth rate. This fell from 30.7 per thousand in 1929 to 18.5 in 1939, and in part this was due to aspirations for a better standard of living.

Enhanced spending power enabled people in general to purchase a wide variety of goods, and so the inter-war years, and particularly the 1930s, saw a great growth in the consumer and service industries. Locally, department stores such as Binns, Joplings and Blacketts prospered.[10] Rayon stockings, chocolate bars and ice-cream, were just some of the cheaper consumer goods that were increasingly in demand. More expensive items were often bought on hire purchase. In the mid 1930s when working-class incomes seldom exceeded £4 a week, and were generally substantially lower, electric toasters could be bought from about 17s. 6d., electric clocks from about £1, and wirelesses costing upwards of £5 were commonplace. Among the well-to-do car ownership increased, with lower range models such as the Austin 7 costing about £100. Houses could also be purchased from around £300, and in March 1934 new semi-detached homes on Side Cliff Road in Fulwell were advertised as costing £565.[11]

And what of the state of public health? Though, as noted, the Depression had an adverse effect on some people, on the whole a general improvement in the state of health occurred between the wars.[12] There were no cases of smallpox in Sunderland after July 1929. In addition, despite fluctuations, deaths from diseases such as bronchitis, tuberculosis and pneumonia fell. The overall death rate dropped from 16 to 14 per thousand between 1920 and 1939. Furthermore, malnutrition and rickets became increasingly rare.

Smartly dressed Wearsiders in 1928

Changes in the medical facilities also happened. In the 1920s, for example, the Royal Infirmary on Durham Road was extended. Moreover following the abolition of the Board of Guardians in 1929, a hospital located in part of the buildings of the workhouse erected in the Victorian era on Kayll Road, came under the corporation's control and was henceforth known as the Municipal Hospital. North of the river, in 1932 the Monkwearmouth and Southwick Hospital (founded in 1873 on Roker Avenue) moved to new premises on Newcastle Road.

The improvement in health noted above was mitigated by overcrowding, which remained a significant problem and in 1926 the town's newspaper noted that 'deplorable' conditions existed in the East End where, for example, three adjoining houses were occupied by a total of 59 people who shared a water tap, two water-closets and a yard 14ft by 9ft.[13] Indeed, according to the census of 1931, Sunderland was the most overcrowded county borough in England and Wales. Overcrowding was measured as a density of more than two people per room, and on this basis 19.2 per cent of the borough's families were overcrowded—the worst place in London's East End, Shoreditch, had 18.4 per cent of its families residing in such circumstances. Subsequently, when a census of overcrowding was undertaken by the council in 1936 on the basis of two or more per room (as required by the Housing Act of 1935), 20.6 per cent of Sunderland's families were found to be in this category.

Living conditions for some Wearsiders were certainly very poor, a point noted by George Reed, who lived in the East End during the 1930s:

> The houses in our area were mainly tenements. Some were like slums...and there were usually plenty of rats about.... We lived in two rooms.... In one room there was a large double bed for mother and father and a sideboard bed which I shared with my two brothers. The other room was the kitchen and also had a bed in it which my sisters shared. Eventually the two rooms housed my parents and ten children.[14]

Appalling conditions existed elsewhere, as the author Vera Brittain discovered when she visited Sunderland in November 1935. Her diary entry for Thursday 7th contains the following:

> Went round Monk Wearmouth housing...[and saw] terrible slums, & crowded rooms with indescribably filthy bedding. In one house saw family of man & woman with nine children all living in two rooms—man an ex-serviceman who had never had a job since the War; woman looked very ill, shapeless & entirely overwhelmed by life. Children only semi-clothed. The couple had been there 20 years & obviously had not turned out the rooms all that time as there was nowhere but the street to put the furniture. Realised as so often what an expensive luxury cleanliness is. Have never seen such terrible housing before—not even in Glasgow.[15]

Local authorities tried to improve matters. For one thing, shortly after the war they started to provide new homes to meet growing demand. In the 1920s Sunderland Corporation undertook major council house building at Plains Farm. Moreover, in 1920 Southwick Urban District Council purchased farmland at Marley Pots for housing. Six years later, it was reported that since the war the UDC (which would soon cease to exist) had erected 214 homes, mostly at Marley Pots, and that further dwellings were planned.[16]

Nationally, the 1930s witnessed a housing boom, partly due to slum clearance programmes. Sunderland played its part in this development with both private and council houses being constructed. For instance, 1,002 council houses were built on 'greenfield' sites between 1931 and 1935 at estates such as Ford, Marley Pots and High Southwick, and their provision played a part in improving the state of public health.[17]

Prior to removal from condemned slum homes, tenants' possessions were disinfected, except for verminous articles inspectors considered too infected, which were destroyed. Consequently, Sunderland's Medical Officer of Health was able to note: 'A survey made of Council houses into which slum clearance tenants have been moved has shown that 2 per cent only have been found to be re-infested.'[18]

The same report contains the findings of a survey made of 445 families moved to the new estates, primarily those named above, since 1933. The families (comprising 2,250 people) had previously occupied 881 rooms at a rental of £123 17s. 5d. a week. Between them they now had 1,671 rooms with the addition of baths, sculleries, separate WC's, gardens and amenities, for £205 1s. 10d. The average weekly increase in rent per family was 3s. 8d. Nonetheless, 91 per cent of the tenants said that they were satisfied with the move. 'Better house and plenty of good air', and 'hot and cold water a luxury, garden a pleasure, and health improved', were some of the favourable comments.[19]

Among those dissatisfied, the distance from shops, buses and schools were subjects of complaint as was the rent. Moreover, 60.2 per cent of the families surveyed were of the opinion that the cost of food was higher in the new neighbourhoods. The average income of the families was £2 3s. 4d. per week. After expenditure on rent etc, each had an average of £1 2s. 3d. for food and so it is not surprising that 22.7 per cent of the families answered 'yes' to the question is any member of the family short of proper foodstuff? In addition, other respondents admitted that they could do with more food.

Religion and Education

During the inter-war years, church and chapel attendance continued to decline and in some cases spirituality was undermined by hardship. In 1928 the Reverend Henry Cheeseman of St Andrew's, Deptford, informed the Bishop of Durham that unemployment 'makes many bitter against religion and fosters a spirit of discontent

Bishopwearmouth Parish Church, which almost completely dates from the 1930s

In 1929 Bede School moved from premises at West Park to this purpose–built site on Durham Road, now part of the City of Sunderland College

and envy towards the well to do, and makes them in some instances cherish hard thoughts against the clergy & affects the attendance at the services of the Church, and chapels, and draws them towards Communism.'[20]

In the years 1932–5 one of the town's historic churches, St Michael's in Bishopwearmouth, was almost entirely rebuilt in the Gothic Revival style— £35,000 was donated for the construction work by Sir John Priestman. The architect was William Caröe, an elderly and highly respected figure who had partially rebuilt Hartlepool's ancient parish church in the mid 1920s.

Sunderland's churches and chapels, of course, continued to provide Sunday Schools. In addition, some children attended schools with a strong emphasis on Christian values, such as the Catholic St Mary's Grammar School (now St Aidan's) which opened in Bede Tower in 1928–9, and moved to the Briery, likewise in Ashbrooke, in 1936.

Bede Collegiate Schools (sometimes referred to in the singular) moved to premises on Durham Road in 1929. The buildings, which cost £112,000 were opened on 19 October by the left-wing baronet Sir Charles Trevelyan, the President of the Board of Education, and a supplement in the same day's paper noted:

> The Bede Collegiate Schools are situated on a magnificent site comprising 20 acres on the western outskirts of Sunderland…and [the location] has bus and tram stopping places at the entrance giving easy approach from all parts of the town and district. The new buildings are designed in a compact and symetrically balanced group…and comprise a boys' school to the west and a girls' school to the east.[21]

For older students, the main centre of higher education was the Technical College. It was located near Bishopwearmouth Green in the Galen Building, which was extended in the 1920s. Primarily, the college was devoted to teaching engineering but another subject was pharmacy, which had been introduced as a part-time course in 1914. In September 1921, though, a young academic named Hope Constance Winch was appointed the first full-time lecturer in pharmacy. Winch, who came from London, initially had 28 students and facilities were basic and centred on a double bench located in the chemistry laboratory. Winch was an able scientist and the subject's profile at the college became increasingly important, so much so that in 1930 a separate pharmacy department was formed and she remained its head until her death in 1944.

Other well-established places of higher education were Sunderland Training College and the School of Art. From 6 October 1922 the former was housed in Langham Tower, which had been acquired by Sunderland Council. The college became a women-only institution at the time of its move to the more spacious premises.[22] On the other hand, the latter met in rooms in the Town Hall until 6 June 1934 when the College of Arts and Crafts (as it had become known) moved to Ashburne House, a substantial residence located on the northern fringe of Backhouse Park.[23]

Entertainment

On the whole, the entertainment industry benefited from the rise in real incomes. For one thing, more and more people flocked to the cinemas, which enjoyed a boom period even in the silent era.

The Havelock was Sunderland's first cinema to switch to sound. It did so in the summer of 1929 and the first 'talkie' shown was *The Singing Fool* starring Al Jolson, which attracted tens of thousands of patrons between 15 July and 10 August. Within a year or two, many of the other cinemas had likewise gone over to sound and others had ceased to exist. In fact, over 50 per cent of the town's cinemas did not survive as they were 'unable to finance the conversion from silent to sound.'[24]

In 1932 Sunderland gained its finest cinema when the Regal opened in Holmeside. It was a prestigious establishment with over 60 staff and seating for 2,500 patrons. Another picture palace, the Ritz, opened at Holmeside in 1937, with a seating capacity of 1,700. For many people the prices charged at the town's finest cinemas were too high (the Regal's ranged from 2s. down to 7d. for the front stalls, with reductions for Saturdays and holidays), and so they attended less savoury establishments. These included the little Cora cinema near the *Wheatsheaf*, Monkwearmouth, which was temporarily closed in 1930 as a health hazard. Here seats cost 3d. or 2d. and were thus affordable to the unemployed.

Cinemas also existed in peripheral areas, as was true for example of the Savoy, which had opened in late 1912 at Southwick. The 1930s saw the opening of three suburban cinemas, the first of which, the Marina on Sea Road, Fulwell, opened in July 1935. Next came the Plaza, on Pallion Road in the summer of 1936, and filmgoers entered the Regent at Grangetown for the first time in May 1937. The Marina was the best cinema on the north side of the river, but arguably pride of place among the outlying cinemas belonged to the Regent.

The increasing popularity of cinemas occurred at the expense of theatres and other places of entertainment, and in 1931 the Empire went over to films—*All Quiet on the Western Front* had its North East premiere there. In this case, though, the change of direction proved brief for in 1933, after being closed for a few months to undergo redecoration, the Empire reverted to a variety role.

Football remained the major spectator sport, most of whose devotees were male. League football, in abeyance for most of the First World War, resumed in 1919 and for Sunderland AFC the succeeding decade was not particularly successful despite the fact that the club spent large sums building up expensive squads. Yet although no trophies were won, on a number of occasions Sunderland finished near the top of the League. Better results ensued in the mid 1930s. They were First Division runners up in 1934–5, and in the following year won the championship for the sixth time— only one other team at this date, Aston Villa, had done likewise. Sunderland went on to win their first FA Cup on 1 May 1937 by beating Preston North End 3–1. Two of the winning goals were scored by outstanding players, Bobby Gurney and Raich Carter, the team captain. The former joined the club in 1925 and is its highest scoring player of all time, with a total of 228 goals in 388 League and Cup games.

The victorious team returned to Sunderland by train and, upon alighting at Monkwearmouth Station, received a rapturous reception. Carter recalled:

> Stepping outside [the station] was like stepping onto an alarm signal. Suddenly everything went off. The tugs and ships in the river were hooting and blowing their sirens, railway engines shrilled their whistles, bells rang and rattles clacked, there was shouting and cheering. It was like a thick concrete wall of deafening din. Then the cheering resolved itself into a Sunderland roar: 'Ha-way the Lads!' And the cry was taken up and surged round, echoing and re-echoing through the crowd who spread further than the eye could see.[25]

Improvements to Roker Park were undertaken between the wars, enhancing the football ground's capacity. In 1929 the main stand, which replaced the original wooden structure, was built at a cost of £25,000. It was designed by Archibald Leitch, and he was subsequently commissioned to redesign the Clock Stand which was rebuilt in 1936. Although mass unemployment during the Depression adversely affected attendance figures, in March 1933 for a cup-tie against Derby County, 75,118 people crammed into Roker Park. It was, and remains, the largest crowd to have ever watched a football match in the North East.

Boxing also attracted popular support. In the 1920s capacity crowds of 3,000 people attended fights at Holmeside Stadium. This was a purpose-built boxing arena that had opened in 1920. It remained a venue for the sport until 1930 when its owners, the Black family, announced its closure to make way for the construction of the Regal Cinema and the Rink dance hall; a decision which meant that Sunderland would be without a large boxing stadium. The last bouts at Holmeside were fought on 31 May 1930. One of the victors was a local hero named Charlie McDonald, whose father was from the West Indies. His opponent was the East End's redoubtable Jack Casey, the 'Sunderland Assassin.'[26]

Among other pastimes were amateur dramatics, of which Gordon Stott has recalled:

> The Sunderland Drama Club was a flourishing source of entertainment. In 1931, they opened the Little Theatre at 19 Tavistock Place and their major productions were staged at the Victoria Hall. A cartoonist…would give their presentations

publicity with sketches in the *Echo*, which always included my father [Jack Stott] with hammer and nails, as the assistant Stage Manager.[27]

Visiting the seaside continued to be extremely popular (during the 1930s Seaburn's fortunes in particular soared) and late in the period the Mayor of Sunderland, Myers Wayman, observed:

Sea Lane, Seaburn, in 1929

Year by year Sunderland is coming into greater prominence as a seaside resort, and that its claims in this respect are justified, cannot be denied. Every year further progress is being made in the development of the sea-front and the provision of facilities for the recreation and entertainment of residents and visitors.[28]

The town's attractions included annual illuminations that had commenced in September 1936. The initial display was a fortnight long, but proved so popular that the length was extended to a month in subsequent years. The display of 1939, advertised as 'brighter and better than ever', failed to take place. Although everything was ready (a preview happened on 1 September for members of the illuminations committee) the event was cancelled following the outbreak of war a couple of days later.

Children riding donkeys at Roker in the 1920s

Politics and Municipal Services

Surprising as it may seem, local politics was dominated by the Conservatives. In the general election of December 1918, when all men over 21 and most women over 30 were allowed to vote for the first time, Sir Hamar Greenwood, a Coalition Liberal, and the local Tory shipowner Ralph Hudson, were elected to represent Sunderland, the former for the second time. Despite the increased franchise, which meant that there were 73,131 registered voters, there was little enthusiasm among the public. Turn-out was 56.4 per cent, a marked contrast from previous general elections and the subsequent one in 1922 when the figure was 81.6 per cent. Two local businessmen, the Conservatives Walter Raine and Luke Thompson, were elected that year and retained their seats until May 1929 (by which time all women over 21 could vote) when they were ousted by Labour candidates. The victors were Alfred Smith and the Australian-born Dr Marian Phillips, the party's national Women's Officer, a robust figure who, as MP, 'always boasted that she was "a better man than most."'[29] The number of registered voters was 101,875 and the turn-out was 81.1 per cent.

Labour's triumph was short-lived. In a by-election in March 1931 caused by Smith's death, Luke Thompson won. Conservative dominance was achieved in the election of October when Thompson retained his seat and was joined by Samuel Storey (the proprietor of the *Echo*, a paper founded by his grandfather) who supplanted Phillips.[30] The Conservatives easily defeated Labour owing to the weakness of the local Liberal Party whose supporters abandoned ship in favour of the Tories. Labour fared badly again in the election of November 1935 when Storey and a National Liberal, Stephen Furness, were victorious.[31]

For most of the inter-war era Labour also played second fiddle on the council. For instance, they failed to win a single seat when 14 of the 16 wards were contested on 1 November 1926, when one of the victors was Mrs Ellen Elizabeth Bell, an independent candidate who had become the town's first female councillor in October 1919. She represented Hendon and took a keen interest in the welfare of children. However, Labour narrowly gained control of the council for the first time in November 1935, by which date the borough's boundaries had been extended (in 1928) and the most notable additions were Fulwell and Southwick.[32]

Labour's hold on power proved brief, though, for on 1 November 1938 the Moderates, an alliance of Tories and Liberals under the leadership of Myers Wayman (who became mayor several days later) regained the council. As a result, the *Echo* triumphantly proclaimed that power was now 'in the hands of businessmen who have pledged themselves to the utmost economy...a planned policy of eschewing that which the town cannot afford will be entered into.'[33] Though not all non-Labour councillors were staunch economisers, the borough was nevertheless dominated for almost the entire period by people with that outlook.

Turning to other matters, in the 1920s the town's street lighting was changed from gas to electricity. Furthermore, the Corporation Electric Tramways Department declared in 1927 that it provided trams every five minutes on the majority of its routes.

The tramcar service remained the dominant means of public transport in the town centre throughout the 1930s. New routes that opened between the wars included one running to Barnes Park via Durham Road. This service commenced in 1925 and was extended to Humbledon Hill in 1929. Almost a decade later, in May 1937, the Fulwell Lane service was extended to Seaburn via Dykelands Road. In addition, trams were supplemented from 1928 by corporation buses. Private buses likewise plied the roads.

As a result of increasing traffic, in April 1927 construction work began on a new Wearmouth Bridge, a structure designed by Mott, Hay & Anderson. It was built around the old bridge, which thus remained in operation until the new structure was completed. The replacement was

Sunderland Town Hall from the southwest in the 1930s. The Central Station can also be seen to the left

officially opened by the future George VI on 31 October 1929 and cost well over £250,000. The same year also saw the introduction of the first traffic lights—at MacKie's Corner and at the junction of Waterloo Place and Holmeside.

Moreover, the port was enhanced by the provision of the Corporation Quay, and Sunderland Council received financial support from the government to meet construction costs.[34] Excavation of the site commenced in October 1930 and the impressive 1,062ft long deep water quay was officially opened on 10 October 1934 by Sir John Priestman. However, the first vessel to berth alongside the quay was the cargo liner *Lochkatrine*, which had done so on 1 June after arriving from Rotterdam.

Some of the corporation's other undertakings were also subsidized by the government. This was true of council house building. In the 1930s the state also rendered assistance for schemes such as the construction of the sea wall and promenade at Seaburn and the installation of sewers. It also contributed to expenditure on hospitals.

Industry

The Medical Officer of Health's report of 1936, as usual, commented that the borough's principal industries were shipbuilding and repairing, marine engineering and allied industries, as well as coalmining and furniture and glass manufacture.

Firms involved in the latter industry included James A. Jobling & Co Ltd, which had operated the Wear Flint Glass Works in Millfield since 1886. Significantly, in 1921 it acquired the exclusive right from an American company to produce and market Pyrex heat-resistant glass in Britain and the British Empire, excluding Canada.[35]

A much larger source of employment was the coal industry and local pits included Hylton Colliery at Castletown and Wearmouth, formerly known as Monkwearmouth Colliery. Both mines were owned by the Wearmouth Coal Company and their combined workforces in the mid 1920s numbered approximately 4,000 men and boys.[36] Local miners participated in the abortive nationwide miners' strike of 1926, caused by employers' attempts to introduce wage reductions and longer hours. The strike commenced in the spring and, unlike the brief General Strike, lasted until the end of November, by which time many miners had however already returned to work.[37] Subsequently, in the mid 1930s most of the mines experienced a reduction in manpower. The most hard hit was Hylton (also known as Castletown Colliery) whose workforce more than halved.[38]

As noted earlier, Sunderland's foremost industry, shipbuilding, enjoyed prosperity in the immediate post-war era. 1920 was the best year—the Wear's 15 shipyards launched a total of 333,335 gross tons. But as the year progressed it became clear that the boom was giving way to hard times; a general trade slump was underway. As R.H. Tawney has commented: 'In April 1920 all was right with the world. In April 1921 all was wrong.' Rising costs of construction and falling freights led shipowners to cancel contracts for new vessels. Not surprisingly 1921 proved a bad year, with output less than half that of the previous year. The downward trend continued. Seventeen vessels grossing 56,522 tons was the output for 1923, a year in which five yards launched nothing at all. A revival followed, but was short-lived. In 1925 output fell again, and dropped to only eight ships totalling 36,979 tons in 1926. Indeed, eight yards launched no ships in that grim year. Mercifully, 1927–9 saw a significant improvement, but in 1930 harder times returned. The output of the following year was a mere seven vessels (8,814 tons) and this was good in comparison with 1932 when only two colliers amounting to 2,628 tons were launched. The Wear's greatest yard, Doxford's, was idle at this time. It had not launched a ship since 18 December 1930 and only reopened in May 1934.[39]

Inevitably, thousands of Sunderland shipbuilders lost their jobs in the slump years. The census of 1931 gives an indication of the problem. 2,375 people were employed in the yards, whereas 11,794 of their former colleagues were unemployed. Yards that failed to survive included Robert Thompson's at Southwick, which closed in 1933.

When, as was the norm in the first half of the 1930s, there were few or no contracts in hand, yards attempted to find alternative tasks for at least some of their employees. Several took up shipbreaking while others, Pickersgill's and Bartram's for instance, respectively engaged in furniture making and the construction of caravans. Where possible preparation was also made for the expected upturn. New machinery was installed and experimentation and research undertaken, with the aim of building ships of the highest possible efficiency.

It was not until the second half of the decade that the situation improved significantly. In 1938, 35 ships grossing 169,898 tons were constructed, the best output since 1930. Government action was partly responsible for the upturn. In 1935 it had introduced the British Shipping (Assistance) Act under which the Board of Trade was empowered to provide loans at a low rate of interest to shipping firms on condition that they scrapped two tons of shipping for every ton they built. The scheme, which ended in 1937, undoubtedly had had a positive effect and Sunderland benefited the most. Of the 50 vessels constructed under the scheme, 24 were built on the Wear.

By the beginning of 1939 things looked bleak again. There were only nine contracts in hand and only four of the yards were open. In March the government finally responded to appeals for financial assistance so that the industry could compete against subsidised foreign competition. Orders immediately began to flow in—in less than three weeks 40 orders were placed for ships from the Wear and others followed so that the river's eight surviving yards once again became hives of activity.[40]

The Gathering Storm

The government's decision to subsidize merchant shipbuilding in March 1939 was due to its belief that war with Germany seemed inevitable. Tension had been growing for some time. Among actions that had caused concern was Hitler's annexation of Austria in March 1938. As Churchill later wrote, Europe was 'confronted with a programme of aggression, nicely calculated and timed, unfolding stage by stage.'[41] By late September 1938 most Britons felt that the United Kingdom would soon be involved in a war with the Third Reich, owing to Hitler's designs on Czechoslovakian territory. However, at the Munich conference the Prime Minister Neville Chamberlain, and his French counterpart, surrendered Czechoslovakia to Hitler's mercy in return for peace. Tension, though, soon returned, and worsened when Hitler annexed the whole of Czechoslovakia in March 1939, by which date Britain's rearmament programme was well underway and civil defences were in the process of being put in order.

SUNDERLAND DURING WORLD WAR TWO

On the morning of Sunday, 3 September 1939, many families on Wearside, like others throughout the nation, were huddled beside their radios listening intently to the Prime Minister, Neville Chamberlain. In sombre mood, he reluctantly announced that Great Britain had declared war on Germany in response to its recent invasion of Poland, and was thereby honouring a promise made in March to that now hard-pressed country.

Sensible people realised that Britain was thus to be engaged in a daunting undertaking for the Germans were courageous and formidable. Some Wearsiders, no doubt, upon hearing Chamberlain, cast their minds back to the First World War and remembered the horrific battles fought at the Somme and elsewhere. If so, they were soon stirred from their recollections by an air raid siren. However, no raid was forthcoming. Moreover none occurred here, or elsewhere in Britain, for many months, a period known as the 'Phoney War.' Nonetheless the days would come—from the summer of 1940 onward—when the skies over Sunderland would reverberate to the droning sound of German bombers and the screaming whistle of falling bombs.

One measure taken by the local authority to prevent sections of Sunderland's population suffering from the expected air raids was evacuation. Plans for evacuating children had been drawn up in the wake of the Munich crisis of September 1938, but for a time it had seemed as though these would come to nothing owing to the attitude of the government. In December of that year a report issued by the Secretary of State declared that 'Sunderland was not considered to be one of the centres from which the population would be evacuated,'[1] and in May 1939 the town was officially designated a neutral zone. This decision was subsequently reversed following the visit of a deputation—including the town's MPs—to the Minister of Health which argued that as a centre of shipbuilding, Sunderland was likely to be bombed. Furthermore, it was pointed out that the average density of population in the town was 36 per acre, slightly higher than that of Newcastle which had been designated an evacuation zone.

On Sunday 10 September, shortly after the declaration of war, 7,910 youngsters were evacuated from Sunderland, and on the following day 1,785 mothers and children under five likewise went. In mid July, a leader in the town's newspaper had stated that if 'parents think the matter over calmly and rationally they can hardly fail to come to the conclusion that it will be in the best interests of the children, as well as the country, for them to be taken away from the immediate danger zones into places of comparative safety.'[2] When it is borne in mind that 24,500 of Sunderland's total school population of 31,439 lived in the central areas of the town designated an evacuation zone, and were therefore eligible to be moved (as were others elsewhere who attended schools in the zone), it becomes clear that the majority of youngsters on Wearside remained at home.

One factor that contributed to this situation was the desire of many families to avoid the pain of parting. Financial considerations also played a part. For some families the cost of providing their offspring with suitable attire was simply too high. In an attempt to meet this need the government subsequently released funds to assist parents who wished to have their loved ones evacuated: a recognition of the fact that 'essential garments for children...living in the country are different from those used in...towns. Many children have long distances to walk to school and they need strong shoes, Wellington boots and macintoshes.'[3]

Evacuees from Sunderland were billeted elsewhere in County Durham and in the North and East Ridings of Yorkshire. Selection of the children in the reception areas was often a painful experience. W.W. Lowther's book, *Wish You Were Here*, contains the reminiscence of a woman who relates: 'I went to the village hall with my mother to choose a child. It was dreadful....just like a market. The little girls seemed to go first and the ones from poor homes, dirty and tired little beings, crying and sobbing, weary and hungry, just sat...wondering why they were not wanted.'[4] While parties of elementary school children were scattered among the villages of the reception areas, pupils of Bede Collegiate Schools, and the Junior Technical School in Villiers Street, were moved as units to facilitate the continuance of their secondary education. Some 816 Bedans were evacuated. The boys, 484 pupils, were billeted in and around Northallerton whilst the girls were sent to Richmond and its environs.[5] Pupils from the Junior Technical School went to Askrigg.

Some youngsters enjoyed life as an evacuee. One, from Sunderland's East End, has recalled how she had a bed to herself: 'At home I...shared a bed with two brothers and two sisters.' Another, a former Bishopwearmouth pupil, remembers: 'We used to love the lambing season when we could go and see the lambs after they were born. It was all new to us.'[6] In similar vein, a former evacuee from Southwick states: 'We were able to roam around the farm freely, picking apples and pears as we went, or could wander down to the river and fish for sticklebacks. We also enjoyed watching the cows being milked as we chatted to the milkmaid. There were so many interesting things for us to do.'[7] Others, though, had a miserable time. Homesickness and the neglect or downright nastiness of resentful strangers with whom they were billeted, caused much pain. One woman recalled: 'The whole experience blighted my life and caused problems in my relationships.'[8]

Indeed, the unhappiness of many children and the desire of parents to have their loved ones back, coupled with the absence of air raids, led to the return of many youngsters. The *Echo* of 14 October 1939 contained an appeal by a member of Sunderland Education Committee entreating mothers 'to refrain from bringing their bairns home.'[9] He was fighting a losing battle. More and more children returned, as did mothers with under fives. By November 1940—despite two lesser evacuations in November 1939 and July 1940, and the commencement of air raids—there were only 3,094 Sunderland children in reception areas and by October 1942 this had dropped to 964.[10]

Poignant view of an evacuee

As Lowther comments: 'The long struggle of the local authority to gain government approval to classify the bulk of the town as an evacuable area, resulted in a real determination to make the scheme work.'[11] As the above figures show, it was a struggle that failed. A notable example of this concerned the Bede Collegiate Schools. In February 1940 a meeting of parents of Bedan evacuees resolved to notify the Education Committee that they intended 'bringing home their children…at the end of the present term.'[12] However, on the 21st it was announced by the committee that though there was to be a partial reopening of 'the Bede' only pupils who had not been evacuated or had returned before 21 December were to be admitted. This proved the case on Monday, 18 March. But owing to growing pressure Mr Thompson, the Director of Education, soon relented and stated that all Bede pupils would be able to enrol in April. Hence within a short time, the vast majority of Bedans were attending their school again.

By this date a general resumption of school reopenings had commenced. In the early months of the war schools had stayed closed—partly to encourage people to participate in the evacuation scheme—and under pressure from parents of children who remained on Wearside the Local Education Authority had had to resort to ad hoc measures: the Board of Education would not allow schools to open in the danger zone. Consequently from 16 October 1939 onward, classes had been held in private houses and other suitable locations such as Boys' Brigade huts.

Air Raids

Prior to the outbreak of war, a variety of measures were taken by the local Air Raids Precaution Committee. Paid personnel and volunteers were formed into squads to perform various functions such as rescue and demolition. Moreover air raid shelters were provided, as was true of over 7,000 householders issued with free Anderson shelters.

During the 'Phoney War' some of Sunderland's residents may have felt that the preparations had been a waste of time. If so, they were wrong. As a major ship-building town, it was inevitable that sooner or later German aircrews would attempt to wreak havoc on Wearside—the airmen mostly belonged to Luftflotte 5 based in Scandinavia, one of three air fleets from which aircraft were sent against Britain.

A foretaste of what would occur took place early on the morning of 22 June 1940 when a solitary plane flew in from the sea. It soon turned back, but before recrossing the coast, dropped several bombs shortly after midnight. Fortuitously they fell on open ground between the Old Rectory, Whitburn, and the nearby Fishermen's Cottages (now known as The Bents) which suffered some damage. An old barn was destroyed by one of the bombs, killing at least one horse in the process.

During July, as a preliminary to invasion, the Luftwaffe began a concerted campaign against airfields and other targets in Britain and Sunderland experienced this at first hand. A notable raid occurred on Thursday 15 August, by which time the town had experienced its first air raid casualties of the war—four workers had been killed at Laing's shipyard six days earlier during a lunchtime raid by one German aircraft, and a young woman injured during the sortie had later died. Now, on 15 August, all three air fleets sent planes on daylight raids against Britain. For instance, approximately 100 aircraft belonging to Luftflotte 5, and consisting of Heinkel 111 bombers escorted by Messerschmitt Bf 110 fighters, approached Sunderland from the northeast, having already been intercepted by RAF fighters. Thus the raid was not as effective as the Germans presumably wished. No bombs, for example, fell on Usworth air base on the western outskirts of Sunderland, from where 12 Hurricanes of 607 squadron scrambled to confront the raiders and claimed three kills. Sunderland itself was less fortunate. A number of fatalities were sustained and a fair degree of damage was done to property on the north side of the river.

Among heartwarming escapes that happened during the war was that of an 18-month-old child who survived an air raid which took place on the night of 23 February 1941. Several houses were destroyed in Tunstall Vale, Ashbrooke, shortly after the alert sounded at 8.46pm, and rescue workers dug through the night in search of survivors. At dawn a faint cry was heard from a partially wrecked bedroom in a badly damaged house. The youngster (the baby of Mrs Violet Cowell who had been killed in the raid), was found in a cot near a bed smothered in rubble. The infant had survived for ten hours despite having been partly exposed to the elements on this cold winter's night. The cold spell had resulted in the worst blizzards of the century so far on Wearside on 19 February, and not surprisingly snow was still covering the ground on the night of the raid.

Sadly, of course, enemy activity could wipe out entire families, as was the case on the night of 3/4 May 1941. Sunderland was on the flight path of aircraft sent to bomb Belfast and at around midnight, as the planes flew over the town, some loosed off bombs. The Redby School area, Monkwearmouth, was hardest hit. Twelve houses were destroyed in Osborne Street and Duke Street North, where the four members of the Storey family were killed; one of the young Storey children was only 14 months old. Among other fatalities that night were nine people who perished in nearby Westcott Terrace, part of Brandling Street.[13]

This raid was just one of several that made the first half of 1941 the worst

Snow being cleared from Mowbray Park in early 1941. In the background is the
Victoria Hall. It was destroyed in an air raid in the early hours of 16 April 1941

period of the war so far for Sunderland, a period which witnessed an intensification of German air raids on Britain as a whole. One of the places badly affected was Hull. There in March-July 1941, of 93,000 houses in the town, only 6,000 escaped bomb damage, a much worse state of affairs than existed on Wearside.

Fortunately, Hitler's invasion of the Soviet Union in June greatly reduced the Luftwaffe's capacity to strike at Britain, for prior to the invasion many aircraft were moved east and the German High Command concentrated on supporting the army as it proceeded to smash its way into the heart of Stalin's empire.

Sunderland's welcome respite from air raids ended on the morning of 13 August 1941 when, just before noon, four people were killed and five injured in Mayswood Road, Fulwell, after bombs were dropped from a solitary Heinkel. One of the survivors, Mrs Gibson, was in her kitchen with the window open when she heard the bomb fall. She therefore grabbed her baby son and dashed into the dining room where she sheltered under an oak table that was soon covered in debris when the bomb landed nearby.

Sporadic attacks continued until mid January 1942, after which none befell the town until 1 May when the Fulwell area again experienced death and destruction and Fulwell Fire Station was largely destroyed.

The most serious raid of 1942 happened on Friday 16 October (the sirens sounded at 9.38pm) when 14 people were killed and 16 injured after bombs fell in Tatham Street and nearby Tavistock Place, Hendon. One of the bombers involved was illuminated by searchlights and brought down by anti-aircraft fire. It crashed into the sea just off the harbour mouth.

More serious still, was a raid on 14 March 1943 which did much damage to the town centre, killed 16 people, and seriously injured 31 others. Among the fatalities was Reverend James Orton, the Vicar of St Thomas' Church, John Street, which was partially destroyed.

By this date the air war over Sunderland was drawing to a close, for the Luftwaffe's capacity to send aircraft against targets in Britain had diminished further. Sadly, though, before raids on the town ceased there was a sting in the tail. It came in May. Indeed, Sunderland was subjected to the two worst air raids it experienced of the war.

The first was endured on Sunday 16 May when the sirens sounded at 1.44am. With the aid of moonlight and flares the raiders were able to concentrate their bombing, and during the course of the next hour the town was hit by parachute mines, high explosive bombs and hundreds of incendiaries. Though industrial targets, such as J.L Thompson's North Sands shipyard were hit, the town in general bore the brunt of the bombing in which 70 people were killed and 73 seriously injured.

Among the fatalities was 25-year-old George Peel, home on short leave from the Royal Navy. He was killed by a parachute mine that devastated Fulwell Crossing where George's wife Stella and baby son were living with his family at Railway House. George's father and brother were seriously injured.

On the same night, in Atkinson Road, Fulwell, Margaret Henderson (whose husband was serving with the Seaforth Highlanders) was trapped in her Anderson shelter when a parachute mine exploded:

Duke Street North and Redby School, following an air raid early on 4 May 1941

> When the All Clear sounded, the wardens shouted and I answered. I said I was all right and they told me I would have to wait to be dug out as they had to rescue some injured people first. More than two hours later, they got me out. They told me to prepare myself for a shock, and when I got out I saw 11 of my neighbours lying dead along the middle of the road.[14]

One of Sunderland's most popular entertainment venues, the King's Theatre, on Crowtree Road, was also among the night's losses. The Edwardian structure was completely destroyed. 'In the midst of all the justifiable praise heaped on the Empire', comments Albert Anderson, 'one must not forget the King's, which opened before its more illustrious neighbour and was just as popular among local cinema and theatregoers alike.'[15]

A week later, early on the morning of 24 May, history repeated itself but with greater intensity, when 83 people were slain and some 109 seriously hurt. At least 18 of the deaths occurred at St George's Square, which received a direct hit. Among others who lost their lives were 16 people, including six youngsters, who had sought safety in the brick and concrete shelter at Lodge Terrace, Hendon. It received a direct hit at 3.15am. William Ord, the husband of one of the survivors, was on fire-fighting duty nearby and dashed to the scene with his colleagues: 'we sailed right in and got to work' he recalled. 'There were several fellows…who knew their wives and kiddies were trapped, so they needed no urging on. Working by the light of a fire nearby, they lifted and heaved on the blocks of stone with their bare hands until we got some tools from a garage.'[16] In so doing, they rescued 40 people. Fortunately this raid, which left 3,500 homeless, was the last Sunderland had to endure.

Despite the pain and hardship, Wearsiders could draw comfort from the general course of the war. In Russia, for instance, things were going from bad to worse for the Germans in the wake of the titanic and calamitous Battle of Stalingrad.

In addition, within weeks of the relatively heavy raids on Sunderland just referred to, the front page of the *Echo* of 10 July featured a map of Sicily and reported that the 'Battle of Europe' had commenced. The allies had just launched an invasion of the island by conducting a successsful moonlight landing. The same page of the newspaper also reported that the allied 'Air Blitz' (massive raids on German cities had commenced in the spring of 1942) was being maintained and that the RAF 'was active day and night.' Indeed, shortly thereafter, in the last week of July and the first days of August, Hamburg was subjected to such heavy bombing by the RAF and Americans that at least 45,000 civilians were killed.[17]

One of the pilots involved in the war over Germany, was an exceptional young man named Cyril Barton who was born in Suffolk in 1921. At the end of March 1944, he was the pilot of a Halifax bomber that took off in Yorkshire to participate in a raid against Nuremberg. However, when about 70 miles from the target, his plane (one of almost 800 allied aircraft that participated) was badly damaged by German night fighters. Owing to a misunderstanding, some of Barton's fellow crewmen, including the navigator, bailed out but he pressed on, determined to accomplish the mission. En route home, the state of the Halifax deteriorated. By the early hours of 31 March

the plane was well off course, low on fuel, and approaching Ryhope. Shortly thereafter, Barton took evasive measures to avoid houses and crashed near Ryhope Colliery.
Two miners walking to work were hit and one of them died as a result. Fellow miners
dashed to the scene and pulled Barton and the three other remaining crewmen from
the wreckage, but Barton died soon after arriving at Ryhope General Hospital. In
recognition of his bravery, he was duly awarded a Victoria Cross. Of Barton, it was
aptly said: 'In gallantly completing his last mission, in the face of almost impossible
odds, this officer displayed unsurpassed courage and devotion to duty.'[18]

Life During the War Years

In addition to the evacuation and air raids, the war obviously affected the lives
of Sunderland's residents in other ways. Unemployment, of course, dramatically
declined. By August 1943 there were only 429 unemployed men in the town; a
figure in marked contrast to those before the war.

Moreover, for most of the conflict Sunderland's beaches were out of bounds—they
were mined and sealed off with barbed wire in case of a German invasion. Rationing
was another way in which people were affected. Petrol was the first item whose use
was restricted, and other rationed commodities included clothes, soap and paper.[19]
Food rationing commenced on Monday 8 January 1940, with butter, bacon or ham
each rationed at 4 ounces, and sugar 12 ounces, per person a week. The system later
became more restrictive: allowances were tightened and more commodities rationed.
Works' canteens provided important supplementary meals. Homegrown produce
also augmented the basic diet. Some of the townsfolk willingly used their gardens
and allotments to grow food, but others had to be cajoled. 'In May 1940', notes Peter
Hepplewhite, 'Sunderland Council tenants who refused to cultivate their gardens
were threatened with eviction.'[20] Furthermore, two months later local restrictions
prohibiting the keeping of pigs, rabbits and poultry, were rescinded.

There was also a significant change in behaviour. Immorality, for example,
increased, with a consequent growth in the number of illegitimate births and a
higher rate of venereal disease, paralleling developments nationally. Crime also
went up between 1939 and 1945, though at a more modest level: 14.7 per cent for
indictable offences contrasting with a rise of over 50 per cent nationwide. Looting
bomb-damaged property was one of the lawless activities undertaken, and brought
a stern response from magistrates dealing with anyone apprehended for doing so.
On the other hand, another set of statistics showed an improvement. Restrictions
on the use of petrol resulted in safer streets: 'Road accidents fell from 561 with 25
deaths in 1939 to 296 with 19 deaths in 1944.'[21]

Among ways of seeking fun and trying to ease tension, were attending the
cinema or theatre. In common with other places of public entertainment, due to
fear of air raids, they had been closed by the government upon the commencement
of hostilities. But from 15 September 1939 official policy changed. It was realised
that entertainment was essential for the continuance of a high state of morale. This
period thus saw a boom in audience ratings for theatres and cinemas and led to the

opening of new premises. A wide variety of tastes were catered for, and not surprisingly many of the films shown were of propaganda value. One of the most popular films screened on Wearside was *The Great Dictator* (1940), a comedy lampoon of Hitler starring Charlie Chaplin.

Needless to say, the Empire was well attended. Artists who performed included the Tyneside comedian Frank E. Franks, the singer Vera Lynn and Sadler's Wells Opera Company. There were also musicals and several nude shows intended to titillate audiences without being lewd—the performers were required to remain motionless. Dance halls experienced a boom. Jitterbugging was all the rage in some, but others prohibited the dance and catered for people with less exuberance or more refined taste. Sunderland's libraries also experienced a growth in demand and among the popular authors of the period was the gifted Scottish novelist A.J. Cronin, whose work included a classic novel set in the North East, *The Stars Look Down*.

In addition, some Wearsiders went on holiday to Weardale or further afield. In at least one case, though, this led to tragedy. On Saturday 8 April 1944, during the Easter holidays, Miss Hope Winch, an experienced amateur climber and the head of Sunderland Technical College's Department of Pharmacy, fell 150ft to her death on Scafell Pike in the Lake District.[22]

And what of football? Upon the war's commencement, League football in Britain was discontinued and players' contracts suspended: some of the Sunderland squad entered the Armed Forces or went to work in 'protected essential industries' such as coalmining. For several months the club was in limbo, but in early 1940 it entered the League War Cup and reached the final of this competition two years later: Raich Carter, a hero of Sunderland's FA Cup win of 1937 and at this date employed as an RAF Physical Training Instructor at a local base, was one of the few members of the team whose face was familiar.

In the summer of 1944 a welcome development occurred. On August bank holiday weekend (several weeks after British, American and Canadian troops had landed in Normandy) the beaches at Seaburn and Roker were opened to the public. Nevertheless, they were only permanently reopened in March 1945.

Shipbuilding, the Port and Merchant Marine

The war had a dramatic effect on Sunderland's shipyards. At the beginning of 1939 only four yards were open and there were only nine contracts in hand. But orders subsequently flooded in, new workers were taken on, and idle yards once again reverberated to the sounds of shipbuilding. In all, nine yards operated in Sunderland during the war: the ninth, Wear Shipbuilders Ltd, opened at Southwick and witnessed its first launch in 1943.

Most of the vessels constructed were merchant ships. In the period from September 1939 to the end of 1944, 249 vessels totalling 1,534,980 tons were constructed. This amounted to around 27 per cent of the total output of merchant shipping from all British yards during that period. The best year was 1942 when 58 vessels (374,794 tons) were produced. Not surprisingly, the biggest single contribution to the Wear's overall tonnage was made by the largest yard, Doxford's. From September 1939 to September 1944, it produced 71 merchant ships whereas the yard in second place, J.L. Thompson's, produced 40 merchant vessels in the same period. In contrast, the figure for the much smaller yard of John Crown & Sons was inevitably far lower, namely eight ships.

Naval vessels produced on Wearside included frigates, corvettes and landing craft. In 1943, to hasten the task of fitting out after launching, the Admiralty decided to establish a fitting-out base at Hendon Dock and by the beginning of 1944 it was in operation. In all, 13 vessels were fitted out there and an additional 20 naval craft used the facilities for repairs before the war ended.

Fast construction was vital to the war effort, to make good the heavy losses sustained at sea. Hence a degree of modernization took place. Although riveting was not entirely displaced, welding became widespread, as did the prefabrication of large sections. Moreover, as in World War I, women were employed (from about early 1942 onward), though as before they were few in number in comparison with the men. On the whole they were engaged in tasks—like sweeping up or painting under-coats in accommodation areas—that required little or no skill. But others worked as crane drivers or were taught to weld.

Initially, the war had an adverse effect on the amount of trade the Port of Sunderland handled. In part, for a time this was due to the transference on stra-tegic grounds of shipping from the east to the west coast ports. In August 1941 the government decided to use Sunderland Corporation Quay for the handling of cargoes of war material. Pleased by the resultant work, it subsequently arranged—in 1943—that a berth in the South Docks would also be devoted to the handling of government cargoes. In addition to such traffic, thousands of tons of US Army stores were landed. Ordinary trade of the port involved the landing of imports such as cement, grain and petroleum spirit; while the principal exports were coal (about two million tons were shipped annually to London and other UK ports in the latter years of the war) bottles, chemicals and machinery.

The port was, of course, subjected to enemy activity. During air raids some damage was caused to the docks' area. In addition, magnetic and acoustic mines were laid off the harbour by aircraft—therefore minesweeping became a frequent undertaking—and at times the German efforts were rewarded as happened on the evening of Friday 26 July 1940. A Norwegian steamer, the SS *Balzac* was rocked by an explosion after leaving port and six lives were lost. One of the fatalities was a local man, George Hall, a 33-year-old pilot. A number of the injured crew duly received treatment at the Royal Infirmary. Overall, though, the Germans failed to affect the port to a great extent.

On the other hand, they made life for members of the merchant navy extremely hazardous further afield and over 300 mariners from Sunderland perished at sea. The worst incident occurred shortly before midnight on 25 August 1940 when the SS *Harpalyce* was torpedoed north of the Hebrides. Among the crew members lost were 14 from Sunderland, two of whom were a father and son from the East End, namely Frederick and Robert Gregory.[23]

Victory and Reflection

From the steps of the Town Hall late on Tuesday 8 May 1945, the Mayor of Sunderland, John Young, announced the declaration of Germany's surrender. Sunderland's residents were generally ecstatic. A festive spirit prevailed in Fawcett Street (where thousands gathered) and throughout the town. However, amid the rejoicing some reflected on their experiences and their thoughts were marred with sadness at the suffering and loss the war had entailed for them and their loved ones.

Others worried about relatives still fighting against Japan, or held captive by the Japanese. For instance, the 600-strong 125 Anti-Tank Regiment, comprising men from Sunderland, had been captured in its entirety when British forces surrendered en masse at Singapore in February 1942. The men subsequently endured terrible conditions in POW camps. Many of them were also forced to work on the Burma Railway. Death took its bitter toll and by the time Japan finally surrendered in August 1945 approximately one third of the captive members of the 125 Anti-Tank Regiment had perished.

Sunderland certainly played a full part in the war and suffered accordingly. For one thing, it ranks among the seven most heavily bombed towns and cities in Britain. It experienced 42 air raids (in all the sirens sounded 247 times) and according to figures given by the Town Clerk to the Imperial War Graves Commission in 1947, civilian deaths totalled 267, while 29 Civil Defence personnel also perished, all but one of them on duty. In addition, 362 Wearsiders were seriously injured and 639 slightly so. In view of heavier casualties elsewhere, particularly in the devastated cities of Germany and Japan, one could tend to view the town's fatalities as almost irrelevant. They were not. Each was a personal tragedy, and most, if not all, blighted the lives of countless other people.

Significant damage was also done to property—1,030 houses were demolished, 2,700 seriously damaged, and 30,000 affected to a lesser extent. Hence the raids exacerbated Sunderland's housing problem, especially in view of the fact that the corporation's endeavours to redress the housing shortage had been brought to a standstill by the war and private house building had likewise ceased.

Sunderland's contribution to the war effort is noteworthy. For example, of the sterling effort of the shipyards (where industrial relations were second to none and the output was first class), T. Holden has observed, it was a 'remarkably fine performance which it is hardly possible to overpraise.'[24] Thus, with the return of peace, Sunderland could be proud of its war record. But what of the future? Would history repeat itself, with many Wearsiders having to experience again the poverty they had known in the inter-war years? Or, finally, would they live in a land fit for heroes?

SUNDERLAND SINCE 1945

Despite the general euphoria when the nightmare of the Second World War came to an end, the standard of living in the immediate post-war period was inevitably affected by the former conflict for the country was deeply in debt and austerity remained part of daily life. True, some items became more readily available—paint was one such, and late 1945 reportedly witnessed numerous local householders sprucing up their property. However shortages of more vital items such as petrol, clothing and food still plagued Wearsiders and the nation at large and rationing continued.[1]

In December, an editorial in the *Sunderland Echo* observed:

> Everybody seems to agree that in many ways things are 'worse' this Christmas than last. There is less food in the shops, hardly any turkeys or geese, almost no fruit, no nuts, few toys to buy and most of them crude and expensive, little choice in presents, with books scarce and greetings cards of poor quality.

Even so, the leader continues: 'Austerity cannot quench or even dim the spirit of Christmas. War itself could never do that.... The great thing is that the shadow of war is lifted.'[2] The front page of the same issue of the newspaper declared: 'Most cheerful news for Wearsiders to-day is that a large delivery of oranges is expected in the town to-morrow, for distribution on Monday. It is expected that the quota will be suffi-cient for 1lb. per ration book, so it will not be a "fruit-less" Christmas...after all.' In the event, although the oranges did arrive some Wearsiders had to wait until after Christmas to receive their quota.

Several Christmases would come and go before food rationing ceased, and in April 1949 a trained nurse calling herself 'Old Mother Hubbard', expressed dismay at a recent reduction in the meat ration: 'I suggest that allo-cations to canteens and priority meat rations to miners be cut in half so that we can look after the mothers and children at home, who have long been having a lean time.'[3]

By this date, the end of food rationing had commenced. It did so with flour in July 1948, and sooner

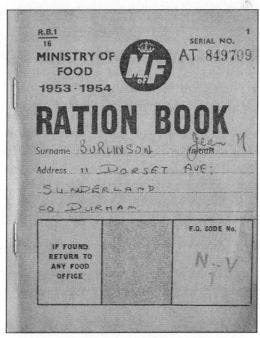

The ration book of a Seaburn resident

223

or later other restrictions were lifted, as was true for instance of treacle, chocolate biscuits and canned and dried fruit in May 1950. On the other hand, meat and bacon continued to be rationed until 4 July 1954.

Harsh weather sometimes also contributed to hardship. Indeed, Sunderland experienced its worst winter weather on record when it was subjected to extreme conditions in early 1947. After a generally mild winter, the cold spell began on 23 January. Initially, conditions were not severe but this soon changed. Several inches of snow fell as January drew to a close. Worse still, in February the sun was not seen for days on end and a total of 36 inches of snow fell and some drifts were 7ft or so high.[4] It was not until 17 March that the front page of the *Echo* was able to proclaim: 'Freeze-Up Time is Over.'

Boundary Changes and Housing

In 1950, the County Borough of Sunderland was extended to include part of the parishes of Ford, Herrington, Hylton and Silksworth. In 1967 a much greater increase in the size of the borough happened when the boundary was extended to embrace the remainder of these parishes, as well as the parishes of Offerton, Ryhope, Tunstall and part of Whitburn, namely South Bents. An even more significant event occurred in 1974. The boundary was changed to encompass Houghton-le-Spring, Hetton-le-Hole and Washington Urban District, and Sunderland became a new borough within the newly established Metropolitan County of Tyne and Wear.

Furthermore, much of the farmland surrounding Sunderland disappeared as the town expanded physically. Inevitably, this process was painful for some people. For example, in February 1949 the *Sunderland Echo* noted that 57-year-old Nicholas Hutchinson of High Ford Farm was the third South Hylton farmer in six months to have had his land taken over as a result of compulsory purchase and was thus about to leave his farmhouse. As late as the previous December, Hutchinson's farm had comprised over 170 acres but building work had reduced his holding to under 40. In a vain attempt to find another farm that he could afford, Hutchinson (who said 'farming is in my blood'), had travelled as far afield as Ayreshire and Devon.[5]

Much of the farmland lost during these years was covered by new housing. Major projects were undertaken, aimed at addressing Sunderland's longstanding housing problem, a state of affairs that had of course been exacerbated by the war and was worsened by a moderate renewal of population growth. In addition to a shortage of dwellings, the quality of many homes was substandard and a considerable number also lacked basic amenities. In 1951, for instance, a quarter of the town's homes did not have an internal water supply. This was the highest proportion of abodes without such a facility among the 157 towns in England and Wales with populations of 50,000 or above.

The council tackled the task of providing well-equipped additional accommodation with gusto. It built just under 20,000 houses between 1945 and 1964. An indication of the magnitude of this undertaking can be gained from the fact that the rate of council house building per head of population in the years 1945–58 was the third highest among 157 towns studied by Moser and Scott.[6] Moreover, according to the census of 1961, more houses per thousand families were built in Sunderland following World War II than in any other town of comparable size.

The first of the new council estates was Springwell Farm Estate, where the town's first permanent post-war council house opened on 25 May 1946. Springwell was soon followed by Thorney Close. Other estates, likewise of predominantly two-storey semi-detached houses with gardens, ensued. These included Hylton Red House, Pennywell and Farringdon. In the 1960s more estates such as Town End Farm, Downhill, Witherwack, Gilley Law and Mill Hill, were created, the last of the corporation's major house building programmes.

Most of the council dwellings were constructed west of the town centre, but the corporation also erected residences in the inner areas. These included tower blocks in the town centre, the East End, and Monkwearmouth. In addition, maisonettes were also built in the East End and in Monkwearmouth where, moreover, three- and four-storey blocks of flats such as Williamson Court and Barclay Court were likewise constructed.[7]

In 2001 the percentage of homes in Sunderland that were owner-occupied was 60.2, whereas the average for England and Wales was 68.9 per cent. Many of Sunderland's private houses post-date the Second World War, as is the case of the substantial Seaburn Dene estate that was developed on Sunderland's northern periphery in

Modern housing around the Marina – the former North Dock

the late 1950s and 60s. More recent private homes erected north of the river include the houses and luxury flats constructed around the North Dock at the turn of the 21st century. However, as with council properties, the majority of private dwellings have been built south of the river. Here notable expansion occurred, with estates springing up further and further southward, including Leechmere and Moorside which date from the 1960s and 1970s.

The post-war decades witnessed major slum clearance by the corporation. This commenced in the 1950s (in accordance with a statutory development plan approved in 1952), and resulted in the demolition of many dwellings in the East End and elsewhere. This is true of Monkwearmouth, where unfit properties near St Peter's Church were destroyed in the late 1950s and early 1960s.

Overcrowding had been a major problem in the slum areas. For example, 62 per cent of the families rehoused during the Central area clearances of 1959 had lived in the same dwelling as at least two other families. The removal of many households to outlying council estates built on 'greenfield' sites greatly reduced population levels in the old parts of the town. Although Sunderland's population rose between 1951 and 1961 (from 181,524, to 189,686), eleven of the town's wards experienced a decrease in the number of their inhabitants and all were centrally located. In Central Ward the population fell by 54 per cent. Moreover the residual populations had a significantly higher percentage of older folk.

One of the areas earmarked by the council in 1952 for redevelopment by 1972 was Millfield, a respectable working-class neighbourhood, mainly consisting of Sunderland Cottages built in the 1870s and 1880s (many of which were owner-occupied), and where the majority of people were Millfielders born and bred. In May 1965 the corporation approved a clearance plan entailing the demolition of the majority of dwellings by 1970. Some residents were eager to be rehoused. The *Echo* of 5 October 1965 contains the following from a resident of one of Millfield's worst streets:

> May I, through the medium of your paper, inquire when we in Rutland Street will be re-housed. My husband and I and four children are living in a one-bedroomed cottage which is soaking wet and overrun with blacklocks.... They say they are harmless, but you can't tell the children that when they wake up through the night and find them crawling across the pillows. We are not the only ones living in these conditions.

However, a sample survey showed that many Millfielders did not wish to have their homes demolished and for themselves to be moved to another area. There were several reasons why most respondents felt like this. Millfield's proximity to the town centre and major sources of employment such as the shipyards were mentioned, as was the fear of receiving unpleasant new neighbours. Some residents were not impressed by the fact that certain amenities which many of the homes lacked would be gained as a result of removal—for a start, according to some of the respondents outdoor WC's were preferable to indoor lavatories.

In November 1967 a residents' association was formed at a meeting of Millfielders called by Jim Taylor, the Vicar of St Mark's. One of the locals in attendance was Norman Dennis who lived at Rosslyn Terrace and was a sociology lecturer at the University of Newcastle upon Tyne.[8] He was to become the association's secretary and discusses this phase of Millfield's history in two important works: *People and Planning: the sociology of housing in Sunderland,* and *Public Participation and Planners' Blight.*[9]

Shortly after the association's formation, the chairman of the Planning Committee stated that the plans concerning Millfield would be re-examined and that public participation would be sought. The first participation meeting took place in November 1968 at which revised plans were put forward concerning East Millfield, where 31 of 688 dwellings scheduled for demolition in the plan of 1965 had already been flattened. According to the new plan, many of the extant properties were now in improvement areas, the fate of 39 was unspecified, and the majority were to be knocked down by 1983. The association raised several objections. For one thing, the extension of demolition until 1983 meant that East Millfielders would live in an area blighted by prolonged clearance. Subsequently, new plans were presented at another participation meeting on 7 February 1969: the demolition of many homes was brought forward.

On 9 April, the corporation approved the plans for East Millfield. It also approved new plans for West Millfield. The 1965 plan had scheduled the demolition of 361 dwellings there, to which another 23 were added later. None had been demolished. Now, save for a few homes that were spared, demolition was scheduled to occur in 1970 and 1972.

In June an exhibition was held in which Millfielders could examine the plans and see what was said about their individual properties. Ever since the first participation meeting, the Planning Department had claimed that its plans were based on reliable information and maintained that internal inspections of all the dwellings had been undertaken by the Health Department, a claim that many locals had disputed. But now, at the exhibition, there was widespread anger and amazement from residents who declared, among other things, that their homes were said to lack certain basic amenities when in fact they had them. Furthermore, as Dennis states: 'Local opinion contradicted the Planning Department's assertion that Alfred Street was the worst street in the area, and that Granville Street was worse than Westbury Street.'[10]

The residents' association had been promised that public participation would ensue concerning West Millfield. No such meeting was forthcoming. So in late July and August the association pursued this matter by sending letters to the Town Clerk's department, in which it also expressed concern regarding the plans for East Millfield. However, unbeknown to the association, on 27 August the Planning Department submitted a report to the Planning Committee misrepresenting the association's correspondence, thus killing off participation on terms the department had sought to dictate.

The report was leaked to the association in October, after which it used ordinary channels, the press (some letters had already been sent to the *Echo*), the local MP and councillor, to achieve its objectives. On 2 July 1970 an *Echo* editorial thus noted: 'Seldom has any local issue so dominated the correspondence and news columns of this newspaper as have the proposals and counter-proposals for the revitalization of Millfield during the past few years.'

As Dennis comments, the council 'was forced by public pressure to devise for the first time a scheme which allowed householders to take advantage of borrowing power granted to the corporation by the central government for mortgage loans for the purpose of house purchase and improvement.' As grants were made piecemeal, 'there was a slow but eventually steep rise in morale and extensive improvements proceeded apace.'[11] Hence the extensive demolition planned for the area never happened and an important part of Sunderland's housing heritage was retained.

Granville Street, Millfield, in 1994

Elsewhere on Wearside, a housing boom had commenced at Washington New Town, which as noted above would soon become part of Sunderland. Washington was designated a 'new town' by the Department of the Environment in July 1964, and in the following September Washington Development Corporation was established. A long-awaited master plan was made public on Tuesday 3 January 1967 and Sir James Steel, the chairman of the Development Corporation Board, was quoted on the first page of the *Sunderland Echo* as saying: 'Washington of the future will be a place where people will be proud to live and the showpiece of the North.' In addition to the historic village of Washington, the 'new town' would comprise 18 distinct estates or 'villages' (houses were already in the process of construction) as well as several industrial estates. The plans also included the construction of the Galleries, a two-storey enclosed shopping and business centre located adjacent to Washington's only high rise building.

Finally, as far as housing is concerned, a momentous development occurred shortly after Margaret Thatcher and the Conservative Party came to power at the general election of 1979, for the government introduced a policy enabling council tenants to purchase the property in which they were living. In 1980 there were approximately 55,000 council houses in Sunderland, but by mid 2000 nearly 17,000 of these had passed into private hands. In that year, the corporation transferred its remaining properties to the Sunderland Housing Group, of which Neil T. Sinclair comments:

> The Housing Group, the third largest social landlord in the United King-dom … embarked on refurbishing existing houses and on building the first new houses in the rented sector for over quarter of a century. The Group also … started on the conversion of existing buildings in the Sunniside area to provide luxury apartments for sale.[12]

Industry and Employment

'Sunderland is a town of precarious economic health.' So wrote B.T. Robson in 1967.[13] It was an apt statement. The local economy was dominated by heavy industry, notably shipbuilding, an enterprise well known for marked changes of fortune.

In 1945 nine yards were operating on Wearside. Subsequent closure and amal-gamation reduced their number. For a start, a yard established at Southwick during hostilities shut a couple of years after the war. Nevertheless, although output of the town's shipyards fell following the return of peace, the industry remained buoyant for some time. This is illustrated by the fact that 20.6 per cent of Sunderland's male population aged 15 or over was engaged in shipbuilding or repairing in 1951. The industry was, of course, also a source of employment for individuals in ancillary fields such as marine engineering.

However, in 1954 output fell significantly. During that year Austin's merged with Pickersgill's, and Laing's did so with J.L. Thompson's. A revival ensued but produc-tion was again low in 1960 and further closures and mergers followed.

In 1961 Doxford's became part of a new conglomerate—Doxford and Sunder-land Shipbuilding and Engineering Company, which included the already merged Laing's and J.L. Thompson's. Three years later, the Pallion shipyard of Short Brothers closed and was demolished. The same year also witnessed the closure of Austin's shipyard, located on the south bank of the Wear just below Wearmouth Bridge. Since the merger with Pickersgill's, the yard had been of secondary importance to the latter's Southwick shipyard, which benefited from major investment (including the construction of new berths) to enhance competitiveness.

Another significant development happened in 1968. Austin and Pickersgill amal-

The bulk carrier *G.M. Livanos* shortly after being launched at North Sands, Monkwearmouth, in April 1968

gamated with Bartram's. By this date Austin and Pickersgill had recently developed a medium-sized general cargo ship, the SD14, and as Ray Nichols has commented, this 'proved to be a world-beater.'[14] It made A&P the most profitable merchant ship-builder in Britain. The first SD14, the *Nicola*, was launched in December 1967 and in due course another 125 SD14's were built on Wearside.

These ships had a dead-weight of approximately 15,000 tons (a thousand tons or so greater than originally planned) and were thus small compared to some other vessels produced on the Wear. The largest were constructed at North Sands by the conglomerate formed in 1961 that included Dox-ford's, a conglomerate that became known as Sun-derland Shipbuilders Ltd

Aerial view of the shipyard at North Sands in 1973

in early 1973 after being acquired by the Court Line the previous year. Some ships launched at North Sands exceeded 150,000 tons deadweight, as was true in 1972 of the ore bulk tanker, *Naess Crusader.*

Two years later the Court Line collapsed and Sunderland Shipbuilders was taken into public ownership. Shortly thereafter, in 1977, Austin and Pickersgill was likewise nationalized and the Wear's shipyards came under the umbrella of British Ship-builders. In 1986, though, the Wear yards were privatized and on 1 April merged to become North East Shipbuilders Ltd.

The shipbuilding industry had experienced a worldwide slump since the late 1970s, and by the close of that decade production had ceased at North Sands and the yard was mothballed. But shortly after the formation of NESL, the future for the industry locally looked assured for the company won a contract to provide a Danish firm with 24 ferries. Sadly, things went sour thereby threatening NESL's survival. The Danes changed their minds following the delivery of two of the vessels. Twelve more of the ferries were built on Wearside, but selling these proved difficult. Eventually, another six were sold to the Danish firm in question and buyers were found for the others. The last ferry left the Wear in the spring of 1990.

By that date shipbuilding in Sunderland had come to an end. Following the re-election of the Conservatives in 1987, the Prime Minister, Margaret Thatcher, appointed Lord Young and Kenneth Clarke to the Department of Trade and Industry with the brief of privatizing remaining nationalized industries. Young reportedly told the prime minister that he would do so by Christmas 1988. The heavily subsi-dized merchant shipbuilding yards of Govan (on the Clyde) and NESL were a high priority.

Govan was sold to a Norwegian firm in 1988, which received a very substantial grant from the British Government to help with the modernization of the yard. However, the European Economic Community's Commission on State Aid and Competition had to ensure that the shipbuilding interests of member countries were not adversely affected by state subsidizing of yards above permitted limits. The DTI had done just that concerning the sale of Govan (and other British Shipbuilders' interests). A secret deal was thus made between DTI civil servants and the commis-sion. The latter would only grant its approval of the sale on condition that there was a closure of a yard, i.e., NESL, to reduce the number of subsidized yards in Europe.

In July, prior to the deal's being struck in December 1988, Clarke was replaced as Young's deputy by Tony Newton. Wearsiders were now well aware that NESL's future was on the line and a vigorous campaign involving locals of all classes and political persuasions was underway. One of the campaign's principal figures was Alan Milburn of the Newcastle-based Trade Union Studies Information Unit, who observed: 'Few communities could have marshalled such overwhelming support in such a short time and shown the determination and spirit to fight for the industry's survival.'[15]

Tony Newton—who was subsequently unaware of the deal referred to—also wished to save the yards (among the most advanced in the world) and hoped that

Superflex ferries from the ill-fated Danish order berthed at Monkwearmouth in 1989

a suitable buyer would appear. None did so, and in the Commons on 7 December he reluctantly announced the closure of NESL. He also mentioned an aid package of £45 million and the introduction of an Enterprise Zone for Sunderland intended to provide new jobs. Nonetheless, the news was met with widespread anger and sadness on Wearside, for the closure of NESL meant that Sunderland's already higher than average rate of unemployment would be swollen by around 2,000 redundant shipyard workers, as well as by people who would lose jobs indirectly. It also meant the end of a centuries-old facet of Sunderland's existence: five days after the announcement, the Wear saw its final launch when the last of the ferries, watched by sombre onlookers, slid into the river on the evening of 12 December 1988.

But hopes soon revived. Established firms, prepared to build unsubsidized ships if necessary, came forward to purchase the yards. In June 1989 expectations that British Shipbuilders' chairman, Sir John Lister, would name a preferred bidder were high. Sadly, this did not prove the case. On 27 June Newton went to Brussels to meet Leon Brittan, the newly appointed head of the Commission on State Aid and Competition, taking the finalized bids with him. As has been stated, Newton was unaware of the secret deal struck the previous year between DTI civil servants and the commission, a deal which, according to a brief prepared for Brittan, stated that the 'closure of North East Shipbuilders Ltd was a determining factor' in the commission's approval of the DTI's oversubsidizing of Govan and other privatizations. Newton was told that even if the government allowed unsubsidized shipbuilding to commence on the Wear, not only would the aid package for Sunderland be jeopardized but the issue of state aid to Govan etc would be reopened.

According to Bob Clay (one of Sunderland's MPs who was heavily involved in the fight to save the town's shipbuilding industry), Newton returned from Brussels 'absolutely devastated', and shortly after doing so he made an announcement that destroyed hopes of the resumption of shipbuilding on Wearside. This whole saga is made more poignant by the fact that the world was about to witness a significant upturn in demand for ships.

Sunderland's coalmining industry has also sunk into oblivion. In 1947, when coal mines were nationalized, there were 127 collieries in County Durham including several on Wearside. The local pits were a major source of employment, as can be gained from the fact that 18,133 people were employed in the industry in 1960, about 20 per cent of Sunderland's male workforce. But the 1960s witnessed a marked decline in demand for coal, a decline that was not allayed, and so pits closed. Ryhope and Washington F Pit did so in 1966 and 1968, whereas Silksworth Colliery shut in 1971. Hylton Colliery went the same way in 1979.

Only three pits remained in the borough by the mid 1980s, namely Wearmouth, Herrington and Eppleton (all of which dated from the 19th century) and they were affected by a nationwide miners' strike that commenced in 1984. The headline of the front page of the *Sunderland Echo* of Friday, 9 March, reads 'All-Out Strike' and notes that the 14,000 miners of the Durham coalfield were expected to commence strike action on the following Monday.

The decision was certainly not universally welcome in pit communities. This was apparent on Saturday, 10 March, when Arthur Scargill visited Sunderland. The militant leader of the National Miners' Union, a figure revered by some and viewed as a left-wing egomaniac by others, came to speak to Wearmouth miners at the Barbary Coast Club, Monkwearmouth. There, angry women from Hetton opposed to strike action—their husbands worked at Eppleton and Murton pits—had gathered and loudly vented their feelings.

Two days later, Monday's *Echo* declared 'Durham Pitmen Obey the Call' as the miners, like the majority of their counterparts nationwide, commenced strike action. Indeed, locally the only pits that continued to work were Dawdon and Vane Tempest Collieries in the Seaham area. However, the following day flying pickets, some of whom were from Wearmouth Colliery, made their way to the two pits where the miners duly refused to cross the picket line and returned home.

The strike engendered a great deal of bitterness, as a few men contemptuously described as 'scabs' by fellow miners, began returning to work. They did so in late August and their treacherous, or valiantly pragmatic stance, led others to do likewise, a process that really began to gain momentum in November. Consequently, heated clashes occurred at the picket-lines between irate strikers and the police. In addition, the homes of some strike-breakers were attacked and members of their families subjected to abuse. By early 1985, substantial numbers of miners were back at work. On Monday, 4 February, it was reported that this was true of over 700 of Wearmouth's 2,000 pitmen. Almost a month later, on 1 March, the number of returnees at the pit totalled 1,583.

The strike was all but over and four days later, on Tuesday 5 March, the most die-hard strikers marched back to work behind union banners. As feelings were still running high, clashes took place and several men were arrested, one of whom was the local MP, Bob Clay. He had allegedly shouted obscenities at the police and declared that Britain was 'a police state.'

Shortly thereafter, in December, Herrington Colliery was closed and Eppleton Colliery went the same way at the end of March 1986. Subsequently, in October 1992 the President of the Board of Trade, Michael Heseltine (a flamboyant figure nick-named 'Tarzan') announced that 31 pits were to be closed or mothballed nationally. Among these was Wearmouth, one of the most advanced mines in the country—an innovative air system had been introduced in the late 1980s. Although the colliery had massive under-sea coal reserves, the pit was to be mothballed. Nationwide public outrage at Heseltine's announcement led to a policy rethink, and one result of this was that Wearmouth was reprieved for market testing. But in November 1993 British Coal announced that the mine—the last in the Durham coalfield—would close on 10 December. This proved the case, with the loss of 670 jobs.

Vaux Breweries, another historic part of Sunderland's industrial life, has likewise ceased to exist. It closed on Friday, 2 July 1999, an event that affected 430 local employees. They each received engraved glasses and bottles of the last beer to be produced—'Time Gentlemen Please!' Referring to the closure, an *Echo* editorial concluded: 'We say, simply and with respect, Cheers, to a dear, departed friend.'

Given that the UK market was suffering from overcapacity in brewing, there had been doubts about Vaux's future for a number of years. Analysts had forecast that the parent company, Swallow, would sell Vaux off to concentrate on their other interest—hotels. With closure looming, a management buy-out bid aimed at saving Vaux took place, led by the Managing Director, Frank Nicholson, a descendant of the founder Cuthbert Vaux. Nicholson described the closure as 'achingly sad.' Among those who shared this sentiment was Peter Wood, a Vaux forklift driver who had worked for the firm for nearly twenty years. He told Ray Nichols of the *Echo*: 'It's absolutely terrible. If you worked at Vaux you thought that you had a job for life. It just seems to me that nothing is safe in Sunderland now.'[16]

Other traditional industries, the manufacture of paper and glass have likewise disappeared. Ford Paper Mill closed in 1971 and Hendon Mill did so nine years later. In the latter case, the plant was reopened in 1981 by the Edward Thompson Group (a well-established local firm) to produce low-grade paper for bingo tickets. However, major production at the site ended in 2005 and it was earmarked for redevelopment, including housing.

The most notable local glass manufacturer was the firm of James A. Jobling, whose factory on Wearside was the Wear Glass Works at Millfield, a plant supplemented in the early 1960s by additional facilities erected at Deptford. The best-known product was Pyrex. Output also included car headlamp lenses and heated glass. Of the firm, it was noted in the late 1960s when the workforce numbered around 3,000:

> The Wear Glass Works, together with a new laboratory apparatus factory at Deptford, is among the Commonwealth's largest producers of glassware for industry, laboratories, and for kitchens and dining tables all over the world. Joblinglass from the firm's Industrial Division goes out to over 114 different lands…and 'Pyrex' oven and tableware to even more….The group has during the past five years increased its exports by 65 per cent.[17]

In 1973 the business was acquired by an American firm, the Corning International Corporation, whereupon additional facilities were erected and production increased, although owing to modernisation in production methods the number of employees subsequently fell. Production continued into the 21st century, but on 2 October 2006 it was announced that Cornings had decided to close its Sunderland operation, a decision that meant the loss of around 100 jobs.

Nevertheless, Sunderland is still the location of significant industrial activity and notable firms with a presence in the city are Rolls Royce and Nissan. In 1966, the former acquired Bristol Siddeley Engines, whose factories included works at Pallion Industrial Estate that had manufactured aero engine parts since the early 1950s when the Bristol Aeroplane Company had established a plant at Pallion. However, in late 2009 Rolls Royce confirmed that it planned to move production from Pallion (where its staff numbered around 400) to Washington New Town and that work on a replacement factory there would commence in 2012.

Sunderland's most notable industrial enterprise is Nissan Motor Manufacturing (UK) Ltd., located between Sunderland proper and Washington New Town, and the largest single investment in Europe by a Japanese company. In January 1981 it was announced that Nissan, Japan's second largest car manufacturer, wished to establish a factory in Britain. Eight sites were thus considered. The final choice was between Shotton in North Wales and the location of Sunderland's nondescript airport at Usworth—the former RAF base had been acquired by the council in 1962 but closed in 1984. Thanks to the combined efforts of the Conservative Government, the Northern Development Council, the Washington Development Corporation and the local authorities, Nissan announced in favour of Sunderland on 30 March 1984.

Construction of a £50 million factory ensued, and in July 1986 production commenced. The initial short-term aim was to produce 24,000 Nissan Bluebirds annually with a workforce of 500. But on 8 September, a second phase was announced sooner than planned. Production was to increase to 100,000 cars annually and the workforce would expand to 2,700. Then, in December 1987, it was announced that additional facilities were to be provided by 1992 in order to manufacture the Nissan Micra, taking employment to around 3,500.

The Nissan factory has been an undoubted success. Of the plant, Marie Conte-Helm has stated: 'With quality standards equalling and sometimes surpassing those in Japan, the workers…have collectively justified the faith placed in them and the North East by the Japanese car giant.'[18] Indeed, on 1 February 1994, Nissan

Nissan Qashqais being fitted out on the production line at their Sunderland plant

announced that it was Britain's biggest car exporter after shipping 182,207 vehicles (84 per cent of total output) to 36 world markets in 1993. Moreover, according to an Economist Intelligence Unit survey of European motor vehicle productivity published in the summer of 1999, the Wearside factory, which had become Britain's largest car plant the previous year, was the most productive car producer in Europe for the third year running in 1998. Production totalled 288,838 cars, with output per head of 105 vehicles. In contrast, the number of vehicles per employee at Rover's Longbridge plant was a mere 30. Hence the journalist Roland Gribben observed:

> The levels of automation at Sunderland are described [in the EIU report] as 'no more than average' but the successful import of Japanese assembly line techniques has helped Nissan maintain its productivity improvement. Workers have adapted trolley-style platform systems to move in parallel with assembly lines and make it easier to instal components.[19]

Although doubts were raised in 2000 about the plant's future[20], the factory continued to operate and commenced manufacturing the Qashqai, a model that went on sale in March 2007 and proved popular with customers both at home and abroad. Nonetheless, in common with other car manufacturers Nissan's fortunes were inevitably affected by the subsequent worldwide economic downturn—the 'Credit Crunch.' So much so, that on 8 January 2009 the firm announced the loss of 1,200 jobs at the factory, thereby reducing the workforce to around 2,600.[21]

Thereafter, although the car market remained volatile, Nissan benefited from a car scrappage scheme introduced by the Labour Government and the plant's deputy manager Kevin Fitzpatrick said: 'Sunderland models—particularly smaller cars like Note and Micra—are proving very popular with scrappage customers.'[22]

In March 2010, Nissan stated that the Sunderland plant would become a production site for Nissan LEAF cars—the world's first mass-produced electric vehicles—which would be launched in 2013. In addition, a press release of 27 April 2010 declared that construction had started on Wearside of a plant to produce batteries for both Nissan and Renault electric vehicles.

Shortly afterwards, on 16 July the last Micra made at the plant rolled off the production line. In all, 2,368,704 of the vehicles were built at the factory—the first was completed on 10 August 1992—over 40 per cent of all cars produced at the plant since it started production in 1986. A new vehicle, the Juke, commenced production in August 2010 as part of a £57 million investment in the plant.

Nissan's arrival in the 1980s was a godsend, because high unemployment had been a marked (though by no means constant) feature of life in Sunderland since the war. The boom years of the 1950s were followed by the depressing early 1960s when many jobs in, for instance, shipbuilding were lost. In 1962–3, the number of unemployed rose as high as 9,000 out of a total insured population of less than 88,000.

Sunderland's unemployment record certainly compared unfavourably with some other places in the region, a point noted by B.T. Robson:

> Among the larger towns [in the North East] the major service centres such as Newcastle and Darlington show consistently lower rates of unemployment than the surrounding towns. This is a function of their more broadly based occupational structures which arise from the tertiary industries which they attract and which provide an employment stability conspicuously lacking in the neighbouring towns. Sunderland, for example, has experienced unemployment rates well above even the regional levels.[23]

Unemployment likewise blighted many lives on Wearside in the 1970s and 80s (Washington New Town fared less badly) and in connection with this, we read:

> The decline in *male* employment in the early and mid-1970s accelerated as the recession deepened, and resulted in an overall decline of 16,200 jobs (-21%) between 1971 and 1981; by contrast, female employment increased over this period by 4,100 (9%) .... The fall in male employment on Wearside was much greater than for the Northern Region (-15.6%) and Britain as a whole (-9.8%) .... The period 1981–84 has seen the continuation of these trends away from male employment (down an estimated 9.3% since 1981) and towards female employment (up by 2.4%), resulting in a situation where women have come to constitute almost half (47.5%) of the Wearside employment total by 1984.[24]

Unemployment during this difficult period in Sunderland's history peaked in September 1985, when 29,686 people were registered as unemployed, a substantial percentage of the workforce when one bears in mind that the borough's total population in 1981 stood at 294,894. Fortunately, the number of jobless then fell very substantially as Sunderland benefited from the nationwide upturn in the economy, but the improvement was short-lived. Recession returned in 1990 and unemployment climbed to 18,653 in January 1993.

A much better situation prevailed at the time of the 2001 census, by which time Sunderland's population had fallen from the peak of 20 years earlier to 280,807. The city had an unemployment rate of 4.8 per cent, which although higher than the national average of 3.4 per cent was a vast improvement on the grim years two decades or so earlier. In line with recent developments, though, a higher proportion of males was unemployed than females.

Inevitably, as a result of the international economic downturn that began in 2008, unemployment levels in Sunderland have risen. In June 2011, for example, 9,510 people were receiving Jobseeker's Allowance, a benefit payable to people aged over 18 but under pensionable age who were out of work and looking for employment.

The Retail Sector

While Sunderland has many moderately prosperous citizens, the vast majority of its inhabitants are not well off and this is reflected in the quality of the shops, for second-rate stores are commonplace.

In the post-war decades, however, several good department stores existed and premier place among them belonged to Binns, one of the few upmarket shops that graced the town centre into the late 20th century. It was located on both sides of the southern end of Fawcett Street, the principal shopping thoroughfare. The premises had been bombed in World War II and thus the business operated on a reduced scale in Holmeside until a new five-storey block opened on one of the bomb-damaged sites.

Work commenced on the new structure in late 1949 and the replacement shop, occupying most of the southwest end of Fawcett Street, partially opened on Monday 2 March 1953—the third and fourth floors did so later. The 'nerve centre' was the basement, where there was 'a switchboard as large as that in an ocean liner, controlling the Neon signs and the lights on every floor.' There was also 'an air conditioning plant—air conditioning is installed in the restaurant, hairdressing rooms and kitchens—boilers for heating the building and the pressure plant which maintains the pneumatic tube system linking every counter with the counting house.'[25] Subsequently, a four-storey building was constructed on the opposite side of the road in 1958–62 and this part of Binns was later connected to the other shop by a subway under Fawcett Street.

By the 1980s Binns was passed its heyday, and in April 1989 the east building closed. More bad news followed, and on Saturday 30 January 1993, the surviving premises likewise shut, with the loss of 140 jobs. One of the members of staff made redundant was 64-year-old Fred Johnson, who told the *Sunderland Star* shortly before closure: 'The Binns store is an institution in Sunderland, and many of the customers have been telling us how sad they are that it's closing. Some have been telling us how they used to shop here with their parents, never imagining a Sunderland without a Binns.'

In the immediate post-war period another fine department store, Joplings, was located in High Street West, three blocks down from the junction with Fawcett Street. However, the shop went up in flames on 14 December 1954, but after using temporary premises, it reopened on 3 May 1956 in a purpose-built four-storey building (with the town's first escalator) on John Street.[26]

Joplings survived into the 21st century, when the future of Sunderland's oldest department store was on the line more than once. In 2007, the shop, which had faced imminent closure, gained a reprieve when it was taken over by Liverpool-based Vergo Retail, although a decline in the quality of some of the stock ensued. Unfortunately, in the spring of 2010 Vergo Retail collapsed. As a result, on 11 May some of Jopling's staff were laid off and it was announced that the shop would shut within four weeks if a buyer did not come forward. Sadly, closure ensued.

The closed Joplings store in July 2011

In the second half of the 1960s (following large-scale demolition and clearance) a pedestrianised shopping complex was developed a short distance to the west of Fawcett Street. Windswept and unattractive, it was soon totally outclassed by Newcastle's indoor Eldon Square development which took custom away from Sunderland, a situation worsened by the opening of the vast Metrocentre near Gateshead in the 1980s. Hence to improve Sunderland's shopping facilities, the centre was overhauled in the late 1980s. It was covered over, enlarged, rendered vastly more attractive and named 'The Bridges.' Customer flow increased from 250,000 to 400,000 people a week. The complex has since been greatly expanded, partly with the aim of attracting additional custom to the city and the extension opened in September 2000.[27]

From the outset the extension has been dominated by a three-storey department store, Debenhams, located at the southwest corner of the Bridges. Although not in the first rank of Debenham shops, the store is the showpiece of the centre.

Sunderland's only department store, photographed in March 2011

The ground floor stocks items such as men's wear, jewellery and fragrances whereas the first floor contains women's clothing, lingerie etc. On the top floor one can find furniture and small electrical items. At this level there is also a restaurant.

Upon exiting the east end of the Bridges, shoppers are in another pedestrianised area, albeit one open to the elements, and where businesses include a branch of W.H. Smith located on the far side of the space in question. Here, too, one finds entrances to the city's underground Central Station, which has occupied the same site since 1879. Little more than a stone's throw to the south, lies Waterloo Place, where two-way motor traffic runs. For many years one of the shops located here was Hills Bookshop, a business that had opened elsewhere in the town during the Victorian era and moved to Waterloo Place in 1929. To the regret of loyal customers, the independently run store ceased trading in early 2006, partly as a result of competition from a branch of Waterstones in the Bridges.

In the opposite direction from the Central Station, lies a pedestrianised section of High Street West that is still a busy retail area. Shops here include Marks & Spencer, which specialises in selling clothing and luxury food and is the most imposing building lining this part of the street. Walking eastward from this point, the junction with Fawcett Street and Bridge Street is soon reached. This location is dominated by old buildings such as Frank Caws' Elephant Tea House (occupied by a branch of the Royal Bank of Scotland) and Hutchinson's Buildings. On the other hand, in the late 1960s another Victorian structure, the *Grand Hotel* in Bridge Street, was demolished. Moreover, at that date the *Sunderland Echo* had its office in Bridge Street, but in 1976 it moved to a purpose-built factory at Pennywell and another building now occupies the Bridge Street site. Recently part of the ground floor of Hutchinson's Buildings contained a confectionery shop named 'Sweet Home Alabama', founded in 2004 by Martin and Joan O' Neill. The business moved to Fawcett Street in 2012.

The centre of Fawcett Street is dominated by branches of banks, namely Barclays and Lloyds, and a branch of Northern Rock is located toward the southern end of the street. Confidence in the financial viability of the latter bank collapsed in the autumn of 2007 and, in line with events nationwide, anxious Wearsiders formed long queues outside the Fawcett Street branch (and others in the city) to withdraw their money—it was the first run on a British bank for 150 years. Although the heart of Sunderland's retail sector has moved westward, the street is still mostly lined with retail outlets such as Wilkinson, part of a high street discount chain, that occupies the former Binns' premises on the west side of the road.

Until the 1970s, corner shops were numerous in Sunderland and people could find butchers, grocers, chemists and so on close at hand. However, the closing decades of the 20th century saw a massive reduction in the number of corner shops as consumers largely abandoned them in favour of supermarkets, a development that also harmed suburban shopping centres. Milk rounds were also affected. Instead of having milk delivered on a daily basis, Wearsiders increasingly purchased it more cheaply at supermarkets. Early supermarkets were modest in scale, as was true of one erected in Sea Road, Fulwell, following the closure of the Marina Cinema in 1963. But much larger stores followed, as is true of Morrisons at Seaburn, which dates from the late 1980s.

The supermarkets belong to national chains, but Sunderland has produced notable entrepreneurs like Tom Cowie. As a young man, on 1 June 1948, he commenced selling used motorcycles at 1 Matamba Terrace in Millfield (owing to franchising restrictions operated by motorcycle manufacturers, the business could only sell secondhand bikes) and T. Cowie Ltd went from strength to strength.

In 1952 the company opened a branch in Newcastle, and another on Hylton Road near the Matamba Terrace headquarters. Other branches duly followed and in 1956 the firm added another string to its bow when it began selling scooters manufactured in Italy, for as Phil Martin comments: 'Far from putting obstacles in the way of dealers keen to sell their product, the Italian scooter manufacturers actively encouraged them.'[28] In the wake of this development, new motorbikes were also soon available from Cowie showrooms. In 1961, by which time Cowies had branches outside the region, motorbike sales nationally plummeted and so the firm switched emphasis to the selling of motorcars, which were becoming increasingly popular, and by March 1963 these accounted for 80 per cent of sales.

Cowies became a public limited company in late 1964, and continued to grow and enter new fields. By 1988 it had Britain's largest fleet of vehicles on contract hire. Tom Cowie received a knighthood in 1992 and retired the following year. In 1997 the Cowie Group changed its name to Arriva (Sir Tom was honorary president) with the aim of appealing more readily to European customers, and now concentrates primarily on running bus operations in the UK and Europe—in 2003, the firm sold its car retail business. The company's headquarters, which had remained at Matamba Terrace well into the 1990s, are located at the prestigious Doxford International Business Park. This opened on the southwest outskirts of Sunderland in the early 1990s, and other enterprises located there include call-centres that deal with such matters as telephone banking.

The Harbour and Transport

In the two decades that followed the war, the River Wear Commission carried out improvements to the port that cost at least £800,000. Among other things, the work included widening the river in two places, reclaiming around 12 acres of land at the South Docks' complex, and erecting the world's first aluminium alloy bascule bridge (over the junction of the Hudson and Hendon Docks), a structure that opened in 1948.

The port remained busy and coal—the staple export—left the harbour in substantial quantities. In the early 1950s over three million tons were shipped annually, mostly for consumption elsewhere in the United Kingdom. By 1960, though, the amount of coal that left the port had dropped to little over two million. The decline continued, a situation exacerbated in the mid 1980s by the opening of new coal handling facilities on Tyneside capable of loading larger vessels. Consequently 1986 witnessed an historic event, namely, the end of the shipment of coal from the Wear. By this date the River Wear Commission no longer existed for it had been replaced by the Port of Sunderland Authority in 1972.

A few years before that event occurred, it was observed:

> The port has a varied general cargo trade which is closely related to the industries of the town and the North East. For example, imports include sisal from East Africa for rope-making; wood pulp from Scandinavia, Belgium, France and Portugal, esparto pulp from North Africa, and china clay from Cornwall, for local paper mills; silver sand and borax from Holland for the town's world-famous 'Pyrex-glassware'; kieselguhr from North Africa for chemical works, and Turkish crome ore for making refactory bricks used in the steel industry; as well as quantities of sawnwood, pitwood and tall oil.[29]

More recently, in 1999–2000, metals comprised 53 per cent of exports, limestone 43 per cent and sundries 4 per cent. On the other hand, oil products accounted for 64 per cent of the cargo landed at the port and aggregates, metals and forest products comprised the remainder.[30] In 2010, the number of ships that cleared the port was 181, a much lower figure than in previous decades. In 1961, for example, 1,568 vessels did so, but the decline was offset to some extent by the fact that the average

The modern reel-lay vessel *Seven Oceans* at Corporation Quay 2011

size of ships had substantially increased. In 2010, the main exports were agricultural lime, scrap metal, crane parts, cargoes for projects offshore, and combinable crops. The principal imports included forest products, mixed dry bulks and non-ferrous metals.

At the beginning of the period, trams were an important component of the town's transport network. However, in 1947 the corporation—which also operated buses—decided to phase trams out of service, partly to save the cost of renewing track and overhead wires. This process culminated on 1 October 1954 when the last tram arrived at the *Wheatsheaf* depot after a ceremonial journey through the town.

On the other hand, the council ran buses until the early 1970s when, as a result of rising operational costs, it handed over the concern to the Tyneside Passenger Transport Executive on 1 April 1973, a body that soon became Tyne and Wear PTE. The latter operated services until the Transport Act of 1985 introduced bus deregulation. The legislation came into effect in October of the following year when local authorities were obligated to transfer municipally owned bus services to separate companies. As a result, bus services again became competitive (unprofitable routes are subsidized by the PTE), a state of affairs that had not existed since the 1930s.

Private bus companies had, however, operated during the days of municipal dominance. Firms included the W.H. Jolly Company, a small concern founded at South Hylton by William Henry Jolly in the early 1920s. Its sphere of operations was very limited. But in the mid 1960s, as a result of the cessation of the rail link between South Hylton and Sunderland in 1964, the firm was licensed to extend its routes and that year saw the arrival of the first Jolly bus to carry passengers into the centre of the town. Jolly's operated until mid 1995, by which time a far greater concern, the Stagecoach Group, had just entered the field. Locally, it is represented by a subsidiary, Stagecoach North East, which is based on Wearside. The main depot is on Dundas Street in Monkwearmouth and its offices are a stone's throw away beside the *Wheatsheaf.*

In the early years of the post-war era, steam-powered ferries operated across the Wear, travelling between Monkwearmouth and a landing beside Wylam Wharf in the East End. Upstream, and outside Sunderland's boundaries, was another ferry

Traffic near the *Wheatsheaf* in March 1954

that used substantial rowing boats to convey passengers between South and North Hylton. However, in 1957 the ferries ceased operating and the following year a rowing boat ferry at Cox Green (further upriver) was replaced by a footbridge.

Changes have also affected the railway network. In 1947, for example, railways that carried coal to staithes on Wearside came under the control of the National Coal Board. As in the past, considerable quantities of coal were conveyed for shipment but, as noted above, a marked decline ensued and in the 1960s coal shipments from the Hetton and Lambton staithes terminated, and likewise ceased at the Wearmouth staithes, thereby bringing an end to a long-established facet of Sunderland's railway activity. But trains continued to convey coal to the South Dock complex (in 1983 the figure was 1,570,529 tons) until shipments ceased in 1986.

In the early years of the period, rail passenger services were operated by the London and North Eastern Railway, formed in 1923 and embracing the former NER. In 1948, LNER was nationalized and a significant reduction in the scale of Sunderland's railway network ensued. In 1952–3, for instance, passenger services on what had once been the Durham and Sunderland line ceased. By the spring of 1967 (almost a decade after diesels had begun to supplant steam locomotives on Wearside) the town only possessed two passenger stations, Sunderland Central, which had been recently modernised, and Seaburn. Passenger services had ended at Monkwearmouth

The Metro at Millfield Station in the summer of 2010

Station on 4 March of that year, which thereafter continued to operate as a freight depot until 1981.

The previous year had seen the opening of the Metro system, a rail service on Tyneside operated by Tyne and Wear PTE and later under the brandname of 'Nexus'. It was expected that the Metro would be extended to Wearside, but the link was delayed for many years. Indeed, the Metro only began operating in Sunderland on 31 March 2002. In addition to using existing stations, new ones, such as the Stadium of Light and Park Lane, were thus provided. Work on the latter, located underground and the most prestigious of the new facilities, was still underway when the Metro's Sunderland service opened and was completed on 28 April of that year. On Wearside, the Metro terminates at a station at South Hylton and the track between there and Park Lane was built along the route of a railway line (the Penshaw Branch) that had carried passengers from 1853 until 1964.

Another form of transport, the motorcar, has of course witnessed a dramatic rise in popularity since 1945. Even so, as late as the 1970s most Wearsiders were still reliant on public transport. In 1977, for example, only 34.7 per cent of households had a car. In 2001, the figure had risen to just over 60 per cent while the average for England and Wales was 73.2 per cent.

Major changes to the road network have included the introduction of one-way traffic systems. In the heart of the town, the first of these was introduced in 1960 when John Street was reserved for south bound traffic and Fawcett Street for vehicles travelling north. Property has also been destroyed to make way for new roads. A case in point affected the northern fringe of the town centre, where a swathe of buildings were demolished in 1968–9 for an inner ring road that runs westward from just above St Mary's Church towards the magistrates courts. This was the first stage of an inner ring road that was completed in the 1990s. Moreover, on Sunderland's western outskirts the mid 1970s saw a major feat of engineering, namely the construction of Hylton Bridge to carry the A19 (a dual carriageway) across the River Wear. Another bridge, closer to the heart of the city, is in the pipeline.[31]

Society

Since 1945, in line with events elsewhere, Sunderland's inhabitants have observed major social changes. For a start, the standard of living has risen considerably. Many items that were either only possessed by the wealthy or did not even exist are now enjoyed, or taken for granted, by growing numbers of Wearsiders and holidays abroad have become increasingly common. Sunderland's population is also more diverse and minority groups, such as Asians and Chinese, are well established. Nevertheless, in 2001 the number of foreign-born residents was 2.5 per cent, well below the figure for many other cities in the country, and 98.1 per cent of the population was white in contrast to the 91.3 per cent for England and Wales. Although the number of non-white residents has since increased, Sunderland still ranks among the least cosmopolitan urban centres in England.

Sunderland has also witnessed a decline in the social fabric. Marriage breakdowns have greatly increased, and criminality and disrespect for authority have become more pronounced than they were in the immediate post-war era, a period that experienced a drop in juvenile crime partly because parental discipline increased as fathers returned from the services. In 1947, for instance, 340 youths had cases proved against them in the Juvenile Magistrates Court, 277 fewer than had been the situation in 1945.

Since then, numerous reports have highlighted anti-social behaviour by youths and others. Early in the period, the corporation's cleansing superintendent, G.M. Sagar, declared that the 'devastation and ruin' caused by the town's vandals was 'enough to make you weep.'[32] In 1970, moreover, an article noted that at Sunderland Juvenile Court four boys whose ages ranged from 12 to 14, had admitted causing damage worth £2,000. At Wade's furniture store in High Street, alone, they had 'slashed three-piece suites, poured paint on carpets and ransacked the manager's office.' Consequently, three of the quartet were 'put on probation for two years, and ordered to spend 24 hours at an attendance centre…[and] ordered to pay £16 11s. 5d. compensation each.'[33]

In addition, large gangs have sometimes caused mayhem. In 1991 the front-page of the *Echo* declared: 'Wearside Teen Gangs Run Riot.' The paper noted that a major bus company, Go-Ahead Northern, was threatening to withdraw its service to a 'no-go' area of the town because approximately 30 youths had stoned one of its vehicles in Pennywell. The incident was 'the latest in a series of violent attacks in Sunderland over the past two weeks. Drivers say they are being stoned by teenagers who, instead of running away, are holding their ground and even climbing onto moving buses, opening their boots and disabling the engines.'[34]

Norman Dennis (1929–2010),
a prominent local academic who
lamented the state of modern society

Certainly, some parts of the city have acquired bad reputations. Empty, boarded-up homes have become a common sight in these areas where ill-mannered, ill-educated and self-centred residents make life difficult for decent neighbours. As the left-wing sociologist Norman Dennis aptly noted, the 'emergence of an unemployable male underclass, depending on state benefits and the proceeds of crime instead of productive work' has undoubtedly had an adverse impact.[35] A comparable view was made by one of Sunderland's MPs, Chris Mullin. On 29 April 2005, he noted that fifteen years after 'The Fall of Thatcher we are still manufacturing semi-literate, unemployable, useless youths, many of them second- or third-generation yob culture.' Mullin was referring to gangs of 'truanting, feral youths' who were making 'a misery of the lives of the law-abiding citizens' living in a terrace in Silksworth.[36]

Nonetheless, despite the above, lawlessness in Sunderland is less prevalent than in some other urban centres—Middlesbrough is a case in point—and large parts of the city experience little significant anti-social and criminal activity and are undoubtedly attractive locations in which to live.

Religion and Education

Since 1945 religion has continued its downward trend. In 2001, according to census returns, 81.5 per cent of Sunderland's residents were Christians but most of these would have been nominally so, for the number of practising Christians has dwindled. For a variety of reasons (including a mistaken belief that all reputable scientists are non-religious) atheism and agnosticism have gained ground.

Hence many places of worship have closed. This process affected two of Sunderland's oldest churches, St John's and Holy Trinity, located in the East End. The former operated until 1970 and was demolished two years later, while Holy Trinity was closed in 1988, although the occasional service continued to be held. In these cases, slum clearance and the removal of many people to peripheral council estates contributed to dwindling congregations, but elsewhere increasing reluctance to attend services proved decisive. One of Sunderland's finest buildings, Christ Church in Ashbrooke closed in 1998 in the face of a major bill for badly needed repairs but in this instance the building was soon taken over by a Sikh congregation.

Other places of worship affected have included St Aidan's Church in Roker (built in 1910) which was converted into a private home in 2000, and the synagogue on Ryhope Road which closed in March 2006 and stands forlorn and empty. The fate of the latter building was sealed by the marked decline of Sunderland's Jewish population, whose numbers fell sharply as families moved elsewhere, in some cases to further careers whilst others emigrated to Israel. In the early decades of the period, the town's Jewish population (which had numbered 2,000 in the mid 1930s) was still substantial and totalled 1,350 in 1965. Subsequently, though, the number of Jews in Sunderland collapsed and there were only 114 in the city in 2001.

On the other hand, Sunderland's oldest church, St Peter's in Monkwearmouth, is still open for worship and underwent an expensive restoration programme after it was set alight by an arsonist on 19 March 1984. Bishopwearmouth parish church—which was renamed Sunderland Minster in 1998—is likewise still a centre of Anglican worship.

For some Wearsiders, religion is certainly fundamental to their existence. This is true, for instance, of Born Again Christians and members of Sunderland's ethnic minorities. In 2001, for example, there were 2,099 Muslims in the city. Moreover, some members of the burgeoning Chinese community worship at the True Jesus Church in Dundas Street, Monkwearmouth, where the congregation is overwhelmingly Chinese. They reject the Trinity doctrine and do not celebrate Christmas because of its pagan origins.

This is also true of Jehovah's Witnesses, who worship in Whickham Street in Monkwearmouth and at Toward Road, as well as at congregations in outlying areas such as Washington. The Witnesses regularly make their presence felt through house-to-house preaching and are not popular for their courageous ministry angers some householders. In addition, their beliefs are sometimes misrepresented. For one thing, because of their refusal to celebrate Christmas, it is said that they do not believe in Jesus Christ whereas he is central to their beliefs. However, they deem Jesus as subordinate to God—Jehovah.

Turning to education, in 1945 Sunderland's educational institutions included the Technical College, which had opened near Bishopwearmouth Green in 1901, and whose facilities had been added to between the wars. Further expansion ensued and in 1958 it was noted that the college was experiencing a phase of 'rapid growth and development' and that student numbers had 'doubled in the last ten years.'[37]

The following year, a major construction project started on Chester Road, and resulted in a new campus that opened in 1964. The facilities included the Edinburgh Building and Wearmouth Hall, the latter a multi-storey residential block. According to Anne Wright, these 'developments meant that Sunderland's Technical College was the first in the region with residential accommodation…and the college was the largest of 25 regional colleges.' She continues, 'Of the student intake a surprisingly high proportion were Norwegian. That group had grown rapidly from 1946 and reached a peak of 260 in the mid 1960s.'[38]

Other higher education establishments were the School of Art, and Sunderland Training College, respectively based in Ashburne House and Langham Tower. Until 1959 the training college was a women-only institution. Interestingly, in 1962 the Cambridge-educated historian Tom Corfe, who moved to Sunderland from Melton Mowbray, joined the staff and in his spare time soon made his mark in the field of local history.[39]

On 1 January 1969 the Technical College and the School of Art merged to form one of the country's first three polytechnics, and were augmented in 1975 by the Sunderland College of Education, as Sunderland Training College had become known.

Over 15 years later (in common with 'polys' elsewhere) Sunderland Polytechnic was granted university status in 1992 and the first vice chancellor was Anne Wright. A splendid new campus, to supplement the existing facilities centred on Chester Road, was constructed on the north bank of the River Wear near St Peter's Church and was officially opened in April 1996 by His Royal Highness, Prince Charles. In addition, major changes have occurred at the Chester Road facilities. For one thing, in 2007–9 Wearmouth Hall was demolished and replaced by CitySpace, a state of the art structure that serves as a sport and social facility. Contemporaneously, the Edinburgh Building was refurbished and given a facelift.

In 2010 the university won the UK's top student experience title at *The Times'* annual Higher Education Awards, and in 2011 it was described by *The Guardian* as the best new university in the North East.

By the time Sunderland Polytechnic was formed, the town's educational facilities also included West Park College of Further Education. This opened in September 1959 (the official opening occurred five months later) and occupied purpose-built premises near the site of the future Civic Centre. The college provided courses on subjects like electrical engineering, naval architecture, and mechanical engineering.

University of Sunderland premises in 2010. The Edinburgh Building is on the left

It was duly replaced by Wearside College (in the Grangetown area) that was officially opened in 1972 by the Conservative Education Secretary, Margaret Thatcher.[40]

North of the river, meanwhile, the early 1960s had witnessed the opening of Monkwearmouth College of Further Education. This initially taught subjects such as nursing and dressmaking, but topics such as O- and A-level history, government, sociology and English literature later became part of the curriculum. The college occupied premises on Swan Street that had just been vacated by Monkwearmouth Grammar School, and later acquired additional facilities such as the former buildings of Stansfield Street School (near Roker Avenue) that had closed in 1974.[41]

In the summer of 1996 Wearside and Monkwearmouth colleges merged to form the City of Sunderland College, which has six main campuses, including the former Bede School buildings and facilities in outlying areas like Shiney Row.[42]

In the opening decades of the period, grammar schools that selected pupils on academic merit via the 11-plus examination, enjoyed pride of place among the town's state schools and this was especially true of 'the Bede', which became a grammar school in 1945. In addition to a strong intake from middle-class backgrounds, the grammar schools also numbered working-class children among their pupils and played a valuable role in facilitating social mobility.

Understandably, in view of the fine education provided by the grammar schools, in late 1964 there was widespread dismay when Sunderland Education Authority (in line with a national trend) announced that it intended to end selective education and replace the grammar schools with comprehensives. Consequently, despite bitter opposition 'the Bede' went comprehensive in 1967 and the same fate befell the town's other grammar schools. For instance, Monkwearmouth Grammar School, which had moved to purpose-built premises at Torver Crescent, Seaburn Dene in 1963, did so ten years after it relocated.

Prior to the introduction of comprehensive education, after attending junior school, the majority of children went to secondary modern schools and several of these were built in the 1950s to cater for children living on estates like Farringdon and Thorney Close.[43] Thereafter, the 1960s saw the construction of purpose-built comprehensives, a development that began at Red House where the school was up and running in 1963. In this case, however, the buildings were demolished in 2009 and the school, henceforth known as Red House Academy, reopened in new facilities on the same site partly funded by the Leighton Group. Although a broad curriculum is taught, emphasis is now placed on engineering subjects.

Private schools also exist. These include Argyle House, founded as a boys' school at Thornhill in 1884 (it is now co-educational) and Sunderland High School in Mowbray Road. The latter was formed in 1992 by merging two well-established independent schools, namely Sunderland Church High School and the Tonstall Preparatory School for Boys. Until September 2012 (when its status changed to a free school), another private school was Grindon Hall, which began on a modest scale at Fulwell Grange in 1988 and moved to the much more spacious premises of Grindon Hall in 2000 as a result of growing pupil numbers.

Health and Hospitals

Since 1945 there has been a general improvement in the standard of health. Immunisation has played a part in this process. For example, in 1951 no child died in Sunderland from diphtheria, the first such year on record.

A particularly notable event was the formation of the National Health Service, which was introduced by Clement Attlee's Labour Government and came into effect on 5 July 1948. Its establishment was a godsend for people with limited means for it enabled everyone to benefit from free medical attention.

Nonetheless despite the improvement in Wearsiders' health, owing to factors such as working conditions, poor diet and lifestyle, Sunderland has had persistently higher death rates than the national average. For one thing, the rate of lung cancer in both men and women is higher than that of England as a whole, and this is also true of heart disease. In addition, for most of the period infant mortality has been above the national average. For instance, in 1948 the death rate for infants aged under 1 was 55 per thousand live births whereas the average for England and Wales was 34 per thousand. Currently, though, the situation is reversed for in 2010 Sunderland's infant mortality was 3.5 and England's, 4.7.

Sunderland's Director of Public Health observed that 'overall life expectancy for people in Sunderland is increasing and... mortality from heart disease and cancer has decreased significantly over the last 15 years.' Nevertheless 'we are not narrowing the gap between average life expectancy for men and women in Sunderland and men and women across England—in fact, for men, the gap has widened slightly. The latest information suggests that average life expectancy for men is 75.4 (England 77.9) and for women 80.4 (England 82).'[44]

The same report also notes that there are marked differences in health levels in different parts of Sunderland. For example, in Fulwell and Seaburn male life expectancy is 79.9 and female life expectancy is 83.8, whereas elsewhere on the north side of the river, the figures for Marley Pots are 69.3 and 75.9. Significant variation, of course, also exists elsewhere in the city. The figures for High Barnes are 79.2 and 82.7, whereas in the Port and East End ward the figures for male and female life expectancy are 67.0 and 76.0.

On the whole, Sunderland has higher rates of smoking, heavy drinking and teenage pregnancy than is true nationwide. For instance, the report states that the city ranked among the 10 per cent of areas in England with the highest rate of alcohol related hospital admissions.

After July 1948, the Sunderland Area Hospitals Management Committee was responsible for administering over 20 hospitals in an area that included Houghton-le-Spring and other peripheral communities such as Seaham. Among the hospitals under the committee's remit were the Royal Infirmary on Durham Road (previously run by a voluntary body) and the Municipal Hospital, on Kayll Road, which had been administered by the corporation and now became known as the General Hospital.

The committee soon began closing the smaller hospitals, and by the mid 1960s their number had almost fallen by half. Moreover, in 1995 the Royal Infirmary closed following the extension of the Sunderland District Hospital, as the General Hospital had become known. The hospital's current name is Sunderland Royal Hospital. It has 970 beds and many of its buildings date from around the year 2000. It is run by City Hospitals Sunderland NHS Foundation Trust, as is the Eye Infirmary on Queen Alexandra Road.[45]

Another body, the Northumberland, Tyne & Wear NHS Foundation Trust (dedicated to caring for people with mental health problems and disabilities) runs Cherry Knowle Hospital and Monkwearmouth Hospital.

The city also has several health centres—the first such was the Springwell Centre founded in 1956—and the overwhelming majority of general practitioners are based in them. Over the years, the number of doctors in Sunderland has been below the national average. For instance, the *Echo* of 14 July 2000 reported that the city had 43.1 GPs for every 100,000 people, compared with a national average of 57.4, with the result that in terms of its number of doctors, Sunderland Health Authority was at the bottom of a league of 109 health authorities in England.

Since 1951 residential homes for the elderly have also been founded by the council, and these are supplemented by many privately run establishments. The corporation also cares for elderly folk in their own homes through meals-on-wheels and the employment of home helps.

'Wearside Jack'

In 1979, Sunderland became the focus of one of the greatest manhunts in British history. It did so as part of a police investigation to apprehend a serial killer—dubbed the 'Yorkshire Ripper'—responsible for the deaths of several women, mostly prostitutes, in Yorkshire.

On 17 June 1979, a cassette recording from someone claiming to be the killer was posted in Sunderland to the head of the investigation, Assistant Chief Constable George Oldfield of the West Yorkshire Police. Public interest in the case was intense and, in front of TV cameras, Oldfield played the tape at a news conference. The nation listened with macabre fascination as a man with a strong Wearside accent declared:

> I'm Jack. I see you are still having no luck catching me. I have the greatest respect for you George, but Lord! You are no nearer catching me now than four years ago when I started. I reckon your boys are letting you down George. They can't be much good, can they?

In March of the previous year, Oldfield had received a letter postmarked from Sunderland and signed 'Jack the Ripper'. The writer claimed to be the killer but told Oldfield not to bother searching for him in Sunderland, for he had only posted the letter in the town while travelling around the country. Now, though, following the arrival of the cassette recording with a Wearside accent (referred to as a 'Geordie accent' by the national press), the police turned their searchlight well and truly on Sunderland. In all, 40,000 men in the town were interviewed and, as voice analysts identified the accent as distinctive to the Castletown area, that neighbourhood in particular came under intense scrutiny.

Meanwhile, killings continued. Indeed, three more women were murdered in Yorkshire before the dramatic arrest of the killer, Peter Sutcliffe, happened in Sheffield in 1981. Much to the embarrassment of the police, Sutcliffe (who duly confessed to the murders) had a Yorkshire accent. The Sunderland tape was a hoax. It had completely misled the police and enabled Sutcliffe to remain at large and continue his murderous campaign.

For years, the identity of the hoaxer remained a seemingly unsolvable mystery. However, in 2005 the police reopened the case in the hope of catching 'Wearside Jack' and a dramatic breakthrough occurred. DNA from envelopes sent to the Yorkshire police in the late 1970s was found to match DNA taken by the Sunderland police from a local man for an unrelated incident in 2000. As a result, on 20 October 2005 a drunken loner named John Samuel Humble, a 49-year-old living on Ford Estate, Sunderland, was arrested. Humble, who had attended a school in Castletown, was tried at Leeds Crown Court where, on 21 March 2006, he was sentenced to eight years in gaol for perverting the course of justice.

Sport

By a considerable margin, Sunderland's principal spectator sport is football and over the years the proportion of female fans has increased significantly. League football, which had ceased at the commencement of the Second World War, resumed in the autumn of 1946 and on the whole Sunderland AFC's record since then is not impressive. This is certainly true of the immediate post-war years. The club finished only one place from relegation in the 1947–8 season and was humiliated in early 1949 when it was ignominiously ejected from the fourth round of the FA Cup by a non-League side, Yeovil Town. Of the lamentable performance, the *Sunderland Echo* of 31 January noted that Yeovil were not giant killers because 'there were no giants to kill.'

League results were generally disappointing during the 1950s, despite the fact that large sums of money were spent on signing players—Sunderland was dubbed 'the Bank of England Club.' On the other hand, in 1955 and 1956 Sunderland reached the semi-finals of the FA Cup. Scandal then ensued. In 1957 allegations that the club was making illegal payments to players surfaced. A joint investigation by the Football League and the Football Association followed. On 10 April, they reported their findings—the verdict? Guilty! Sunderland AFC had furtively paid players more than the maximum of £15 per week (the maximum wage was to be abolished in 1961) and stern measures followed. Among other things, Sunderland was fined £5,000, at the time the largest fine imposed in the game's history. Battered and bruised, the club fared badly the following season. So much so that in 1958 it was relegated to the Second Division for the first time—it had been in the top flight since 1890.

First Division status was regained in 1964 but succeeding seasons proved disappointing. Roker Park, however, served as one of the venues of the 1966 World Cup hosted by England and several matches were played at the ground. Visiting teams included Italy and the USSR.

Sunderland's star player was the Irishman, Charlie Hurley, who had joined the club in late 1957 and left in May 1969. He was an outstanding centre half, so much so that when the club later celebrated its centenary he was voted the best player Sunderland's ever had. Of him, Mark Metcalf comments: 'Hurley was not only brilliant in the air in defence or when Sunderland forced corners, he was also a great tackler and defender. A celebrated leader of players, a natural captain and a determined opponent, Hurley was the ultimate professional.'[46]

Statue recreating Bob Stokoe's finest moment, the 1973 FA Cup final victory

In 1970 Sunderland was relegated to the Second Division and, apart from one season (1976–7) back in the top flight, remained there for the rest of the decade. Undoubtedly, the greatest triumph of this period took place on 5 May 1973 when the club, managed by Bob Stokoe, a miner's son born in Northumberland and an ex-Newcastle United player, won the FA Cup for the second time by beating First Division Leeds United 1–0.

Sunderland's centenary season, 1979–80 proved a triumph, for the club gained promotion. But glory did not ensue. During the next few seasons the team usually finished towards the bottom of the table and in 1985 Sunderland was relegated yet again.[47] Worse still, in 1987 the club sank to new depths when it dropped into the Third Division! But much to the relief of fans, its stay in such uncharted waters proved mercifully brief, just one season.[48]

Shortly thereafter, owing to the formation of the Premier League (which replaced the old First Division) Sunderland started the 1992–3 season as a First Division side and thus in the second tier of the modern English game. Promotion to the Premier League, however, occurred in 1996 and 1999.

By the latter date the club was based at a new home, the Stadium of Light—the last match played at Roker Park, the club's famous old ground, happened on 13 May 1997.[49] Construction work on the stadium began in May 1996 (the year in which Sunderland AFC became a public limited company) and 14 months later, on 30 July 1997, the club's magnificent new home opened. A festive atmosphere prevailed. The capacity crowd of 42,000 fans was entertained with live performances by musicians such as the veteran rock band, Status Quo, before watching an exhibition match between Sunderland and the famous Dutch team, Ajax, that ended in a goalless draw. The historic evening concluded with an impressive fireworks display.

As fans wended their way home they had good reason to be pleased with the awesome £23 million new stadium, one of the finest grounds in Europe.[50] But many were shocked and disappointed by its name, announced only hours before the opening ceremony. Popular alternatives were 'New Roker Park' or the 'Wearside Stadium' and the actual choice came as a complete and unwelcome surprise.

Sunderland AFC's fortunes in the first decade of the 21st century were chequered. Initially results were excellent with seventh place in the Premier League being secured two years in succession under manager Peter Reid. By March 2003 though, the club was struggling. Mick McCarthy (who had previously managed the Republic of Ireland) was appointed manager, and although he was unable to avoid relegation, in 2004–5 he led Sunderland back into the top flight. But it was not a happy return. Defeat soon followed defeat and a national journalist, Matt Lawton, observed: 'With debts of £40 million, money has been tight at Sunderland. McCarthy spent less than £3m last summer and he is unlikely to receive much more in January. Gates have fallen, the one sell-out this season coming when ticket prices were dropped to £5 for adults and £1 for children for a Carling Cup clash with Arsenal.'[51] Utter humiliation thus resulted. Sunderland became a laughing-stock. It plummeted out of the Premier League in truly abysmal style, pitifully amassing a then record total of only 15 points, beating the previous record low of 19 points also set by Sunderland in the 2002–3 season.

Before the season came to its wretched conclusion, McCarthy was no longer

The Stadium of Light in 2000. An additional tier is being
added to the North Stand to increase capacity to 49,000

on Wearside, for he was sacked in March 2006. Shortly afterwards, it emerged that a former Irish international, Niall Quinn, a revered figure who had played for Sunderland in the years 1996–2003, was the driving force behind the formation of a consortium of mostly Irish businessmen intent on taking over the floundering club. This proved the case, and Quinn (who describes his involvement with Sunderland as 'a love affair'[52]) became chairman.

Quinn briefly also managed the club, but in late August another Irishman, Roy Keane, was appointed to do so. Under his formidable leadership, a memorable run ensued and Sunderland, whose supporters included a newly acquired contingent from across the Irish Sea, emphatically gained promotion to the Premier League as First Division champions in 2007.

Keane remained manager until December 2008, by which date less happy times had returned. Indeed, the club only escaped relegation in 2009 by the skin of its teeth.[53] In the wake of this deliverance, it was announced that Sunderland AFC had just been bought by the tycoon Ellis Short, an Irish-American financier who already had a stake in the club. Ellis declared,

> There was a lot about Sunderland that interested me. It's a big proper football club with the best fans in the league, both home and away, with one of the best stadiums in the league and one of the best training facilities in football. It's a very well run club, the scouting organisation and the youth development programme are in place, so it's got all the pieces in place to be a long-term successful, really powerful club.[54]

The city's recreational facilities also include the Ashbrooke Sports Ground, which was the venue for very well attended events in the early decades of the period. Of one such occasion, Dave Dodds, the winner of the Sunderland Police Sports Mile in 1953, recalls

> although I expected to be running in front of a big crowd, I was still amazed to find that we were among such a huge throng.... The renowned police band was playing to a capacity crowd, who had come to watch the best runners and racing cyclists in the North East, as well as a sprinkling of British international athletes who had been invited to take part.... One of the reasons why the Police Sports was such a popular event, was that they awarded better than average prizes, and I took home an attractive silver tea service which was valued at £6. This was £1 more than my weekly wage.[55]

Other venues include Crowtree Leisure Centre (one of the largest indoor sports and recreation centres in the country) which lies in the heart of Sunderland and was officially opened by Prince Charles in 1978, and the Silksworth Sports Complex.[56] The latter, on Sunderland's southern periphery, dates from 1976 and is on the 160-acre site of the former Silksworth Colliery. Among other things, it has the largest artificial ski-slope in the northern region, a boating-lake, sports stadium and cricket ground. In 1988, moreover, the Puma Sunderland Tennis Centre opened at Silksworth. It was revamped and extended in the mid 1990s and is one of the largest public tennis facilities in the country. April 2008 saw the opening of the Sunderland Aquatic Centre, an indoor complex that includes an Olympic-size swimming pool (the only one between Leeds and Glasgow) as well as a diving pool and gymnasium.[57]

Libraries, Museums and Places of Entertainment

Sunderland is well endowed with public libraries, and pride of place belongs to Sunderland City Library in Fawcett Street.[58] Previously, it was known as Sunderland Central Library and was located in the same building as the museum on Borough Road. Although those premises were considerably enlarged when an adjoining extension (officially opened in June 1964 by HRH the Queen Mother) was built on the site of the former Winter Gardens, by the close of the century the facilities were inadequate. Therefore, on 23 January 1995, Sunderland City Library (as it would henceforth be known) opened its doors for the first time at a new location, the former Binns building on the east side of Fawcett Street, premises whose interior was substantially altered as part of the relocation scheme. The new site provided more space and the award-winning library is one of the finest public libraries in the country.

Visitor attractions in Sunderland include several museums, some of which are owned by the corporation, as is true of the museum on Borough Road. In 1999 the museum, whose space had increased thanks to the library's move to Fawcett Street, was closed and given a complete overhaul. It reopened on 21 July 2001 with improved visitor facilities and new galleries that focus more on local history than had been the case. Furthermore, the museum was enhanced by the provision of a new entrance (complete with a shop) at the west end, and the Winter Gardens at the other. Although less substantial than their Victorian predecessor, the Winter Gardens are an attractive feature and include a tree-top walk from which one can gaze down upon a variety of exotic plants from Australia, China, Madagascar, South Africa and elsewhere. Technology controls temperatures and levels of humidity.

Sunderland Corporation also owns Monkwearmouth Station Museum on North Bridge Street, which opened in 1973 and is dedicated to railway history. On the other hand, some museums are run by volunteers, as is true of the North East Aviation Museum, which was formed by a group of enthusiasts in 1974. Initially, it was based at Lambton Pleasure Park near Washington, but by early 1977 it had relocated to occupy part of the site of Sunderland Municipal Airport. The museum has the largest aviation collection between Yorkshire and Scotland.

Beside St Peter's Campus, on the north bank of the river, lies one of Sunderland's most impressive attractions—the National Glass Centre—which opened in June 1998. It was brought about by Tyne and Wear Development Corporation and was partly funded by a £7 million grant from the National Lottery. In its first year the centre, 'the national institution for the development and promotion of excellence in the art and industry of glass', attracted over 150,000 visitors. Nonetheless, after the initial wave of enthusiasm, visitor numbers fell well below expectations and the centre ran at a loss and in May 2010 it became part of the University of Sunderland. Displays recount the history of glassmaking and there are a number of interactive features. In addition, one can witness glass blowing in progress and it is possible for visitors to try their hand at the process. One can also buy items from a wealth of attractive glass objects made locally and elsewhere, and dine in the centre's award-winning restaurant which overlooks the River Wear.

Turning to other matters, in the post-war era Sunderland had several cinemas. Sadly, in common with a trend nationally, a decline in their number ensued as more and more Wearsiders acquired TVs from 1953 onward. An early casualty was Sunderland's first purpose-built cinema, the Villiers, which closed in 1958. Among other venues that soon went the same way were the Regent in Grangetown, which closed in 1961, and the Gaumont (formerly the Havelock) that did so in 1963. Furthermore, the Odeon (once the Regal) became a bingo hall in 1982, a fate shared by other local cinemas.

By the beginning of the 21st century Sunderland had no cinemas at all—in the late 1990s the two remaining venues, the tiny Empire Studio adjoining the Empire Theatre, and Holmeside's Cannon Cinema (which had begun life as the Ritz) had closed. Fortunately, this lamentable state of affairs was short-lived. In 2003 work commenced on erecting the impressive Empire Cinemas, a multi-screen complex that duly opened on Lambton Street.

The post-war years were generally difficult for the Empire Theatre. This was certainly true in the field of high culture. In 1946, for example, the Metropolitan Ballet attracted a lamentably small audience. In other ways, the Empire likewise found these tough years. For one thing, dance bands, which had previously attracted audiences, were increasingly performing in the town's dance halls instead.

The domed Winter Gardens viewed from Mowbray Park

The National Glass Centre, one of Sunderland's most striking buildings

By the late 1950s, therefore, the Empire was struggling to survive. Indeed, it closed on 2 May 1959, albeit briefly thanks to Sunderland Corporation which commendably soon bought the venue for £52,000. As a result, on Boxing Day the Empire resumed operating as Sunderland's civic theatre and did so with a panto-mime, *Robin Hood*.

Although a serious effort was made to provide a balanced programme with wide appeal, the Empire ran at a loss during decades of civic control in the face of stiff competition from other entertainment venues. Stars that performed at the Empire during these years included The Beatles—they did so twice in 1963—the actor Sid James (best known for his roles in the 'Carry On' films) who died of a heart attack on the theatre's stage in April 1976, and the renowned Russian ballet dancer Rudolf Nureyev.

The latter commenced a tour of the UK at the Empire in the spring of 1991 but the concerts (held on 26 and 27 April) were shambolic for the dancer was well past his prime. Unbeknown to the theatre's management and patrons, Nureyev, who was in his early fifties, had contracted AIDS from which he would die less than two years later. The performances caused consternation and annoyance and made national news. As Alaistair Robinson noted in a review of the first concert, the dancer some-times limped. Moreover, he 'had turned down the Empire's offer to provide an orchestra. He insisted on using taped music. The tape stopped and, in a few seconds of deep embarrassment that seemed to last several hours, ran at the wrong speed.'[59] One indignant fan, who had paid £26 for a ticket, declared: 'I have waited 25 years to see this man and I was absolutely shocked. He didn't really dance. I'm surprised he wasn't slow hand-clapped.'[60]

By the close of the 20th century, Sunderland Corporation had decided to place the Empire under private management. Thus in 2000, SFX was granted a 12-year contract to run the theatre. In the event, Clear Channel Entertainment—later renamed Live Nation—soon replaced SFX and in 2004 a £4.6 million refurbishment programme (partly financed by Sunderland City Council) occurred so that the theatre could host larger shows than ever before, including major West End productions. Hence the theatre, the largest between Leeds and Edinburgh, can rightly claim to be 'the West End of the North East.'

During the 1960s, various cabaret and nightclubs were established in Sunderland and one of the first was *le Cubana*, founded by a local enthusiast Eric Punshon at 13 Toward Road. Fourteen months or so later, a sister club, *La Cubana*, opened on the upper floors of the same premises. Although cramped, the venues were extremely popular and attracted able up-and-coming local musicians like Bryan Ferry (born in Washington in 1945) and established artists such as the Spencer Davies Group. Nevertheless, for a variety of reasons, in the late 60s Punshon decided to close the clubs. Among other popular nightclubs of the era was *La Strada* at 52 Fawcett Street, which opened in the same decade and operated until the early 1980s. Nightclubs are still very much at the heart of the city's entertainment industry—particularly on Friday nights—and include *Annabels*, a well-established club at 278–84 High Street West and little more than a stone's throw from the Empire Theatre.

Public houses likewise play an important part in the recreational life of Wearsiders, and include historic pubs such as the *Dun Cow* (next to the Empire) and more recent 'watering holes' like the *New Derby* in Roker, which opened in 1963, and the *Lambton Worm* which did so in 2003 in Low Row, Bishopwearmouth. Even so, the number

A forlorn sight. *The Welcome Tavern* stands empty in 2011

of pubs has diminished. Losses include premises like Bishopwearmouth's *Rose and Crown* (demolished in the late 1960s to make way for the first stage of the town's inner ring road) and *The Welcome Tavern* on Barrack Street and Prospect Row, a pub erected in 1915 on the site of a previous public house. *The Welcome Tavern* closed in 2009 and the landlord, 46-year-old Geoff Moon—who had run the pub for 18 years— told the *Sunderland Echo* that various factors had contributed to its demise: 'There's the smoking ban, the recession and supermarkets pumping beer out for nothing. At one time we were very busy—seven nights a week and doing very well.'[61]

Piano Recitals and other Concerts

Various admirable societies exist in the city and a particular jewel in the crown is the Sunderland Pianoforte Society, which holds concerts in the Pottery Room, Sunderland Museum. The society was formed on 2 February 1943 and its website notes that the aim was to 'encourage the study and playing of piano music by presenting at least four concerts in each season.'

For the first few years, half the programme at every concert was performed by members of the society and the rest was played by a professional classical soloist. For instance, this was the case on Thursday, 27 January 1949, when the professional musician involved was Kendall Taylor, Professor of Piano at the Royal College of Music.[62] This arrangement was, however, soon superseded by the introduction of a 'Members' Evening' and the other recitals were exclusively by professional pianists.[63]

In the early days, the society borrowed and hired pianos before using an old Bechstein. By the late 1950s, as membership was expanding, the decision was made to buy a replacement piano. Fundraising ensued and a founder member of the society named Ted Ducker subsequently visited several piano showrooms in London. He was accompanied by Ronald Smith, a leading concert pianist who had made his Proms debut in 1942 aged 20, and had first performed for the society during the 1952–3 season. Smith tried out a number of instruments and, on his recommendation, in late 1960 a Steinway model D concert grand in a walnut Louis XVI style case was bought. Smith was the first musician to use the excellent piano (one of a handful of that model made in Hamburg in the early 1900s) for one of the society's recitals, and did so at the start of its 1960–1 season.[64]

One of the renowned pianists who has enthralled audiences at the society's recitals (which are open to non-members and have a down-to-earth atmosphere), is Ashley Wass, the first British pianist to ever win top prize at the World Piano Competition. On 9 October 2007, for example, he played music by William Alwyn, Liszt, Debussy and Frank Bridge. Moreover, on 8 March 2011 Jong-Gyung Park—who made her orchestral debut at the age of 13 and won third prize at the Arthur Rubenstein Inter-

The Korean virtuoso, Jong-Gyung Park in Sunderland

national Piano Master Competition in 1998—delighted the audience with music by Schubert, Ravel and Chopin. It was her first appearance in Sunderland.

Another admirable body is the Bishopwearmouth Choral Society. On 18 November 1948 an informal meeting was held to discuss setting up a local society that would perform major choral works. Key figures in these proceedings were the Reverend John Farquar Richardson, Rector of St Michael's Church, Bishopwearmouth, and the church's choirmaster and organist Clifford Hartley. The latter, a highly qualified musician born in Halifax, Yorkshire, had moved to Sunderland in 1946 to take up the post of music master at Bede Grammar School. The core of the proposed choir would comprise the men of St Michael's Parish Church Choir and the Senior Girls Choir of the grammar school.

The first performance was held on Thursday, 31 March 1949, and featured Haydn's magnificent late 18th century oratorio *The Creation*, arguably that composer's greatest work. Hartley conducted the performance and the choir, numbering over 80 singers, was accompanied by Conrad Eden, the organist of Durham Cathedral. The fledgling society had pulled off a major coup, for the renowned Scottish soprano Isobel Baillie performed as one of the soloists during the oratorio.

The society gradually became well established and held its 12th concert on 3 December 1953, an event that commenced with an organ recital and then featured Bach's *Christmas Oratorio*. Of proceedings, we read that 'in last night's performance there was much that was successful and enjoyable....The Society's conductor, Clifford Hartley, directed the oratorio...with a suave yet steady beat...and coaxed some splendid singing from the choir in the chorales.'[65] Hartley remained the conductor until his retirement in 1974 after the society's 56th concert, a performance of Bach's *Mass in B Minor*.

Since 1993 the conductor has been David Murray and concerts rightly still attract favourable comment, for the quality of the choir is high and the soloists are professionals. Hence a review by Roy Horabin of a concert held in 2009 reads: 'Bishopwearmouth Choral Society gave a fabulous performance of Edward Elgar's Dream of Gerontius at Sunderland Minster....Musical director David Murray ensured a convincing interpretation.' Horabin then praises the soloists, John Graham-Hall, Anne Marie Owens, and Philip Smith, before noting:

> In addition to the main chorus a semi-chorus operated from the side gallery, which included Bishopwearmouth Young Singers trained by organist Eileen Bown. The 50-strong orchestra lent colourful support and balanced admirably with singers so the combined ensemble work was notable for its cohesion and subtlety of detail. Serene closing passages made a lasting impression.[66]

On 10 March 2009, Horabin himself participated in another wonderful event at Sunderland Minster. He did so at a meeting of the Sunderland Antiquarian Society which, after meeting at various locations over the years, was based at that church—the society has since moved to Douro Terrace. Horabin provided piano accompaniment for Rupert Hanson, a Sunderland-born licentiate of the Royal College of Music, who enthralled those present as he enthusiastically recounted his life-story and also sang a variety of material, including an aria from Mozart's *The Magic Flute*.

Hanson, who died of cancer only a few months later, was the director of Sunderland Symphony Orchestra, which largely consists of accomplished amateurs. The orchestra was founded in October 1999 to mark the start of the new millennium and was the brainchild of three local councillors, Mark Greenfield, Winifred Lundgren and John Lennox.[67] Although the orchestra's inaugural performance was held in February 2000, its first performance of a complete symphony happened on 7 April 2001 and featured Dvorak's popular *New World Symphony*.

The orchestra is based at West Park Church but has also played elsewhere, including at Sunderland Empire and the Sage, Gateshead. Its first visit to the Empire took place on 27 September 2000 and featured music by Wagner and Johann Strauss. In addition, a work written in honour of the Queen Mother by Derek Gooch, a local composer born in Sunderland in 1973, received its premiere. Further local interest was provided by Sarah Busfield, a 'young pure-toned soprano' from Ryhope. Of the concert, Horabin observed: 'While faulty precision marred one or two passages, there was some very colourful and expressive playing; the overall standard obviously delighted the audience.'[68]

The orchestra's musical director and principal conductor is Ray Farr, who succeeded Hanson in 2009,[69] and on 23 October 2010 West Park Church was the location for a concert that featured the orchestra's first performance of a piano concerto, namely Rachmaninov's famous *Piano Concerto No. 2*. The pianist was Dr Patrick Zuk of Durham University who gave a 'scintillating' performance, and of the orchestra Zuk aptly notes:

Bishopwearmouth Choral Society, following a performance of music by Haydn on 26 March 2011. Eileen Bown and David Murray are pictured front row, eighth and ninth from left

It is greatly to Sunderland's credit that the city can maintain such an active orchestra. Ensembles of this nature not only allow local musicians to play for pleasure, but they also greatly enrich the musical life of the region because they afford opportunities for people to experience live performances of repertoire that they might otherwise never hear in concert.[70]

For a number of years, the Odeon in Holmeside was the town's main venue for rock and pop acts, and artists who performed there included Bill Haley and the Comets on 15 February 1957 and the Rolling Stones (supported by the Hollies) on 9 March 1965. In the late 1960s and early 1970s, the Locarno Ballroom on Newcastle Road also witnessed rock concerts and performers included the blues/hard rock band, Free. The group was very popular on Wearside. A reporter noted in the 4 July 1970 issue of the national music paper *Melody Maker*, that the fans' reaction at a recent Free concert at the Locarno was akin to the hysteria he had only previously observed elsewhere at the height of Beatlemania. From the mid 1970s, however, Sunderland was usually overlooked in favour of Newcastle by touring artists.

The largest concerts on Wearside have been held at the home of Sunderland AFC. On 23 June 1987 Roker Park football ground was the setting for a concert by David Bowie (whose tour band included the acclaimed guitarist Peter Frampton), who played to a packed crowd during his Glass Spider Tour. More recently, on the evenings of 5 and 6 June 2009, the Stadium of Light was full when fans attended concerts by the pop band Take That, on the first leg of a sellout tour that had broken records for the speed of ticket sales nationwide. The concert was spectacular and the music was accompanied by a theatrical display whose centrepiece was a giant mechanical elephant. Days later, on Wednesday 10 June, another major act, the rock band Oasis, likewise performed at the same venue.

Take That on the opening night of their Progress Live tour at the Stadium of Light

On Friday 27 May 2011 an even bigger event commenced. Take That returned to the stadium at the start of their record-breaking Progress Live tour, and the band performed there again the following evening and on the ensuing Monday and Tuesday. Although the weather was colder than it should have been for the time of year, the concerts were a great success and over 200,000 people attended the shows in total.[71] Thankfully, such major concerts raise Sunderland's profile—the opening concert was mentioned by the national press—and the city has become the region's leading centre for massive concerts, events that attract fans from home and abroad.

Sunderland's Twin Resorts

In the early years of the period, Wearsiders and holidaymakers flocked to the beaches and associated amenities at Seaburn and Roker. The former was the most popular and attractions included a fairground, boating pool, recently laid miniature railway and Seaburn Hall. The latter, which had opened in July 1939, was described in 1949 as the 'Mecca of good dancers and dance bands. Only the best bands come to Seaburn Hall. Every week one of the country's leading dance Orchestras is here.'[72] Oscar Rabin, Joe Loss, and Harry Gold were among stars that had provided entertainment.

Naturally, attendance at the seafront soared during good weather, as was true at Easter 1949. The Saturday issue of the local newspaper observed: 'Soon after midday yesterday Seaburn presented a picture reminiscent of last summer. Crowds overlapped from the beaches on to the grass strips along the promenade, long queues stood outside the ice-cream shops, cafes were filled to capacity, and hundreds of holidaymakers patronized the newly-painted fun fair.'[73]

The temperature that day reached 22°c and the Entertainments Manager, Mr. W.N. Jackson, stated that it was 'the best Good Friday on record.' Boats on the miniature pool made 400 trips, whereas ticket sales for the miniature railway (which travelled a total of 100 miles) numbered 2,400. In addition, 600 deck chairs were hired, 400 people played golf and putting, and sales of ice-cream cartons at two corporation kiosks numbered 80,000. There were 600 vehicles on the car park and 1,000 visitors had had their weight measured on the corporation's scales. Moreover, the weather continued to be excellent for the remainder of the bank holiday weekend.

The previous year, after an 11-year gap, Sunderland recommenced displaying annual illuminations. Arthur Suddick subsequently noted their popularity: 'Year after year our great display of Illuminations is receiving favour further afield than ever before. During the Illuminations period of 1953 we estimate that between 300,000 and 400,000 people visited our attractions during the four weeks of their presentation.'[74]

The displays certainly attracted many sightseers, but the illuminations nevertheless ran at a loss. Therefore, the display that commenced on Friday, 3 September 1954, proved to be the last until a revival occurred in 1986 and lasted until 1993. In the interim, Seaburn Hall had been demolished in July 1982 after falling into a state of dereliction, and Seaburn Leisure Centre now occupies the site.

1950s guide depicting the charms of
Seaburn and Roker as tourist resorts

By the beginning of the 1970s, the heyday of the 'twin resorts' of Roker and Seaburn was over for the number of holidaymakers was on the wane as other destinations, such as Spain, became increasingly affordable. Nowadays, the seafront witnesses its greatest level of activity when vast crowds attend the popular annual Sunderland International Airshow, a two-day event first held in 1988 and the largest free airshow in Europe. Overall, the airshow has been a great success. But inevitably, bad weather has sometimes marred the occasion, as was most notably the case on 26 and 27 July 2008. Although most of Sunderland was bathed in sunshine, thick fog shrouded the seafront and almost all the flights were cancelled. Disappointed visitors were able to hear (but not see) at least one fighter plane fly past at speed, and could enjoy using flight simulators and viewing a number of static exhibits which, as usual, were located at Seaburn as part of the event. In addition, since 2009 spec-

Seaburn seafront in 1994. The fountain was an expensive recent feature and is no longer in use

tacular firework displays have been held
on Roker Pier on the Friday evening preceding the airshow, and on Friday 29 July
2011 the entertainment also included
a performance by the well known band,
10cc, at Cliffe Park, Roker.

Politics and City Status

In a general election held in July 1945 the
town's MPs, Stephen Furness, a National
Liberal and the Conservative Samuel Storey, were ousted by Labour candidates.
The victors were Fred Willey (a Cambridge-educated barrister) and Richard
Ewart, and their triumph was part of a
nationwide trend that swept Clement
Attlee's aspirational party to power. One
of those who celebrated Labour's victory was a 13-year-old Wearsider named
Archie Potts, whose family were committed Socialists. He later recalled a speech
made on Wearside during the campaign
by 'Manny' Shinwell, the colourful MP
for Seaham:

An F16 fighter performs a high speed pass at the
2007 Sunderland Airshow. HMS *Albion* looks on

> The highlight of Labour's 1945 election campaign in Sunderland ... was undoubt-
> edly the meeting held at Roker Park football ground with Shinwell as the main
> speaker .... Shinwell was in top form that evening. He built his speech around the
> theme of a game of football, accusing the Tories of being a one-man team with
> Churchill as their only star-player, whereas Labour could field a well-balanced
> team of first-class players .... His jokes were delivered with a skill of timing which
> many music-hall comedians would have envied. It was a virtuoso performance
> and I have never seen it bettered by any other politician.[75]

Sunderland was a two-member constituency. By 1950, though, it was divided into
two single-member constituencies and, in February of that year, Willey and Ewart
were respectively returned to parliament for Sunderland North and Sunderland
South. Willey retained his seat until 1983 when he was replaced by another Labour
MP, Bob Clay, a staunch left-winger who had been educated at a private school and
Cambridge University but had worked as a bus driver since the mid 70s.

In the meantime, Labour's hold on the seat had strengthened. Whereas in the
1950s the Conservative candidates polled only a couple of thousand or so votes less
than Willey—the closest contest was in October 1959 when Willey gained 24,341
votes as opposed to the 22,133 of his Tory rival, thereafter the challenge weakened. So
much so, that at the general election of October 1974 Willey trounced his opponent
by gaining 29,618 votes, well above the 13,947 of his Conservative adversary.

During the 1950s, it was not just in Sunderland North that the Tories enjoyed strong support. The same was true south of the river where both main parties waged closely contested election campaigns. Indeed, in a by-election in 1953 caused by Ewart's death (he was only in his late 40s) the seat was won by a Conservative, Paul Williams, a close runner-up at the general election two years earlier. Williams gained 23,114 votes, 1,175 more than his Labour rival. Williams retained the seat until he was displaced in 1964 by Labour's Gordon Bagier, albeit by a narrow margin. Subsequently, Labour tightened its hold, paralleling events north of the river. Bagier was replaced by Chris Mullin, an accomplished journalist, in 1987 who held the seat until the 2010 election when he declined to stand, a decision likewise taken by Bill Etherington (also Labour) who had replaced Bob Clay in 1992.

For the general election of 6 May 2010—which resulted in the formation of a coalition government between the Conservatives and Liberal Democrats—the constituencies of Sunderland South and Sunderland North were abolished by the Electoral Commission. They were replaced by three new constituencies—Houghton and Sunderland South, Sunderland Central, and Washington and Sunderland West. The seats were won, respectively, by Bridget Phillipson, Julie Elliott and Sharon Hodgson, the first time in Sunderland's history that its MPs are all female. The victors have strong local roots. For instance, Phillipson (who was born in 1983 and studied modern history at Oxford University) was raised on a council estate in Washington, where she attended St Robert of Newminster School.

Late that Thursday, as the nation awaited the results of the election, Sunderland's Puma Centre was the focus of attention by the national media for the city was expected to be the first place in Britain to announce results. This proved the case. The first winning candidate in the country was Bridget Phillipson, whose victory was announced at 10.50pm. Further publicity was gained for Sunderland when the next two successful candidates declared were Hodgson (11.25pm) and Elliott (11.40pm).

That Sunderland's results were announced so quickly was no surprise. At the general election of 1992, owing to good organisation and fast work by those counting the returns, Sunderland South had been the first constituency in Britain to declare its result, an achievement repeated at all subsequent general elections.

Conservative candidates came second in the new Sunderland constituencies, and there was a swing from Labour to the Tories in each of them, most notably in Washington and Sunderland West where the swing was 11.6 per cent, significantly higher than was true nationwide.

Nevertheless, Sunderland is of course staunchly pro-Labour and one of the party's strongholds. Many Wearsiders view the Conservative Party with outright hostility, convinced that it is the enemy of the working class and the North East. Such animosity was strongest in the days of Margaret Thatcher, the prime minister in the years 1979–90. Many referred to her contemptuously as 'that Woman!' and, in local parlance, declared: 'She wants shooting.' Strong dislike (no doubt partly based on class bigotry) also exists towards the current prime minister, David Cameron, the most socially exalted premier since Sir Alec Douglas-Home in the 1960s.

At parliamentary level, and to a large extent in council elections, the Liberals, and more recently the Liberal Democrats, have not fared well in Sunderland. In fact, between 1952 and 1974 the Liberals did not even bother to contest any of the parliamentary elections. Their candidates have invariably trailed well behind their major rivals. To illustrate the point, in 1950 the Liberal candidates for Sunderland North and Sunderland South respectively gained 3,614 votes and 5,604 votes, whereas the Conservative candidates (who came second) obtained 17,469 and 22,012 votes.[76] In 2010, the Liberal Democrats came third in all three of the new constituencies, albeit by a less pronounced margin.

Needless to say, since 1945 Labour has dominated the council. For instance, following municipal elections on 1 November of that year, the party controlled the council for over 20 years. A succession of Labour mayors—including the town's first female mayor, Jane Huggins, who was elected in May 1954—came to an end in May 1967 when Norman Waters, a Conservative, was elected to the mayoralty and Conservatives held the office until May 1972. Afterwards, for most of the period until 1990, the leader of the council was the lawyer Charles Slater, a moderate Labour councillor under whose firm leadership Sunderland Council was spared from 'loony-leftism when so many other towns were devastated by it.'[77]

On the same day as the 2010 general election, council elections also happened in Sunderland and Labour was successful in the vast majority of the city's 25 wards where, with three exceptions, they were triumphant. In particular, the party made gains at the expense of the Tories who lost seats in Barnes, St Peter's and Washington East. On the other hand, the Conservatives held St Michael's, Fulwell and St Chads. Although they witnessed a rise in support, the Liberal Democrats failed to add to their one seat. As a result of the election, the number of Conservative councillors fell to 18 and Labour's total rose to 52. Moreover, four independent candidates were also elected.

The council meets in the Civic Centre on Burdon Road and the premises were erected on a 15-acre location opposite Mowbray Park in 1968–70. The architects were Sir Basil Spence (best known for designing Coventry Cathedral), Bonnington and Collins. The centre has three main sections and includes a two-storey council chamber. The complex cost £3.5 million and was officially opened by HRH Princess Margaret, Countess of Snowdon, on Thursday 5 November 1970.

The Civic Centre was built to replace the Town Hall in Fawcett Street. Sadly, despite a public outcry, that attractive building was demolished in 1971, a lamentable act of destruction that robbed Sunderland of a historic and imposing landmark.

Since 1992, Sunderland has enjoyed the status of a city. In the summer of 1991 Kenneth Baker, the Conservative Home Secretary, invited the council to make a bid for city status because the queen had decided to confer such status upon a town to commemorate her 40th year on the throne. The corporation responded enthusiastically to the invitation.[78] Among other things, it argued that Sunderland deserved to become a city in view of its long history and the contribution it had made to the nation. There were 22 other bidders but on 14 February 1992 it was announced

The innovative Civic Centre

that Sunderland had triumphed and would become Britain's 54th city. Hence on 23 March 1992 the queen formally signed and sealed letters patent bestowing city status on Sunderland.

At the beginning of this period, few Wearsiders could have envisaged how much Sunderland would change as World War Two became an increasingly distant memory. As has been noted, some of the changes have been beneficial while others have been very painful. To what extent Sunderland will change in the future is of course uncertain. Of this we can be certain. Sunderland has a long, and on the whole, honourable history of which Wearsiders can be proud.

ENDNOTES

Chapter One

1. Quoted in J.F. Clarke, *Building Ships in the North East: A Labour of Love, vol.1, c.1640–1914*, 1997, p. 93.

2. I have discussed the city's prehistory at some length in 'The Prehistory of the Sunderland Area', in *Sunderland's History* 8, 1995, pp. 1–19.

3. Some prehistorians are of the opinion that the Mesolithic period in the British Isles commenced in about 10,000 BC and concluded around 4000 BC.

4. In connection with lithic material uncovered during a programme of excavations at St Peter's Church in the second half of the 20th century, Robert Young comments: 'The area around Wearmouth may well have been a "preferred location" or base camp area for human habitation in the Mesolithic period'. R. Young, 'The Flint from Wearmouth', in R. Cramp, *Wearmouth and Jarrow Monastic Sites* vol. ii, 2005, p. 455. Mesolithic dwellings were not necessarily rudimentary. At Howick on the coast of Northumberland, archaeologists have uncovered evidence of a structure that comprised a large stout timber-framed circular residence that could provide comfortable accommodation for up to eight people. At Monkwearmouth, no evidence of subsequent prehistoric activity was uncovered during the excavations.

5. R. Young, *Lithics and Subsistence in North East England: aspects of the prehistoric archaeology of the Wear valley, County Durham, from the Mesolithic to the Bronze Age*, BAR (British Series) 161, 1987, p. 96.

6. Although there is a degree of consensus for the dates of the Neolithic, prehistorians are certainly not in total agreement as is evident from a number of recent publications discussing the prehistory of the North East. For instance, some archaeologists believe that the period commenced around 4,000 BC and ended c.2,500, whereas others are of the opinion that the period roughly spanned the years 4,200–1,800 BC.

7. T. Adey, C. Harvey, and C. Haselgrove, *County Durham Through The Ages*, 1990, p. 8.

8. On the summit of Humbledon Hill, in April 1873 Bronze Age cremations and pottery were found in a barrow while a reservoir was under construction. In 2001 a geophysical survey revealed features that suggest that a prehistoric enclosure or fortification may have been erected around the hilltop and future excavation may confirm that this was the case.

9. C.T. Trechmann, 'Prehistoric Burials in the County of Durham', *Archaeologia Aeliana* third series vol xi, 1914, p. 156.

10. T.C. Squance, 'Description of the Human Remains Found in Hasting Hill barrow', *ibid.*, p. 173.

11. A.M. Gibson, *Bronze Age Pottery in the North East of England*, BAR (British Series) 56, 1978, p. 26.

12. Trechmann, 'Prehistoric Burials', p. 156.

13. This paragraph is based on notes taken by the author at a lecture given by Mr. Speak to members of the Architectural and Archaeological Society of Durham and Northumberland, on 9 December 1992. I wish to thank Mr. Speak for subsequently confirming the accuracy of my notes and for providing me with an unpublished paper, *A Prehistoric Site at Carley Hill, Sunderland*, that he co-wrote with M.E. Snape.

14. N.R. Whitcomb, 'Two Prehistoric Dugout Canoes from the River Wear at Hylton, near Sunderland, County Durham', *Archaeol. Ael.* fourth series, vol. xlvi, 1968, p. 300. Interestingly, David Heslop plausibly suggests that dugout canoes may have been deliberately buried in waterways during the Iron Age as votive offerings: 'Newcastle and Gateshead before A.D. 1080', in D. Newton, & A.J. Pollard, *Newcastle and Gateshead Before 1700*, 2009, pp. 4–6.

15. A. Breeze, 'The Name of the River Wear', *Durham Archaeological Journal*, vol.13, 1997, p. 87.

16. Some homes of this period were certainly not rudimentary. A recently excavated late Iron Age palisaded site at Fawdon Dean (near Ingram in the Cheviots) contained stone roundhouses with paved floors.

17 R. Cramp, *Wearmouth and Jarrow Monastic Sites*, 2005, vol. 1, p. 24.

18 *Ibid.*, p. 24.

19 W.C. Mitchell, *A History of Sunderland*, 1919, (reprinted 1972), p. 19.

20 J.A. Petch, 'Roman Durham', *Archaeol. Ael.*, fourth series, vol. 1, 1925. p. 31. The authenticity of the inscribed stone, bearing lettering often found on Roman altars, has since been called into question and has been dismissed as only dating from the 18th century.

21 Sunderland thus differs from Newcastle, where archaeologists have excavated the site of a Roman fort (now partly occupied by a medieval castle) and an adjacent civilian settlement. On the other hand, evidence of prehistoric activity at Sunderland is stronger than it is at Newcastle.

22 J. Robinson, 'Roman Road and Remains at Bishopwearmouth', *Antiquities of Sunderland* vol. v, 1904, p. 5. In addition, Robinson wrote: 'There were also fragments of ancient pavements [cobbled roadway] uncovered when making some deep excavations some years ago for Langham Towers, near Christ Church, and on the direct line between the Seaham pavement and that discovered in Low Row'. *Ibid.*, p. 6.

23 E-mail to the author on 9 August 2010.

24 R. Selkirk, *Chester-le-Street and Its Place in History: a regional archaeological history*, 2001, p. 83.

25 As with historians and archaeologists, unanimity on the matter likewise does not exist among geneticists. Certainly, the view that the Anglo-Saxon invasions led to the virtual extermination of the native population is now discredited. On the other hand, I am not wholly convinced by the revisionist point of view and am of the opinion that the number of Anglo-Saxon settlers was greater than is widely accepted.

26 Local place-names are overwhelmingly of Old English origin. A case in point is Ryhope, whose name means 'rough or rugged valley.'

Chapter Two

1 Bede, 'Lives of the Abbots of Wearmouth and Jarrow', trans. by John Gregory, in J. Marsden, *The Illustrated Bede*, 1989, p. 160.

2 *Ibid.*, p. 160. For a discussion of the structures that received glazed windows, see 'The Monastic Site' (by R. Cramp) in M.M. Meikle & C.M. Newman, *Sunderland and its Origins, monks to mariners*, 2007, pp. 31–2.

3 'The Anonymous History of Abbot Ceolfrith,' trans. by D.H. Farmer, in *The Age of Bede*, 1998, p. 216. The biography is more well known as the *Life of Ceolfrith*.

4 Bede, 'Lives of the Abbots of Wearmouth and Jarrow', trans. by D.H. Farmer, *ibid.*, p. 192.

5 *Ibid.*, p. 192.

6 *Ibid.*, p. 195.

7 *Ibid.*, p. 196.

8 *Ibid.*, p. 197.

9 F.M. Stenton, *Anglo-Saxon England*, 3rd ed. 1971, p. 185.

10 'The Anonymous History of Abbot Ceolfrith', in *The Age of Bede*, p. 216.

11 J. Marsden, *The Illustrated Bede*, pp. 162–3.

12 'Lives of the Abbots', in *The Age of Bede*, p. 203. From later evidence, it has been plausibly suggested that the monks of Wearmouth also held other estates south of the river, at for instance Silksworth and Ryhope, whereas holdings north of the river may have included Fulwell and Southwick.

13 Presumably, many of the brethren were dispersed at various points around the monastic lands of Wearmouth and Jarrow, possibly to man churches and to engage in pastoral activity.

14 'The Anonymous History', in *The Age of Bede*, pp. 222–3.

15 Whether the *Codex Amiatinus* was produced in its entirety, or in part, at either Wearmouth or Jarrow is unknown. More often than not, it is unwarrantably attributed to the latter house.

16 M.P. Brown, *The Lindisfarne Gospels—Society, Spirituality & the Scribe*, 2003, pp. 155–6.

17 A. Thacker, 'Bede and Wearmouth' in Meikle & Newman, *Sunderland and its Origins*, p. 25. Ezra, a fifth century BC Jewish scribe, in addition to penning the Bible-book that bears his name, was credited by Jewish tradition with beginning to compile and catalogue the books of the Old Testament. He was therefore a figure whom those involved in the editorial programme at Wearmouth and Jarrow that culminated in the *Codex Amiatinus* and its companions evidently viewed as a source of inspiration.

18 Marsden, *The Illustrated Bede*, p. 167 and p. 16.

19 P.H. Blair, *The World of Bede*, 1970, p. 4.

20 'The Anonymous History', in *The Age of Bede*, p. 218. The same passage of text notes that as a 'small boy' this member of the monastic community had, along with Ceolfrith, been the only survivor of a plague that had devastated Jarrow's monastic community. However at the time of the pestilence, Bede would have been around 13 and so may not have been the individual referred to.

21 Blair, *The World of Bede*, p. 178. Hwaetberht is a possible alternative identification.

22 H.L. Robson, 'Bede of Wearmouth or Bede of Jarrow', *Antiquities of Sunderland* vol. xxiii, 1964; *The Great Days of Wearmouth*, (undated).

23 T.W. MacKay, 'Bede's Hagiographical Method', in G. Bonner (ed.), *Famulus Christi—Essays in Commemoration of the Thirteenth Centenary of the Birth of the Venerable Bede*, 1976, p. 80.

24 Quoted by P.H. Blair, *Northumbria in the Days of Bede*, 1976, p. 199.

25 *Ibid.*, p. 213.

26 Archaeological excavations highlighted a telling lack of pre-Conquest coinage after the period c.840. Likewise, there is a dearth of late Anglo-Saxon metalwork, and of pottery from the late 9th to the late 11th century.

27 The church at Chester-le-Street was rebuilt in stone in the mid 11th century. A preference for stone construction is also a hallmark of churches in Yorkshire from around the same time.

28 D. Rollason, 'St Cuthbert & Wessex', in G. Bonner, C. Stancliffe & D. Rollason (eds.), *St Cuthbert, his Cult and his Community until AD. 1200*, 1989, p. 420.

29 E. Cambridge, 'Early Romanesque Architecture in North-East England: a Style and its Patrons', in D. Rollason, M. Harvey & M. Prestwich (eds.), *Anglo-Norman Durham 1093–1193*, 1993.

30 As a young lecturer, Cramp had moved from St Anne's College, Oxford, to the University of Durham in 1955. She was appointed Professor of Archaeology at the latter in 1971. The programme of excavation continued in phases from 1959 until 1974. In 1986, moreover, part of the interior of St Peter's Church was excavated.

31 S. Anderson, C. Wells, & D. Birkett, 'People and Environment: The Human Skeletal Remains', in R. Cramp, *Wearmouth and Jarrow Monastic Sites*, vol. ii, 2005, p. 501. It has been estimated that juveniles comprised 35.5 per cent of the deceased, a figure based on the possibility that the bone assemblage contained remains from 327 people. *Ibid.*, p. 482. However, the authors also note that it is more likely that the bones came from some 200–230 individuals.

32 *Ibid.*, p. 485. Elsewhere, in a *Report on Human Remains from Monkwearmouth, Durham County*, Calvin Wells concluded that adults at Wearmouth had lived rather longer than was the case at three other sites—all in East Anglia—with which he was familiar. He stated that the average age of death at Wearmouth for males was 40.8 years and 37.6 years for females. However, when summarising Wells' findings, Rex Gardner argued that these figures were probably too low—R. Gardner, 'Medicine in Anglo-Saxon Northumbria', in D. Gardner-Medwin (et al.), *Medicine in Northumbria: Essays on the History of Medicine in the North East of England*, 1993, p.48. Subsequently, owing to the poor condition of many of the human remains, no attempt to provide average ages of death was attempted in volume two of Cramp's *Wearmouth and Jarrow Monastic Sites*.

33 Wells, *Report on Human Remains*, cited by Gardner in 'Medicine in Anglo-Saxon Northumbria.'

34 R Cramp, 'Monastic Sites', in D.M. Wilson (ed.), *The Archaeology of Anglo-Saxon England*, 1976, p. 234.

35 P. Wormald, 'Monkwearmouth and Jarrow', in J. Campbell (ed.), *The Anglo-Saxons*, 1982, p. 75.

Chapter Three

1 *The Anglo-Saxon Chronicles*, translated and edited by Michael Swanton, 2000, p. 203.

2 *Ibid.*, p. 219.

3 W. Aird, *St Cuthbert and the Normans: the Church of Durham 1071–1153*, 1998, p. 83.

4 Quoted in R. Cramp, *Wearmouth and Jarrow Monastic Sites*, 2005, vol. 1, pp. 35–6. Cramp also notes: 'The only surviving architectural feature which is universally accepted as belonging to the Aldwinian period is the bulbous base of the south pier of the chancel arch', *ibid.*, p. 117.

5 Quoted in E. King, *Medieval England*, 1988, p. 26.

6 R.A. Lomas and A.J. Piper (eds.), *Durham Cathedral Priory Rentals, I: Bursars Rentals*, Surtees Society vol. lxxxii, 1889, p. 204.

7   A.L. Poole, *Domesday Book to Magna Carta, 1087–1216*, 2nd ed., 1954, pp. 351–2, & 223.

8   G.T. Lapsley, 'Boldon Book', in W. Page (ed.), *Victoria County History of Durham*, vol. I, 1905, p. 307.

9   G.V. Scammell, *Hugh du Puiset, Bishop of Durham*, 1956, p. 214.

10 R. Surtees, *The History and Antiquities of the County Palatine of Durham*, vol. 1, 1816, p. 297.

11 M.M. Meikle, & C.M. Newman, *Sunderland and its Origins—Monks to Mariners*, 2007, pp. 85–6.

12 The borough court was operative again by 1609, a point noted by Christine Newman, *Sunderland and its Origins*, p. 96.

13 One of the things that contributed to Newcastle's prosperity was the fact that from the mid 14th century it served as the staple port for the exportation of the region's wool.

14 Scammell, *Hugh du Puiset*, p. 165.

15 D. Austin (ed.), *Boldon Book*, 1982, p. 50. A mark was a unit of account worth two-thirds of a pound.

16 *Ibid.*, p. 16. According to Madeliene Hope Dodds, the Wearmouth entry solely refers to 'the profits of the court, tolls, and house rents: this accounts for the fact that it is much less than the farms [payments] of Gateshead and Darlington, which include the profits of the bakehouses and fisheries.' M.H. Dodds, 'The Bishops' Boroughs', *Archaeologia Aeliana* 3rd series, vol. xii, 1915, p. 99.

17 H.S. Offler, 'Re-reading Boldon Book', in A.J. Piper and A.I. Doyle (eds.), *North of the Tees: Essays in Medieval British History*, 1996. The same point was made by M.H. Dodds in her article (cited above) on the episcopal boroughs.

18 Austin, *Boldon Book*, p. 14.

19 *Ibid.*, p. 12.

20 F. Bradshaw, 'Social and Economic History,' in W. Page (ed.), *Victoria County History* vol. ii, 1907, p. 184.

21 'Husewiva' is an example of an English word used in a Latin text.

22 Austin, *Boldon Book*, p. 16.

23 Poole, *Domesday Book*, p. 43.

24 Four manuscripts of the survey have survived and some textual differences occur.

25 P.D.A. Harvey, 'Boldon Book and the Wards between Tyne and Tees', in D. Rollason, M. Harvey, and M. Prestwich, (eds.), *Anglo-Norman Durham 1093–1193*, 1993, p. 404.

26 W.E. Kapelle, *The Norman Conquest of the North*, 1979, p. 186.

27 Austin, *Boldon Book*; Washington, p. 12; Herrington, p. 52. William de Hartburn's descendants, the Washington family, continued to hold the manor until 1399.

28 W. Greenwell (ed.), *Boldon Buke, a survey of the possessions of the See of Durham*, Surtees Society, xxv, 1852, appendix p. vi.

29 Lomas and Piper, *Durham Bursars Rentals*, p. 17. The valuations given are as follows: de Silksworth xiii s. iiii d.; de Wermuth lx s.; de Fulewell xx s.; de Suthwyk vi li. ix s. ii d.; de Schelis xxxiii s. iiii d. Like Fulwell and Monkwearmouth, South Shields lacked a mill: tenants there had to use a mill in adjacent Westoe.

30 *Ibid.*, p. 205.

31 Meikle, & Newman, *Sunderland and its Origins*, p. 71.

32 The administration of the Bishop of Durham also held halmote courts. Lay lords, like the Hylton family on Wearside, held manorial courts on their estates but very little is known about them, a point noted by Peter Larson: 'In stark contrast to the abundance of material in the bishopric and priory archives...evidence about courts held by lay lords is surprisingly rare...[and] only a handful of records survives for villages in lay hands....What does survive largely conforms to the picture drawn from the bishopric and priory courts.' P. Larson, 'Local Law Courts in Late Medieval Durham', in C. Liddy, & R.H. Britnell (eds.), *North East England in the later Middle Ages*, 2005, p. 99.

33 W.H. Longstaffe, & J. Booth, (eds.), *Halmota Prioratus Dunelmensis*, Surtees Soc. lxxxii, 1889, p. 4.

34 *Ibid.*, p. 10. A rood was a unit of land of around a quarter of an acre. By modern reckoning, the third in the series of halmotes of 1296, at which this case was heard, was held in early 1297: New Year's Day was 25 March.

35 *Ibid.*, p. 36. The Latin word *averia* that appears in this entry can mean draught animals or goods and merchandise. However, draught animals seems the most likely reading.

36 *Ibid.*, p. 69. White bread was made from wheat flour whereas other bread was made from barley and rye.

37 *Ibid.*, p. 166.

38 *Ibid.*, p. 85.

39 *Ibid.*, p. 177.

40 The earliest known reference to the village at Hylton dates from 1323, but the settlement had undoubtedly existed for a long time by then.

41 The earliest reference to a settlement at Houghton-le-Spring dates from 1112. Although the church is essentially 13th century, the oldest parts of the structure are a Norman doorway and window in the north wall of the chancel.

42 Richard Holme, a graduate of Cambridge University, was a Yorkshireman appointed Rector of Bishopwearmouth in 1401 by the Bishop of Durham, Walter Skirlaw, who likewise came from Yorkshire. In addition to serving as rector, Holme was a canon of York. He also served as the spiritual chancellor of Skirlaw and his successor, Bishop Langley.

43 Some of the spiritual revenue from the parish went to Durham Cathedral Priory, as was the case with the corn-tithes of Hylton and Southwick. However, in 1425 these were granted to the cell when its fortunes were at a particularly low state: the grant of the tithes from Southwick only lasted until 1434. Of the farm the monks managed, usually approximately 80 to 90 acres were under cultivation—the total was 91 acres in 1321—and wheat, barley, peas and beans were the main crops. Livestock included oxen for the ploughs, as well as pigs and geese. In 1321, for example, there were 10 oxen, 45 pigs and piglets, and 11 geese. Sheep are also listed among other livestock in the account for that year (the number of sheep and lambs totalled 41) but are sometimes absent. It appears that a flock of around 30 sheep was the norm during the 15th century.

44 R.B. Dobson, *Durham Priory, 1400–1453*, 1973, p. 312.

45 Records show that fish were also purchased at Sunderland on the cellarers' behalf by a buyer termed a 'provisor.'

46 The accounts of the cell mention expenditure on buying and repairing boats that plied between Monkwearmouth and Sunderland, and record income derived from this ferry. However, this was not always the case. The account for the year 1438–9 notes that nothing was received from the ferry that year: '*De passagio batelli inter Wermouth et Sunderland nichil hoc anno.*' J. Raine (ed.), *The Inventories & Account Rolls of the Benedictine Houses or Cells of Jarrow and Monkwearmouth*, Surtees Soc. xxix, 1854, p. 202.

47 John FitzMarmaduke, a formidable figure with a reputation for cruelty, died in Scotland during the winter of 1310–11. His estates were confined to County Durham, where he possessed eight manors, and his main residence was at Silksworth and was located near a chapel dedicated to St Leonard. An inventory of Fitzmarmaduke's possessions drawn up after his death, lists among other things, a dozen golden spoons, his peacock and two peahens. FitzMarmaduke's family are the earliest recorded landholders at Silksworth. The family held Silksworth in its entirety at one time but, as noted above, by the close of the 12th century part of it had passed into other hands.

48 Quoted by M. McKisack, *The Fourteenth Century, 1307–1399*, 1959, p. 31.

49 J. Scammell, 'Robert I and the North of England', *English Historical Review*, no. cclxxxviii, July 1958, pp. 385 & 389.

50 The right of wreck along the coast of County Durham belonged to the Bishop of Durham.

51 Through marriage, Silksworth passed to the Middletons of Belsay in Northumberland.

52 Thomas was likely a member of the Menvill (also spelt Menville) family, lords of the manor of Horden in the parish of Easington. John Menvill, a lawyer from Northumberland, began acquiring land in the parish in the 1330s. Durham Cathedral Muniments show that he was granted the manor of Horden by Ralph Neville of Raby in December 1340, and the Menvills extended their property portfolio in the parish in the second half of the 14th century. They also held land at Silksworth in the parish of Bishopwearmouth.

53 E. King, *Medieval England*, p. 194.

54 F. Bradshaw, 'The Black Death in the Palatinate of Durham', *Archaeologia Ael.* 3rd series, iii, 1907, p. 156. It is usually said that the plague arrived in the county by road and first affected southeast Durham.

55 R. Lomas, 'The Black Death in County Durham', *Journal of Medieval History* 15, 1989, p. 129. The least badly affected of the 28 townships was Monkton (near Jarrow) where 21 per cent of the tenants died.

56 Bradshaw, 'Social and Economic History', in *Victoria County History* ii, p. 212.

57 In the 1350s, there was a rise in production and on this point Ben Dodds comments:

'Rising productivity is explicable in terms of the changing relationship between population and resources. Whilst land had never been scarce between Tyne and Tees, the 'Great Pestilence' bequeathed a new abundance of the county's most fertile land to its survivors…[who] were able to use their resources more efficiently and, in so doing, improved their own standards of living.' B. Dodds, 'Peasants, Landlords and Production Between the Tyne and the Tees', in Liddy & Britnell (eds.), *North East England in the later Middle Ages*, p. 184.

58 Four 48-acre husbandlands also existed at Fulwell, but Richard Lomas comments that they had 'become unrecognizable' by 1340; R. Lomas, 'Developments in Land Tenure on the Prior of Durham's Estate in the later Middle Ages', *Northern History*, vol. xiii, 1977, p. 31. A husbandland had also existed at Southwick but had disappeared by 1340: perhaps it had become a freehold.

59 *Ibid.*, p. 31.

60 R.H. Britnell, 'Feudal Reaction after the Black Death in the Palatinate of Durham', *Past & Present*, August 1990, p. 40. By the second half of the 14th century only a small proportion of the peasantry were personally unfree. In County Durham, '*nativi* [i.e. neifs] made up approximately ten to twenty per cent of the customary tenants in the late fourteenth century. The rest were personally free, even though dependent on their lords because they held customary lands.' P. Larson, 'Local Law Courts in Late Medieval Durham', in Liddy & Britnell (eds.) *North East England in the later Middle Ages*, p. 106.

61 W. Greenwell (ed.), *Bishop Hatfield's Survey: a Record of the Possessions of the See of Durham*, Surtees Soc., xxxii, 1857, p. 132. Surnames of other tenants at Bishopwearmouth mentioned in the survey include Hobson, Gray, Rudd, Shepherdson, Marshall, Gamell and Warden.

62 Exchequer holdings were well represented elsewhere in the parish of Bishopwearmouth. They were especially notable at Ryhope, where there were 22 small plots of exchequer land, each comprising an acre and three roods (almost two acres in total), on neighbouring moorland.

63 The Hedworths were free tenants of the Prior of Durham and, since the 1330s, were at the forefront of Southwick's tenantry. During the late Middle Ages the family rose into the ranks of the county's lesser gentry. A key marriage was into the Darcy family, landholders in Lincolnshire who were granted land on Wearside (the manors of Harraton and West Herrington) by Bishop Antony Bek of Durham in the early 14th century. By 1432 John Hedworth, whose mother was a Darcy, had acquired (as a co-heir) two-thirds of the manor of Harraton and had made it his base. He retained his property at Southwick, however.

64 Greenwell, *Hatfield's Survey*, p. 137. Interestingly, the late Victor Watts noted the 'overwhelmingly English character' of the names of the fisheries on the Wear and that they contained traces of the Old English inflectional system. He thus declared: 'There is no doubt that the majority of these names predate the Norman conquest and may well go back to the foundation period of the Jarrow-Monkwearmouth monasteries or beyond.' V.E. Watts, 'Some Northumbrian Fishery Names 1,' *Transactions of the Architectural and Archaeological Society of Durham and Northumberland* new series vol. 6, 1982, p. 90.

65 Greenwell, *Hatfield's Survey*, p. 132.

66 In connection with the early history of the Hyltons, W. H. Longstaffe has commented that 'it would be endless to refute all the absurd statements' that have been made about the family, such as tales that they were lords of Hylton in the days of King Athelstan (924–39); W.H. Longstaffe, 'The Church of Guyzance', *Archaeol. Ael.* new series vol. iii, 1859, p. 134. In addition to Roman's agreement with the Prior of Durham in 1157, the next head of the family, Alexander, also made a covenant respecting a chapel at Hylton. He did so with Prior German of Durham on 11 November 1172 (in the presence of Hugh du Puiset) and confirmed, and clarified, aspects of the previous agreement. Hence the Hyltons (and their tenants) could worship at Hylton provided that they did not neglect St Peter's Church, Monkwearmouth, which they had to attend for festivals such as Easter and Christmas, and to which they had to render certain dues, including thraves of corn.

67 Barons of the bishopric were identical to honorial barons—leading vassals of great lords such as the Earls of Chester—found elsewhere in England.

68 Robert de Hylton (who had fought on the side of the rebels against Henry III during

the Barons' War of the mid 1260s) is often identified as the grandson of Alexander de Hylton, who died in the early 1240s after departing for the Holy Land. In fact, he was Alexander's son as is evident, for instance, from a document of 1297 or later, in *The Percy Chartulary*, Surtees Soc. vol. cxvii, 1911, p. 457. Robert was summoned to parliament in 1295 and 1296. The next head of the family to receive such summonses, Alexander, did so in 1332–6. In contrast, County Durham's most important lay lords, the Neville family of Raby, were also first summoned to parliament in 1295 but were continuously summoned thereafter and were undoubtedly members of England's nobility, whereas the Hyltons, whose wealth was not comparable, were greater gentry.

69 Hylton's patrimony included the same three knights' fees recorded in 1166, as well as additional property elsewhere, such as Shilbottle, Guyzance and Rennington in Northumberland that had been acquired through marriage into the Tyson family in the late 12th century.

70 Hylton and Lumley were friends and the latter, when he built Lumley Castle in the late 14th century, placed a shield bearing the Hylton arms above the entrance on the east front. Interestingly, Sir William Washington was part of the affinity of the mighty Neville family of Raby, whereas the arms of the Nevilles are conspicuously absent from the heraldic display that adorns Hylton Castle. Instead, Sir William Hylton was closely aligned with the Percys, the only family in the North East whose power rivalled that of the Nevilles. Sir William Washington was the last of his line to hold the manor of Washington. Upon his death in 1399 the estate passed, through the marriage of his daughter, to the Tempests of Studley whose property mostly lay in Yorkshire.

71 B. Morley & S. Speak, 'Excavation and Survey at Hylton Castle, Sunderland', *The Archaeological Journal*, vol. 159, 2002, pp. 260–1. Geophysical investigation on an artificial terrace lying further to the east, indicated the site of a substantial structure. Speak and Morley suggest that the presumed building may well have augmented, or supplanted, the castle as the Hyltons' residence 'between the late medieval and Georgian use of the castle proper', ibid, p. 263.

72 His mother is sometimes wrongly identified as Joan (or Jane) of Biddick.

73 J. Raine (ed.), *The Inventories and Account Rolls of the Benedictine Houses of Jarrow and Monkwearmouth*, Surtees Soc. xxix, 1854, p. 241. The old church ('ye ald kirke') is believed to have been one of the secondary churches of Benedict Biscop's former monastic house. The cell's accounts for the year 1360 (*ibid.*, p. 159) mention the existence of an old church, presumably the same structure as that mentioned in the Hylton dispute, in which tithe-barley was stored.

74 *Ibid.*, pp. 241–3.

75 A.J. Pollard, *North-Eastern England during the Wars of the Roses*, 1990, p. 48. The accounts of the cell at Monkwearmouth are in line with the regional downward pattern. Of the cell's parochial revenues from tithes etc, Alan Piper notes: 'Before 1400 these amounted to some £20–25 a year, dropping to less than £15 between 1400 and 1450, and recovering a little after that.' A.J. Piper, *Durham Monks at Wearmouth*, 1974, p. 4.

76 Meikle, & Newman, *Sunderland and its Origins*, p. 88. The Bowes likely came from the North Riding of Yorkshire and became members of County Durham's gentry in the early 14th century. The founder of the family fortunes was a lawyer named Adam (died c.1347) who married the heiress of Sir John Trayne of Streatlam.

77 Pollard, *North-Eastern England*, pp. 1–2.

78 Accounts of the cell of Wearmouth from the mid 15th century onward, sometimes record that vessels visiting the Wear paid the monks anchorage.

79 Quoted by E. Watts Moses in 'The Williamsons of East Markham, Monkwearmouth and Whitburn', *Antiquities of Sunderland* vol. xxiii, 1964, p. 73.

80 Wearside's most famous Anglican clergyman of this era was Bernard Gilpin (c.1510–83). Born in the North West, he was educated at Oxford and served as Rector of Houghton-le-Spring from 1557 until his death. The 'Apostle of the North', Gilpin undertook far-flung preaching tours that included annual visits to the wild valleys of North Tynedale and Redesdale where he preached to the notorious Border Reivers. He was, nevertheless, a conscientious rector of Houghton where, moreover, he co-founded Kepier Grammar School in 1574.

One of the Bishops of Durham during this period was Richard Barnes, who held the see for a decade. In 1577, shortly after becoming bishop, he instructed his clergy that they were to teach their parishioners that if an infant died 'without publique babtisme first to it ministred, that the same is not to be…adiudged as a damned sowle, but to be well hoped of, and the body to be interred in the churche yearde, yet without ringinge or any divine service or solemnity.' Moreover, the clergy were among other things instructed not to frequent 'any comon tavernes or aile howses, or any onlawfull games, as cardinge, dicinge, bowlinge, dauncinge, or such like.' J. Raine (ed.), *The Injunctions and other Ecclesiastical Proceedings of Richard Barnes, bishop of Durham from 1576 to 1587*, Surtees Soc. xxii, 1850, p. 18.

81 *The Rising in the North—the 1569 Rebellion, being a reprint of the Memorials of the Rebellion of the Earls of Northumberland and Westmoreland edited by Sir Cuthbert Sharp*, 1840, (reprinted 1975), pp. 30–1.

82 He is sometimes described as a younger son of Sir Ralph Bowes. In fact, his father was Sir Richard Bowes.

83 Some Wearsiders were sympathetic to the rebel cause, and Diana Newton has highlighted evidence that during the rebellion and its immediate aftermath Catholic rituals were practised at St Peter's Church, Monkwearmouth; D. Newton, *North-East England, 1569–1625: Governance, Culture & Identity*, 2006, p. 120. Following the rebellion, a local rebel was hanged at Fulwell.

84 J.A. Myerscough, *The Martyrs of Durham and the North East*, 1956, p. 82.

85 *Calendar of State Papers, domestic series, 1601–3, with add. 1547–65*, p. 573.

86 Meikle and Newman, *Sunderland and its Origins*, p. 98.

87 *Ibid.*, p. 47.

88 H.L. Robson, 'George Lilburne, Mayor of Sunderland', *Antiquities of Sunderland*. vol. xxii, 1960, p. 91. Most Wearsiders, of course, continued to derive their livings from agriculture. Rural affairs were sometimes marred by acrimony. For example, at Fulwell on 28 December 1599 a resident of that township named Richard Haddock, a yeoman, 'assaulted George Jackson and wielding a pitchfork worth 8d. prevented an ox belonging to Michael Calverley, gent., yoked to a cart…laden with muck from being

taken from Fulwell to the town fields, to the injury of Jackson and Calverley and against the queen's peace.' C.M. Fraser (ed.), *Durham Quarter Session Rolls, 1471–1625*, Surtees Soc. cxcix, 1991, p. 115. Haddock was thus fined 12d. for his wayward behaviour.

Chapter Four

1 Quoted by W. Dumble, 'The Durham Lilburnes and the English Revolution', in D. Marcombe (ed.), *The Last Principality, Politics, Religion and Society in the Bishopric of Durham, 1494–1660*, 1987, p. 227. Thomas Triplet (also spelt 'Triplett') was a graduate of Oxford University and had been Rector of Whitburn since 1631. He also became Rector of Washington in April 1640.

2 P. Gregg, *Free-Born John—A Biography of John Lilburne*, 1961, p. 24.

3 J. Hatcher, *The History of the British Coal Industry, I: Before 1700: Towards the Age of Coal*, 1993, p. 493.

4 The chaldron was a measure of volume that differed around the country. During the 17th century, a Newcastle chaldron came to equal 53 hundredweight (2.65 tons) and this may have been the norm for the measure on Wearside as well. In view of the uncertainty that exists, historians who have calculated the amount of coal that left the Wear have come to different conclusions about the tonnages involved. In 1695, parliament standardised the North East chaldron at 53 hundredweight.

5 M.M. Meikle & C.M. Newman, *Sunderland and its Origins—Monks to Mariners*, 2007, p. 117. Hatcher states that in 1616–7 (from Christmas to Christmas) 39,665 tons were shipped from the Wear. Most of the coal went to English ports, but 4,240 tons were sent overseas. Hatcher, *The History of the British Coal Industry*, p. 493. A different figure for the Wear's coal shipments in 1617 has been provided by B. Deitz, who calculated that a total of 31,432 tons left the Wear in 1617. B. Deitz, 'The North-East Coal Trade, 1550–1750, Measures, Markets and the Metropolis', *Northern History*, vol. 22, 1986, p. 291.

6 Hatcher, *The History of the British Coal Industry*, p. 494. Deitz's estimate for total shipments of coal from the Wear in 1634 was 56,933 tons.

7 Deitz, 'The North-East Coal Trade', p. 288.

8   Meikle & Newman, *Sunderland and its Origins*, p. 116.

9   Gregg, *Free-Born John*, p. 96. By this date George Lilburne had remarried (his first wife had died in late 1627 and was buried at Whitburn) for on 13 April 1629, 'Mr. George Lylburne, Sunderland, and Elianor Lambert, widow, dau. of Mr John Hickes, pson [parson] of Whitburne, and of Alice his wyfe', married at Whitburn. H.M. Wood (ed.), *The Registers of Whitburn in the County of Durham*, vol. x, 1904, p. 93. Lilburne's new father-in-law, John Hicks, died less than two years later and was buried at Whitburn on 31 December 1630, *ibid.*, p. 144. His successor was Thomas Triplet.

10 J.G., Garbutt, *A Historical and Descriptive View of the Parishes of Monkwearmouth and Bishopwearmouth and the Port and Borough of Sunderland*, 1819, appendix page 10. Morton's charter is quoted in full, pp. 9–35.

11 Richard Hedworth of Chester Deanery, head of a junior branch of the Hedworths of Harraton, also ranked among the aldermen, as did Francis James of Hetton-le-Hole and Washington Hall, now known as Washington Old Hall.

12 The previous year, 1636, Newcastle had experienced a particularly devastating outbreak of plague, one that reached Tyneside from Holland. Parish records show that it killed approximately 47 per cent of the town's population.

13 In connection with this aspect of Morton's charter, Christine Newman suggests: 'This may have been a confirmation of fairs and markets already existing.' Meikle & Newman, *op. cit.* p. 88. Madeliene Hope Dodds was more emphatic and declared that Morton's charter 'was a confirmation of fairs and markets which had long existed'; M.H. Dodds, 'The Bishops' Boroughs', *Archaeologia Aeliana*, 3rd series, vol. xii, 1915, p. 110. Dodds suggests that Sunderland may have been granted a market in the early 14th century, as was Stockton on Tees in 1310.

14 J. Briggs *et al*, (eds.), *Sunderland Wills and Inventories, 1601–1650*, Surtees Society, vol 214, 2010, p. 190.

15 On this point, Robert Surtees wrote that the will produced 'litigations and chancery suits in abundance.' *The History & Antiquities of the County Palatine of Durham*, vol ii., 1820, p. 22.

16 As I have said elsewhere, one of the king's failings was that 'he was prone to bad judgement. More often than not he misread a situation: more often than not he was sanguine in circumstances which would have alarmed others. In the short term this was good for his health: in the long-term it cost him his head.' G.L. Dodds, *Battles in Britain 1066–1746*, 1996, p. 160.

17 P.H. Osmond, *A Life of John Cosin, Bishop of Durham 1660–1672*, 1913, p. 59.

18 An incident affecting Burgoyne, and likely a dispute over tithes, is mentioned in court records from 1609. At Durham, on 21 August of that year, it was presented that at Bishopwearmouth on 24 July, 'in a close called *Hollow Crosse*', seven men had 'assembled riotously and broke into the same and seized 3 measures of hay worth 12d. of Francis Burgoyne…rector of Bishopwearmouth.' C.M. Fraser (ed.), *Durham Quarter Session Rolls, 1471–1625*, Surtees Society, vol. cxcix, 1991, p. 190. The men in question, described as yeomen of Bishopwearmouth, were William Pattison, Thomas Hilton, Nicholas Bryan, William Robinson, Thomas Roxby, John Thompson and John Shiperdson. Shortly thereafter, on 4 October the defendants appeared in person at Durham and pleaded not guilty.

A more serious incident (albeit unconnected to Rector Burgoyne) occurred on Wearside later that year. At Durham on 11 April 1610, it was declared that Robert Milner of Monkwearmouth 'deliberately on 27 December 1609 between 9 a.m. and 11 a.m. at Monkwearmouth attacked Adam Watson, cast him to the ground and knee'd him so that he languished from his injuries from 27 December to 5 March following when he died at Sunderland by the Sea.' *Ibid.*, p. 196.

19 Quoted by H.L. Robson, 'George Lilburne, Mayor of Sunderland', *Antiquities of Sunderland*, vol. xxii, 1960, pp. 105–6. The living of Monkwearmouth was controlled by a member of the gentry, Henry Hylton, who was evidently well disposed to Puritan views. So too, was Richard Hicks (the son of Triplet's predecessor at Whitburn), a graduate of Oxford University who had been licensed to the perpetual curacy of Monkwearmouth on 13 September 1638.

20 Quoted by Dumble, 'The Durham Lilburnes', p. 228.

21 The Durham High Commission was a body founded in the Elizabethan era, whose members were appointed by the Crown, and which dealt with spiritual and ecclesiastical matters.

22 Quoted by Robson, 'George Lilburne', p. 104.

23 In connection with this development, we read: 'The House of Commons, having discovered many dangerous Designs plotted against the Parliament, and especially that of the Fourth of this Instant *January* [the king's attempt to arrest the MPs]…have thought fit once again to recommend the taking of this Protestation.' H.M. Wood (ed.), *Durham Protestations*, Surtees Soc., vol. cxxxv, 1922, p. xi.

24 'A note of all ye names of all those yt tooke the protestation in the Burrowe of Sunderland this present twentie third day of februarie, 1641', *ibid.*, p. 149. By modern reckoning, the Protestation was signed on 23 February 1642, for before 1752 the year began on 25 March. None of Sunderland's menfolk refused to sign.

25 Surnames of people in the parishes of Bishopwearmouth and Monkwearmouth at this date include: Atkinson, Ayre, Bell, Browne, Cotterall, Foster, Gibson, Hall, Henderson, Jopling, Kell, Leighton, Myres, Pemberton, Roddam, Roxby, Swann, Thompson, Wake, Watt, Weatherall. In the parish of Washington, 119 people signed the Protestation and eight refused. In the neighbouring parish of Houghton-le-Spring, 469 signed and nine refused, three of whom were members of the Lisle family of West Herrington.

26 The other counties were Northumberland, Westmorland, Cumberland and Newcastle-upon-Tyne. The latter, with the exception of the castle, had been severed from Northumberland and made a county in 1400.

27 R. Welford (ed.), *Records of the Committees for Impounding, 1643–1660*, Surtees Soc. vol. cxi, 1905, p. 279.

28 Anon., *An ordinance with severall propositions of the Lords & Commons assembled in Parliament…to reduce the town of Newcastle to obedience to the King and Parliament*, 1643.

29 Quoted by C.S. Terry, 'The Scottish Campaign in Northumberland and Durham', *Archaeol. Ael.* 3rd series vol xxi, 1899, p. 165.

30 At this date, the New Bridge was the closest of the bridges on the Wear to Sunderland. Of the Scots' advance, the letter of 12 March states: 'Upon Saturday, March 2, we passed the Ware [Wear] at the new bridge neer Lumley…. We quartered that night at Harrington [Herrington] and the villages adjacent where we did rest all the Lords Day and entered Sunderland upon Monday the 4. of March.' Quoted by Terry, 'The Scottish Campaign', p. 165. In contrast, it is sometimes said that after crossing the New Bridge, the Scots spent the sabbath at Harraton (which would have entailed recrossing the river to reach the north bank) and then arrived at Sunderland after fording the river yet again, with part of the army crossing at Hylton and the remainder at Ford or Pallion. Given that the Scots' advance south of the Wear was not barred by the presence of an enemy army blocking the route to Sunderland, it seems likely that the version of events recounted in the letter of 12 March is correct and that Leven and his army (or at least part of it) headed towards Sunderland via Herrington.

31 *Ibid.*, p. 165.

32 Meikle & Newman, *Sunderland and its Origins*, pp. 125–6.

33 'Diary of Robert Douglas', in *Historical Fragments Relative to Scottish Affairs from 1635 to 1664*, 1833, pp. 52–3.

34 Quoted by Terry, *op. cit.*, p. 166.

35 *Ibid.*, p. 167.

36 *Ibid.*, p. 171. According to a Royalist source, the 30 March 1644 issue of *Mercurius Aulicus*, 'The fight began at about three in the afternoon.'

37 Quoted by Terry, *op. cit.* p. 171.

38 *Ibid.*, 172.

39 One of Lambton's sons, also named William, had lost his life fighting for the king at Wakefield the previous year.

40 Meikle and Newman, *Sunderland and its Origins*, p. 135.

41 Welford, *Records of the Committees for Compounding*, p. 61.

42 *Ibid.*, p. 313.

43 Fenwick's second wife was Catherine Haslerig, one of whose brothers subsequently married Elizabeth, the colonel's eldest daughter by his first wife.

44 Dumble, 'The Durham Lilburnes', pp. 233–4.

45 Fenwick's heirs, Elizabeth and Dorothy, were daughters from his first marriage.

46 Although an important living, Bishopwearmouth (worth around £160 per annum in 1647) was outclassed by an even more lucrative ecclesiastical post in the neighbour-

hood, the rectorship of Houghton-le-Spring. Of the latter, we read: 'to the said Rectory or Parsonage…there is belonging a great large and spacious Parsonage House with Barnes stables dovehouse and other outhouses and houses of office gardens Orchard fishpond and Glebeland and Tythes of all sorts as well as Grand Tythes as petit Tythes and other Ecclesiasticall duties worth p.a. £300 and above and that one Mr Reuben Easthorpe is now incumbent there by order from the Parliament upon the delinquency [Royalism] of Hamlett Marshall Doctor of Divinitie late Parson thereof.' A. Kirby (ed.), *Parliamentary Surveys of the Bishopric of Durham* II, Surtees Soc., clxxxv, 1972, p. 147.

47 Enclosure occurred elsewhere in the locality, a point noted by Gillian Cookson: 'Most arable and moorland in the Wearmouth parishes was enclosed before 1700, following the general trend in Co. Durham', G. Cookson, *Sunderland, Building a City*, 2010, p. 28. Not surprisingly, several mills existed in the locality. For example, in 1647 a certain Martin Watson was 'possessed of a windmill at Bishop Weremouth being a Corne mill…which hath neither house nor ground belonging to the same neither are any Tennants bounde to grinde thereat & it is worth per ann besides the Lords rent £4 which is in good repair.' Kirby, *Parliamentary Surveys*, p. 144.

48 Quoted by Robson, 'George Lilburne', p. 118.

49 The woman in question, Hester Hobson—who continued her journey to the meeting on foot—was the wife of a prominent figure in Baptist circles at Newcastle, Colonel Paul Hobson. He was a close associate of Lilburne's nephew, Colonel Robert Lilburne, a fellow Baptist who had played a leading role in establishing a congregation of that sect at Newcastle. Robert, the eldest son of George Lilburne's elder brother, had signed Charles I's death warrant and was a successful soldier.

50 Unpopular measures enforced by Cromwell's regime were a ban on Christmas because of its pagan origins, (the ban was introduced by the Puritans in the 1640s), and a prohibition on church weddings imposed from 1653: instead, magistrates solemnized marriages.

51 Quoted by Dumble, 'The Durham Lilburnes', p. 242.

52 G. Ornsby (ed.), *The Correspondence of John Cosin, D.D., Lord Bishop of Durham* Part II, Surtees Soc., vol. lv, 1870, p. 21.

53 The second intruder had been Samuel Hammond, a Cambridge-educated minister who benefited from the patronage of Sir Arthur Haslerig, by whom he was made Rector of Bishopwearmouth in 1651. Hammond held the post until late the following year, when he moved to St Nicholas' Church, Newcastle.

54 Robert Grey (also spelt 'Gray') had been educated at Cambridge University and had served as the curate at Bishopwearmouth in the years 1640–3. He was the half-brother of William, Lord Grey of Wark in Northumberland.

55 Quoted by Dumble, 'The Durham Lilburnes', p. 245.

56 Ornsby (ed.), *The Correspondence of John Cosin*, p. 327. On 10 October of the same year, a number of parishes in County Durham contributed to a relief fund for 'those who have been undone by the late dreadfull fire in London', *ibid*, p. 331. The parish of Monkwearmouth contributed £1 11s.; the parish of 'Houghton in le Springe' £5 15s.; and the parish of Washington, £1. 15s. 2d.

57 On 18 July 1665, Dean Carleton wrote as follows: 'The plague is in Sunderland and Warmouth [Bishopwearmouth]…seven houses shut in the former already, and one in the latter. This morning intelligence is brought to Durham that nine died yesterday in Sunderland.' *Ibid.*, p. 317.

58 Of the legal dispute, Robert Surtees observed that the 'Citizens of London, who derived very little direct advantage from the will…were wearied out with the contest; and after the Restoration an amicable decree was pronounced, by which the possession of the estates was restored to the heir, on condition that he should discharge all the particulars of the trust created by the will.' R. Surtees, *The History & Antiquities of the County Palatine of Durham*, vol ii., 1820, p. 22. In the event, the payments were reduced by one-third owing to the poor condition of the neglected properties.

59 'Free-Born John' (c.1614–57), a notable radical, is sometimes said to have been born in Sunderland but is usually thought to have come into the world at Greenwich, London. He was a younger son of George Lilburne's elder brother, and was educated at grammar

schools in Bishop Auckland and Newcastle before being apprenticed to a London cloth merchant. After serving as a Roundhead officer in the Civil War, he became a leading member of the radical Leveller movement. In the early 1650s, during George Lilburne's clashes with Haslerig—partly over Harraton Colliery—John outspokenly supported his uncle and was so critical of Haslerig and a parliamentary committee established to investigate the affair, that he was heavily fined and banished from England, to which he returned in 1653. Of him, Harry Robson commented: 'There is no definite proof that [he]…ever set foot inside Sunderland, although he may have done so in visiting his Uncle George at the time of the Harraton Colliery dispute.' Robson, 'George Lilburne', p. 86.

60 Not surprisingly, other people whose surname was Williamson appear in earlier records connected with Wearside. For instance, in the early 1380s a certain Robert Williamson had ranked among the peasants who were tenants of the Bishop of Durham at Tunstall: W. Greenwell (ed.), *Bishop Hatfield's Survey: a Record of the Possessions of the See of Durham*, Surtees Soc., vol. xxxii, 1857, p. 135.

61 Surtees, *The History & Antiquities of the County Palatine of Durham*, vol ii., 1820, p. 9. Monkwearmouth Hall was destroyed by fire in 1790.

62 Dorothy purchased the share of the Monkwearmouth estate from her late sister's son, Sir Thomas Haslerig, whose grandfather had served as Newcastle's governor after the Civil War. Dorothy bequeathed the share to her husband, Sir Thomas Williamson. The history of the Monkwearmouth estate during this era is further complicated by the fact that in 1672, in return for £800, Sir Thomas and Dame Dorothy had settled part of the estate on three gentlemen, one of whom was a Haslerig. Sooner or later, however, the entire estate passed into the hands of the Williamson family.

63 Ferries also crossed the river further upstream, as was the case with the Hylton ferry, which operated between the township of Ford and North Hylton.

64 According to John Hatcher, total coal exports from the Wear for 1665–6 (Christmas to Christmas) were 53,798 tons, well below the amount shipped in some previ-

ous years, of which a paltry 307 tons went to foreign ports. J. Hatcher, *The History of the British Coal Industry*, p. 494. Deitz also notes a significant drop in the amount of coal that left the Wear. He estimated that 42,258 tons were shipped in 1666, of which 244 tons went abroad: B. Deitz, 'The North-East Coal Trade, 1550–1750', *Northern History*, vol. 22, p. 291.

65 Quoted in J. Summers, *History & Antiquities of Sunderland* 1858, p. 26.

66 Hatcher, *The History of the British Coal Industry,* p. 494.

67 S.T., Miller, 'The River Wear Commission, 1717–1859', *Antiq. of Sund.* vol. xxvii, 1977–1979, pp. 57–8.

68 Quoted in J.G. Garbutt, *A Historical and Descriptive View of the Parishes of Monkwearmouth & Bishopwearmouth and the Port & Borough of Sunderland*, 1819, appendix, p. 39.

69 As Hatcher notes, 'Sunderland's harbour, and the shallowness of the Wear, would not provide access to large vessels, and throughout the seventeenth century vessels from Sunderland carried on average only a third as much coal as those frequenting the Tyne.' Hatcher, *op. cit.*, p. 474. The same author also states that in 1682–3, the average cargo of colliers leaving the Wear was 64 tons, much less than the average, 174 tons, from the Tyne.

70 Quoted in W. Page (ed.), *Victoria County History: Durham*, vol. ii, 1907, p. 281.

71 According to Hatcher, in 1684–5 (Christmas to Christmas) 164,976 tons were shipped from the Wear, of which 22,350 tons went overseas. By way of comparison, Newcastle's total coal shipments for that year were 621, 883 tons, likewise the highest known figure for that port in the 17th century.
In addition to London, important domestic markets for coal from the Wear included Hull, King's Lynn and Yarmouth. In this respect, Sunderland's coal trade differed from Newcastle's which was overwhelmingly dominated by the London market. For example, only 21.6 per cent of the coal shipped from the Wear to other ports in Britain went to the capital in 1682–3, whereas 70.9 per cent of Newcastle's domestic coal shipments during the same period went to London. In contrast, in the same year 20.9 per cent of the Wear's domestic coal shipments went to Yorkshire whereas a paltry 1.2

per cent of the Tyne's did so. An even higher figure, 27.3 per cent of the Wear's coal, went to East Anglia in contrast to the 18 per cent of the Tyne's coastal shipments.

72 Meikle & Newman, *Sunderland & its Origins*, p. 154.

73 The Goodchilds were well established on Wearside. In 1572, John Goodchild (who came from Ryhope) had acquired 'the whole tenement and grounds called the Pallyon', located on the south bank of the River Wear a short distance upstream from Bishopwearmouth. The Pallion estate Goodchild obtained comprised a messuage, toft, garden, 20 acres of arable land, 30 of meadow, 200 of pasture, 100 of moor and 100 of furze in Pallion and Bishopwearmouth, as well as a fishery.

74 Contrary to what is sometimes said, the freemen and stallingers are not mentioned in Bishop Morton's Charter, the text of which appears in Garbutt's *Historical and Descriptive View*, see note 10 above. The consensus of scholarly opinion is that the freemen and stallingers originated in medieval times. See, for instance, Vernon Ritson: 'A Critical Enquiry into the Origin and Status of the Freemen and Stallingers of Sunderland, in two parts', *Antiquities of Sunderland* vol. vi, 1905, and Madeliene Hope Dodds, 'The Bishops' Boroughs', in *Archaeol. Ael.* 3rd series vol. xii, 1915, pp. 128–32.

75 Quoted by W.A. Speck, 'The Revolution of 1688 in the North of England', *Northern History xxv, 1989*, p.197.

76 J. Miller, 'A Suffering People': English Quakers and their neighbours, c.1650–c.1700', *Past and Present*, vol. 188, 2005 p. 101.

77 W. Camden, *Camden's Britannia, Newly Translated into English: with large additions and improvements*, 1695, p. 785.

Chapter Five

1 *Local Acts 1, Sunderland Improvement 1719–1885*, p. 1.

2 Before becoming known as Church Street, the road went by other names: 'Deeds of 1719 refer to it as Leadgate Lane alias Watt's Lane and now Church Lane', *What's In A Name: Street names of Sunderland*, 2010, p. 16.

3 Anon., *Some Account of Edward Browne of Sunderland*, 1842, p. 8. The same source states that the house was 'a handsome building, commanding an extensive sea view, and

having large gardens belonging to it', p. 3. Browne was an Irishman who had settled in Sunderland by 1715, and was a prosperous merchant and coalfitter. He was also a leading figure in the town's Quaker community. Browne's business fortunes collapsed in 1729, two years after he had built Fitters Row and his splendid residence. As fellow Quakers observed at a meeting held in Sunderland, Browne 'had launched forth in his dealings, adventures to sea, and building houses beyond his ability, (against which he was several times cautioned) which, together with some considerable losses in trade, reduced him to straits and failure of payments, whereby in the end he was declared a bankrupt.' *Ibid*, pp. 18–19. Browne thus returned to Cork, Ireland, 'beset by calamities and misfortunes' as he noted in a letter of 1730, *ibid.*, p. 8.

4 G.E., Milburn, *Holy Trinity, Sunderland, Tyne and Wear*, 1990, p. 3. William Etty of York designed the interior and is sometimes also credited with designing the building as well.

5 *Local Acts 1*, pp. 3–4.

6 Sir F.M. Eden, *The State of the Poor*, 1797, p. 186. Inmates of workhouses received 'indoor relief', whereas the poor who dwelt at home and were deemed in need of assistance, were given 'outdoor relief.'

7 *Ibid.*, p. 182.

8 Quoted in G.E. Milburn, & S.T Miller, *An Eye Plan of Sunderland and Bishopwearmouth 1785–1790, by John Rain*, 1984, p. 39.

9 The assembly hall appears on a map of 1737 by Burleigh and Thompson, where it is described as a 'town hall.'

10 I have been unable to relocate the source of this quotation.

11 In connection with the legal dispute of 1731, Madeliene Hope Dodds notes, among other things, that 'witnesses stated that there were twelve freemen and eighteen stallingers, who had always enjoyed rights of pasturage on the town moor, intack, and coney warren [the latter was near the harbour], namely every freeman four cattle gates, *i.e.* pasture for four cows or two horses, and every stallinger one cattle gate, and the widows of freemen two cattle gates...[a] deponent stated that the freemen, exclusive of the stallingers, held meetings at which they made by-laws and orders for the regulation of the common and for their own affairs.' M.H. Dodds, 'The

Bishops' Boroughs', *Archaeologia Aeliana*, 3rd series, vol. xii, 1915, p. 126.

12 G. Morgan, & P. Rushton, *The Justicing Notebook 1750–64 of Edmund Tew, Rector of Boldon*, Surtees Society, vol. 205, 2000, p. 38.

13 *Ibid.*

14 When St John's opened, Thornhill had recently moved to an imposing house in Bishopwearmouth parish, but had previously resided a stone's throw to the west of Holy Trinity in a lane that would subsequently become known as Coronation Street.

15 The Hyltons had obtained the advowson of St Peter's (the right of presentation to the benefice) shortly after the Dissolution of the Monasteries in the reign of Henry VIII, and it was acquired by Sir Hedworth Williamson in 1751 upon the sale of the Hylton estates.

16 Laurence was baptised at Stamford Baron, Northamptonshire, in October 1668. Before becoming Rector of Bishopwearmouth, for many years he was Rector of Yelvertoft in his native county. *A New System of Agriculture* was published in 1726. Daughters of the green-fingered rector married three local gentlemen, Edward Dale of Tunstall, John Goodchild of Pallion Hall, and John Pemberton of Bainbridge Holme.

17 The chapel was ransacked on the morning of 22 January. Reportedly, around 300 men, bearing pistols and cutlasses, were involved in the incident and, upon their arrival, 'they found several people at prayers and a couple to be married who, with Mr Hankin, their priest, all fled out' of the building. Quoted by L. Gooch, *The Desperate Faction—the Jacobites of North-East England, 1688–1745*, 2001, p. 172.

18 The chapel stood on Half Moon Lane, not far from where the Exchange Building now stands.

19 The Robinson family of Middle Herrington were local gentry, present at Herrington since the 14th century. They were heavily involved in Sunderland's urban expansion in the early and mid 18th century, a point highlighted by Gillian Cookson in *Sunderland, Building a City*, 2010, pp. 68–9. One of them, Richard Robinson, a younger son who died in 1723, lived in Church Street.

20 *New Catholic Encyclopedia*, vol. xiv, 1967, p. 299.

21 Quoted by G.E. Milburn, in *The Travelling Preacher*, (revised ed.) 2003, p. 51.

22 *Ibid*, p. 51.

23 *Ibid.*, p. 56. A fellow clergyman, the aristocratic Spencer Cowper, had a negative view of Sunderland. Apart from admiring the pier, he wrote as follows in September 1751: 'Sunderland is a large filthy Town inhabited by more filthy people…there is a mighty pretty *Parish Church*…but it is kept so filthy as makes one regret the original expense they were at in building it.' E. Hughes (ed.), *Letters of Spencer Cowper, Dean of Durham, 1746–74*, Surtees Soc. vol. clxv, 1956, p. 142. For his part, John Wesley knew the church. He sometimes worshipped there when visiting Sunderland, as was the case for example on Trinity Sunday, 1755.

24 The marriage, to Anne Robinson of Middle Herrington, occurred in 1807 and proved childless. Robert Surtees died in February 1834, after catching a cold while returning to his estate at Mainsforth following a visit to Sunderland.

25 Quoted by G.E. Milburn, in 'Education and Learning 1780–1914', in G.E. Milburn and S.T. Miller (eds.), *Sunderland, River, Town & People, A History from the 1780s to the Present Day*, 1988, p. 142. John Hampson (1760–1819) wrote the first major biography of John Wesley, whom he had known personally. It was published in 1791. Four years later Hampson became the Rector of Sunderland, a post he held until his death.

26 Quoted by Stuart Miller in 'The Establishment of the River Wear Commissioners', *Durham County Local History Bulletin* no. 26, May 1981, p. 19.

27 *Ibid*, p. 14.

28 Quoted by S.T. Miller, in *Port of Sunderland Millennium Handbook*, c.2000, p. 18.

29 In 1760 (the year after the RWC's jurisdiction of the river had been reduced to the stretch downstream from Biddick Ford), a widely travelled visitor to Sunderland named Richard Pococke aptly observed: 'They are at great expense in improving the harbour. They have large decked boats on which women throw up all the earth and gravel they can get up, and then the boat is taken out, and 'tis shovel'd into the sea; and they also dredge for the earth, and draw harrows backward and forward in the water in order to loosen the earth that it may be carried out by the current.' 'Northern Journeys of Bishop Richard Pococke', in J.C. Hodgson (ed.), *North Country Diaries* II (Surtees Soc.) cxxiv, 1914, p. 248.

30 In the early decades of the 18th century, the number of quays increased. Among the new facilities was Ettrick's Quay, built for the coal trade near Sunderland's Customs House in 1705. It was erected by William Ettrick, who had succeeded his father, Walter, as collector of customs in 1700 and held the post until 1717. William and his brother Anthony constructed another quay (c.1710) a short distance further downstream. They did so after abandoning an attempt to erect a quay even closer to the river mouth, an endeavour thwarted by tidal damage.

31 J.M. Ellis, 'Cartels in the Coal Industry on Tyneside, 1699–1750', *Northern History* vol. xxxiv, 1998, p. 138.

32 M.W. Flinn, *The History of the British Coal Industry, 1700–1830*, 1985, p. 220. Of Sunderland's coal trade, Flinn further notes that by '1749, an even smaller share went to London—only eight per cent, while Yarmouth took twenty-one per cent, and Whitby eight per cent.' *Ibid.*

33 Quoted by E. Hughes, in *North Country Life in the Eighteenth Century: the North East 1700–1750*, 1952, p. 159. Two years later, in 1727 the Wear's coalowners, a group that included Henry Lambton, John Hedworth and the Earl of Scarborough, made an agreement among themselves to maintain the price of their coal for the following seven years. Among other things, it was decided that fitters were not to be sold coal below 11s. 6d. a chaldron [a measure equalling 53 hundredweight], and that the price fitters would charge ship masters would not be under 14s. a chaldron. Anyone who broke the agreement would be required to pay a fine of 2s. 6d. a chaldron to their fellow members of the concord. The Earl of Scarborough, like other parties to the agreement, partly owned a number of ships. He co-owned 64 vessels, of which 25 had Sunderland as their homeport.

34 *Universal British Directory 1793–1798*, vol. 4, Part I, N-S, (reprinted 1993), pp. 510–11. It was however, the practice of vessels involved in the shipment of coal from the Tyne to await their cargoes at the river mouth: the coal was brought downstream by keels.

35 In the mid 18th century, small-scale pottery production occurred at Silksworth.

36 Hendon Lodge stood near the Town Moor.

37 The firm was known as Atkinson and Co., but became Anthony Scott & Co. at the turn of the century.

38 J.F. Clarke, 'Shipbuilding on the River Wear, 1780–1870', in R.W. Sturgess (ed.), *The Great Age of Industry in the North East*, 1981, p. 80.

39 In addition to noting that there were six yards in constant production at Sunderland, Hutchinson wrote as follows about Monkwearmouth Shore: 'This place is very greatly increased in buildings, population, and wealth within the last twenty years. There are now five carpenters yards constantly employed for ship-building; which, with the dependent articles of manufactory, engage a multitude of workmen.' W. Hutchinson, *The History and Antiquities of the County Palatine of Durham*, vol. ii, 1787, pp. 506–7.

40 *Universal British Directory*, p. 511.

41 Burleigh was a prosperous Sunderland businessman and a member of the town's Quaker community, whereas Thompson was a Newcastle printer and surveyor. They produced the map on behalf of the River Wear Commission.

42 Sir William married Elizabeth, one of the daughters and co-heiresses of John Hedworth of Harraton. In 1714 Williamson sold his share of the Harraton estate to his brother-in-law, Ralph Lambton.

43 It is sometimes said that the Williamsons moved to Whitburn Hall after Monkwearmouth Hall was destroyed by fire in 1790. However, the move had already occurred. For instance, William Hutchinson noted in 1787 that 'Monkweremouth-Hall…is the property of Sir Hedworth Williamson, and was for some time the place of his family's residence', *History and Antiquities* vol ii, p. 506. Moreover, on 20 September 1749 William Huddleston Williamson, the son of Sir Hedworth Williamson and his wife Elizabeth, was baptised at Whitburn Parish Church, as was another son of the couple in 1751. H.M. Wood (ed.), *The Registers of Whitburn in the County of Durham*, vol. x, 1904, pp. 44–5.

44 In 1866 Sir William George Hylton Jolliffe Bt., a descendant of John Hylton's sister Anne (who married Sir Richard Musgrave), was created Baron of Hylton. The present holder of the peerage is Sir Raymond Hervey Jolliffe, fifth Baron of Hylton. He was born in 1932 and was educated at Eton and Oxford.

He served in the Coldstream Guards and inherited the title in 1967.

45 The hall was demolished in 1797. Instead, between 1796 and 1802 the Lambtons built a new Lambton Hall. They did so on the site of Harraton Hall, which enjoyed a finer setting on the opposite side of the River Wear. Subsequently, in the 1820s, the new house was rebuilt on a more lavish scale and renamed Lambton Castle.

46 Henry's father, Ralph Lambton of Barnes, had married Dorothy, one of the daughters and co-heiresses of John Hedworth of Harraton. Several of the couple's children were baptised at Bishopwearmouth, as was true of Henry (their eldest son) who was born in 1697 and inherited the main Lambton estates from an uncle.

47 The Lambtons had held land in Bishopwearmouth parish since the late 16th century. The house in Sunderland replaced their previous town house in Bishopwearmouth Panns, which became the home of their steward.

48 G. Patterson, *Sunderland's First Theatre and Music Hall*, 2009, p. 7.

49 *Ibid.*, p. 6.

50 S. Sadie (ed.), *New Grove Dictionary of Music and Musicians, vol. 1*, 1980, p. 748.

51 John Lambton (1710–94), a former officer in the Coldstream Guards, had raised a regiment of foot in 1758 that would subsequently become known as the Durham Light Infantry. In 1761 he inherited the Lambton estates upon the death of his brother, Henry. Rain's 'Eye Plan' shows other plots of land owned by Lambton, who was made a general in 1782.

52 In 1768 the bank, 'Russell & Co.' received over £27 following a benefit concert held on behalf of the Corsicans who were involved in a conflict with France. The Russell family had settled in Sunderland in 1717 and had become very wealthy as a result of various business enterprises. At the time of Rain's *Eye Plan*, the head of the family was William Russell (who later became known as the 'richest commoner in England') and his partners in the bank were Robert Allan, John Maling and a Mr. Wade.

53 Villiers Street was located on land that belonged to the Lambtons, and was named after Lady Anne Villiers, a daughter of the Earl of Jersey. In 1791 she had married William Henry Lambton, the eldest son and successor of General John Lambton (see note 51 above). William Henry died in 1797 and was succeeded by his young son, John, the future first Earl of Durham.

54 Of the town, Hutchinson observed in the 1780s: 'the chief or high street of Sunderland is nearly a mile in length, the houses well built with brick; the low street, which runs parallel thereto, and adjoins upon the quay, is narrow and extremely populous. There are some new streets which run from the upper [south] side of the high street, containing several elegant buildings.' Hutchinson, *History and Antiquities*, vol. ii, p. 525.

55 Sunderland's first freemasons had been members of Ambrose Crowley's workforce at his factory in the 1680s, a venture that he soon moved to Tyneside.

56 W.B Griffiths, *Wylam Wharf, Sunderland, 1994 Excavation Report*, p. 2.

57 The closest bridge was Newbridge, just downstream from Chester-le-Street.

58 Who deserves the credit for designing the bridge is unclear. Traditionally, the honour has been bestowed upon Thomas Paine, but more recent scholarship has rejected this opinion and given greater prominence to figures like the Rotherham ironmaster, Joshua Walker (who had links with Paine), and a Sunderland schoolmaster and mathematician named Thomas Wilson. On this point, the late John G. James commented: 'Most modern writers accord the design honours to Wilson, who was undoubtedly the official architect/engineer, although it is probable that most of the ironwork details were due to the foundry experts at Rotherham.' J.G. James, 'The Old Cast Iron Bridge 1793–1796', in Milburn & Miller (eds.) *Sunderland, River Town & people*, p. 9.

59 *Universal British Directory of 1793–1798* p. 511. An example of impressment affecting the Wear dates from the spring of 1779. As T.W. Beastall comments, 'Sunderland was empty of ships in late April and early May 1779, many having been "detained to the Southward by the badness of the prices and by the impress of seamen" in the American war.' *A North Country Estate: the Lumleys and Saundersons as Landowners, 1600–1900*, 1974, p. 31.

60 Quoted by N. McCord, 'The Impress Service in North-East England During the Napoleonic Wars', in T. Barrow, (ed.), *Pressgangs and Privateers, Aspects of the Maritime History of the North East*, 1993, p. 25

Chapter Six

1 T. Dibdin, *A Bibliographical, Antiquarian and Picturesque Tour in the Northern Counties of England and in Scotland*, 1838, vol. 1, p. 313.

2 *Ibid.*, vol. 2, pp. 1070–1.

3 R. Surtees, *The History & Antiquities of the County Palatine of Durham*, vol 1, 1816, p. 253. The Exchange Building was designed by John Stokoe of Newcastle and was erected in the years 1812–4 by a local builder, George Cameron. The latter was killed in Nile Street on 16 December 1814 when Wearside was hit by a vicious storm. According to the diary of Bernard Ogden: 'about one o'clock pm a large portion of a very high wall…gave way with a dreadful crash and buried a respectable mason of the name of Cameron in the ruins. He was taken up with his skull sadly fractured and died this afternoon.' Quoted by Dennis Wheeler in 'Sunderland's 19th Century Weather Observers', *Sunderland's History 7*, 1993, p. 3. Cameron was the posthumous grandfather of the scientist Joseph Wilson Swan.

4 *Sunderland Herald*, 25 January 1850, p. 5.

5 P. Gibson, *Southwick-on-Wear: an Illustrated History*, 1985, p. 3.

6 *Report on the Proposed Municipal Boundary and Division into Wards of the Borough of Sunderland*, 1836. p. 1.

7 Cited by Graham R. Potts, 'Growth of Sunderland', in G.E. Milburn and S.T. Miller (eds.), *Sunderland, River, Town and People, A History from the 1780s*, 1988, p. 59. Among middleclass homes that existed on the north side of the river, were ones erected in Dundas Street and Barclay Street in Monkwearmouth Shore, from around 1820, streets running east from North Bridge Street.

8 S. Muthesius, *The English Terraced House*, 1982, p. 104.

9 A. Long, 'The Sunderland Cottage', in T.E. Faulkner (ed.), *Northumbrian Panorama*, 1996, p. 103.

10 D.B Reid, *Report on the Sanitary Condition of Newcastle, Gateshead, North Shields, Sunderland, Durham and Carlisle—Appendix to Second Report*, 1845, p. 192.

11 A.B. Granville, *The Spas of England and Principal Sea-Bathing Places*, 1841, p. 268.

12 S.T. Miller, *The Book of Sunderland*, 1989, p. 58.

13 S.T. Miller, 'Cholera in Sunderland', in Milburn & Miller, *Sunderland, River Town & People*, p. 73. Many other Wearsiders, however, also resented the imposition of quarantine.

14 The infirmary opened in 1823 at the foot of Chester lane (now Chester Road) and was designed by one of the region's leading architects, Ignatius Bonomi of Durham City. It replaced a previous infirmary, located in Sans Street from 1810.

15 Jack Crawford died of cholera on 9 November 1831, after falling ill early on the morning of the 7th. The outbreak of the disease that claimed his life was followed by others on Wearside, such as in 1849 when 435 people died, and again it was the East End and other poor areas that suffered the most.

16 D.B. Reid, *op. cit.*, p. 191.

17 *Ibid.*, p. 191.

18 *Ibid.*, pp. 199–200.

19 *Ibid.*, p. 182, & p. 161.

20 *Ibid.*, p.132.

21 *Ibid.*, p. 198. Sir Hedworth Williamson (1797–1861) had inherited the family baronetcy and estate in 1810.

22 R. Rawlinson, *Report to the General Board of Health on a Preliminary Inquiry as to the Sewerage, Drainage, Supply of Water and the Sanitary Condition of the Borough of Sunderland in the County of Durham*, 1851, p. 85.

23 *Ibid.*, p. 59.

24 *Ibid.*, p. 85.

25 *Ibid.*, p. 38.

26 *Sunderland Herald*, 1 February 1850, p. 1.

27 One of the former sailors who received support was Harding Hall. He was born in Sunderland in 1758 and began serving in the Navy in 1803 as a member of the crew of HMS *Colossus*. Two years later he was one of over 70 local men present at the Battle of Trafalgar, and was wounded in the epic encounter. He later survived a shipwreck and was eventually invalided out of the Navy in February 1814, whereupon he returned to Sunderland. By the early 1820s Hall was resident at Assembly Garth, where he was also living at the time of the 1841 census. When he died seven years later, he was at no. 15 Robinson Lane. Of his life, Douglas Whiteley Smith aptly notes: 'Altogether it had been quite a story!' D.W. Smith, 'Now Safe Returned From Dangers Past', *Sunderland's History 9*, 2000.

28 Churches further afield included Washington parish church, Holy Trinity, a medieval structure. By the early 1830s, the fabric was in such a lamentable condition that the

building was demolished and replaced in 1831–3. Part of the cost was paid by Henry Perceval (the son of a former murdered prime minister) who was Rector of Washington in the years 1826–37. The church was later enlarged.

29   J.G. Garbutt, *A Historical and Descriptive View of the Parishes of Monkwearmouth & Bishopwearmouth and the Port & Borough of Sunderland*, 1819, p. 176.

30   G.E. Milburn, *Church and Chapel in Sunderland 1780–1914*, 1988, p. 16.

31   W. Paley, *Natural Theology*, (Oxford World's Classics) 2006, pp. 7–8.

32   *Ibid.*, p. 16.

33   *The New Encyclopædia Britannica*, vol. 9 (Micropaedia), 15th edition, 1997, p. 84. I have discussed Paley at some length in *Paley, Wearside & Natural Theology* (2003). Of course, following the publication of Darwin's *On The Origin of Species* in 1859, the design argument was widely dismissed by members of the scientific community and continues to be derided by many scientists, including Richard Dawkins, the author of books such as *The Blind Watchmaker* (1986) and *The God Delusion* (2006).
But this is not universally the case. For instance, a well known scientist, Paul Davies, aptly noted that 'many practicing scientists are also religious', *The Mind of God: Science and the Search for Ultimate Meaning*, (1992), p. 15. Moreover, Alan Hayward states 'that Paley's design argument really is a force to be reckoned with once again', *Evolution and Creation: the Facts & the Fallacies*, (revised ed.) 1994, p. 58. Furthermore, in *The Language of God* (2007) one of the world's leading scientists, Francis Collins, links his belief in God with evolution, and another eminent scientist, John Lennox, concludes that 'far from science having buried God…the results of science point to his existence', *God's Undertaker—Has Science Buried God?* (2007), p. 179. For one thing, Lennox comments: 'Since Paley's time, developments in science have shown that there are many kinds of systems within living organisms for which the term 'molecular machine' is entirely appropriate and among which are to be found biological clocks that are responsible for the vital molecular timekeeping function within the living cell and which are of vastly greater sophistication than Paley's illustrative watch.

Indeed, "machine" language is ubiquitous in cutting-edge molecular biology.' *Ibid.*, p. 83.

34   Quoted by W.B. Maynard, 'Pluralism and Non-Residence in the Archdeaconry of Durham, 1774–1856: the Bishop and Chapter as Patrons', *Northern History* vol. xxvi, 1990, p. 126. Dr Wellesley was present at a grand dinner held at the Exchange in Sunderland on 4 October 1827, when the guest of honour was his brother the Duke of Wellington. Other prominent figures who attended the memorable occasion included Lord Londonderry, Lord Ravensworth and the author Sir Walter Scott.

35   Garbutt, *A Historical and Descriptive View*, p. 367.

36   C.S. Collingwood, *Dr Cowan and the Grange School, Sunderland, with recollections of its scholars,* 1897, p. 9. Collingwood was born at Sunderland in 1831 and was an old boy of the school. He served as Rector of Southwick in the years 1863–98 and married the sister of the author Lewis Carroll in 1869.

37   *Ibid.*, p. 23.

38   M.E. Swan, and K.R. Swan, *Sir Joseph Wilson Swan—Inventor and Scientist*, (1968 edition) p. 14.

39   *Ibid.*, p. 23.

40   *Ibid.*, p. 24.

41   Quoted by T. Corfe, *Swan in Sunderland*, p. 7.

42   Surtees, *History & Antiquities*, vol. 1, p. 262.

43   Garbutt, *op. cit.*, p. 91.

44   J.W. Smith, & T.S. Holden, *Where Ships Are Born: a History of Shipbuilding on the River Wear*, (revised ed.) 1953, p. 4.

45   'There are…at present 31 shops empty in the High Street, whereas four or five years since there was not a shop to be obtained', observed the *Sunderland Herald* of 17 February 1843; quoted in the *Sunderland Herald*, 25 January 1850, p. 5.

46   *Sunderland Herald*, 25 January 1850, p. 5.

47   J.F. Clarke, 'Shipbuilding 1780–1914', in Milburn and Miller, *Sunderland, River, Town & People*, p. 34.

48   *Ibid.*, p. 34.

49   Quoted by G. Patterson, 'Victorian Working Life', *ibid.*, p. 52.

50   W. Fordyce, *The History & Antiquities of the County Palatine of Durham*, 1857, vol. ii, p. 509.

51   *Ibid.*, p. 509.

52   Clarke, 'Shipbuilding 1780–1914', p. 37.

53 The Hetton Coal Company was formed in 1819. Sinking the pit began the following year and the first coal from Hetton Colliery (also known as Hetton Lyons Colliery) was conveyed to Sunderland in November 1822. Hetton-le-Hole's population, which had been only several hundred strong before work on the mine commenced, thus rose dramatically. Augustus Granville, who subsequently travelled through the neighbourhood en route to Sunderland, observed that 'the famed Hetton Colliery' was 'one of the most extensive in England...and not fewer that 1000 men are employed in it....The population above ground amounts to nearly six thousand, who have eleven places of worship and seven Sunday-schools.' A.B. Granville, *The Spas of England and Principal Sea-bathing Places*, 1841, pp. 244–5. In nearby Houghton-le-Spring, significant growth also occurred following the sinking of Houghton Colliery in the years 1823–7.

54 J.R. Leifchild, *Children's Employment Commission Report*, 1842, p. 660.

55 Quoted by J.E. McCutcheon, *A Wearside Mining Story*, 1969, p. 34. Other members of the workforce were 'putters' who pushed tubs part of the way along the tramways. Leifchild's report includes the following about one of these individuals at the colliery, 18-year-old Alexander Ball: 'Gets up at 4 o'clock...begins work about 5....Takes a bait in a bag down with him, and a bottle of coffee.... The first thing he does every morning is to prepare the tub by taking off the drags; then goes in bye, perhaps a mile—does not know exactly—to where the hewers are at work. There with the help of the men (hewers) fills the tub; then puts it along the tram ways, perhaps 60 or 70 yards, then returns for another.... The putting is hard, but the hardest thing is the heat, and the hours are very long.' Leifchild, *op. cit.*, p. 643. Ball made about 3 shillings a day and finished by 6pm.

56 Patterson, 'Victorian Working Life', p. 46.

57 *Chambers' Edinburgh Journal, 30 March 1850*, p. 194.

58 *Ibid.*, p. 195.

59 *Ibid.*, p. 196.

60 Dibdin, *op. cit.* vol. ii, p. 1071.

61 Charles Stewart (1778–1854), third Marquess of Londonderry, was a major landowner in County Durham as a result of his marriage in 1819 to a baronet's daughter, the heiress Frances Vane-Tempest, and his property included collieries in the Rainton area. His County Durham residence was Wynyard Park near Stockton-on-Tees.

62 Dibdin, p. 1071.

63 N.T. Sinclair, 'Industry to 1914', in Milburn & Miller, *Sunderland, River, Town & People*, p. 24.

64 Quoted by J. V. Stirk, *The Lost Mills: A History of Papermaking in County Durham*, 2006, p. 134.

65 Surtees, *op. cit.*, p. 261.

66 *Ibid.*, p. 261.

67 Garbutt, *op. cit.* p. 419.

68 J. Burnett, *The History of the Town & Port of Sunderland, and the Parishes of Bishopwearmouth and Monkwearmouth*, 1830, p. 109.

69 Quoted by D.J. Rowe, in 'Trade Unions and Strike Action in the North-East before 1871', in E. Allen *et al.*, *The North East Engineers Strikes of 1871*, 1971, p. 69.

70 A case in point is William Story, who was born in Sunderland in 1753 and lived in the town with his wife and daughter. He was the owner of a merchant ship named the *Jane* and in March 1805 was on board the vessel when it sailed north from London, carrying ballast. The ship (en route to Quebec) duly arrived off Sunderland where it halted to take on supplies and also enabled Story and members of his crew to see their families. Subsequently, after rounding Scotland, the *Jane* headed into the Atlantic where, on 14 April, it was soon intercepted by an 18-gun French ship. Story and his crew were compelled to transfer to the enemy vessel and the *Jane* was plundered and scuttled. Several weeks later, after landing in Spain (to which they had been driven by bad weather), William Story and his fellow captives were marched northward to be detained in France. Story regained his freedom in the spring of 1814 after allied troops entered Paris and Napoleon abdicated. En route home, upon landing at Dover on 5 May, William recorded in his journal that 'after a captivity of nine years and twenty one days, I was again a free man in a free country' (quoted by Peter Clark, 'William Story, Merchant Captain of Sunderland, A Prisoner of Napoleon', in *Sunderland's History*, 2003, p. 123). Extracts from Story's diary were published in Sunderland by George Garbutt in 1815, the year in which Napoleon, who had briefly regained power, was finally defeated

at Waterloo. Story died in 1829 and was buried at Houghton-le-Spring.

71 M.A. Richardson, *Local Historian's Table Book*, vol. iv, p. 37.

72 John George Lambton (1792–1840) was a major landowner in the Chester-le-Street/Washington area. He also possessed land in Sunderland where, for instance, Villiers Street and Lambton Street were built on ground he owned. The former street bears his mother's maiden name.

73 N.T. Sinclair, 'Sunderland's Railways', in Milburn & Miller, *Sunderland, River, Town & People*, p. 26. Stephenson, who was born at Wylam in the Tyne Valley in 1781, built his first steam locomotive, *My Lord*, in 1813–4 for the waggonway at Killingworth Colliery on Tyneside.

74 T. Corfe, 'Sunderland and the Railways', in H.J. Bowling (ed.), *Some Chapters on the History of Sunderland*, 1969, p. 65.

75 Granville, *The Spas of England*, p. 244.

76 Miller, *The Book of Sunderland*, 1989, p. 38.

77 S.T. Miller, *Port of Sunderland Millennium Handbook*, c.2000, p. 24.

78 T. Corfe, *Sunderland—a Short History*, (2nd ed.) 2003, p. 58. The Durham and Sunderland Railway became part of Hudson's business empire in 1846.

79 Archives of the Sunderland Antiquarian Society.

80 *Sunderland Herald*, 21 June 1850, p. 4.

81 *Sunderland Herald*, 21 June 1850, p. 5.

82 Garbutt, *op. cit.*, p. 324.

83 T. Corfe, *Swan in Sunderland*, 1979, pp. 26–7.

84 *Chambers' Edinburgh Journal*, 30 March 1850, p. 194.

85 *Sunderland Herald*, 25 January 1850, p. 5.

86 Garbutt, *op. cit.*, p. 286.

87 Quoted by G.E. Milburn, *Church and Chapel in Sunderland 1780–1914*, 1988, p. 8.

88 Garbutt, *op. cit.* p. 113.

89 J. Burnett, *The History of the Town & Port*, p. 92. Subsequently, a local chemist named John Young was an enthusiastic bather, a point the 23-year-old noted in his diary in August 1843: 'I have "Bathed" in the sea every day this week.... I gather every time more confidence and I am certain that a little diligent practice will speedily enable me to acquire such a facility in the noble art of flotation as will prove the probable means of safety in the event of any sudden and unexpected casualty.' G.E. Milburn (ed.), *The Diary of John Young*, p. 128.

90 R. Rawlinson, *Report to the General Board of Health*, 1851, pp. 56–7.

91 *Report of the Commissioners of H.M. Woods and Forests, etc., enclosing the report of the Surveying Officers: Sunderland Markets, Bridges, Ferries etc., Sunderland Improvements, Market and Bridge*, 1847.

92 Quoted by J. Pearson, 'Local Government 1810–1851', in Milburn & Miller, p. 83.

93 N. Gash, *Aristocracy and People, Britain 1815–1867*, 1979, p. 168.

94 Pearson, 'Local Government', p. 84.

95 *Ibid.*, p. 88.

96 Sir William Chaytor (1777–1847) was born into Yorkshire's gentry and became a barrister. In 1816 he purchased Witton Castle (in lower Weardale, County Durham) which became his seat, and in 1831 he was created a baronet. Chaytor had a rather rough, scruffy, appearance and was nicknamed 'Tatie Willie.'

97 *The Times*, 30 July 1845, quoted by A.J. Arnold and S. McCartney, *George Hudson: the Rise and Fall of the Railway King*, 2004, pp. 138–9.

98 A. Heesom, 'Parliamentary Politics 1830 to the 1860s' in Milburn & Miller, p. 94.

99 The gang began throwing stones as the victory procession travelled along Whitburn Street in Monkwearmouth Shore, and one of those struck as a result was Sir Hedworth Williamson who was seated in a carriage with Lady Howick. The leader of the stone-throwers also discharged a firearm, albeit one loaded with paper pellets. Howick recorded what ensued: 'The people very naturally forced the door of the house & destroyed every article it contained. They would also very probably have killed the man but happily he got into another house behind & was not discovered till Williamson & a party of constables got there & they were able to protect him & take him to the lock up room.' Quoted by Alan Heesom, 'The Sunderland By-Election, 1841', *Northern History* vol. ix, 1974, p. 77.
Lord Howick had family links with Wearside. At St Peter's Church, Monkwearmouth, in June 1762 his grandfather Charles Grey—a member of Northumberland's gentry who later became the first Earl Grey—had married Elizabeth, the daughter of George Grey of Southwick. One of the couple's children

was Howick's father, the second earl, who is commemorated in Newcastle upon Tyne by the imposing Grey monument. Howick succeeded to his father's peerage in 1845, something which resulted in the by-election won by Hudson.

100 *Ibid.*, p. 74.

101 *Ibid.*, p. 74.

102 Heesom, 'Parliamentary Politics', in Milburn & Miller, p. 102.

103 quoted by Heesom, *ibid.*, p. 99.

Chapter Seven

1 J. Murray, *Handbook for Travellers in Durham and Northumberland*, 1864, p. 124, & p. 127.

2 L. Irving, *Henry Irving*, 1951, p. 79.

3 Sunderland was granted the status of a county borough in 1889, as a result of the Local Government Act passed the previous year. County boroughs were politically independent from the administrative counties—which in Sunderland's case, was of course County Durham—and had populations of at least 50,000 inhabitants. In the North East, Newcastle, Gateshead and South Shields also became county boroughs in 1889.

4 J. Patterson, *Guide to Sunderland and its environs*, 1891, p. 31.

5 G.R. Potts, 'Growth of Sunderland', in G.E. Milburn & S.T. Miller, (eds.), *Sunderland, River, Town & People: A History from the 1780's to the Present Day*, 1988, p. 60.

6 St George's Place later became known as St George's Square. It was badly damaged in an air raid in World War Two and the site is now partly covered by the Civic Centre.

7 C.L. Cummings, 'Some Account of St George's Square and the People Connected Therewith', *Antiquities of Sunderland*, vol., vii, 1906, pp. 79–80.

8 W. Fordyce, *The History & Antiquities of the County Palatine of Durham*, 1857, vol. ii, p. 422.

9 *Sunderland Year Book*, 1904, p. 11.

10 Fordyce, *op. cit.*, p. 480.

11 A. Long, 'The Sunderland Cottage', in T.E. Faulkner (ed.), *Northumbrian Panorama, Studies in the History & Culture of North East England*, 1996, pp. 114–15.

12 Potts, 'Growth of Sunderland', p. 66.

13 *The East End of Sunderland. St John's Parish: its work and its limitations*, 1896, pp. 14–15.

14 *Ibid.*, p. 11.

15 *Report of the East End Commission to the Ruridecanal Conference*, 1896, p. 19.

16 *Ibid.* p. 9.

17 *The East End of Sunderland. St John's Parish*, 1896, p. 17.

18 Fordyce, p. 479.

19 'The Insanitary State of Sunderland: and its Consequences', *The Builder*, Sept. 30, 1871, in *Sunderland's History 9*, 2000, p. 60.

20 T. Corfe, 'Prosperity and Poverty' in Milburn & Miller, *op. cit.* p. 78.

21 G. Patterson, 'Harrison's Buildings—Sunderland's first council houses', *Sunderland's History 3*, 1985, p. 32.

22 *Sunderland Yearbook*, 1906, p. 130.

23 A key player in the establishment of the Ebenezer Chapel (which he partly designed) was a lively and well-informed young man named Robert Whitaker McAll (1821–93). Hitherto, McAll had served at the Bethel Congregational Chapel founded on Villiers Street in 1817. However, as a result of a clash with some of the deacons, McAll and over 200 members of the congregation left Bethel in 1851 and soon erected the Ebenezer Chapel. McAll served as its first minister, but left Sunderland in 1855.

24 N. Pevsner, & E. Williamson, *The Buildings of England: County Durham*, 1983, p. 469. John Priestman (1855–1941) was born in Bishop Auckland (the son of a master baker), and came to Sunderland where, at the age of 14, he commenced working in the shipbuilding industry. He opened his own yard at Southwick in 1882. On the other hand, E.S. Prior (1852–1932) was the son of a London lawyer and, after receiving training in the firm of the eminent architect Norman Shaw, commenced his own practice in 1879.

25 J. Betjeman, *Collins Pocket Guide to English Parish Churches: the North*, 1968, pp. 128 & 132. Literature on the church includes my own article, 'St Andrew's Church, Roker', in the *Durham Archaeological Journal* vol. 10, 1994, pp. 105–11.

26 R. Sharpe, 'Emily Marshall of Sunderland: A Victorian Campaigner for Women's Work in Anglican Parish Life', *Sunderland's History 6*, 1992.

27 Quoted by D.W. Smith, 'Priscilla Maria Beckwith—A Forgotten Victorian Lady', *Sunderland's History 6*, 1992, p. 18.

28 *The East End of Sunderland. St John's Parish*, 1896, p. 17.

29 *Ibid.*, pp. 19–20.

30 Quoted in Fordyce, *op. cit.*, p. 455.

31 *Ibid.*, p. 465.

32 Among other school boards on Wearside were Barmston (1875) and Washington (1890).

33 G.E. Milburn, 'Education and Learning, 1780–1914', in Milburn & Miller, *Sunderland, River, Town & People*, p. 149.

34 The Central School of Science and Art, as it had become known, moved to the Town Hall in 1891 and was based on the uppermost floor. In 1894 the corporation began providing the school with significant funding and it passed into the control of the local authority in 1902.

35 J. Patterson, *Guide to Sunderland*, 1891, p. 27.

36 *Ibid.*, p. 29. High Street was in fact divided into High Street East and High Street West.

37 *Ibid.*, p. 49.

38 *An Illustrated Guide to Sunderland & District*, 1898, p. 114.

39 *Ibid.*, p. 127.

40 *Ibid.*, p. 88. Calvert's was located three blocks down from the junction of High Street West and Fawcett Street and the site is now occupied by a bowling alley.

    Among other things, Calvert's included a showroom for cycles and a cycle track for learners, as well as a glass and china department. These were in the basement, whereas on the ground floor were men's and boys' clothing, stationery, and carpets. Progressing to the next level, shoppers could purchase furniture, boots and shoes, general drapery, curtains etc., and ladies' clothing. As was customary, the upper floors contained the residential quarters of members of staff.

    Calvert's held an annual 'Dressed Doll Competition', of which we read: 'This event is one of the most popular features of the Christmastide celebration, handsome prizes being offered for the six best dressed dolls, which are eagerly competed for by the deft fingered damsels of Sunderland', *ibid*, p. 88.

41 Of Robert Ferry (1820–90), Patricia Storey comments: 'He was prominent in the revival of the Sunderland Philharmonic society c.1860, being presented with a gold watch and chain and a testimonial in recognition of his services in January 1863.' P. Storey, 'Mayors of Sunderland Part IV, 1902–1910', *Sunderland's History 10*, 2003, p. 32. One of his daughters, Emily, married Frederick Foster (1853–1920) in 1879. As noted, Foster, who had been born in North Shields, went into partnership with his father-in-law and ran the shop as the sole partner following Ferry's death. In addition, Foster became a town councillor in 1895 and served as Mayor of Sunderland in 1904–5.

42 P. Curtis, *Sunderland, a Century of Shopping*, 1999, p. 32. In the East End, one could find a comparable site, namely the Old Market, which dated from 1830 and linked High Street East with Coronation Street.

43 Fordyce, p. 509.

44 William Pile (1823–73), an affable, generous character and first-rate ship designer, was the most famous of the Wear's shipbuilders during this period. Pile was born at Southwick and was fascinated by ships from his youth. He worked at several of the river's yards and from 1853 operated a yard at North Sands, Monkwearmouth Shore, that became the leading one on the Wear, reportedly employing 3,000 workers. Although greatly admired for the quality of his ships, Pile was not a good businessman and when he died his liabilities totalled £170,000.

45 Quoted by D. Dougan, *The History of North East Shipbuilding*, 1968, p. 86.

46 J.F., Clarke, 'Shipbuilding 1780–1914', in Milburn and Miller, *Sunderland, River, Town & People*, p. 39.

47 P. Gibson, *Southwick on Wear: an Illustrated History*, 1985, p. 3.

48 The head of the firm was Sir William Theodore Doxford (1841–1916). He took over the management of the yard in 1882, following the death of his father, and continued to head the firm (a business that he ran with great ability and a willingness to innovate) until his own death. In 1878 he joined the Institution of Naval Architects and duly served as a vice-president. Moreover, in 1884 he was a founder member of the North East Coast Institution of Engineers and Shipbuilders and served as its second president. Among other things, he sat on Sunderland Council and served as a Conservative MP for Sunderland in the years 1895–1906, during which period he received a knighthood. He also served as the Chairman of the Employers' Association in the years 1908–12 and had a conciliatory approach to labour relations. On a lighter note, in 1906 he joined the Sunderland Antiquarian Society and remained a member until his death.

49 The strike, with the aim of reducing the basic working week from 59 hours to 54, had commenced on 3 April 1871. It did so after employers rejected a petition respectfully calling upon them to shorten working hours—the petition was drawn up as a result of a meeting of around 800 workers held at the Theatre Royal on 25 March. After the strike commenced, some of Wearside's engineering employers soon threw in the towel, and the resistance of other masters collapsed shortly thereafter. Consequently, a month after the strike had begun it ended in victory for the workers.

50 J. Wilson, *A History of the Durham Miners Association 1870–1904*, 1907, p. 3.

51 M. Anderson, *Durham Mining Disasters, c.1700–1950s*, 2008, p. 100.

52 John Candlish (1816–74) was born into humble circumstances near Bellingham in North Tynedale, and was a member of a family of Scottish origin. In the early 1820s, the family moved to Sunderland where John and his father gained employment at the Ayre's Quay Bottleworks which were managed by John's paternal uncle and owned by the Pemberton family. Later, at the age of 20 after serving an apprenticeship as a draper, Candlish began his own drapery business but it failed and a variety of jobs ensued. His fortunes were at a very low ebb, but took a turn for the better in 1853 when he formed a partnership and began the Seaham Harbour Bottleworks (subsequently known as the Londonderry Bottleworks), a venture that proved very successful and enabled him to purchase Diamond Hall Bottleworks.

53 J. Stirk, *The Lost Mills—A History of Papermaking in County Durham*, 2006, p. 147.

54 *Sunderland Times*, 24 October 1873, quoted by Stirk, *op.cit.*, p. 173.

55 D.J. Rowe, 'Occupations in Northumberland & Durham', *Northern History*, vol. viii, 1973.

56 G. Patterson, 'Victorian Working Life', in Milburn and Miller, *Sunderland, River, Town & People*, p. 49.

57 Quoted by Patterson, *ibid.*, p. 52.

58 K. Gill, *Sunderland Volunteer Life Brigade*, 2010, p. 37. Gill further notes: 'The brigade at Sunderland initially covered an area bounded by Whitburn Steel to the north and Ryhope to the south—approximately six miles of busy coastline.' *Ibid*, p. 42. The first recorded rescue mission was undertaken on the night of 14/15 October 1877 when a vessel named the *Loch Cree* got into difficulties when being towed into the harbour during a gale: 'By 3.00 a.m. the gale had reached an alarming height and the crew signalled for assistance. The brigadesmen fired ... [a] rocket which was made fast by the crew and, using ... breeches bouy equipment, the eighteen crew members and a pilot were taken off and landed safely within an hour.' *Ibid.*, p. 42.

59 *Sunderland Echo*, 23 September 1903, p. 6.

60 *Ibid.*, p. 6.

61 Freight traffic commenced on the line in 1852, whereas a passenger service started the following year.

62 Thomas Elliot Harrison (1808–88) was educated at Kepier Grammar School, Houghton-le-Spring, and ranks among the most eminent civil engineers of his generation. He was born at Fulham in Middlesex, but spent much of his childood in Sunderland to which his family had moved by 1813. Three years later the family was resident at Thornhill House, Sunderland, a home they shared with a wealthy friend. In around 1830, the Harrisons moved to Fulwell Grange, also known as Monkwearmouth Grange.

Thomas Harrison's first major engineering project was the Victoria Bridge, which he designed for the Durham Junction Railway formed in 1834. Work on building the structure—to span the River Wear between Washington and Penshaw—commenced on 17 March 1836 and was completed on 28 August 1838. Of this project, we read: 'The main span of the bridge still remains the largest for a masonry railway bridge in England—not a bad achievement for the first major structure by an engineer still in his twenties.' J. Addyman & B. Fawcett, 'Thomas Elliot Harrison, North Eastern Railway Engineer', *Archaeologia Aeliana* fifth series, vol. 37, 2008, p. 223. Later, he played a major role in the construction of Robert Stephenson's High Level Bridge across the Tyne at Newcastle in 1849–50, and became the chief engineer of the North Eastern Railway in 1854. In addition to designing Sunderland's railway bridge, Harrison partly designed the town's Central Station. He died on 21 March 1888 at his substantial home overlooking the green at Whitburn.

63 Southwick UDC was formed in 1895, and was the successor of Southwick Local Board formed in 1863.

64 *Guide to Sunderland and its environs*, 1891 p. 161.

65 *Ibid.*, p. 162.

66 Fordyce, *op. cit.*, p. 477.

67 In contrast to Sunderland, it was only in 1873 that South Shields library and museum opened. Moreover, Newcastle lacked a municipal museum and art gallery until 1904.

68 *Antiquities of Sunderland*, vol. i, 1900, p. xiv.

69 *Ibid.*, p. 39.

70 *Antiq. of Sund.* vol. vii, 1906, p. 83.

71 Quoted by G. Patterson, *Sunderland's First Theatre and Music Hall*, 2009, p. 14.

72 *Ibid.*, p. 21.

73 *Sunderland Yearbook*, 1902, pp. 137 and 139.

74 A. Anderson, *A Century of Sunderland Cinemas*, 1995, p. 8.

75 *Sunderland Echo*, 1 July 1907, p. 3.

76 *Sunderland Echo*, 2 July 1907, p. 3.

77 *Ibid.*, p. 3.

78 J. Patterson, *Guide to Sunderland and its environs*, 1891, p. 87.

79 *Ibid.*, p. 86.

80 *An Illustrated Guide to Sunderland & District*, 1898, p. 84.

81 P. Gibson, *Southwick-on-Wear volume 3*, 1991, p. 40.

82 By mid century various forerunners of the bicycle had already been invented and included cumbersome treadle-operated three or four-wheeled velocipedes. A local enthusiast was the Sunderland shipbroker, H.F. Wilcox. In the late 1860s, he purchased a four-wheeled velocipede made by Willard Sawyer of Dover, and, in a letter published by the *English Mechanic and Mirror of Science* in February 1869, noted: 'in my Sawyer I have climbed all the steepest hills in this neighbourhood except the celebrated Houghton Bank.'

In the same year, the first pedal-powered two-wheeled velocipedes started to arrive from France. Riding such machines could be an uncomfortable experience—especially on surfaces like cobbled roads—and as a result of the jarring effect on arms and legs velocipedes were nicknamed 'bone shakers.' In subsequent years, numerous bicycle shops were established in the North East (in many cases manufacturing their own cycles) and by 1900 over 20 existed in Sunderland. One such was Turvey and Co. in Holmeside, run by Fred Turvey, one of the town's leading cyclists.

83 The club, formed as a result of the merger of Bishopwearmouth Cricket Club and Hendon Terrace Cricket Club, was based at the Blue House Field at Hendon. In 1864 it moved to Holmeside, where it remained until 1876 when it relocated to Chester Road.

Two years later, several thousand spectators attended the latter ground to witness a memorable encounter between 18 players from Sunderland and its environs and a formidable Australian national team that was visiting Britain for the first time where it won the majority of its matches. During the innings at Sunderland, played on 16 and 18 September 1878, Sunderland and District won by 71 runs. Spectators were however disappointed that the Australian squad lacked its star player, Fred Spofforth, 'the Demon Bowler.'

84 Quoted in E. Watts Moses (ed.), *To Ashbrooke and Beyond: the History of the Sunderland Cricket and Rugby Football Club*, 1963, p. 16.

85 *Ibid.*, p. 27.

86 Helen Aitchison (1881–1947) the eldest daughter of a shipbuilder, was born in Sunderland the year after the first recorded lawn tennis tournament was held in the town. It took place at Chester Road but was poorly attended, and rain led to the departure of most of the spectators.

At the 1912 Olympics, Aitchison won the silver medal in the mixed doubles. Prior to that success, she had won the Ladies' Doubles title at Wimbledon in 1909. She played there again four times before the First World War and reached three semi-finals. In addition, she won the World Covered Court Championship in 1913.

87 J. Hudson & P. Callaghan (eds.), *Sunderland AFC: the Official History 1879-2000*, 1999, p. 21.

88 Quoted by Alan Heesom, 'Parliamentary Politics, 1830 to the 1860s', in Milburn and Miller, *Sunderland, River, Town & People*, p. 97.

89 P. Storey, 'Personalities and Power, 1860s to 1914,' *ibid.*, p. 124.

90 Of Thomas Summerbell (1861–1910), Archie Potts comments, he 'was, without doubt, the dominant personality' in Sunderland's Labour movement at the time. 'He was born in Seaham Harbour and left school at the age of 12. He served an apprenticeship as

a printer, became resident in Sunderland, and in 1894 he set up his own printing business in the town. His political development was from right to left: moving from Conservatism to Liberalism and then to Socialism....He was a keen advocate of municipalisation and was instrumental in persuading the Council to buy out the privately-owned tramway company.' A.A. Potts, 'Forty Years On: the Labour Party in Sunderland 1900–1945', *North East Labour History bulletin* no. 24, 1990, p. 13.

91 Storey, 'Personalities and Power', in Milburn and Miller *op. cit.*, p. 135.

92 *The Sunderland Yearbook of 1902* , p. 13.

93 One of the editors of the *Sunderland Times* was William Brockie (1811–90), a Scot who moved to Sunderland from South Shields in 1860 (he had been the first editor of the *Shields Gazette* founded in 1849) in order to edit the *Times*. He retained the post until December 1873 when his health worsened, but his association with the paper continued for he wrote material that appeared in its pages. Brockie also wrote articles for other newspapers and was the author of several books. Four years after his death, a compilation of biographical articles was published entitled *Sunderland Notables*.

94 M. Milne, *The Newspapers of Durham & Northumberland: A study of their progress during the 'Golden Age' of the Provincial Press*, 1971, p. 150.

95 *The New York Times*, 23 November 1980.

96 P. Hall, 'The First World War', in Milburn and Miller, *op. cit.*, p. 189. One of Wearside's earliest fatalities was Private Walter Darcey Thompson, who had worked at Hylton Colliery (also known as Castletown Colliery) and lived at 5 John Street (now Darwin Street) in Southwick. A former professional soldier, Thompson was a reservist and was called up to serve in the Coldstream Guards when hostilities began. He took part in his first engagement of the war on 25 August 1914. Less than a month later, he was killed in action on 16 September aged 31. He left a pregnant wife and two young children.
One of Sunderland's last fatalities was Bombadier Robert Wilson who was killed on 14 October 1918, aged 22. Wilson, who had worked as an apprentice butcher on Chester Road, had enlisted in 1914. His parents lived at 106 Sorley Street.

97 J. Sheen, *Wearside Battalion, the 20th (Service) Battalion of the Durham Light Infantry in the Great War*, 2007. The battalion was raised in Sunderland in 1915 (recruitment began on 19 August) and was mostly manned by men from Wearside. The battalion, which included many miners, was sent to France in May 1916 and was soon in action. Later that year, the 'Wearsiders' took part in the Battle of the Somme and subsequent fighting included service in the Ypres Salient and elsewhere.

98 One of the officers killed in action was Lieutenant Geoffrey Lambton, a nephew of the third Earl of Durham. The 26-year-old lost his life on 1 September 1914 while serving in the Coldstream Guards.

99 J.F. Clarke, 'Shipbuilding, 1780–1914', in Milburn and Miller *op. cit.*, p. 41.

100 One of the people killed was Thomas Dale, a magistrate and the leader of the local Labour Party. Property affected included Monkwearmouth's Star Picture Hall, which was destroyed. The cinema, one of the town's smallest, had opened in 1911.

101 *More Monkwearmouth Memories, Book no.3*, 1991, p. 47. On the other hand, the town's newspaper commented that the 'attack caused absolutely no panic, but the prevailing feeling is one of indignation. The victims include a baby and several children, while the damage was practically confined to small working-class property.' *Sunderland Echo*, 3 April 1916, p. 3.

102 At around noon on the 11th Sunderland's mayor, William F. Vint, appeared on the steps of the Town Hall to address a huge crowd that had gathered to hear the news that the war was over. Vint was 'received with a great outburst of cheering and flag waving.' He said that he was lost for words on such a momentous occasion but declared that 'After four years of strain and sacrifice, of doing our duty to our country and to mankind...we had arrived at the consummation of our hopes.' At the end of his speech cheers were 'given for the King, the Mayor and Mayoress, and the "lads", and the crowd, having sung the National Anthem, dispersed.' *Sunderland Echo*, 11 November 1918, p. 6.

Chapter Eight

1 The strike was called by the general council of the Trades Union Congress in the hope

that it would force the Conservative Government (headed by Stanley Baldwin) to renew a subsidy to the hard-pressed coalmining industry.

The strike began at midnight on the night of 3/4 May, and as the deadline for action drew near Sunderland's mayor, John Nicholson, called upon Wearsiders to volunteer to run essential services. The following issue of the *Echo* states: 'The effects of the strike were seen in Sunderland this morning, when there was none of the regular tramcar and bus services and all sorts and conditions of vehicles were plying for hire. On the whole the people accepted the position with all good humour.' *Sunderland Echo*, 4 May 1926, p. 3. The same issue also mentions that the Central Railway Station had virtually closed and that only one train had arrived at, and left, Sunderland.

Violent incidents occurred during the General Strike. For example, late on the afternoon of 11 May passengers on a train that travelled from Durham to Sunderland encountered considerable hostility from irate strikers and women who pelted the train with stones, bricks and other missiles almost throughout the journey between Leamside and Penshaw. Terrified passengers thus sheltered under their seats. Fortunately though, Sunderland witnessed little violent disorder during the strike and when it ended on 12 May, the mayor thanked the townsfolk for their good behaviour.

2   This was the total on Sunderland's 'live' register of unemployment on 14 May 1934. The figure comprised 26,300 men, 862 boys, 1,454 women and 455 girls. Shortly thereafter, an article published in the *Sunderland Echo* of 29 May aptly noted that although unemployment nationwide was lower than at any time since 1929, this was not the case in the North East.

3   G. Patterson, 'Between the Wars', in G.E. Milburn & S.T. Miller (eds.), *Sunderland, River, Town & People—a History from the 1780s to the Present Day*, 1988, p. 171.

4   C. Mowat, *Britain Between the Wars, 1918–1940*, 1955, p. 484.

5   Anon., *Them Were The Days, or were they? Life in Sunderland's East End in the 1930s*, 1985, p. 17.

6   Anon., *Men Without Work: a Report made to the Pilgrim Trust*, 1938, p. 139.

7   *Ibid.*, p. 112.

8   J.B. Priestley, *English Journey*, 1934, p. 306.

9   Patterson, 'Between the Wars', p. 177.

10   Since the mid 1880s, Binns had occupied a site at the southwest end of Fawcett Street. By 1921, the shop also had premises on the opposite side of the same road. Joplings had started on a modest scale in 1804 and from 1882 onward was owned by Hedley, Swan and Co. The business was located at 174–78 High Street East. However, in 1921 it moved westward to 126 High Street West, premises once part of Calvert's department store, a shop that no longer existed. Blackett's lay further west. The shop celebrated its centenary in 1926 and was located at the junction of Union Street and High Street West.

11   The homes in question were constructed by Bell Brothers of Sunderland, and comprised five rooms plus a bathroom and kitchenette containing an up-to-date stove.

12   At the beginning of the period, Sunderland was affected by the influenza pandemic that swept around the world. When the Great War ended, deaths had already happened on Wearside for the first wave of the disease occurred between late June and late July 1918. The second wave struck in late October and peaked a month later (shortly after the armistice) when 37 deaths happened on 29 November. Further deaths ensued until 4 January 1919. According to the Medical Officer of Health's annual report for 1918, the epidemic of influenza caused 654 deaths. Moreover, the outbreak caused complications to respiratory diseases, and thus the total number of deaths directly or indirectly due to the epidemic was approximately 754. The death rate in the town was 24.0 per thousand, whereas the figure for the previous year was 18.2.

13   *Sunderland Echo*, 30 July 1926, p. 4. The same article also notes that: 'In one house of eight rooms there are five tenants and 25 persons, there is no yard, and two water-closets serve the 25 occupants of the house.'

14   Sunderland Antiquarian Society Newsletter Oct/Nov. 2008. Reed further notes: 'Our furniture was the bare essentials, tables and chairs, chest of drawers etc. [and]…our clothes were bought mainly from the second-hand clothes stalls down the old market.'

15   A. Bishop (ed.), *Chronicle of Friendship, Vera Brittain's Diary of the Thirties, 1932–1939*, 1986, p. 232. Brittain came to Sunderland to

support her husband who was standing for parliament as a Labour candidate.

16 *Sunderland Echo*, 17 April 1926, p. 5. Southwick became part of Sunderland in 1928.

17 In marked contrast to such peripheral development in the 1920s and 30s, the Garths (large square blocks of council dwellings) were erected in the late 1930s near the East End's Trafalgar Square almshouses.

18 *Medical Officer of Health's Report*, 1936, p. 128.

19 *Ibid*, p. 134.

20 Quoted by R. Lee, 'That Priest-Ridden City: Politics, Power and the Church of England in Durham, 1820–1930', *Durham County Local History Society Journal*, no. 74, September 2008, p. 57. Although poverty no doubt did undermine religious belief, few Wearsiders actually embraced Communism. Cheeseman, a Yorkshireman, had served as Vicar of St Andrew's since coming to Wearside in 1909 and held the post until the end of April 1934. By that time he was approaching his 83rd birthday and was the town's oldest vicar.

21 In his opening address, Trevelyan commented: 'You have two equal wings of your new school which shows that you intend an equal chance to both sexes…In the same way let this school always be free of access to boys and girls from every kind of home.' *Sunderland Echo*, 19 October 1929, p. 7. Trevelyan was squire of Wallington Hall in Northumberland and an MP for Newcastle.

22 The college's initial home was Westfield House (opposite the Technical College) in Green Terrace. The premises were however unsuitable and had been described by the Board of Education as 'dingy and disagreeable.' *Sunderland Echo*, 6 October 1922, p. 5. At the time of the move to Langham Tower the college had 146 pupils, most of whom were local.

23 The house, which was in existence by 1841, had been bequeathed to the town by Thomas William Backhouse (1842–1920), a wealthy banker and a keen amateur astronomer. He likewise donated the park, which was opened to the public in 1923. Reportedly, as a result of the move to Ashburne, the college was 'the most modern institution' of its kind in the North, *Sunderland Echo*, 6 June 1934. The college had approximately 300 students attending day and evening classes.

24 A. Anderson, *The Golden Age of the Silver Screen*, 2001, p. 4.

25 R. Carter, *Footballer's Progress*, 1950, p. 136. Horatio Stratton Carter was born on 21 December 1913 in Hendon, Sunderland, and joined Sunderland AFC in the autumn of 1931. He became extremely popular with the fans, whom he enthralled with his agile playing skills, and scored a total of 130 goals in 279 appearances for the club. Shortly after World War Two, he signed for Derby County and retired as a player in 1952, by which time he was playing for Hull City. In addition, during his career, he was capped 13 times for England. He died near Hull in 1994.

26 Casey was born in 1908 and his career began as a flyweight in 1926. He was Wearside's most celebrated local boxer between the wars and his career was avidly followed by many locals. He was the Northern Area Middleweight Champion in 1932 and retained the title until 1934 when he relinquished it after his weight had increased to 12 stone. Following the closure of the Holmeside Stadium, Casey rarely fought in Sunderland. On one such occasion, in 1935, he was defeated in a bruising encounter at the Theatre Royal in Bedford Street, after which he announced his retirement. Although he later made comebacks, the glory days were over. During the 224 fights of his career—148 of which he won—Casey was never knocked out. Of him, one of his former opponents, Marcel Thil, recalled years later: 'Your Jack Casey was the toughest and bravest man I ever fought.' (Quoted by A. Potts, *Jack Casey, The Sunderland Assassin*, 1991). The fight took place at the Royal Albert Hall in 1931 when Thil was the French Middleweight Champion: he later became world champion.

27 Letter to author.

28 *Roker & Seaburn, Sunderland, the Official Handbook*, 1939, p. 7. Partly as a result of Seaburn's growing popularity, Seaburn Railway Station opened in 1937. Sadly, of course, not all visits to the seafront had happy endings. For instance, almost a decade earlier the *Echo* of 18 October 1929 mentioned the details of an inquest held following the recent death of a 13-year-old boy named Sidney Ward, of 1 William St, who had been badly burned on Roker Beach. Ward was playing among rocks at low tide on Good Friday (29 March) when he picked up a 'yellow stone' that he thought looked 'bonny'. Tragically, the 'stone' proved to be phosphorous and set his clothes on

fire. He received prompt assistance and was taken to the Life Brigade house, before being conveyed to Monkwearmouth and District Hospital where he eventually lost his fight for life.

29 F. Willey, *The Honourable Member*, 1974, pp. 9–10.

30 Samuel Storey (1896–1978) was educated at Haileybury (a public school) and at the University of Cambridge. He became a barrister and, following his grandfather's death in 1925, succeeded him as chairman of the group of newspaper companies that he had established, a chain of papers that had started with the *Sunderland Echo* in 1873. Moreover, Storey served as a councillor for Monkwearmouth ward in the years 1927–30 (thereby also following in his grandfather's footsteps) and as an MP for Sunderland from 1931 to 1945. He was later granted a baronetcy and a life peerage.

31 One of the unsuccessful Labour candidates was the academic George Catlin. His wife was the author Vera Brittain, from whom he received enthusiastic support during the three-week election campaign he waged in Sunderland. Of her, we read: 'Arriving in Sunderland on 3 November Vera threw herself into canvassing and public speaking. In ten days she made thirty-three speeches, and although at first George was concerned that she might come across as too lady-like, it was evident before long that she was winning supporters over to him.' P. Berry & M. Bostridge, *Vera Brittain–A Life*, 2008, p. 343. The defeat of Catlin and the other Labour candidate, Leah Manning (who was more left-wing), was partly due to 'well-orchestrated smear campaigns: Manning at the hands of the local Conservative newspaper [the *Echo*] which made much of her past Communist associations, and George from a scarcely credible story that Catlin, in reality an old Bedfordshire name, was of Polish-Jewish origin.' *Ibid.*, p. 343.

Subsequently, Manning became the Secretary of the Spanish Medical Aid Facility after Spain was engulfed by civil war in 1936, and travelled there to help victims of Franco's Fascist troops. A small number of Wearsiders also went to Spain. They did so to fight against Franco, as was true of Frank Graham (1913–2006). Graham was born in Sunderland and attended Bede Collegiate Boys' School from where he won a scholar-ship to King's College at the University of London. However, owing to financial pressures he did not complete the course and returned to Sunderland, where he became a member of the Communist Party. Following the outbreak of the Spanish Civil War, he played a decisive role in organizing a small band of volunteers in Sunderland to join the British Battalion of the International Brigade. Graham arrived in Spain at Christmas 1936 and soon took part in ferocious combat. During the course of the civil war, some of the Wearside volunteers were killed and Graham was severely wounded in March 1938, whereupon he returned to Britain. In later years he ran a successful publishing firm specialising in publications on the North East, one of which, Tom Corfe's *A Short History of Sunderland*, appeared in 1973.

32 In 1936, the boundary was extended again to take in East and Middle Herrington and other land south of the river.

33 *Sunderland Echo*, 2 November, 1938, p. 2.

34 Construction of the quay entailed large-scale demolition of property in the East End, including many homes on Low Street.

35 Production of Pyrex on Wearside commenced on a modest scale within a year or so and by the close of the decade was gaining momentum, thereby transforming the fortunes of the Sunderland factory, which James A. Jobling & Co. renamed the Wear Glass Works in the late 1920s.

36 The workforces at Wearmouth and Hylton numbered around 2,300 and 1,700 respectively.

37 At Silksworth Colliery, for instance, (a pit owned by the Lambton, Hetton and Joicey Company) a small number of the workforce of around 2,800 had resumed work on 20 October. In the opening weeks of November, the number of miners who gave up the struggle in the Durham coalfield and elsewhere increased significantly. Of Wearmouth, we read: 'Wearmouth Miners' Lodge decided last night by a large majority in favour of the coal peace terms, a result which was rather in the nature of a surprise in view of the strong antagonism locally against the owners' eight hour and reduced wages proposals.' *Sunderland Echo*, 16 November 1926, p. 5. Subsequently, on 30 November representatives of the Durham coalfield declared that the strike was at an end.

38 The number of people employed at the mine dropped from 1,841 in 1930, to 893 in 1935. At Wearmouth the respective figures were 2,529 and 1,866. Silksworth and Ryhope also experienced a significant reduction in the same period. On the other hand, Herrington's workforce was 1,054 strong in 1930 and numbered 1,001 in 1935 whereas Hetton's workforce totalled 859 in 1935, 70 more than had been the case five years earlier.

39 It did so to build a 9,150-ton vessel for a Newcastle firm, the Sutherland Steamship Company, a task that would employ approximately 450 men. As the *Echo* noted: 'The placing of this order brings the work in hand on the Wear up to six vessels.' *Sunderland Echo*, 9 May 1934, p. 1. The other yards with work were Austin's, which had orders for four colliers, and Crown's which was building a pleasure steamer for a Scarborough yard.

40 The remaining yards were Austin's, Bartram's, Crown's, Doxford's, Laing's, Pickersgill's, Short's and J.L. Thompson's.

41 quoted by C. Mowat, *op. cit.* p. 601.

Chapter Nine

1 W.W. Lowther, *Wish You Were Here, Sunderland's Wartime Evacuation*, 1989, p. 12.

2 *Sunderland Echo*, 15 July 1939, p. 2.

3 *Sunderland Echo*, 11 November 1939, quoted by Peter Hepplewhite, 'The Home Front 1939–1945', in G.E. Milburn & S.T. Miller (eds.), *Sunderland, River, Town & People, A History from the 1780s to the Present Day*, 1988, p. 187.

4 Lowther, *Wish You Were Here*, p. 22.

5 'Within a month' recalled one of the teachers of Bede Collegiate Girls' School, 'we were working full examination syllabuses. Every Friday morning we saw instructive films through the generosity of Sunderland Education Authority. Despite drawbacks, we enjoyed our "exile" ... [and] as I look back, I realise how nobly the work of the school went on.' Sunderland Antiquarian Society newsletter, September 2009.

6 Quoted by Lowther, *op. cit.*, pp. 56–57.

7 D. Dodds, *Running Shoes to Racing Silks, A North-East man's action-packed life*, 2009, p. 65.

8 Quoted by Lowther, p. 57.

9 The letter was written by Councillor Wilton Milburn, who continued: 'Do not foolishly exaggerate the little vexations and discomforts ... [evacuees] may be feeling in their new homes .... Mothers of Sunderland, please, please, be warned.' *Sunderland Echo*, 14 October 1939, p. 5.

10 Tragically, in 1940 nine Wearside evacuees (aged five to 13) who were en route to Canada perished when the *City of Benares,* which left Liverpool on 13 September, was torpedoed early on the 18th. Two other evacuees from Wearside survived. The affair was made more poignant because two sisters, and a brother and sister, were among the children from Sunderland who died.

11 Lowther, *op. cit.* p. 54.

12 *Sunderland Echo*, 19 February 1940, p. 3. However some Bede parents were not in favour of their children returning as is evident from letters published in the paper.

13 Robert Moore, a retired policeman who had been on firewatch duty near his house, no. 5 Westcott Terrace, was one of the people who lost loved ones in the raid. During a lull, he returned to his home to have a cup of coffee and see how his wife and daughter were coping. He told the *Echo* that as he approached his home, 'another bomb fell right in the street and I saw the debris thrown into the air. Getting nearer I saw it was my own house and I realised what had happened to my home and my family. My wife and daughter I knew were sheltering under the stairs. They would have no chance at all. They must have been killed outright.' *Sunderland Echo*, 5 May 1941, p. 4. Several neighbours sheltering in the same house also perished. Incidentally, in the same month, 107 men, women and children in an underground air-raid shelter at North Shields died when a bomb-damaged building collapsed on them. It was the region's worst loss of life in a single incident during an air raid.

14 Quoted by C. Roberton, in *Wearside at War, A Sunderland Echo Souvenir*, 8 May 2005.

15 A. Anderson, *A Century of Sunderland Cinemas*, 1995, p. 40.

16 *Sunderland Echo*, 24 May 1943, p. 4.

17 Over two years earlier, an *Echo* correspondent whose letter was signed 'Bomb 'Em', had called for retaliatory air raids on Germany: 'Retribution must be our watchword ... give Germany a real blitz.' *Sunderland Echo*, 5 May 1941, p. 4. This desire for vengeance was

now certainly being meted out on a scale far greater than the correspondent could have imagined. Indeed, whereas the total number of British civilians who died during the war was over 60,000, at least half a million German civilians perished.

18   *The London Gazette*, 27 June 1944, quoted by W.W. Lowther, *Cyril Joe Barton, V.C.*, 1994, p. 51.

19   Petrol rationing was introduced in September 1939 and lasted until 1942, when the fuel was reserved for use by the armed forces, emergency services and bus operators. For most of the war, the vast majority of vehicles were thus out of use.

20   Hepplewhite, in *Sunderland, River, Town & People*, p. 192.

21   *Ibid.*, p. 194.

22   Winch, who lived in 11 Beechwood Terrace, was aged 49 at the time of her death.

23   This information is derived from Alan Burns' *Sunderland Mariners Lost at Sea 1939–1945*, 2007, p. 15. As Burns comments, for the men of the Royal and Merchant Navies there was no period of a 'phoney war' and for nearly six years mariners 'faced their own private hell of torpedoes, bombs, shells and mines, as well as facing the perils of the cruel sea.' *Ibid.*, p. 2.

24   T.S. Holden, & J.W. Smith, *Where Ships Are Born: a History of Shipbuilding on the River Wear*, revised edition, 1953, p. 124. On 19 June 1941 the king and queen paid tribute to the work of the town's shipbuilders by visiting Doxford's. They later visited J.L. Thompson's on 8 April 1943.

Chapter Ten

1   Petrol rationing for civilians, which had ended in 1942 when petrol was reserved for the armed services etc, was reintroduced when the war ended and lasted until May 1950.

2   *Sunderland Echo*, 22 December 1945, p. 2.

3   *Sunderland Echo*, 6 April 1949, p. 3. The previous year, another correspondent had commented with dismay on persistent theft from allotments, a practice that appeared to be getting worse. 'Within recent months on Plains Farm allotments nightly marauders have removed whole tool sheds, stripped a green-house of all the glass, and last week a large flock of ducks disappeared. A man who steals from gardens now is no mere sneak thief; he is an enemy of the country, and he should be treated as such.' *Sunderland Echo*, 2 January 1948, p. 2.

4   In mid March, for example, Wearsiders were informed: 'Weary and hungry passengers who had left Sunderland railway station at 8 o'clock this morning on a train bound for Hartlepool and Middlesbrough, arrived back at their starting point five hours later. Combined efforts of four locomotives had moved the train, in a blizzard, from six-foot deep snowdrifts near Ryhope.' *Sunderland Echo*, 13 March 1947, p. 1.

5   *Sunderland Echo*, 12 February 1949, p. 5. Hutchinson's family had farmed at South Hylton for several generations.

6   C.A. Moser, & W. Scott, *British Towns—A Statistical Study of their Social & Economic Differences*, 1961.

7   In the latter half of the 1980s, Williamson Court and Barclay Court, which had become slums shortly after their construction due to sociological factors, received such treatment. Williamson Court was transformed into council houses and bungalows, whereas Barclay Court (which had a worse reputation) was mainly transformed into two-storey council houses or bungalows and the remainder became private flats. Subsequently, such work occurred elsewhere, including at Downhill.

8   The son of a Sunderland tram driver, Norman Dennis was born at 29 Booth Street, Millfield in 1929, and both his parents were likewise born and raised in the neighbourhood.
      After attending Bede Collegiate Boys' School in 1940–8, Dennis won entrance to Corpus Christi, Oxford, but decided to study at the London School of Economics instead.
      When a member of the Millfield Residents' Association, Dennis lived at 10 Rosslyn Terrace, from where he used to ride his bicycle to lecture at the University of Newcastle upon Tyne. He subsequently moved to the northern suburbs of Sunderland, where he lived at 26 Westcliffe Road (1974–c.1982) and 3 Thompson Road. In 2000, four years after retiring, he moved to Hamilton Court, North Haven, next to Sunderland Marina. He died at his home there late on Saturday, 13 November 2010.
      His funeral was held at Sunderland Crematorium on the 26th, and was followed by a memorial service at St Andrew's Church,

Roker. Among those in attendance was Chris Mullin, a fellow member of the Labour Party and a former Sunderland MP, a man whom Dennis held in high regard.

One of the eulogies was delivered by Ray Mallon, the Mayor of Middlesbrough, whom Dennis had known since the mid 1990s. Among other things, Mallon declared that on one occasion when he was a guest at Hamilton Court, within a three-hour period journalists from four national newspapers, including the *Daily Telegraph* and *The Times*, all phoned Dennis to ask his views on a particular relevant issue. This incident, Mallon told the mourners, clearly indicated how highly Dennis was regarded.

9   Professor Bob Hudson (who represented Millfield ward on Sunderland Council in the early 1970s, as did Dennis), aptly describes *Public Participation and Planners' Blight* as 'an excoriating analysis of the unwillingness of the bureaucratic-professional machine to listen to residents, and the failure of local politicians to challenge the narrative presented by their officials.' *The Guardian*, 29 November 2010, p. 38.

10 N. Dennis, *Public Participation and Planners' Blight*. 1972, p. 151.

11 *Ibid.,* p. 213.

12 N.T. Sinclair, *Sunderland, City and People Since 1945*, 2004, p. 97.

13 B.T. Robson, *Urban Analysis—a Study of City Structure*, 1967, p. 83.

14 R. Nicholas, *Changing Tide: the Final Years of Wear Shipbuilding*, 1990, p. 21.

15 *Ibid.,* p. 32.

16 *Sunderland Echo*, 2 July 1999, p. 3. As closure loomed, in a supplement on Vaux in the *Echo* of 29 June 1999, Frank Nicholson is quoted as saying to Sunderland's residents: 'I would like to say a big thank-you on behalf of all Vaux people for the tremendous support you have given us and which has kept us at the heart of the city for more than 160 years. From everyone here at our late, great brewery: thank you and goodbye.'

17 *Port of Sunderland, 1967–1968*, souvenir edition, p. 58.

18 M. Conte-Helm, *Japan and the North East of England from 1862 to the present day*, 1989, p. 152.

19 *The Daily Telegraph*, 18 August 1999, p. 23.

20 In the summer of 2000, Nissan made headline news nationwide following comments by the company's president Carlos Ghosn, that added fuel to the strongly debated issue of whether Britain should abandon the pound in favour of a new currency, the Euro, which had come into use in most European countries. On 30 June, Ghosn warned that future investment at the Sunderland plant (employing 5,000 people) was being called into question by the high rate of the pound against the Euro for the strong pound was adversely affecting exports. A £150 million expansion plan to produce the next generation Micra at Sunderland was thus threatened. In *The Journal* of 1 July, Ghosn was quoted as saying: 'How much we rely on Sunderland is at stake. We could be interested at limiting output at Sunderland and increasing output at other European plants. We have important decisions to make.'

21 Among those affected were 400 staff whose short-term contracts would not be renewed. However, in May of the same year Nissan announced that 150 staff would be re-hired on 4 month fixed term contracts, and in June it was reported that another 100 jobs would be created on the same basis.

22 *Sunderland Echo*, 8 June 2009, p .2.

23 Robson, *op cit.* p. 83.

24 I. Stone & J. Stevens, 'Employment on Wearside: Trends and Prospects', *Northern Economic Review*, winter 1985/86, no. 12, pp. 39–40. As Jane Lewis has noted, there has been a dramatic increase in female employment in Sunderland where 'female employment increased enormously between 1951 and 1976 and at a higher rate than the national average.' 'Women, Work and Regional Development', *Northern Economic Review*, summer 1983, no. 7.

In 1951 women comprised 29 per cent of total employment in Sunderland, compared with 31 per cent nationally. In 1976, the figures were respectively 43 per cent and 40 per cent. The percentage has continued to rise. Today about 50 per cent of Sunderland's workforce is female. The majority work in the service sector and part-time jobs are common.

25 *Sunderland Echo*, 27 February 1953, p. 15. Items available on the ground floor included jewellery, umbrellas, handbags, dress silks and woollen fabrics etc. Goods stocked on the lower ground floor included ladies' and children's shoes, toys and games. The first floor contained millinery and clothing whilst the second floor had, among

other things, prams and nursery furniture, household and fancy linen. A month after opening, Binns became part of the House of Fraser Group.

26 Of the shop, an *Echo* supplement noted: 'Latest ideas have been brought from the Continent, including Rotterdam lighting that casts no shadows. The wall papers are in contemporary designs and the floors are covered in attractive tiles or luxurious pile carpets specially woven for Joplings.' The first floor was devoted to fashions and there were 50 fitting-rooms.

27 As part of the extension programme, the middle section of Crowtree Road became part of the Bridges complex and is thus now an enclosed pedestrianised area lined with shops.

28 P. Martin, *The Tom Cowie Story*, 1998, p. 21.

29 *Port of Sunderland 1967–1968*, souvenir edition, p. 43.

30 In September 2000, during a nationwide protest against the high cost of petrol and diesel, the port was briefly blockaded to prevent landed fuel being transported by road elsewhere. Demonstrators began their protest on Monday, 11th, and two of their number were arrested on the following Wednesday (the only arrests to occur in the country during the dispute) when petrol tankers began leaving the port in the face of little resistance.

31 Sunderland Corporation has confirmed plans to erect a bridge between Wessington Way and Pallion New Road. The structure, expected to be built by 2014, will be 1,102ft long and will have two eye-catching towers soaring 590ft above the Wear, higher than any other bridge in the country.

32 Sagar cited the case of public conveniences located near the Town Moor, where repair work had been completed the previous Friday. However, on the following Sunday he discovered that 14 panes of glass brick had been broken, and another 23 had been smashed by the following day. 'The point about this case', he told a reporter, 'is that these glass bricks cannot be broken easily', an indication of how determined the vandals had been to inflict damage. *Sunderland Echo*, 9 February 1949, p. 7.

33 *Sunderland Echo*, 11 June 1970, p. 17.

34 *Sunderland Echo*, 3 April 1991.

35 N. Dennis, 'Beautiful Theories, Brutal Facts: the Welfare State and Sexual Liberation', in D. Smith (ed.), *Welfare, Work and Poverty*, 2000, p. 55. In the same chapter, Dennis mentions that a study of Pennywell conducted in August 1999 showed that a high level of illiteracy contributed to the number of jobless (in some parts of the council estate the figure was 80 per cent) and this was one of the reasons why local businessmen did not employ residents of the estate. So, too, was the poor work ethic of some of the locals.

36 C. Mullin, *A View From The Foothills, the Diaries of Chris Mullin*, 2009, p. 554.

37 *Port of Sunderland*, 1958, p. 53.

38 A. Wright, 'Pioneers of Education and the University of Sunderland', in *Sunderland's History 2000*, 1999, p. 36.

39 Tom Corfe (1928–2006) was born in London. He lived in Sunderland from 1962 until 1986 when he retired from his post as a lecturer at Sunderland Polytechnic and moved to Hexham where, with characteristic enthusiasm and energy, he soon breathed new life into the local history society.

40 Wearmouth College continued to provide vocational training. In the late 1980s, it also used the buildings of the former Bede School.

41 In the early 1980s, the Stansfield site was demolished to make way for private housing.

42 The Swan Street site now serves another function and the ground once occupied by Wearmouth College is covered by homes constructed in the early 2000s.

43 Thorney Close County Secondary Modern School was opened on Wednesday, 7 October 1953, by the Mayor of Sunderland, McGregor English. Work on building the school, which could accommodate 900 pupils and cost £425,000, had commenced in 1950. At the time, it was the largest and most expensive post-war school in the town.

44 *Director of Public Health Annual Report 2008–9*, p. 2 and p. 12. The difference between average life expectancy in Sunderland and the country as a whole is long established, but the gap widened in the 1980s and early 90s.

45 The Eye Infirmary, founded in the 1830s, was based on Stockton Road from 1893 until it moved to premises on Queen Alexandra Road in 1946.

46 M. Metcalf, *Charlie Hurley, 'the Greatest Centre Half the World has ever Seen'*, 2008, p. xiii.

47 Violence added to gloom felt by fans during the course of the 1984–5 season. The headline on the front page of the *Echo* of 14 February 1985 reads: 'Stones and Bottles fly in Roker's night of Rioting.' The paper notes that 96 fans had been arrested, dozens of people injured, and thousands of pounds worth of damage caused 'in the worst scenes of soccer violence and hooliganism in Sunderland for many years.' Among the injured were two Chelsea fans with suspected fractured skulls, and five police officers. Two-thirds of the fans arrested were supporters of the visiting team. Among those affected by the trouble were patrons of the *Blue Bell* pub in Fulwell who were subjected to a terrifying onslaught by a coach-load of drunk Chelsea supporters, who 'punched and kicked their way' into the premises where they proceeded to hurl bottles, glasses and tables at the hapless people they encountered.

48 More often than not subsequent years, mostly spent in the Second Division, proved disappointing. Indeed, there was a real possibility that Sunderland would again be relegated to third-flight football. In 1992, though, Sunderland reached the FA Cup final, only to be defeated by Liverpool.

49 Roker's capacity had been greatly reduced from the early 1980s onwards, largely to meet increasingly stringent safety regulations. In the early 80s, the ground could hold 48,000 people but this had dropped to under 23,000 by 1996. In view of this and the aging facilities and cramped location, the board of directors decided that Roker was no longer suitable for an ambitious, forward-looking club. A quest for a new ground thus commenced. In the early 1990s, Sunderland AFC hoped to move to an out-of-town site near the Nissan car factory but Nissan blocked its plans. Later, owing to the closure of Wearmouth Colliery, a site near the town centre became available and the club acquired the location.

50 On 10 October 1999, the Stadium of Light's status as a superb footballing venue was underlined when it played host to an international match between England and Belgium. The game ended 2–1 to England, and a member of the winning team was a member of the Sunderland squad, Kevin Phillips, one of the most prolific goalscorers in the history of the club.

51 *Daily Mail*, 26 November 2005, p. 107.

52 *Niall Quinn—the Autobiography*, 2002, p. 252.

53 For some fans, the club's nailbiting survival was made all the more sweet because Newcastle and Middlesbrough were relegated from the Premier League.

54 *Sunderland Echo*, 28 May 2009, p. 1. Shortly thereafter, in June of the same year, Steve Bruce (who was born in Corbridge, Northumberland) was appointed to manage the club. Under his management, Sunderland ended the 2010–11 season in tenth place in the Premier League, two places higher than Sunderland's arch-rivals, Newcastle.

55 D. Dodds, *Running Shoes to Racing Silks, A North East man's action-packed life*, 2009, pp.103–104. Dodds was born in Sunderland in 1930. He subsequently became an accomplished international athlete and ran in marathons in Southern Africa, Greece and elsewhere, including the British Empire and Commonwealth Games at Cardiff. He later became a successful amateur jockey and won the Rhodesian Grand National in 1965.

56 Of the Crowtree Leisure Centre, we read: 'The centre's main features are a sports hall, a multi-purpose sports area, eight squash courts, a tropical leisure swimming pool and diving pool, an eight-lane indoor bowling green, an ice rink, a restaurant, bars and exhibition area, sauna suites, creche and shop units.' *Guide to Sunderland*, 1977, p. 42.

57 As a result, the swimming pool at Crowtree Leisure Centre closed. A swimming bath (dating from between the wars) on Newcastle Road has also shut.

58 Some of the branch libraries date from the Edwardian era, but others are of more recent date such as Grindon which opened in 1955, Fulwell in 1965, Ryhope Branch Library in 1973, and Washington New Town Library which did so in 1976.

59 *Sunderland Echo*, 27 April 1991, p. 7.

60 *Ibid.*, p. 1. Some of the disgruntled audience had paid even more for their tickets.

61 *Sunderland Echo*, 29 July 2009, p. 11.

62 One of the three members of the society who performed that evening was Winnifred Elstob, who had joined in late 1943 and remained a devoted member until her death in 2007.

63 In 2000, however, the Members' Evening was discontinued for there were not enough people capable of performing.

64 Over the years many pianists have commented on the quality of the society's piano.

For example, the young Italian maestro Alessandro Taverna did so on 12 April 2011, following his first performance in Sunderland. Taverna mentioned that the instrument is one of the best he has ever played, and examined it carefully after the recital. His programme had begun with Beethoven's *Eroica Variations*, and included a very diverse range of material. It elicited thunderous applause from a particularly large audience for the event had been more well publicised than usual thanks to Newcastle's *Evening Chronicle*.

65 *Sunderland Echo*, 4 December 1953, p. 2.

66 *Ibid.*, 2 April 2009, p. 57. The society's president is Anne-Marie Owens, who was born at South Shields and is one of Britain's finest mezzo sopranos whereas David Murray, the society's permanent conductor, is head of keyboard studies at the University of Newcastle upon Tyne. Eileen Bown was born in Sunderland and attended the University of Durham. Her career included a spell as a music teacher at Monkwearmouth Comprehensive School, c.1975–80, and she gave a recital for the Sunderland Pianoforte Society in 1988. She has also performed piano duets with David Murray throughout the country.

67 The orchestra had a long defunct predecessor, also named the Sunderland Symphony Orchestra, which performed its first concert at the prestigious Meng's Restaurant in Fawcett Street on 2 June 1934. The 50-strong orchestra played Beethoven's *Fifth Symphony* and accompanied Robert Hooker who performed Grieg's *Piano Concert in A minor*.

68 *Sunderland Echo*, 28 September 2000, p. 2.

69 Farr, who was born in Hereford in 1948 and attended the Royal Academy of Music, has been a guest conductor in Europe and elsewhere. For instance, he conducted the Stavanger Symphony Orchestra. In 2003, he became conductor in residence at Durham University.

70 E-mail to author, 18 March 2011. Patrick Zuk was born in Cork, Ireland, in 1968 and is of Irish/Polish descent.

71 To add to many fans' excitement, Take That had been rejoined by Robbie Williams (who had left fifteen years earlier) and he gave a barn-storming performance. For some he was the highlight of the show, but others were irritated by his brash, and sometimes crude, behaviour.

72 *Welcome to Roker and Seaburn*, 1949

73 *Sunderland Echo*, 16 April 1949, p. 4.

74 *Roker and Seaburn — The Sun-Spot of the North East*, 1954.

75 A. Potts, 'The Other Victory, Sunderland, July 1945', *North East Labour History*, no.19, 1985, p. 44.

76 The winning candidates, Willey and Ewart, gained 24,810 and 27,192 respectively. Turnout in the constituencies was 84.3 per cent and 83.3 per cent, higher than at any other time after the war.

77 The quotation, by Norman Dennis, was posted on the Civitas Blog on 6 January 2005. Charles Slater, whose maternal ancestors had lived in Sunderland since the late 19th century, attended Bede Collegiate Boys' School and became a solicitor. He was elected to the council in 1958 and in the early 1960s played a crucial role in bringing about the pedestrianised shopping centre in the heart of the town, the forerunner of today's Bridges complex. In 1968 he succeeded his uncle, Sir Jack Cohen, as leader of the Labour Group on the Council. Slater was passionate about Sunderland's welfare—for instance, he played an important part in bringing Nissan to Wearside—and was not frightened to ruffle feathers in pursuit of his objectives. His strength of character, debating skills, and no nonsense approach did not endear him to all his colleagues and he quit as leader of the Labour Group in 1990. Slater was born into Sunderland's Jewish community which, as is so often the case, made a contribution out of all proportion to its size in the local population.

78 Several previous attempts to gain city status for Sunderland had occurred; the first such was in 1932.

BIBLIOGRAPHY

In addition to primary sources, the following have been used.

Abbreviations

AA	*Archaeologia Aeliana*
AS	*Antiquities of Sunderland*
BDCLHS	*Bulletin of the Durham County Local History Society*
DAJ	*Durham Archaeological Journal*
NH	*Northern History*
SH	*Sunderland's History*
VCH	*Victoria County History*

Anderson, A., *The Dream Palaces of Sunderland*, 1982.

Bain, G.W., 'The Antient Chappel in the Corn Market, Sunderland-near-the-Sea', AS vol. V, 1904.

Bain, G.W., 'The Early Banking Houses of Sunderland', AS vol. VI, 1905.

Bain, G.W., 'The Early Printing Presses of Sunderland', AS vol. VII, 1906.

Bain, G.W., 'The Topography of Bishopwearmouth', AS vol. VIII, 1907.

Bain, G.W., 'The Topography of Bishopwearmouth' (Part III), AS vol. XI, 1910.

Betjeman, Sir John, *Collins Pocket Guide to English Parish Churches: the North*, 1968.

Blair, P.H., *The World of Bede*, 1970.

Blair, P.H., *Northumbria in the Days of Bede*, 1976.

Bovill, D.G., 'The Sunderland Orphan Asylum and the education of boys for the Mercantile Marine 1850–1902', BDCLHS no.39, December 1987.

Bowling, J. (ed.), *Some Chapters on the History of Sunderland*, 1969.

Bradshaw, F., 'Social and Economic History', VCH vol. II, (ed.) W. Page, 1907.

Bradshaw, F., 'The Black Death in the Palatinate of Durham', AA, third series, vol. III, 1907.

Brady, K., *Sunderland's Blitz*, 1999.

Breeze, A., 'The Name of the River Wear', DAJ vol. 13, 1997.

Breihan, J.R., 'Army Barracks in the North East in the Era of the French Revolution', AA, fifth series, vol. XVIII, 1990.

Bretherton, F.F., 'John Wesley's visits to Sunderland', AS vol. XX, 1932–1943.

Brett, A., *Sunderland Public Houses*, 2003

Brett, A., & Royal, J., *Old Pubs of Sunderland*, 1993.

Britnell, R.H., 'Feudal Reaction after the Black Death in the Palatinate of Durham', *Past and Present*, August 1990.

Brockie, W., *Sunderland Notables*, 1894.

Burnett, J., *History of the Town and Port of Sunderland*, 1830.

Callcott, M., 'Dr Marion Phillips, Labour MP Sunderland 1929–1931', *North East Labour History*, no. 20, 1986.

Cambridge, E., 'Early Romanesque Architecture in North-East England: a Style and its Patrons', in D. Rollason, M. Harvey and M. Prestwich (eds.) *Anglo-Norman Durham 1093–1193*, 1993.

Clarke, J.F., 'Shipbuilding on the River Wear 1780–1870' in R.W. Sturgess (ed.), *The Great Age of Industry in the North East*, 1981.

Clarke, J.F., *Building Ships on the North East Coast: a Labour of Love, Risk and Pain*, (two volumes) 1997.

Clay, M., Milburn, G.E., & Miller, S.T., *An Eye Plan of Sunderland and Bishopwearmouth 1785–1790 by John Rain*, 1984.

Conte-Helm, M., *Japan and the North East of England from 1862 to the present day*, 1989.

Cookson, G., *Sunderland, Building a City*, 2010.

Cornett, J.P., 'Local Paper Mills', AS vol. IX, 1908.

Corder, J.W., 'Bishopwearmouth Village in 1790', AS vol. XIX, 1929–1932.

Corfe, T., *A History of Sunderland*, 1973.

Corfe, T., *Swan in Sunderland*, 1979.

Cramp, R.J., 'Monastic sites', in D.M. Wilson (ed.), *The Archaeology of Anglo-Saxon England*, 1976.

Cramp, R.J., *Wearmouth and Jarrow: Monastic Sites* (2 vols.), 2005.

Crangle, L.P., 'The Roman Catholic community in Sunderland from the 16th century', AS vol. XXIV, 1969.

Cummings, C.L., 'Some Account of St George's Square and the people connected therewith', AS vol. VII, 1906.

Curtis, P., *Wearside In Winter*, 2001.

Curtis, P., *Sunderland's Shopping Heritage*, 2004.

Curtis, P., & Brett, A., *Once Upon A Time In Sunderland*, 2009.

Dale, T.C., 'Notes on the Owners of Pallion, 1572–1815', AS vol. XVIII, 1918–25.

Dennis, N., *People and Planning: the sociology of housing in Sunderland*, 1970.

Dennis, N., *Public Participation and Planners' Blight*, 1972.

Dobson, R.B., *Durham Priory, 1400–1450*, 1973.

Dodds, G.L., *The Historic River Wear* (unpublished).

Dodds, G.L., 'St Andrew's Church, Roker', DAJ vol. 10, 1994.

Dodds, G.L., 'The Prehistory of the Sunderland Area', SH 8, 1995.

Dodds, G.L., *Historic Sites of County Durham*, 1996.

Dumble, W., 'The Durham Lilburnes and the English Revolution', in D. Marcombe (ed.), *The Last Principality: Politics, Religion and Society in the Bishopric of Durham, 1494–1660*, 1987.

Dunn, M., *Coal Trade of the North of England*, 1844.

Ede, T.W., 'Cholera in Sunderland', BDCLHS no. 13, November 1970.

Finch, R., *Coals from Newcastle: the story of the North-East coal trade in the days of sail*, 1973.

Flinn, M.W., *The History of the British Coal Industry, 1700–1830*, 1985.

Garbutt, G., *A Historical and Descriptive View of the Parishes of Monkwearmouth and Bishopwearmouth, and the Port and Borough of Sunderland*, 1819.

Gardner, R., 'Medicine in Anglo-Saxon Northumbria', in D. Gardner-Medwin *et al* (eds.), *Medicine in Northumbria: Essays on the History of Medicine in the North East of England*, 1993.

Garside, W.R., *The Durham Miners 1919–1960*, 1971.

Gash, N., *Aristocracy and People: Britain 1815–1867*, 1979.

Gibbs, G.B., 'Early History of the Water Supplies of Sunderland and South Shields', AS vol. XII, 1911.

Gibbs, G.B., 'Neolithic Man in County Durham', AS vol. XIX, 1929–1932.

Gibson, A.M., *Bronze Age Pottery in the North East of England*, 1978.

Gibson, P., *Southwick-on-Wear: an illustrated history*, 1985.

Gibson, P., *Southwick-on-Wear*, vol. 2, 1988.

Gibson, P., *Southwick-on-Wear*, vol. 3., 1991.

Gill, K., *Sunderland Volunteer Life Brigade*, 2010.

Gregg, P., *Free-Born John: a biography of John Lilburne*, 1961.

Griffiths, W.B., *Wylam Wharf, Sunderland: 1994 Excavation Report*, (unpublished), 1995.

Hall, J., 'The Dates of the Monastic Remains at St Peter's Church, Monkwearmouth', AS vol. XVIII, 1918–1925.

Hall, J., 'The Hilton Monument & Stone Effigy, St Peter's Church, Monkwearmouth', AS vol. XX, 1932–43.

Hatcher, J., *The History of the British Coal Industry, I: Before 1700: Towards the Age of Coal*, 1993.

Heslop, G., 'The Copperas Works at Deptford, Sunderland', AS vol. III, 1902.

Hill, B.R., 'Rowland Wetherald, Printer, (1727–1791)', AS vol. III, 1902.

Holley, S., *Washington: Quicker by Quango: the history of Washington New Town 1964–1983*, 1983.

Hawkins, F.H., *History of the Presbytery of Durham*, 1973.

Heesom, A., 'The Sunderland By-Election, 1841', NH vol. IX, 1974.

Howard, T.D., & Miller, S.T., 'Reform of the Policing System in Sunderland in the early nineteenth century', BDCLHS no.32, May 1984.

Hudson, J., & Callaghan, P., (eds.), *Sunderland AFC: the Official History 1879–2000*, 1999.

Hughes, E., *North Country Life in the Eighteenth Century: the North-East 1700–1750*, 1952.

Hutchinson, W., *The History and Antiquities of the County Palatine of Durham*, vol. II, 1787.

Hyslop, R., 'The Fawcett Estate, Sunderland', AS vol. XIX, 1929–1932.

Jessop, L., & Sinclair, N.T., *Sunderland Museum: the People's Palace in the Park*, 1996.

Kapelle, W.E., *The Norman Conquest of the North*, 1979.

Kirtlan, N., 'The Stately Homes of Suddick', *Sunderland Antiquarian Society Newsletter*, January 2010.

Kitts, J.J., 'The Subscription Library', AS vol. IX, 1908.

Kitts, J.J., 'The Poor Laws—with special reference to Sunderland Workhouses', AS vol. X, 1909.

Lapsley, G.T., 'Introduction to Boldon Book', VCH vol. I, 1905.

Leighton, H.R., 'The Family of Goodchild of Pallion Hall: their Ancestors, Descendants & Relatives', AS vol. III, 1902.

Liddy, C.D., *The Bishopric of Durham in the Late Middles Ages*, 2008.

Lomas, R., 'Developments in Land Tenure on the Prior of Durham's Estate in the later Middle Ages', NH vol. XIII, 1977.

Lomas, R., 'The Black Death in County Durham', *Journal of Medieval History 15*, 1989.

Lomas, R., *North-East England during the Middle Ages*, 1992.

Lomas, R., *An Encyclopaedia of North-East England*, 2009.

Lowther, W.W., *Wish You Were Here: An Account of Sunderland's Wartime Evacuation*, 1989.

MacKay, T.W., 'Bede's Hagiographical Method: his knowledge and use of Paulinus of Nola', in G. Bonner (ed.), *Famulus Christi: Essays in Commemoration of the Thirteenth Centenary of the Birth of the Venerable Bede*, 1976.

Martin, P., *The Tom Cowie Story*, 1998.

McCord, N., *North East England: the region's development 1760–1960*, 1979.

McCutcheon, A.W., *A Wearmouth Mining Story*, 1960.

McKitterick, T.J., *Bishopwearmouth Church*, 1923.

Mearns, N.W., *Sentinels of the Wear: A History of Sunderland's River Police and Fireboats*, 1998.

Meikle, M.M., & Newman, C.M., *Sunderland and its Origins, monks to mariners*, 2007.

Middlemiss, J.T., 'Sunderland Ferry', AS vol. III, 1902.

Middlemiss, J.T., 'Some Account of Sunderland Bridge', AS vol. VIII, 1907.

Milburn, G.E., 'Wesleyanism in Sunderland in the later 18th and early 19th century', AS vol. XXVI, 1974–1976.

Milburn, G.E., *The Christian Lay Churches*, 1977.

Milburn, G.E., 'Wesleyanism in Sunderland (Part Two)', AS vol. XXVII, 1977–1979.

Milburn, G.E., 'Thomas Dixon of Sunderland', SH 2, 1984.

Milburn, G.E., & Miller, S.T. (eds.), *Suunderland, River, Town & People: a History from the 1780s to the Present Day*, 1988.

Milburn, G.E., *Church and Chapel in Sunderland 1780–1914*, 1988.

Milburn, G.E., 'John Hampson's Life of John Wesley', SH 9, 2000.

Milburn, G.E., *The Travelling Preacher: John Wesley in the North East 1742–1790*, (revised ed.), 2003.

Miller, S.T., 'The River Wear Commission 1717–1859', AS vol. XXVII, 1977–1979.

Miller, S.T., 'The Establishment of the River Wear Commissioners', BDCLHS no. 26, May 1981.

Miller, S.T., 'This Unpleasant Affair . . . Cholera in Sunderland in 1831–1832', BDCLHS no. 29, December 1982.

Miller, S.T., *The Book of Sunderland*, 1989.

Miller, S.T. & Brett, A., *Cholera in Sunderland*, 1992.

Mitchell, W.C., *History of Sunderland*, 1919.

Morley, B., *Hylton Castle*, 1979.

Morley, B., & Speak, S., 'Excavation and Survey at Hylton Castle, Sunderland', *The Archaeological Journal*, vol. 159, 2002.

Morton, B., 'Assembly Garth and Trafalgar Square Merchant Seamen's Houses', AS, vol. IV, 1903.

Moses, E.W., 'The Williamsons of East Markham, Nottinghamshire, Monkwearmouth and Whitburn', AS vol. XXIII, 1964.

Moss, M., & Turton, A., *A Legend of Retailing: House of Fraser*, 1989.

Mowat, C.L., *Britain Between the Wars, 1918–1940*, 1955.

Muthesius, S., *The English Terraced House*, 1982.

Myers, B. A., *The Rectors of the Ancient Parish Church of Bishopwearmouth A.D. 1195 to 1975*, 1982.

Myerscough, J. A., *The Martyrs of Durham & the North East*, 1956.

O'Brien, P., & Gibson, P., *Seaburn and Roker*, 1997.

Offler, H.S., *North of the Tees: Essays in Medieval British History*, 1996.

Patterson, G., 'Samuel Plimsoll and Sunderland', SH 1, 1983.

Patterson, G., 'Harrison's Buildings—Sunderland's first council houses', SH 3, 1985.

Patterson, G., *Sunderland's First Theatre and Music Hall*, 2009.

Patterson, J., 'The Volunteer Movement in Sunderland at the time of the Napoleonic Wars', AS vol. V, 1904.

Patterson, J., 'The Birthplace of the Venerable Bede', AS vol. XII, 1911.

Petch, J.A., 'Roman Durham', AA, fourth series, vol. 1, 1925.

Pevsner, N., & Williamson, E., *The Buildings of England: County Durham*, 2nd ed., 1983.

Piper, A.J., *Durham Monks at Wearmouth*, 1974.

Pocock, D. and Norris, R., *A History of County Durham*, 1990.

Pollard, A.J., *North-Eastern England during the Wars of the Roses: lay society, war and politics, 1450–1500*, 1990.

Potts, A., *The Wearside Champions*, 1993.

Potts, A., *Jack Casey, the Sunderland Assassin*, 1991.

Potts, T., *Sunderland: A History of the Town, Port, Trade and Commerce*, 1892.

Ritson, V., 'A Critical Enquiry into the Origin and Status of the Freemen and Stallingers of Sunderland, in two parts', AS vol. VI, 1905.

Ritson, V., 'A Chapel of Ease: the Early Records of St John's Church, Sunderland', AS vol. IX, 1908.

Roberton, C., *Sunderland—the making of a 21st century city*, 2000.

Robinson, J., 'Some Historic Houses in Sunderland, illustrated with plans and photographs', AS vol. IV, 1903.

Robinson, J., 'Roman Road and Remains at Bishopwearmouth', AS vol. V, 1904.

Robson, B.T., *Urban Analysis: A Study of City Structure with special reference to Sunderland*, 1969.

Robson, H.L., 'George Lilburne, Mayor of Sunderland', AS vol. XXII, 1960.

Robson, H.L., 'Bede of Wearmouth or Bede of Jarrow', AS vol. XXIII, 1964.

Robson, H.L., 'Maintenance of the poor in Sunderland under the Parish Vestry', AS vol. XXIV, 1969.

Robson, H.L., *The Great Days of Wearmouth* (undated).

Rollason, D., 'St Cuthbert and Wessex', in G. Bonner, C. Stancliffe and D. Rollason (eds.), *St Cuthbert, his Cult and his Community to A.D. 1200*, 1989.

Routledge, M., 'A History of Sunderland's Fire Brigades', SH 7, 1993.

Sayers, A.B., *Sunderland Church High School for Girls: a centenary history 1884–1984*, 1984.

Scammell, G.V., *Hugh du Puiset: Bishop of Durham*, 1956.

Scammell, J., 'Robert I and the North of England', *English Historical Review 73*, 1958.

Sharpe, R.A., 'Emily Marshall of Sunderland: a Victorian campaigner for women's work in Anglican parish life', SH 6, 1992.

Simmons, W., & Graham, R., *History of Sunderland AFC*, 1987.

Sinclair, H., *Cycle Clips: A History of Cycling in the North East*, 1983

Sinclair, N.T., *Railways of Sunderland*, 1985.

Sinclair, N.T., *Sunderland, City & People Since 1945*, 2004.

Smith, D.W., 'Priscilla Maria Beckwith: a forgotten Victorian lady', SH 6, 1992.

Smith, H.J., 'The Sunderland and South Shields Water Company', SH 3, 1985.

Smith, J.W. & Holden, T.S., *Where Ships are Born: Sunderland 1346–1946 (and later years), a history of shipbuilding on the River Wear*, 1953.

Smithwhite, J.H., 'Biscop's Twin Churches', AS vol. XX, 1932–43.

Sockett, E.W., 'A Concrete Acoustical Mirror at Fulwell, Sunderland', DAJ vol. 6, 1990.

Speak, S. & Snape, M.E., (unpublished) 'A Prehistoric Site at Carley Hill, Sunderland.'

Squance, T.C., 'Description of the Human Remains found in Hasting Hill Barrow', AA, third series, vol. XI, 1914.

Staddon, S.A., *The Tramways of Sunderland*, 1964.

Stone, I., Stevens, J. & Morris, M., *Economic Restructuring and Employment Changes on Wearside since 1971: employment potential in Sunderland*, 1986.

Storey, P.J., 'Sunderland Newspapers', AS vol. XXVII, 1977–1979.

Storey, P.J., 'Mayors of Victorian Sunderland', SH 6, 1992.

Storey, P.J., 'Mayors of Victorian Sunderland (Part 2)', SH 7, 1993.

Storey. P.J., 'Mayors of Victorian Sunderland (Part 3)', SH 8, 1995.

Storey, P.J., 'Mayors of Sunderland Part IV, 1902–1910', SH 10, 2003.

Summers, J.W., *History and Antiquities of Sunderland*, 1858.

Surtees, R., *The History and Antiquities of the County Palatine of Durham*, vol. I, 1816 and vol. II, 1820.

Thompson, A.H., (ed.), *Bede, his Life, Times and Writings: Essays in Commemoration of the Twelfth Century of his Death*, 1935.

Trechmann, C.T., 'Prehistoric Burials in the County of Durham', AA, third series, vol. XI, 1914.

Whitcomb, N.R., 'Two Prehistoric Dugout Canoes from the River Wear at Hylton, near Sunderland, County Durham', AA, fourth series, vol. XLVI, 1968.

Wormald, P., 'The Age of Bede and Aethelbald', in J. Campbell (ed.), *The Anglo-Saxons*, 1982.

Walker, H.L., 'Ships, Sunderland and Lloyd's Register of Shipping', BDCLHS no.12, April 1970.

Wilson, K., 'Sunderland and the 1832 Reform Bill', *North East Labour History*, no. 17, 1983.

Wright, A., 'Pioneers of Education and the University of Sunderland', SH 9, 2000.

Young, R., *Lithics and Subsistence in North East England: aspects of the prehistoric archaeology of the Wear Valley, County Durham, from the Mesolithic to the Bronze Age*, 1987.

INDEX

PICTURE CREDITS

Printed in Great Britain
by Amazon